# THE EVOLUTION
# OF CAPITALISM

# THE EVOLUTION
# OF CAPITALISM

Advisory Editor
## LEONARD SILK
Editorial Board,
*The New York Times*

Research Associate
## MARK SILK

# ECONOMICS

## AN ACCOUNT OF THE RELATIONS BETWEEN
## PRIVATE PROPERTY AND PUBLIC WELFARE

BY

ARTHUR TWINING HADLEY

### ARNO PRESS
A NEW YORK TIMES COMPANY
New York • 1972

Reprint Edition 1972 by Arno Press Inc.

Reprinted from a copy in
The State Historical Society of Wisconsin Library

The Evolution of Capitalism
ISBN for complete set: 0-405-04110-1
See last pages of this volume for titles.

Manufactured in the United States of America

- - - - - - - - - - - -

Library of Congress Cataloging in Publication Data

Hadley, Arthur Twining, 1856-1930.
    Economics: an account of the relations between
private property and public welfare.

    (The Evolution of capitalism)
    1. Economics.  I. Title.  II.  Series.
HB171.H13  1972                330            77-38259
ISBN 0-405-04124-1

# ECONOMICS

## AN ACCOUNT OF THE RELATIONS BETWEEN
## PRIVATE PROPERTY AND PUBLIC WELFARE

BY

### ARTHUR TWINING HADLEY

Professor of Political Economy in Yale University ; sometime Labor Commissioner
of the State of Connecticut ; Author of " Railroad Transportation, its History and its Laws "

### G. P. PUTNAM'S SONS

NEW YORK                     LONDON
27 WEST TWENTY-THIRD STREET      24 BEDFORD STREET, STRAND
The Knickerbocker Press
1896

The Knickerbocker Press, New Rochelle, N. Y.

# PREFACE.

THIS book is an attempt to apply the methods of modern science to the problems of modern business.

Within the last thirty years there have been important changes in economic theory. One school of investigators has employed the principle of natural selection to explain the development and present shape of industrial ideas and institutions. Another school has used some of the results of recent psychological study to account for the actions of individual men in pursuing their own interests under the ideas and institutions thus developed. Both these things have combined to make the economic science of the present day very different, in its methods of analysis and powers of explanation, from that which formed the basis of John Stuart Mill's *Principles of Political Economy*.

Meantime new problems have been developing in modern business life ; most conspicuously, perhaps, in connection with large investments of capital in factories and railroads. The time which elapses between the rendering of labor and the utilization of the products of labor is now so long that the work of the speculator has far greater importance than it did a generation ago. The size of the units of capital is so large that free competition often becomes an impossibility, and theories of economics which are based upon the existence of such competition prove blind guides in dealing with modern price movements. We have to study, far more closely than we once did, the effect of combinations upon the interests of the consumers on the one hand and the laborers on the other; to examine the results of meeting organizations of capital with organizations of labor, and of controlling them by special legislation or by direct government ownership. We have to deal with socialism, not as the theory of a few visionaries who try to destroy property rights, but as a series of practical measures urged by a large and influential body of men who are engaged in extending the functions of government.

There is no general work in the English language which deals at all comprehensively with these problems of modern economics. As long as Marshall's book remains incomplete there is nothing which attempts to do for the readers of to-day that which Mill did with such signal success for those of half a century ago. The field thus left open I have tried to cover to the best of my ability in the book now offered to the public. It is written for students—that is, for those readers who are willing to give the time and trouble necessary for understanding subjects which are at once important and perplexing. In a professional experience which has been about equally divided between the editorial room and the lecture room, I have generally found that, barring certain necessary differences in form of presentation, what is good teaching in one place is good in another. I have attempted to make the book available for students in the broad sense of the term as well as in the narrow sense; for those who are engaged in doing the world's work as well as for those who are preparing themselves to do it.

I have put things as plainly as I could; but there are some parts of economics where no amount of effort by an author will relieve the reader of the necessity of doing independent thinking on his own account. There are many problems of business life which are so complicated in reality that it is unwise to treat them as if they were simple. There is no foundation for the popular belief that questions of money, of the tariff, or of the relations between labor and capital, are easy to understand if properly presented. The simplicity obtained by looking at them from one side only is apt to be secured at the expense of thoroughness and too often of candor.

Dealing as the book does with matters of active controversy, sometimes clouded by party loyalty or by personal interests, I am far from expecting everyone to agree with its conclusions. But I trust that everyone will recognize my intent to state both sides of disputed questions as clearly as possible, and to treat the controversies as an arbiter rather than as an advocate, even in those cases where the arguments on one side have seemed decidedly stronger than those on the other.

Where these controversies involve important differences of legislative or commercial policy, the arguments have been presented in the text of the book ; where they involve differences of explanation or theory rather than of practice, they have been outlined in the foot-notes. These notes are not to be regarded as exhaustive discussions of economic theory, but as summaries of opinion on controverted points, which may serve to pave the way for detailed study on the part of those who are interested to pursue the subject farther than the limits of the present book will allow.

Without going into the more complicated details of modern mathematical economics, I have occasionally employed diagrams in cases where they seemed necessary for a thorough explanation of the subject. For most people who are likely to use this book I am confident that time spent in studying the diagrams will be more than repaid. I have used one of Cournot's methods of presentation, not because it is any better than those employed by his successors, but because it is simpler.

The separation which is made in so many modern books between economic theory and economic practice seems to me a mistake. I have tried to keep theory and application together; and, just as far as possible, to make the study of practical problems a means of developing and explaining scientific theories. Where this method can be employed it gives increased interest to the study of economics; and, what is still more important, it guards us in some measure against the danger of disproportionate and one-sided deductions from certain parts of economic science, to which the student is always liable if he develops his theory first and makes its practical applications afterward. No writer on economics has had as wide an influence as Adam Smith; and while Smith's power was in large measure due to those personal qualities in which he stands pre-eminent, it was in perhaps equal measure due to his habit of keeping theory and practice closely combined. People studied his reasoning carefully because it was applied to things which they really wanted to understand, and was constantly supported by an appeal to the observed facts of business life.

I am very far from trying to substitute economic history for economic theory. In a book like this, the explanations are the important thing; the presentation of facts is not an end in itself, but a means of making the explanation clear and comprehensive. The reader will be disappointed if he expects to find a complete and well-ordered history of the financial and industrial policy of various nations. For such a history, he should look to the various works that deal with the special departments of finance, commerce, or industry. A work like this is designed to enable him to make use of such books, not to dispense with them.

In thus connecting theory and practice and giving due prominence to the work of the speculator in modern industry, I have found myself obliged to abandon the time-honored division of the science into the departments of production, distribution, exchange, and consumption. The subjects which are commonly treated under the head of production are chiefly found in chapters ii, v, and vi; those which are commonly treated under the head of exchange will be found in chapters iii, iv, vii, and viii; while the last six chapters deal principally with questions of distribution, and incidentally with those of consumption.

My obligations to previous writers, in general and in detail, are something which I cannot possibly express in full. When a scientific principle is specially identified with the name of some particular author, I have taken pains to credit it to its proper source—especially in the case of work which, from its newness or for any other reason, has not become part of the general stock of economic discussion. In other cases, I have limited my citations to those books which are likely to prove most accessible and useful to the reader who desires to pursue special subjects farther than can be done within the limits of a general text-book. The titles of such books have been for the most part placed at the head of the chapters bearing on the specific subjects with which they deal; thus forming a bibliography which, while very incomplete, may yet prove serviceable to some readers. Other things being equal, I have included works which are written in English, rather than in foreign languages, and have cited English translations rather than originals.

I am indebted for material aid to my colleagues Messrs. Irving Fisher and J. C. Schwab; and still more to my wife, on whom I have depended both for criticism and for assistance at every stage of the work.

YALE UNIVERSITY, NEW HAVEN,
March, 1896.

# CONTENTS.

## CHAPTER XII.

## CHAPTER XIII.

## CHAPTER XIV.

# ECONOMICS:

## AN ACCOUNT OF THE RELATIONS BETWEEN PRI-VATE PROPERTY AND PUBLIC WELFARE.

---

### CHAPTER I.

#### PUBLIC AND PRIVATE WEALTH.

Preliminary Definitions—History of Economic Science—Individualism and Socialism—Standards of Public Good.

Luigi Cossa : " An Introduction to the Study of Political Economy " ; translated by L. Dyer. London, 1893. An admirable history and bibliography. Its title is a little misleading, as the book is of more use to advanced students than to beginners.

J. N. Keynes : " The Scope and Method of Political Economy." London, 1891.

Among the many critical histories of socialism the most useful is perhaps that of John Rae : 2d ed., London and New York, 1891. A good presentation of the ideas and aims of moderate socialists is given in " Fabian Essays in Socialism " ; edited by G. B. Shaw. London, 1890. New York, 1891. For a brief statement of extreme individualistic views see W. G. Sumner : " What Social Classes Owe to Each Other " New York, 1883 ; for a fuller development, W. Donisthorpe : " Individualism " London, 1889.

§ 1. IN the Middle Ages questions of industrial policy were treated by most writers as incidental details in a system of theology or of law. But in the sixteenth and seventeenth centuries people began to separate the study of matters affecting a nation's commerce and finance from the more general consideration of its politics or its morals,

and to develop an art of *political economy* which should
guide the statesman in his efforts to promote public wealth,
as the arts of personal and industrial economy guide the
individual in his pursuit of private wealth. In their attempts to formulate the rules of this art, writers of the
eighteenth century discovered certain laws which are the
basis of the modern science of *economics.*

§ 2. But what is public wealth?

In the first place it is *not* the same thing as government
property. It is something far wider. The individual
citizens are a part of the nation just as much as the
government is; their property, no less than that of the
government, must be included in any rational attempt
to estimate the industrial resources of the community. Waterworks and railroads owned by private companies are just as much part of the public wealth as are
municipal waterworks or national railroads. Whether
the public wealth is likely to be increased in any particular case as an indirect result of making more of it public
property, can only be decided by examining the circumstances of that case. It will depend upon how well such
property is managed. If the agents of the government
are disinterested and wise enough, the public property
will probably be made to render more service than private property; if they are not disinterested and wise, it
will probably be made to render less service. In the
latter case, the "nationalization" of a piece of property
will tend to diminish the public wealth instead of increasing it.

§ 3. Nor can we estimate the public wealth of a nation
by taking the sum of the property of its individual members. Many things like pure air and abundant water supply, which form most valuable elements of public wealth,
are hardly counted as private property at all. A property-
right is a title to part of the public wealth; but the
amount of these titles outstanding forms no indication

of the amount of enjoyment which the public can command. The exchange value of a property-right is connected with its exclusiveness. It depends not so much upon the enjoyment which the property can be made to afford as upon the completeness with which its owner can monopolize that enjoyment for himself or his friends to the exclusion of the general public.

The total value of these rights of exclusion does not necessarily correspond in any way with the resources available for the public. It is quite misleading to measure a nation's wealth by a census of the property of its members. Property-rights may be created without increasing public wealth or destroyed without diminishing it.[1] Under the English system of enclosures, land which had formerly been free to all the public was made the subject of private ownership. By this practice there was a creation of property-rights without production of wealth. The landlords now had something valuable which could be bought or sold and which did not exist before; but the wealth of the community was in no wise increased. There were no more means of enjoyment in existence than there had been previously. On the other hand, the abolition of slavery involves a diminution of private property without a corresponding loss of public wealth. It sweeps away an enormous mass of exchangeable wealth of individuals. Systems of compensation to the owners of such wealth, though they may shift the burden, cannot annul the loss. Yet such a loss is simply a destruction of titles and transferable rights. It does not destroy means of happiness. The wealth of the community, judged by public standards, is as great after abolition as it was before.

A curious instance where loss of private wealth went hand in hand with gain in public wealth is furnished by the history of the waterworks in the city of Venice. For-

---

[1] But see § 12.

merly water was so scarce that it commanded a price, and a good well was a source of considerable private wealth to its possessors. But when an abundant supply of water was furnished at slight cost, the commercial character of the water changed, and it could under all ordinary circumstances be had for nothing. But the very abundance of water, which makes it commercially worth nothing, is an element of public wealth; and the scarcity which makes it a valuable article of property is a symptom of public poverty.

The high price of real estate in New York City, which forms an enormous item of private wealth, is partly connected with causes that promote the public wealth and partly with those that antagonize it. So far as it is due to the excellence of the harbor and other things which make New York an admirable trade centre, it connotes a public good. So far as it is connected with the narrowness of Manhattan Island and other things which limit the number of people who can most conveniently avail themselves of these privileges, it connotes a public evil.

§ 4. Improvements in the arts have had a beneficial effect on the public wealth of nations wholly out of proportion to any gains which they have enabled individuals to appropriate for their own exclusive advantage. This benefit cannot be measured in money. If an improvement enables the same number of laborers to produce twice the amount of useful products, it may happen that the price of each product will fall one half. In this case there is no apparent gain in private wealth; but if the article is a really useful one, there is a great gain in public wealth and social well-being through its increased abundance.

The true basis for an estimate of a nation's wealth is to be found in the enjoyments of its members. The wealth of a community does not depend on the money value of its means for such enjoyment, nor even on their physical amount, but on their utilization. Public wealth is "a flow and not a fund "; it is to be measured as *income* and not as *capital.*

§ 5. The distinction between capital and income as *modes of measuring* [1] resources is almost as important as the distinction between public and private wealth, and is quite as much neglected in current economic discussion.

If a man for a series of years earns $10,000 a year and spends it all, he is always rich in one sense, and never in another. He has much income and no capital—unless we stretch the idea of capital wide enough to include the skill which enables him to earn the large income. In like manner a nation whose members habitually produce much and consume much, will have large enjoyments and small accumulations. Measured as income its public wealth will be large; measured as capital it will be small.

The distinction between capital and income is not due to a difference in the things themselves, but to a difference in methods of measurement. The capital of an individual or a community is an amount of wealth in existence *at* a particular moment. The income of an individual or a community is an amount of wealth obtained *during* a specified period. Capital is being constantly converted into income and income into capital. But capital, under all times and conditions, is measured as a quantity, while income is more properly measured as a rate. Capital is a static conception, independent of time; income a dynamic conception involving the time element.

We see this distinction illustrated in the balance sheets of any large industrial enterprise. The capital account of a railroad company gives the property which it owns at a particular moment—road, equipment, land,

---

[1] For the development of this distinction, which involves a combination of the ideas of Knies and Newcomb, I am much indebted to my colleague Dr. Irving Fisher.

buildings, stocks of other corporations, accounts payable, materials and cash on hand. The income account gives its earnings during the year preceding—from passengers, freight, mail, express, and other sources. The two accounts deal with the same road, but with a totally different set of items; and while the amount of the one has a great influence on the other, there is no direct connection between the two.

§ 6. As a matter of pure mathematics, a quantity of capital and a rate of income should be as incommensurable as a line and an angle. In practice, however, we are constantly comparing the two. The rate of interest furnishes a basis on which we compare and exchange capital and income with one another. If we say that the rate of interest is five per cent. we mean that we regard an income of five dollars a year as equivalent to a capital of a hundred dollars. The causes which determine this basis of comparison are extremely complicated; they are treated at length in chapter ix.

§ 7. Of the two methods of measuring wealth, the income standard is of more primary importance; that of capital is secondary. Accumulations of capital have their chief usefulness as means of producing income. For this reason the term capital is confined in ordinary usage to things which are valued in connection with productive industry. As thus limited, the word capital, in its public sense, means wealth used for producing more wealth. A nation's capital consists mainly of food, necessary clothing and shelter, materials, machinery, means of transportation, and instruments of exchange. It is impossible to say just which objects are capital and which are not. It is very far from being possible to form an accurate money valuation of the amount of such capital. On the other hand, private capital is property used for acquiring more property. We can tell with substantial accuracy what property each individual is using as capital, and can estimate its money value very closely. Just as the acquisition of property is usually attended with production of wealth, so the investment of property as private capital is usually attended with accumulation of public capital. But there are cases where one takes place without the other. The burglar's outfit or the roulette table of the gamester is private capital—property used for acquiring more property; but it certainly is not wealth used for producing more wealth. On the other hand, the pioneer in science often adds greatly to the wealth of the country by the use which he makes of existing wealth; but the cases are very rare where he increases his property in so doing, or where the attempt to acquire property is a dominant motive in directing his action. Public capital is not the sum of the private capital of individuals, any more than public wealth is the sum of individual property rights. Public capital consists of useful things; capital *goods*, as Clark calls them. Private capital consists of titles and rights to a part of those things.[1] The increase or diminution of such titles is not synonymous with an increase or diminution of the things themselves.

§ 8. The relations between the different forms of wealth may be summed up as follows :

[1] Some economists, who see that there is a distinction of this kind, fail to recognize its true nature. Both Marx and Clark, for example, speak of capital as a permanent thing, independent of the transmuted and changing goods of which it is at each moment composed. But Clark regards this thing as permanently productive and its increase as normal and natural ; while Marx regards it as an unproductive dead-weight, whose increase is a spoliation of the laborer. But what is this thing which is permanent while the goods change ? It is nothing else than the titles to property in process of industrial transmutation ; titles which carry with them the control and direction of the process. Whether the existence of these titles increases the production of the community depends on the wisdom with which the control is exercised. They are not necessarily productive as assumed by Clark ; still less are they necessarily unproductive as held by Marx. They are more likely to be productive than not, because our industrial arrangements are such that, if men fail to use their capital for things the community needs, they lose money and are eliminated from control of the next period of production.

Wealth in the public sense consists of all means of enjoyment, whether they have a commercial value or not. The use obtained from these things in a given period is the public income for that period. The amount in existence at any given moment is the public capital at that moment in the broadest sense of the word. But it is customary to confine the term capital to wealth which is actually used for producing more wealth.

Wealth in its private sense, better designated as property, consists of rights to part of the public wealth. The amount of such rights which accrues to any person in a given period is his income for that period. The aggregate amount which he has at any moment is his capital in the broadest sense of the word. But here again it is customary not to apply the term capital to a man's whole property, but to confine it to that part which he uses as a means of acquiring more property.

§ 9. These distinctions are something which the student of economics must master at the very outset. This is not so easy as it appears. The political economists of the sixteenth, seventeenth, and early part of the eighteenth centuries habitually confused public and private wealth. The theories of that time constitute what is known as the *mercantile system* of political economy, because they involve the idea that a nation should strive to make money in the same manner as an individual merchant. Just as a prudent business man so manages his affairs as to produce more than he consumes and make money by the excess of his sales over his purchases, it was thought that a prudent statesman should so manage the affairs of the nation as to make it produce more than it consumes and export more than it imports. It was considered by many that this excess of exports over imports constituted an index of national prosperity and the true measure of the increase of national wealth. Just as the money which an individual has made represents his power of industrial control over other individuals, it was thought that the money which a nation had thus saved represented its power of control over other nations. In fact, no small part of the commercial legislation of all countries has been framed under the influence of these ideas.

§ 10. The error of the mercantile system was pointed out by a school of French economists known as *physiocrats*, because they laid stress on the powers of nature as the basis of national prosperity and public wealth. These economists indicated that the true source of national power lay, not in the supply of gold or silver, but in the supply of food ; not in the power to command other nations' labor, but in the power to develop its own labor. A nation might be prosperous with very little money *per capita*. This would simply result in a lower scale of prices. But with little food *per capita* great misery and industrial inefficiency must inevitably follow. Instead of encouraging manufactures, as the mercantile school has done, the physiocrats were led to undervalue them. No manufacture, they said, could exist except on the basis of a surplus of food produced by the agricultural laborers ; and the real cost, not to say the real worth, of every manufacture was measured by the amount of food consumption which it represented. Food was therefore the true measure of wealth, no less than the true source of national prosperity.

§ 11. This was a great advance from the conception of wealth embodied in the mercantile system. But the physiocrats made a mistake in laying too much stress on the quantity of food as a measure of public wealth and too little on its utilization. The prosperity of a nation depends far more upon the use made of its wealth than upon the amount of such wealth in existence at any time. The public income is not represented by an amount of money, but by a series of purchases made with that money ; not by an amount of unconsumed food, but by a series of things made and used by those who consume it. A nation which has a large amount of capital and utilizes it badly may be far less prosperous than one with a smaller capital which it transmutes more rapidly.

The full importance of this process of transmutation was first recognized by Adam Smith, whose *Inquiry Into the Nature and Causes of the Wealth of Nations*, published in 1776, is usually regarded as the starting-point of modern political economy.[1] He agreed with the physiocrats in their strictures on the mercantile system, but his conception of public wealth was broader and truer than theirs. He also showed, far more clearly than any of his predecessors, the relation between the pursuit of private wealth and the utilization of public wealth. He proved that the former was a most powerful agency for furthering the latter; that the actions of men in their pursuit of money-making were a means of serving others even when they had no intention or consciousness of so doing. Modern economists have followed in the lines laid down by Adam Smith. Their inquiry into the causes of the wealth of nations has connected itself with an inquiry into the results of the property rights of individuals and the motives connected with them. This twofold aspect of the science is recognized in the definition given on the title-page of the present work,—An Account of the Relations between Private Property and Public Welfare.

§ 12. The perception of this relation between the acquisition of property and the production of wealth has had several important consequences. In the first place, it has changed the attitude of the public mind toward trade. In ancient times trade was regarded as a fight between buyer and seller; to-day it is looked at as a means of

---

[1] The best edition is that of J. E. Thorold Rogers, Oxford, 1880. W. J. Ashley has published an excellent abridgment (New York and London, 1891), which presents the most important parts in very narrow compass.

mutual service. To the mediæval economist the business man was a licensed robber; to the modern economist he is a public benefactor. Five hundred years ago it was thought that a man could make money only by buying goods for less than they were worth, or by selling them for more than they were worth; that each business transaction involved the temptation to cheat; and that if a man was successful in business it showed that that temptation had been too much for him. To-day we believe that money is made on a large scale by doing the public a service. If a man's goods command a high price we assume that he has met an actual need. If this price furnishes him a large margin of profit, we believe that he has so organized the labor under his control as to diminish not only his own expenses but the actual labor cost of producing the goods. So confident are we of the substantial identity of interest between the business man and the community as a whole, that we give our capitalists the freest chance to direct the productive forces of society to their own individual profit. Even the mistakes of private enterprise may prove a means of progress to society, since they show at comparatively small cost what is to be avoided in the future.[1]

§ 13. A second result is a change in the attitude of economists toward state interference. When people thought that every business man was trying to serve himself at the expense of the community, a large number of restrictions of all kinds were brought into play. The commercial legislation of past centuries was a mass of such restrictions. Adam Smith and his successors showed that the bulk of this legislation had a very different effect from what was intended. Instead of preventing extortion, it prevented mutual service. Instead of enabling the nation as a whole to make money, it interfered with the

[1] Compare J. S. Mill, "On Liberty," London, 1839; John Morley, "On Compromise," London, 1877.

development of its resources and the wise application of its labor. To so great an extent were the economists able to point out the evil results of mistaken legislation, that in the popular mind the teaching of economics has become synonymous with the effort to reduce the activity of government to a minimum. The phrase *Laissez faire, laissez passer* (let things take their own course), which was the motto of the physiocrats, has taken an exaggerated hold on the public imagination, and has been regarded as a fundamental axiom of economic science, when it is in fact only a practical maxim of political wisdom, subject to all the limitations which experience may afford.

§ 14. A third result is to make people treat political economy as a science instead of an art. The earliest students of the subject thought that political economy was the art of managing the business affairs of a community in the same way that domestic economy is the art of managing the business affairs of a household. The modern economist rejects the idea of paternalism involved in this conception. He sees that the attempts of government authorities to manage the economy of a nation, however well meant, are apt to defeat their own ends ; that the growth of national wealth depends upon causes far deeper and more powerful than those which the statesman or legislator can control ; and that more is to be accomplished by trying to observe and study these causes than by seeking to repress their operation. In this modern view we are able to develop a true science of political economy. It is one which concerns itself primarily with explanations rather than precepts. It bears the same relation to the arts of statesmanship and legislation that the science of physiology bears to the art of medicine, or the science of mechanics to the art of engineering. It does not prescribe to the statesman or legislator exactly what he shall do, as the ancient art of political economy would have attempted ; but it indicates limits which he cannot pass without defeating his own ends. Economics does not say that all men must be left free to make their own contracts, any more than mechanics says that all buildings must be constructed on geometrical patterns. But each science sets forth the conditions of stability and the laws of structural strain, which the statesman or the builder disregards at his own peril.

§ 15. In the modern conception of economics the word *law* is necessarily used in two quite distinct senses. In the majority of cases the economist is primarily occupied with establishing and investigating *natural* laws, or observed sequences of cause and effect. In spite of individual variations, it is now recognized that the average or typical conduct of masses of men operates with a high degree of regularity. The modern science of statistics is based on the existence of such regularity, and concerns itself exclusively with natural laws of this kind. But the economist also includes in the scope of his investigations the *positive* laws or commands relating to wealth, whether moral or jural in their character ; the former deriving their authority from the moral sentiments or religious beliefs of the community, while the latter are promulgated and enforced by the government.

§ 16. With the growth of these modern ideas of scientific method, the name *economics*, which is essentially that of a science, is gradually being substituted for the older term *political economy*, which was in some respects more applicable to an art.

§ 17. It was not by mere chance that the Declaration of Independence and the *Wealth of Nations* were published at so nearly the same time. Each involved the recognition of the same principle in different fields of human activity. In modern politics we have seen that society is better governed by allowing individuals, as far as possible, to govern themselves. In modern economics we have seen that society is made richer by allowing individuals, as far as possible, freedom to get rich in their own ways. Each of these principles has its limits ; but each marks an immeasurable advance, in politics and in economics, over the system of police government which had preceded it.

This development of individualism in economics is part of the general trend of modern thought and modern life. A few centuries ago, the principle of individual freedom was not recognized in law or in morals, any more than in trade. It was then thought that liberty in trade meant avarice, that liberty in politics meant violence, and that liberty in morals meant blasphemous wickedness. But as time went on, the modern world began to see that this old view was a mistake. Human nature was better than it had been thought. Man was not in a state of war with his Creator and all his fellow-men, which it required the combined power of the church and the police to repress. When a community had achieved political freedom, its members on the whole used that freedom to help one another instead of to hurt one another. When it had achieved moral freedom, it substituted an enlightened and progressive morality for an antiquated and formal one. When it had achieved industrial freedom, it substituted high efficiency of labor for low efficiency, and large schemes of mutual service for small ones. Constitutional liberty in politics, rational altruism in morals, and modern business methods in production and distribution of wealth have been the outcome of the great individualistic movement of the nineteenth century. The individualist has taught people not to confound public morality with a state church, public security with police activity, or public wealth with government property. He has taught men that, as society develops, the interests of its members become more and more harmonious ; in other words, that rational egoism and rational altruism tend to coincide. In fact his chief danger lies in exaggerating the completeness of this coincidence in the existing imperfect stage of human development, and in believing that freedom will do everything for society, economically and morally.  He is prone to assume that private property would necessarily be managed in the public interest, and is in danger of treating the increase of such property as a good in itself instead of a means to the public good.[1]

§ 18. These mistakes and exaggerations of individualism have afforded a legitimate field for socialistic criticism.  A socialist, in the proper definition of the word, is a man who distrusts these conclusions of the individualist and who believes that the loss from the exercise of individual freedom in most of the debatable cases outweighs the gain.  Scientific socialists have done admirable work in pointing out where the evils arising from individual freedom may exceed its advantages, and when society must use its collective authority to produce the best economic and moral results.  Men of this type must recognize that the point of issue between individualism and socialism is not a question of ends, but of means.  Both sides have the same object at heart, namely, the general good of society.  One side believes that this good is best achieved by individual freedom in a particular line of action ; the other side believes that the dangers and evils with which such freedom is attended outweigh its advantages.

§ 19. Unfortunately the contest between individualists and socialists has not been carried on in a spirit which could lead to mutual understanding.  The individualist is apt to regard the socialist as revolutionary, in the face of the fact that in conservative countries like England a great many of the ideas of socialism have been carried out by constitutional methods and in the most

---

[1] An illustration of this danger is seen in the writings of the brilliant French economist Bastiat, whose " economic harmonies " are sometimes as overstrained as the " economic antinomies " of socialists like Proudhon.

peaceable fashion.  The socialist is apt to regard the individualist as hard-hearted and immoral, in the face of the
fact that the group of individualist thinkers at the close
of the last century, headed by Jeremy Bentham, did more
to promote practical morality and enlightened care for
the unfortunate than had been accomplished for centuries
previous.  The socialist thinks that the individualist's
ideal of a good citizen is the " economic man," solely occupied with the pursuit of wealth, whom some economists
have used as a lay figure on which to exhibit their deductions.  He charges the individualist with glorifying the
pursuit of wealth and making it the chief end of man.
This is exactly the reverse of the truth.  The individualist views the pursuit of private wealth, not as an end, but
as a means to the general well-being of society.  He
shows that the effort to make money is a most powerful
incentive to work in the service of the community—in
fact the most powerful incentive the world has yet known;
and that within certain limits the commercial success or
failure of an enterprise is dependent upon the question
whether the community needs it.  To this extent he may
be said to glorify the pursuit of wealth, in showing that it
is a means of mutual service instead of mutual robbery,
an honorable ambition instead of a base one.  But in thus
elevating it to its proper place in the social order, he also
reduces it to its proper place.  By understanding the uses
of the commercial system, he is able the more effectively
to criticise its abuses.  The day is past, if ever there
was one, when indiscriminate condemnation of business
methods and business ambition can be effective.  The
moralist who tries to show that money-getting is a mean
thing overshoots the mark.  His own acts, in his daily
life, are usually enough to convict him of inconsistency.
The economist, on the other hand, in pointing out the
reasons why modern business methods are approved by
society, puts himself in a position to condemn those

methods when they are carried to a point where they cease to be of social service, and violate instead of furthering the purposes which have justified their existence.

§ 20. Individualism is not a creed or a platform, but a way of looking at things; and the same may be said of socialism. The difference between individualists and socialists is largely a matter of temperament. It comes from a difference in constitution which leads the individualist to calculate the large and remote consequences of any measure and ignore the immediate details, while the socialist feels the immediate details so strongly that he distrusts the somewhat abstract lines of thought which the individualist is prone to follow. There is always some danger that the individualist will undervalue the emotional element in dealing with economic matters. Men of the more purely intellectual type are liable to mistakes of this sort. Reasoning about human conduct is full of chances of error; and if the outcome of such reasoning is to leave a considerable number of human beings in hopeless misery, the socialist is justified in demanding that every premise and every inference in the chain of reasoning be tested, and every rational experiment be made to see whether such a consequence is really inevitable. Instances have not been wanting where the conclusions of the economists have proved wrong, and the emotions of the critics have been warranted by the event. The factory legislation of England furnishes an historic example. The economists, as a rule, condemned this legislation as wrong in principle and likely to do harm; but the results showed that these economists had overlooked certain factors of importance with regard to public health and public morals which vitiated their conclusions and justified public opinion in disregarding them.

But while the men of emotion may sometimes be right and the men of reason wrong, the chances in matters of legislation are most decidedly the other way. It is safe to say that the harm which has been done by laws based on unemotional reasoning is but a drop in the bucket compared with that which has been done by laws based on unreasoning emotion. The tendency to overvalue feeling as compared with reason is a far greater practical danger than the tendency to undervalue it. For legislation is essentially a matter of remote consequences. The man who tries to reason out these consequences will occasionally make mistakes; the man who refuses to reason them out will habitually do so. The good which state interference does is often something visible and tangible. The evil which it does is much more indirect, and can only be appreciated by careful study. The man who has his mind so fixed on some immediate object as to shut his eyes to the results of such study, is almost certain to advocate too much state action. He may succeed in passing a few good laws, but he will be responsible for a vastly larger number of bad ones.[1]

§ 21. But how are we to determine what constitutes the general good of society, or to decide, in doubtful cases, whether a law is to be regarded as good or bad? What is to be our standard of public wealth? Shall we judge it by some preconceived ethical code? This begs the whole question, for every race and every generation has a different ethical code of its own; and the very point we have to decide is, which of these several standards is the best. Or shall we judge a law by its effect on the happiness of the human race as a whole? The difficulty of measuring happiness of groups of men renders this standard wholly unpractical except in a very limited range of cases. Or shall we try to discover in which direction human evolution is tending, and call a thing good or bad according as it perpetuates itself by conforming to this tendency or destroys itself by resisting it? This is the standard which Hegel, Comte, and Darwin,

[1] Herbert Spencer, "The Man versus The State," 1884.

each in their several ways, have gradually taught the modern world to apply and accept.

The modern observer sees in human history, no less than in natural history, the record of a process of elimination and survival. He sees that laws and institutions no less than genera and species are the result of natural selection instead of being ordained by Providence for all time. He sees that the explanation, not to say the justification, of national customs and feelings must be sought in the historical reasons for their survival. The modern world is coming to look at history as a record of a struggle between different ideas and different institutions, whose issue is chiefly decided by the moral qualities of the contesting races and has its chief importance in determining the moral standards of those races in the immediate future.

§ 22. The struggle for existence among men is probably quite as severe as that among the lower forms of organic life. Among men as among animals or plants, we find a number of young brought into being which is far in excess of the number that reaches maturity. We have a constant process of elimination of the weak and selection of the strong ; a process by whose workings we may explain the formation of different types of man, as we have learned to explain the origin of species in plants or animals. In some respects the application of the doctrine of natural selection to human history is easier and clearer than its application to biology. In biology, no satisfactory explanation has been given of the preservation of acquired characteristics. Whether we hold with Darwin that they are transmitted by heredity, or with Weissmann that they are not thus transmitted, our reasoning is in either case beset with difficulties. But the student of human history is troubled with no such dilemma. Imitation and education will account for the perpetuation among the children of the useful qualities which their fathers have developed, and for the quick suppression of some qualities which have proved disastrous, without the necessity of calling in the aid of any doubtful theory of heredity.

§ 23. But while the intensity of the struggle is the same, the conditions under which it is waged are different in certain important respects. In the first place, the human struggle for existence is between groups more than between individuals. In the second place, it is a struggle for domination more than for annihilation,—a struggle which has in it the possibility of losing part of its character as a strife and giving place to an arrangement for mutual service between those whose interests at first seemed to conflict. Neither of these things is wholly confined to the human race. All the higher animals make some sort of arrangements for the protection of their young until they reach years of maturity. They have some measure of family life, in which one or both parents will readily sacrifice themselves for the preservation of their offspring; so that the struggle is to a certain extent for the preservation of families rather than of individuals. In a great many cases larger groups of animals band themselves together for mutual defence and support, so that, within the limits of the group or herd, coöperation takes the place of conflict. In a few cases, especially among the higher forms of articulate life (*e. g.* ants), we even find domination substituted for annihilation as the result of the struggle between races. The race of ants which has proved stronger in the fight no longer regards the members of the weaker race as rivals to be killed, but as helpers to be utilized in labor for which the fighting race is unfitted. Under such circumstances we find institutions and usages which are in many respects strikingly like those of semi-civilized man.

§ 24. What really distinguishes the evolution of human habits and institutions from those of the beaver or the ant is that their progress and differentiation are not accompanied by changes of corresponding importance in the physical structure of the members of the race. The fighting ant is of a different species from the working ant. All its physical characteristics are different. They cannot have a common offspring. But the fighting man and his slaves belong to the same species. Their races can and do mix. Their physical characteristics are strikingly alike. The development of distinctive habits and usages among the lower animals is coincident with, and probably incidental to, obvious changes of physical structure. But in man the variations of habit and usage are the conspicuous phenomena, while the variations of physical structure are, by comparison, neither permanent nor important. Among the lower types of organic life, instances where domination rather than annihilation is the outcome of the struggle for existence are marked by sharp structural distinctions between the groups involved; distinctions which are even more conspicuously marked in groups which render mutual service without one-sided domination. In the lower forms of life this is almost confined to organisms that stand wide apart—*e.g.*, flowers and insects. But in the human race it is most fully developed among those who stand nearest together in their plane of civilization, and who in their physical characteristics would seem to be designed for rivals rather than helpers.

§ 25. There may have been a time at the beginning of its existence when the human race lived in isolated families; when its organization was like that of the lion rather than that of the wolf. The evidence on this subject is quite untrustworthy. But the earliest and lowest races of humanity about which we can safely generalize are conspicuously gregarious. The horde is the unit, and not the family. There seems to be no reason for modifying the old word of Aristotle, that man is a political animal, and that the man without a community is either less than man or more.

When we have a struggle for existence between communities, we no longer find the stronger individuals preserved at the expense of the weaker. It is the stronger form of organization which survives ; or perhaps we can better say that survival proves which of the forms of organization is the stronger. We have a natural selection of ethical types rather than physical ones. In fact the very strength of the bonds which hold the organization together may prevent the elimination of weaker individuals and pave the way for physical degeneration of the race as a whole ; realizing Goethe's fear that the world would turn into a vast hospital where the best energies of the strong would be taxed to take care of the weak.

§ 26. To avoid this danger, which becomes more imminent as civilization advances, every good organization provides for a certain amount of struggle within the group itself. Such a struggle between individuals is of importance, in order to prevent the group type from becoming so rigid, and its laws and customs so inflexible, as to render it unable to adapt itself to changed conditions. But these conflicts within the group are to be regarded as means for preserving the whole group and making it strong. Where an institution gives the best individuals the chance to set the pace for the whole community and force it up to their level, it affords to the race that enjoys it an advantage in the struggle for existence ; where it gives them the chance to exalt themselves by pushing down their fellows, it has an opposite effect. The individual conflict must be judged as good or bad according to its bearings on the outcome of the race conflict. If the individualist can show that freedom will really contribute to the success of a nation or community in its struggle for existence with rival nations or communities, no one is likely to dispute the advantages of freedom. If, however, the socialist can show that this freedom enriches a few in the nation at the expense of the many, and thus makes any increase in material wealth a source of weakness rather than of strength, his criticism and demand for change will be accepted. No economist of reputation at the present day would attempt to ignore the ethical aspects of an institution, as might have been done fifty years ago. Instead of asserting the complete independence of economics and ethics, the modern economist, whether individualist or socialist, would insist on the close connection between the two sciences. He would say that nothing could be economically beneficial which was ethically bad, because such economic benefit could be only transitory. He would insist with equal force that nothing could be ethically good which was economically disastrous, because in this case also destruction must ensue with equal certainty. The economist must understand the ethical bearings of the results which he discusses ; the moralist must understand the economic consequences of the action which he advocates.

§ 27. Now that the world has come to recognize the true position and importance of economic history, it is useless to try to divide the economists of today into deductive and historical schools, according as they employ one method or the other. Every good economist now employs both methods by turns; being guided in his choice by the character of the problem he is investigating. The old antithesis between deductive and historical schools is giving place to a distinction between static and dynamic problems. In a static problem we assume that the character and institutions of a people remain fixed while the relations between the individual members change. In a dynamic problem we take account of the progressive changes in national character which result from the altered conditions of individuals. If the economist takes human nature and human society as he finds them in the most civilized communities, with all their habits and their motives, their institutions and their theories, and on the basis of this assumption inquires what will be the effect of any proposed line of action upon the production and distribution of wealth, and the general well-being of society, this is called the deductive method of investigation. It deduces consequences from a given set of social conditions; it is the method chiefly used in dealing with static problems. But the economist may go one step farther back and inquire how these motives and institutions have arisen; how far they are themselves capable of modification; what causes at the present day may be contributing to modify them. This is called the historical method of inquiry, and is of special importance in the study of dynamic problems.

§ 28. Most of the every-day work of economists involves the deductive method rather than the historical. If we ask why the price of wheat is falling; or why wages are high in a certain locality; or what is the probable effect of a proposed tax law upon production and prices; or how the various classes in the community are influenced by the use of silver as money;—we take human nature as we find it, and consider how commercial motives operate in affecting demand and supply in various lines of industry. But in the more difficult questions which involve moral judgment, the historical method must be combined with the deductive. If we ask whether trades-unions are a good thing or a bad thing, it is not enough to consider their momentary effect on wages, prices, and demand for labor. We must study this carefully; but we must also study something more. We must look at the educational effect of such organizations upon successive generations of workmen and capitalists. Have they, in actual history, been wisely or unwisely led? Have they taught workmen to do better work or worse work than was obtained by free competition? Have they secured a more equitable distribution of wealth among the members of the community? Are they likely to mitigate or to intensify those conflicts between capital and labor which form such a source of social weakness in the present economic system? All these questions must be answered, and the probable gains and losses carefully balanced, before we are in a position to pass judgment on the question in its most fundamental aspect. In a broad problem of this kind, deductive economics and deductive ethics are equally helpless. The two sciences must be studied historically in connection with one another.

# CHAPTER II.

## ECONOMIC RESPONSIBILITY.

Slavery — Property — Emancipation — The Persistence of Poverty — The Malthusian Theory—Poor Relief—Compulsory Insurance.

For a fuller account of the sociological basis of economics the reader is referred to F. H. Giddings, "Principles of Sociology," New York, 1896. A. Wagner, "Grundlegung" (vol. i. of his "Lehrbuch der Politischen Oekonomie"), 3d ed., Leipzig, 1893 ; and A. Loria, "Les Bases Économiques de la Constitution Sociale," Paris, 1893, may be read with advantage. The latter deals with economic history from a distinctly socialistic standpoint.

J. Bonar : "Malthus and his Work," London, 1885.

H. Fawcett : "Pauperism," London, 1871.

G. Drage : "The Unemployed," London, 1894 ; "The Aged Poor," London, 1895.

§ 29. PRIMITIVE man seems to have lived in much the same way as did the animals about him. He obtained his food by hunting, by fishing, or by consuming such vegetable products as lay ready to his hand ; in other words, by the destruction of the lower forms of organic life. But as civilization began to develop, he learned to utilize animals and plants instead of destroying them. Instead of killing all the animals which he captured in the chase, he found that they could serve him more usefully by being domesticated. Some, like the dog or the horse, could assist him in hunting and increase the certainty of spoils. Some, like the goat or the cow, could give him a steady supply of milk. Some, like the sheep, could be made to multiply their numbers, and give an assured source of warmth in time of cold and a reserve of food when hunting or fishing proved unproductive. A little later he learned to utilize plants as well as animals. Instead of eating all the fruit which he found, semi-civilized man saved a part for seed, and had more to eat during the coming year. Instead of destroying the means of food supply that nature furnished, he took care to replace them in increasing numbers. Instead of seeking income only, he began to accumulate capital.[1]

§ 30. This change in his attitude toward the lower forms of life paved the way for a change in his attitude toward his fellow-men. When a tribe of men lived by hunting, it looked upon the members of other tribes as rivals, to be killed, if not eaten. So late as Roman times a stranger (*hostis*) was synonymous with •an enemy. Where the available food supply was small, every additional mouth was a positive evil. As a consequence the wars between different tribes were wars of extermination. Prisoners could not be taken ; for the only way in which they could support themselves was by hunting, and if they were given weapons to hunt with, they might use them to the destruction of their conquerors. In a state of society like this female captives were occasionally spared ; male captives almost never, unless for some very exceptional reasons the conquerors were prepared to adopt the captive as a member of their own tribe.

But when the domestication of animals and the cultivation of plants came into use, the case was altered. The captives could be employed to perform labor which was disagreeable to their conquerors. This labor required no weapons and did not render the slaves dangerous ; though we find some tribes where captives were habitually blinded as a precaution against insurrection, as in Herodotus description of the Scythians. The more the arts advanced, the greater was the opportunity to utilize such

[1] In the public sense—not as yet in the private sense.

unwarlike labor and the larger was the proportion of captives whose lives were spared.

Such was the origin of slavery. As compared with the conditions that preceded it, it represented a positive gain for humanity. From the standpoint of the captive, it was better to be spared even for a life of hard labor than to be put to death without mercy. From the standpoint of the conqueror, it was an intellectual and moral advance to forego the cruel delight of torturing enemies for the sake of the future advantages to be obtained from mastery over their persons and powers. From the standpoint of the community as a whole, it was an immeasurable gain to have labor exercised continuously for a remote end, even though it was bestowed grudgingly and under compulsion.

§ 31. Those who look at the virtues of free communities, and the vices which develop in connection with the system of slavery, are often tempted to regard its introduction as a degradation of society. Even if they admit that the new system enables a great many people to live who would otherwise have been put to death, they think that this is accompanied by a lowering of the average moral standard of the community. There is much superficial reason for this view. Where all men were free, and all skilled in the use of arms, there was universal self-reliance and self-respect. Where each man by the same token was able to protect the honor of his daughter, sister, or wife, there was frequently a high degree of respect for women. But these merits were outweighed by an insecurity which rendered progress impossible. So much of the strength of the community had to be spent in fighting, that there was little opportunity for present comfort and no chance to lay the foundation for future improvement. The rose-colored view of the life of free communities which people held a few years ago is no longer universally accepted. Great as were the disadvantages attending it, there is reason to believe that the condition of serfdom gave to the majority of the people who lived under it a positive advance in present enjoyment and in possibility of increased future enjoyment. The mediæval villein who had to give half his time to the service of a feudal lord was better off, materially at any rate, than a man who, though nominally free, had to spend half of his working time in self-protection, and who even on those terms could not protect his family from outrage, nor the results of his labor from arson and pillage.[1]

§ 32. But while slave labor marked an advance over the conditions which had preceded it, it was far from being a good system according to modern standards. It was better than no labor at all. This was about all that could be said in its favor. If people would not work except on compulsion, it was a good thing for society to have that compulsion exercised. But the result was at best unsatisfactory. The slave tended to keep his product at a minimum. He was compelled by the overseer to do a certain amount ; he had no inducement to do more than that amount. He had reason to believe that his master would be forced by self-interest to allow the slave enough to keep him alive ; he was still surer that the master would not allow him more than this. Any extra exertion or care redounded to the profit of the master, not of the slave. The inevitable result was low efficiency and great waste. The more complicated the work to be done, the less was the chance of avoiding these evils. A slave-driver could compel those who were subjected to his rule to perform a certain amount of physical labor: but he could not compel them to exercise intelligence or zeal. These were only to be secured when the hope of reward came in to supplement or take the place of the fear of punishment. When

---

[1] Modern historical criticism has cast doubt on the idea, so universally held a short time ago, that the development of feudalism supplanted a system of free and prosperous village communities.

the habit of labor and the capacity for labor were sufficiently developed in a race of men, the institution of property furnished a far more potent means of getting work done for society than did the institution of slavery. While it allowed the shiftless men to do a little less, it encouraged the prudent and ambitious to do a great deal more.

§ 33. It must not be supposed that property rights originated in considerations of this kind. Though the institution of property is a most important motive to the zealous and intelligent application of labor, it was not devised for this purpose. The earliest property rights were based on occupancy rather than on labor. They were a recognition of the power of the strong man to retain what he had seized, not of the right of the industrious man to enjoy what he had produced. We may fairly grant the claim of the socialist that capital originated in robbery. In like manner, labor originated in slavery. Neither fact has any appreciable bearing on present issues. Neither fact tends in the least to prove either that the capitalist is a thief or the laborer an inferior.

§ 34. At first, property seemed indistinguishable from possession. The so-called property-rights of uncivilized tribes are for the most part customs regulating the claims conferred by possession, rather than guarantees of permanent ownership. True property right is something quite distinct from the fact of possession or from the claims which such possession gives the occupant. It involves a recognition on the part of the community that some individual or group of individuals has permanent authority over certain objects, whether he is actually using them or not. In the hunting stage of society there was very little property right, because most of the useful objects took the form of food for immediate consumption or clothing and weapons for continuous use. In any of these cases the fact of possession was the important matter

and established a right of use. A man was left in possession of the things which he himself made, used, and consumed. But the same progress in the arts which gave
the chance for labor and paved the way for slavery, gave
rise to questions of ownership and to a more complex
system of property rights. Whenever there was an alternative between domination and destruction, as in taming
an animal instead of eating it, or in sparing a prisoner of
war instead of killing him, it was necessary to strengthen
the motives which should lead people to sacrifice obvious
present enjoyment for the sake of large future advantage
to the community. An animal was far more likely to be
domesticated if the man who had captured it was allowed
special and enduring rights to its use. The prisoner of
war was far more likely to be spared by his captor if that
captor was assured that the slave would be recognized as
belonging permanently to him rather than to the community as a whole.

§ 35. Such ancient property rights are for the most part
not well earned, according to modern standards. They
are due to force more than to labor. The men who enjoyed
the most property were, as a rule, the successful fighters
rather than the industrious workers. But such a system
of property, in spite of its apparent violations of justice,
has served an important purpose. It marks the beginning
of a higher civilization. It enables the races that have
lived under it to reach a higher stage of material and
moral development than their rivals who have had no
such system.

In the first place, it tends to the preservation of useful
things. It causes domination to take the place of extinction as a habit in peace and a purpose in war.[1] It gives
the race a larger amount of accumulated wealth of every
sort ; and this wealth, though primarily enjoyed by a few

[1] Compare O. Effertz, " Katechismus der Politischen Oekonomik," Bonn,
1893. Lieferung III.

who have perhaps done least to merit it, nevertheless contributes to the strength and security of the whole people
and their possibilities of enjoyment in the future.   Insecurity of tenure makes wealth likely to be destroyed.   It
was noticed in the American Civil War that when a regi-
ment was ordered to leave a camping ground which it had
gradually made comfortable, a fire was almost certain to
arise which would consume all the non-portable improvements.

§ 36. In the second place, property right, even when
based upon force, creates a class of men more or less
removed from the immediate pressure of poverty.   The
man who holds accumulated wealth can use it for the permanent advantage of himself and his children, and enable
them to develop physically and mentally in the face of
industrial vicissitudes which would otherwise bring the
whole community to the verge of starvation.   Property
of this kind is accumulated not for the individual alone,
but for his family.   Its development is associated with
the development of modern family life.   It paves the way
for a progressive advance of the members of a family from
generation to generation.   By exempting the children of
the fortunate few from the burdens of want which, if
equally shared, would drag the whole race down, it
allows them to advance and to pave the way for a similar
advance on the part of others.   The desire to make provision for one's children is not merely a potent motive for
the preservation of property, but a powerful means for
giving free room to the process of natural selection of the
types most fit for permanent strength and survival.

§ 37. In the third place, such accumulations of property, combined as they are with family life and family
feeling, create a conservative class in the community
which stands on the side of law rather than of violence, of
construction rather than of destruction.   If a strong man
has no property, he has everything to gain and nothing

to lose by the constant prevalence of petty warfare. If, however, he has useful rights which he wishes society to recognize, and, above all, if he desires a permanent recognition of those rights for his children as well as for himself, his powers are enlisted on the side of tranquillity and permanence rather than on that of war and change. He is interested in giving increased power to law and to the sentiment of respect for law ; a process which, as it is carried toward its completion, must work for the benefit of the weak quite as much as for that of the strong. Even if his property right was originally based upon acts of violence, he is led to discourage the continuance of this method of acquisition among his immediate neighbors, and to make usage, rather than force, the basis on which society is to recognize rights of possession.

§ 38. If this point has been reached, and the strong man appeals to customary rights among his neighbors, it is but a short step to the recognition of such customary rights among his slaves. Whether a nation takes this step or not depends very largely upon its foreign relations. If these are such that the supply of slaves from abroad continues rapid and steady, the acknowledgment that slaves have rights makes little progress. The old slaves are worked to death, new ones take their place, and there is no room for the creation of a traditional status which slave laborers may inherit from generation to generation. Even among the most civilized nations of antiquity the progress of emancipation was slow as long as wars of conquest were matters of every-day occurrence. The Romans created a system of property right which enabled them to accumulate wealth, to develop an aristocratic class, and to secure the highest degree of law and order within the Roman dominions ; but it was a long time before the slaves obtained much benefit from this process, because slave labor from abroad was so readily obtained by conquest. In mediæval Europe, on the other hand, while

there was much less accumulation of wealth and much
less respect for law, there was far more rapid recognition
of civil rights on the part of the laborers who were actually engaged in the production of wealth. It is true
that these rights were by no means accurately defined.
Serfs could be sold into foreign parts, and different members of families separated from one another by such
sale, to a far greater degree than is generally supposed.[1]
But a custom grew up and grew stronger from generation
to generation, rendering such infringements of personal
liberty more and more rare as time went on.  In mediæval
serfdom, as we generally see it in western Europe from
the twelfth to the fifteenth century, the villein was bound
to labor for his lord a certain number of days, and on
other days was allowed to work for himself or for his own
community on certain lands set apart for that purpose.
He had thus attained, by custom rather than by law, a
certain measure of freedom and a status in the community
which placed his position far above that of the Roman
slave.

§ 39. Where such customary rights have been once
established and no new sources of supply of slave labor
are opened, the necessity of stimulating production causes
the workmen to be given proprietary rights in the product of their labor.  This is at first most conspicuous in
manufacturing industries.  A few skilled workmen collect
in a town where they can defend themselves against military aggression, and then produce goods so far superior
in quantity and quality to the product of their enslaved
competitors that the feudal lord soon comes to purchase
goods from the town instead of relying on the few rude
articles which can be made on his own domain.  The
towns thus become a centre of free trade and free labor.

§ 40. The same course of events works itself out in

---

[1] D'Avenel: "Histoire Économique de la Propriété," Paris, 1894, pp.
162 *ff.*

agriculture, though as a rule more gradually. The free-man working for himself can produce so much more than the serf that there is a chance for both parties, lord and vassal, to gain by the process of emancipation. If the amount which a man produces in a day when he works for his landlord is worth a halfpenny, and the amount which he produces when he works for himself is worth one and a half pence, it is for the advantage of both the landlord and the laborer to make a contract whereby the laborer agrees to pay the landlord a penny in lieu of each day's labor previously rendered. Such a contract is also advantageous to the public wealth of the community as a whole, by causing increased food supply and consequent increase either of numbers or of strength. The more in-telligent and ambitious the laborer, the greater will be the difference between his minimum product which he creates as a serf and his maximum product which he can create as a freeman ; the greater, therefore, will be the possible advantages to all parties from emancipation. Hence we find that the passage from slavery to freedom came earliest and worked itself out most completely in those countries where the general ability of the villein class was greatest. In England, between the twelfth and the fourteenth century, there was a rapid change in the position of the cultivators of the soil, whereby money rents of small amount were substituted for compulsory labor.[1]  On the continent of Europe the change did not take place so soon, nor was it so complete when it came. Instead of agreeing to pay a certain amount of money, as was generally the case in England, the continental peasants usually contracted to pay a certain share of the product to the owner of the soil. They thus gained a part of the benefit of their industry and ambition, instead of the whole. This system of share rents, whereby the cultivator gives the proprietor a percentage of the pro-

[1] W. J. Ashley : "English Economic History," chap. i.

duct, is known as the *metayer* system. Even this degree of independence was not attained by most of the peasantry in central Europe until the close of the last century, while in Russia the system of serfdom lasted with but slight modifications until 1863.

§ 41. It must not be supposed that this change from slavery to free labor was voluntarily suggested, or even readily accepted, by the feudal lords. It was forced upon them by the conditions of the struggle for existence between different races and different members of the same race. As Europe was constituted in the Middle Ages, the land was by no means well utilized. Scarcely any district produced anything like the amount of food and other supplies which would have been possible under a better system of government. As long as warfare was carried on with rude appliances, this lack of good agriculture, however injurious to the comfort of the mass of the people, did not seriously cripple the fighting power of the privileged classes. But with the improvements in military art, which rendered capital necessary for the successful waging of war, it was impossible for a man to fight to advantage unless his vassals worked to advantage. Where every man was ready to fight on short notice and armies could be supported by plundering the peaceful inhabitants of the country through which they travelled, whether friend or foe, the necessity of large supplies was not clearly manifest. But when war was waged on such a scale that a campaign involved weeks of preparation and days of occupancy of the same ground, victory was apt to rest with the man who had the best commissary service. Under these circumstances, the race that could feed and clothe its army on the largest scale had an enormous advantage in the conflict, and one which generally proved decisive. It was for this reason quite as much as for any other that we find kings so often taking the side of free labor. It was not because they loved serfs and hated nobles, but because, warring on a large scale, they were compelled to maintain large armies and to give their acquiescence to the system by which such armies could best be fed.

§ 42. The force of these considerations is illustrated by the history of emancipation in Russia and in the United States. To the Russian government, the Crimean war had proved that a country living under the old industrial order, however large her population and her army, could not even on her own ground cope successfully with countries which enjoyed modern industrial methods. Emancipation thus became a military necessity. In the United States this necessity was even more strikingly emphasized, because the contending parties were of the same race and on the same general level of civilization, differing only in the fact that the North relied on free labor and the South on slave labor. The contest was decided, not by the direct result of military operations—for if we look at battles alone the victories of the South were more conspicuous than those of the North—but by the fact that the North was able to maintain her supplies of every necessary article almost unimpaired by the stress of war, while the South was brought low by continually increasing exhaustion. The war was not decided by disparity of numbers between the two sections; for this disparity was nearly counterbalanced by the advantage which the South had in acting on the defensive. It was the disparity of industrial systems which decided the issue of the contest.

§ 43. It must not be assumed that emancipation is a good thing for every man or for every race. Compulsory labor is better than no labor at all. If people are not ready to work for fear of starvation tomorrow, they must be forced to work by physical compulsion today. If they are not accessible to motives of ambition, there is danger that the loss by the introduction of free labor will outweigh the gain. Where a body of serfs contributes in large measure to the working out of its own emancipation, there is not much danger of this result. The struggles necessary to obtain freedom form the best preparation for freedom and the best guarantee that it will be wisely used. But where emancipation is imposed from above by outside power, whether from motives of humanity or of self-interest, there is great danger that, for the time being at least, the losses will outweigh the gains. The emancipation of the slaves in South American countries has not always contributed to the commercial prosperity of the countries which set them free or to their general standard of morality and efficiency. Even in the United States it seemed for many years questionable whether the good resulting from the abolition of slavery would outweigh the evil. A population which had never worked except under immediate compulsion was suddenly given the highest degree of freedom. To a considerable part of the negro race this freedom meant liberty to desert their families and to violate all contracts for continuous work. For many years the free labor of the South was too uncertain to be available for industries requiring uninterrupted toil. Iron manufactures failed in regions conspicuously well adapted for iron production, because no laborers could be found to keep a furnace in blàst if a circus unexpectedly appeared in the next county. They were ready to sacrifice all prospects of future employment for the sake of the day's gratification. Of late this state of things has changed for the better. The increasing development of business ability among the leading men of the South, coupled with the adaptability and docility of most of the negroes, has at length enabled the country to secure the advantages of free labor. In spite of many perplexing problems connected with increase of negro population, the worst difficulties of emancipation have been evidently surmounted.

§ 44. In Russia the result is not nearly so good.

Though the Russian peasant was a little more self-reliant than the negro slave, he was by no means so adaptable to new conditions. Nor were the Russian nobility fitted, either by power or by inclination, to take the lead in teaching the peasantry good business habits. Under such circumstances, the condition of the Russian free peasant today seems to be worse than that of the serf a generation ago. He has diminished instead of increasing his productiveness. He has fallen under the control of the money-lender, who proves quité as hard a master as the old noble. Not having been mentally qualified at the start to avail himself of the advantages which emancipation offered, he has gradually sunk into a position where those advantages are out of his reach, no matter how great the industry or the ambition which he might show. People differ as to the remedy ; but there is a general consensus of opinion among all who are versed in Russian affairs that the state of things as it exists at present is a most unsatisfactory one, and that emancipation has failed to accomplish the good which was expected.

§ 45. The gradual progress of emancipation widens the circle of those who can free themselves from the imminent danger of poverty. Instead of being confined to the military chieftain, a fair degree of comfort comes within the reach of a large number of men of industry and ability. Under the system of slavery, the worker had no inducement to increase his output or to diminish his consumption. Under the system of free labor, each increase in the amount that he produces and each diminution in the amount that he consumes goes to make up a fund which will ensure him and his children against danger of starvation. Under these circumstances there is a force constantly at work to build up a race of industrious and prudent men. Poverty is by no means abolished, but it is localized. The ancient world was constantly in dread of famines which swept away large sections of the com-

munity and diminished the strength of those that survived. Today we no longer regard such universal misery
as a probable incident of economic life. When there is
an approximation to such a condition, as in the potato
famine in Ireland in 1846, or in the occasional years of
great distress in the Russian Empire, it is due to exceptional causes which have prevented the laborer from
realizing the benefits of freedom. In the most advanced
communities, extreme poverty is very apt to be associated
with gambling, drinking, or general shiftlessness. The unfortunate but deserving poor, though still far too numerous, are the exception rather than the rule.

§ 46. While it is true that poverty persists in the
midst of advancing wealth, it is not true that it increases,
as so many people are led to suppose. Judged by the
best criteria which we can apply, poverty as a whole is
diminishing rather than increasing. Both the absolute
standard of comfort attained by the average laborer, and
the share of national income which goes to labor, seem
to be better now than in any period for which we have
adequate data for comparison. [1] Perhaps the chief reason
why the evils of poverty are so emphasized in modern
times is to be sought in the very progress which has localized poverty. As long as danger of starvation was regarded as the common lot of mankind, from which only a
favored few were exempt, it seemed as idle to complain
of poverty as it was to complain of heat or cold. But
when most people were relieved from a pressure which
was formerly wellnigh universal, the lot of those who remained under the yoke excited commiseration as something exceptional. As theories of political and social

---

[1] This subject is further developed in subsequent chapters. See also Rae :
"Contemporary Socialism," chapter on "Socialism and the Social Question." Atkinson : "The Distribution of Products," Part i. Reasonings on
either side of this question based on uncritical use of census figures are quite
worthless.

equality make progress, the industrial inequality between richer and poorer members of a community is felt to be a grievance. Even by some of those who grant that the system of free labor has tended to diminish the number of the poor, the fact that any people whatever remain poor and out of work is made an indictment against it. It is felt by many that our theories of political equality and our sense of moral duty are violated if any man who is willing to work cannot obtain the chance to exercise his powers and obtain a living wage by so doing. Admitting, as they must, that much of the poverty is due to causes for which the poor themselves are to blame, they do not feel that society has done its duty as long as any man who is willing to work is deprived of the opportunity.

§ 47. This view was subjected to sharp criticism by Malthus at the close of the last century.[1] He made a systematic attempt to prove that society could not undertake to provide work for all who might desire it, and that poverty was a necessary incident of the struggle for existence rather than an indictment against modern society. It is of the utmost importance to determine the truth or error of the Malthusian theory. According as we accept or reject it we change our mental attitude toward a large number of schemes of social reform. If poverty is inevitable and simply represents a sacrifice of individuals for the sake of the progress of the race, we may and must view with resignation a number of evils which can only be made worse by attempting to eradicate them. If, on the other hand, it is in large measure a preventable thing, then the claims of our present civilization to favorable judgment, in the matter of either material or moral prosperity, can hardly stand for a moment.

§ 48. The Malthusian theory, in brief, is that population has a tendency to multiply faster than subsistence, and that, under such circumstances, some people will neces-

[1] "Essay on the Principle of Population," 1798.

sarily fail to have the food they need; that poverty is therefore inevitable unless the race as a whole adopts preventive means to restrict the increase of its numbers. In the absence of such preventive checks to population, the Malthusian holds that poverty is unavoidable, and that the numbers of the race will be kept down by vice and misery.

§ 49. In order to understand the chain of proof by which this theory is supported,[1] let us look at the relations between the birth and death rates and the prosperity of the community as a whole. By the birth rate, as it is ordinarily expressed in statistics, we mean the number of births per thousand inhabitants per year. If in a city of 100,000 inhabitants the records show 300 births in a month, we say that this represents a birth rate of 36, because the same number continued through the twelve months would make 3,600 in a year for the whole city of 100,000, or 36 per thousand. The physiological possibilities of the birth rate in the human race, when not restrained by intellectual, social, or moral considerations, are thought to be as high as 60 per thousand, though no statistics show a birth rate as large as this over any considerable extent of space or time.

The death rate is computed and expressed in the same manner as the birth rate. For instance, if the number of deaths in the same city during a month was 200, it represents a death rate of 24.

The lowness of the death rate is an index of social prosperity. If the death rate is high it means that there is a large amount of disease and waste and a short average duration of human life. If, on the other hand, the death rate is low, it means that the average duration of human life is long, disease relatively infrequent, and

---

[1] The line of argument which follows differs in some respects from that adopted by Malthus. It represents the modern proof of the theory rather than the one originally advanced.

working power well utilized. A death rate of 20 per thousand means an average duration of life of 50 years. A death rate of 40 per thousand means an average duration of only 25 years, with all the misery which such a state of things connotes.

§ 50. The difference between the birth rate and the death rate in any one year represents the rate of increase of population for that year. If the birth rate is 45 per thousand, and the death rate 25 per thousand, the increase of population is 20 per thousand, or two per cent. Such an increase in any given area means a corresponding increase of the density of population. As long as this increase is accompanied by corresponding improvements in the arts of producing and utilizing food, it has no adverse effect; but when the increase of numbers is more rapid than this, it involves difficulty in obtaining enough for people to eat. For it is a fact thoroughly established by observation, that in any given stage of the arts there is a certain point beyond which increased application of labor and capital does not obtain correspondingly increased supplies of food from a given area. A territory which can support one million men in comfort cannot do the same for two million under the same conditions of cultivation. Either the two million must work very much harder to obtain their food supplies from the land, or they must content themselves with less food *per capita.* This great law of agricultural production is known as the law of the diminishing return. Up to a certain point increased amounts of labor and capital are accompanied by more than proportionate increase in the product; but when this point is passed the additional returns diminish rapidly and not infrequently cease altogether. In order to live at all the laborers have to seek out new lands less advantageous than the old, or to content themselves with obtaining the necessary product from the old lands at an economic disadvantage.

§ 51. Whenever a country has become so crowded that such a state of things as this is realized, the struggle for domination between individuals gives place to a struggle for extinction. Each man in striving to obtain enough to keep himself alive leaves less than enough for some other man. As society is at present organized this pressure will be felt most severely by those who have large families of children. The prudent man, who has not married until assured of his ability to support a family, has placed himself outside of the severest stress of this struggle. But his less prudent competitor, who earns no more and who has more mouths to feed, may find himself, and often does find himself, through no fault of his own except lack of foresight, in a position where he is unable to keep his children alive. Not that in civilized communities they often die of actual and direct starvation ; but that the lack of the food best adapted to their wants makes them succumb to disease where better-fed children would survive.

§ 52. Under favorable circumstances this scarcity of food may be avoided by improvements in the arts, whether of agriculture, of domestic economy, or of good government. Whatever contributes to the better utilization of the products of the land for human support increases the number of people that can be maintained without the danger of starvation. This result is produced by any improvement in agriculture which enables the land to furnish larger crops ; or by better cooking, which enables more nourishment to be obtained out of the same crop. Improvements in clothing and shelter, which keep people warm, may take the place of food which was once needed to produce heat. Methods of government which cause a larger part of the land to be utilized for the support of the nation or diminish losses and waste from violence, may serve to prevent the pressure of overcrowding. But the physiological possibilities of the birth rate are so far in excess of any death-rate which is consonant with social prosperity that the improvement in the art of food supply, direct or indirect, will not generally keep pace with this possible excess. Even if the pressure be momentarily relieved, the reduction of the death rate, which is a consequence of such relief and an index of prosperity, serves to hasten the time when the increase of population reaches the limit set by the possibilities of supporting it.

§ 53. A fact like this may be obscured for a time in a country like the United States, where settlers with a high degree of civilization occupy land which is almost empty. Before such a country has filled up to the level permitted by modern civilization, increase of numbers will for a long time mean increased economic advantage, and the law of the diminishing return will drop out of sight. But the United States is doing, in little more than a century, what it has taken Europe several thousands of years to do. It is passing from a density of population limited by the arts of the hunting stage to one which is allowed by the modern arts of scientific agriculture. Such a state of things is necessarily exceptional, and must terminate in a comparatively short time.[1]

§ 54. This pressure of population upon subsistence serves in no slight degree as a stimulus to improvement in the arts. It was this which forced hunting tribes to practice the domestication of animals. It was this which forced wandering pastoral tribes to settle down and apply themselves to the less exciting and agreeable arts of agriculture. It is this which has done much to accelerate the change from the military organization of society to the modern system of free labor. The attempt to provide for all children that might be born would, in the opinion

---

[1] The criticism of Henry George ("Progress and Poverty," book ii.), which is perhaps to readers of the present generation the most familiar argument against the Malthusian theory, overlooks this exceptional character of American conditions.

of the Malthusian, not only prove futile from the difficulty of finding food enough to go around, but it would also, first, take away the stimulus under which progress had been made ; second, put a stop to the natural selection of the stronger individuals and families and reduce the race to a dead level; third, impair the capital of the community through increased consumption and diminished production so much that it could not maintain the stage of civilization which it had reached, and that its progress must give place to retrogression. The Malthusian therefore argues that society cannot undertake to relieve its members from the pressure and from the evils of poverty unless they will consent to adopt preventive checks to population. They must be prepared so far to reduce the birth rate that the excess of the actual birth rate over the admissible death rate will not outstrip the annual improvement in the arts of producing food. If we wish to reduce the death rate to 25 in the thousand and the increase in food supply from the area available is not likely to average more than one per cent. annually, the birth rate must be kept down to 35. The man who marries recklessly, so as to make the consumption of his family exceed its contribution to the annual product of the nation, is, in the opinion of the Malthusian, assuming the right to do something which must prove disastrous to the race if adopted generally. Against the attempt to burden society as a whole with the results of such imprudence the Malthusian protests emphatically. If the relief of a certain section of the poorer classes results, not in the accumulation of property by those classes, but in the multiplication of the number of their children, society, by the relief which it furnishes, simply transfers its food supplies from the support of the children of the efficient and prudent to the support of the children of the shiftless and imprudent. Such a course must result in degeneration. It is a condition of social progress that society must keep its increase of numbers within the limits set by improvement in the arts. In order to make such a general restriction of numbers possible, the responsibility for diminishing the numbers of his own family must be brought home to every man ; and if this responsibility is ignored, the blame for the condition of the family must be imputed, not to society as a whole, but to the man who has ignored a social necessity.

§ 55. To this view the opponents of Malthus reply :

1. There is almost never, in civilized society, a present or immediate pressure of population upon subsistence. There is always food enough to go around, if it were only better distributed. 2. If such a distribution were made, there is no likelihood of a future pressure of population upon subsistence, because increased comfort is accompanied by a lower birth rate instead of a higher one.

§ 56. These critics overlook the fact that this surplus of food in civilized countries is itself a consequence of that family responsibility on which the Malthusian lays so much stress. In uncivilized countries there is not habitually any such surplus. It is a matter of very great doubt in each year whether there is going to be food enough to go around. Famine and weakness, resulting from too great numbers and too little food, constitute an ever-present danger to an uncivilized or half civilized tribe. The efforts to avoid this danger testify to its existence and its importance. Not a few races have habitually resorted to infanticide as the only means of keeping the numbers of the tribe within the power of the land to support. Others, a step farther advanced, have tried to solve the question of population by leaving the matter to the women,—a system known as the matriarchate. Each of these methods lessened the burden of unproductive consumption, but neither of them fully met the necessities of the case. While they checked consumption and made accumulation possible, they did not provide

security for such accumulations of capital nor means of
natural selection of the strong ; still less did they afford
the stimulus to production which the combination of private property and family life gives to the modern laborer
in all but the very lowest classes.

§ 57.   Nor have we any reason to believe that increased
comfort is necessarily accompanied by a lowering of the
birth rate.   It is true that as society exists at present,
high comfort and low birth rate are commonly associated,
because comfort is made to depend upon prudence.   Let
the comfort be made independent of prudence, as in the
case of the pauper or criminal, and the birth rate tends to
increase rather than diminish.   It may not be exactly
true, as some Malthusians would have us believe, that the
low birth rate is the cause of the comfort, but it is much
farther from the truth to assert that the comfort is the
cause of the low birth rate.   Both are the results of a
common cause—the exercise of prudence, which gives
high comfort and low birth rate to those who are capable
of practicing it, while those who are incapable of so doing
have at once a higher birth rate and a lower level of
comfort.[1]

§ 58.   This line of thought enables us to explain satis-
factorily a phenomenon which has been misunderstood
by many of the opponents of Malthus, namely, that the
fear of starvation does not lower the birth rate so much
as the fear of losing social standing.   In the light of what
has just been said, the reason for this is perfectly clear.   It
is not that social ambition *in itself* constitutes a greater
preventive check to population than the need of subsistence ; but that the need of subsistence is felt by all
men alike, emotional as well as intellectual, while social

---

[1] No amount of facts such as are accumulated by writers like Nitti will
prove anything against the Malthusian theory.  Statistics show that high
comfort and low birth rate go hand in hand.  They are absolutely incapable
of showing which is cause and which is effect.

ambition stamps the man or the race that possesses it as having reached the level of intellectual morality. Ethical selection can therefore operate on the latter class as it does not on the former. The intellectual man has possibilities of self-restraint which the emotional man has not. Give the intellectual man the chance to reap the benefit of such self-restraint, and you will find reduced birth rate and increased comfort going hand in hand.

There are some cases under the existing social order where men who are capable of higher things multiply recklessly through sheer hopelessness. With men like this, a better distribution of the results of labor would doubtless operate not only to increase their productive efficiency but to contribute to their prudence in marrying, and thus to diminish the birth rate. But this result would be accomplished by assimilating the condition of these men to the normal condition of property owners, and would be dependent on the operation of those prudential motives which the majority of the opponents of Malthus habitually decry.

§ 59. The more completely you give the prudent and efficient man control of the results of his labor, the more do you localize the pressure of population upon subsistence, and confine the effects of this pressure to a few. Under such circumstances there is habitually that surplus of food on which the anti-Malthusian lays so much stress. But give the children of the shiftless, by thoughtless charity or various systems of poor relief, the right to eat the substance of the efficient and prudent, and you will soon lose both the capital and the morality under which that capital has been created.

When the comfort of an individual is made dependent upon his foresight and prudence, and when the comfort of a group is made dependent on the existence of intellectual as distinct from emotional morality, we shall find prudent men and prudent races possessing high comfort

4

and low birth rates. The history of civilization is in large measure a history of this development of prudence and comfort. Possibly some nations are carrying this conscious adaptation of means to ends a little too far for their own good. The waste of nerve power connected with the exercise of conscious prudence is a real evil, and if carried to an extreme may offset the gain attendant upon the possession and accumulation of capital. The case of France is an instance in point. The French people, as a rule, logically accept the consequences of the Malthusian theory. The birth rate is low, the national wealth high, the increase of population almost *nil*. Some writers think that this course of events has been attended with moral and physical evils; that less prudence and keener struggle for existence would better serve to protect the race against danger of degeneration. The same criticism has been applied to the conditions prevailing in many parts of the United States.

§ 60. This is a fair point for socialistic criticism. But with the average man, the dangers of this extreme are less than those of the other. The evils of thinking too much, and trusting Providence too little, seem small in comparison with those which arise from trusting Providence for everything and not thinking at all. Doubtless Malthus made a mistake in giving too much countenance to the idea that restrictions upon population must be conscious. But his socialist critics make a greater mistake in holding that they are automatic. The truth would seem to be that they are for the most part institutional. The modern family and the modern law of capital have acted as a powerful system of preventive checks to population. The apparently automatic and often non-conscious operation of these checks must not blind us to the historical power which has established and perpetuated them. The assumption made by so many of the socialistic critics of the Malthusian theory, that the average character of a people will remain unchanged when the economic institutions under which this character has developed are radically modified or abolished, finds no warrant either in ancient or in modern history.

§ 61. It is urged by some of the socialists that the advocates of the Malthusian theory make too much use of the principle of natural selection, and ignore the equally important biological principle of functional adaptation. They urge that natural selection has in large measure done the work which was required of it in inculcating prudence, and that, in order to regulate population properly, we have only to secure those favorable economic conditions to which the race has proved its power to adapt itself. But the history of the English poor-law (§ 65) seems to show that natural selection has not done its work ; that such measure of functional adaptation as has been already secured is extremely precarious, and that it can only be maintained by continuing the stimulus under which it has developed to its present degree of activity.

§ 62. Although society insists as far as it can that each man shall be responsible for himself and his family, it cannot carry this principle out to its logical conclusion. We cannot kill off the weak merely because they have been unable to support themselves. Still less can we leave the unfortunate to die as a result of their incapacity. The ethical loss to the community which adopted such a course would indefinitely outweigh any material or physical gain. The dependent and the unfortunate must, under certain conditions, be taken care of by society, even though the process of natural selection is thereby hampered.

§ 63. Besides these two classes there are two others which habitually defy the principle that every man should earn a living for himself and his children. These are the criminal and the pauper. The case of the criminal, however hard we may find it to deal with him in practice, is easily judged from the standpoint of economic theory.

His activity must be repressed and his power of perpetuat-
ing his race limited. The case of the pauper involves
more difficulty. He is not, like the criminal, actively
hostile to society. He claims charity on grounds which
are often plausible, and which on investigation may possibly turn out to be valid. We often do not know the
real reason why a pauper seeks charity. If it is because
he can work and will not, he approaches very near to the
condition of the criminal; he is trying to get a living
out of society without rendering society an equivalent.
If he is willing and able to work but cannot find an opportunity, he is no longer a criminal but an unfortunate.
If he is mentally or physically unable to work, he is an
incapable. According as he belongs to one or the other
of these three classes he demands different treatment,
both for his own sake and for that of society. Yet it is
frequently a matter of the utmost practical difficulty to
see where he belongs. Perhaps he cannot tell himself.
He may belong to all three by turns, according to the
circumstances in which he is placed.

§ 64. In the treatment of paupers there is a natural inclination, both on the part of individuals and of the
public, to take a charitable view of the matter and give
help in doubtful cases. People think that the harm from
denying charity to a deserving man so far outweighs that
which will result from giving charity to an undeserving
one that they give relief in a great many cases simply because they have no power to make investigations. There
is an evil involved in such free exercise of private charity
which people are slow to recognize, but which is all the
more dangerous on that account. If a man gives money
to a pauper he seems to be doing an unselfish act. He
parts with a certain amount of his own property and gives
it to some one else. But the economic result does not
stop here. The dollar which is given to an undeserving
beggar and is spent by him for his own purposes diverts

the product of the labor of the country from the hands of the industrious to those of the idle. The *property* which the giver has placed at the beggar's disposal diverts *wealth* from some other consumer. It enables the pauper to consume unproductively what otherwise would probably have gone to the support of a hardworking man. If the practice of indiscriminate giving becomes general it causes so many beggars to lead lives of idleness that the production of the country is greatly diminished and the industrious find themselves compelled to maintain an idle population out of a scant product.

§ 65. The evils connected with private charity are more conspicuous in the case of misdirected public charity, because public charity is dispensed on a large scale by officials who have the whole taxable property of the community to draw upon. The operation of the English poor-law in the early part of the present century furnished a memorable instance of the troubles which may arise from this source.

The history of poor-relief in England divides itself into four periods. In the first period, lasting till 1600, the state confined its efforts to the suppression of pauperism, leaving the care of the incapable and unfortunate to other agencies. The Reformation made some of these agencies inoperative ; and during the second period, inaugurated by the Act of Elizabeth (1601) the parish authorities were charged with the duty of relieving the destitute. Every effort was made to prevent such relief from being abused. The tendency of the poor to migrate to parishes where they received the best treatment was met by the acts of settlement, which were framed to prevent people with precarious means of livelihood from changing their legal residence. The laxity of certain justices who ordered relief to be granted on inadequate grounds, was met by the imposition of the workhouse test (1713). Parishes were encouraged to build workhouses and to make resi-

dence in such workhouses a condition of relief. Pauperism was made as unpleasant as possible in order to reduce
the burdens of the rate-payer. But in the latter part of
the eighteenth century a different spirit began to prevail.
The old practice was felt to be unnecessarily hard on the
poor. The use of the workhouse as a test was abolished.
It was made a place of support for the incapable. No one
was to be sent to a workhouse if he could maintain himself elsewhere. By "Gilbert's Act" (1782) the guardians
of the poor were charged with the duty of helping them
thus to maintain themselves; in other words, of finding
work for every one who applied for it. Until they succeeded
in finding work for him, the applicant was to be supported
in his own home at public expense. The effect of this
law on the prosperity of the English agricultural districts
was terrible. It relieved any man who chose to avail himself of its provisions from the responsibility of seeking
work. It gave the overseers more to do than they could
possibly accomplish. They could not find employment
for all who applied. They were compelled to support
these applicants and their families in reasonable comfort.
The burden of this support came indirectly on the industrious laborers. The condition of the man who lived on
charity was in many districts made better than that of
the man who supported himself by honest labor. Conspicuously was this the case with persons who had large
families. The parish allowance for each child was so
great as to constitute a premium on the increase of numbers. In certain districts the operation of the law not
only crippled industry, but had most disastrous effects on
public morality; practically abolishing female chastity
among those classes to whom the ample parish allowance
for the support of children constituted a temptation to
vice.[1] So great were these evils that in the year 1834
Parliament was compelled to reëstablish the workhouse

[1] " Report of Poor-Law Commissioners, 1834."

test. By this change the burden of pauperism, which had increased with such rapidity that it threatened to cripple English agricultural prosperity, was gradually lightened ; but the southern and western counties of England have not yet recovered, either materially or morally, from the evils which were entailed upon them by fifty years of liberal policy in the matter of poor-relief.

§ 66. In the interest of those who are willing and able to work it is absolutely indispensable to reduce the burden of pauperism to a minimum. Any other policy not only puts unnecessary taxes upon the industrious, but tends to increase the number of paupers and diminish the number of those who are charged with the labor of supporting them.

The first step toward reducing pauperism is to separate the wilful paupers from the incapable and unfortunate applicants for relief. By this policy we are able to refuse help to the former class and limit greatly the number of those who seek aid under the pretext of belonging to one of the two latter. A part of the work of separation consists in careful investigation of individual cases. This is our chief means of distinguishing the incapable poor who cannot work, from those who can. The separation of the unfortunate from the pauper is more difficult. To secure this end personal investigation on the part of organized charities or agents of the government must be supplemented by the work test. If we insist that an able-bodied man who applies for help must stand ready to do hard work of some sort, and if we do not give too much help in comparison with the labor required, we avoid putting a premium on pauperism. We make it probable that a man who applies for help under such conditions really deserves it, and is not making the absence of work a convenient pretext for living in idleness. [1]

[1] It is an open question whether the administration of relief, and especially of emergency relief, should be in the hands of the same authority that im-

§ 67. The work test just described is primarily and chiefly used as a means of determining the character of the applicants. If it can be so arranged that the product of the labor which is thus tested is worth something to the community, well and good ; but the attempt to make the labor useful must not be allowed to interfere with its character as a test. If this once happens, the efforts to render the results of relief work valuable to society are worse than useless.

§ 68. These efforts take three forms : 1. Public works to utilize the power of those who are temporarily thrown out of employment. 2. Labor colonies to give permanent occupation to those who are in need of it. 3. Advances of money procured by the credit of the government, and placed at the disposal of those who expect to repay it by their work. None of these plans can be said to have accomplished the object in view.

§ 69. There is a specious argument in favor of public works for the relief of those who are temporarily unemployed. People say that such work would have to be done, sooner or later, in any event ; that the unemployed must be helped in some shape or other; that even if those who are set to work upon these things do not earn the full amount of their wages, the little they may accomplish is better than nothing, as otherwise they would have to be wholly supported at public expense. They also add that employment on useful work of this kind preserves the self-respect of the laborer which the direct giving of charity tends to destroy. But this view of the matter is a somewhat dangerous one. There is reason to fear that public works arranged with this motive and object in view do more harm than good. In the first place, most public works cannot be constructed in the winter

poses the tests.   If the detection of fraud becomes the chief function of any organization, such a body is sometimes handicapped in its attempts to discover and relieve poverty that is not fraudulent.

season, when destitution is greatest and the need of temporary relief most pressing. In the next place, the amount accomplished by laborers who are set to do such work without special training is greatly overestimated by those who have not had experience. It seems a simple matter to build a sewer, but it requires an amount of training for which the man who is given such work as a temporary means of relief has had neither the time nor the opportunity. In the third place, the seeming advantage from the construction of these works causes too many operations of the kind to be undertaken, and diverts to these operations a certain number of laborers who would gradually have found profitable and useful employment in lines for which they were more fitted. The net loss to the tax-payers from this large amount of ill directed labor is greater than that which would have resulted from the bestowal of a smaller amount of direct charity to the persons who, by investigation and by the work test, had been found worthy to receive it. Finally, the preservation of self-respect to the laborer by this process is more apparent than real. If it is known that public works are being constructed for which laborers are employed on something better than a commercial basis, the pressure for these positions makes them an object of political wire-pulling. It is a false notion of self-respect which leads the man who can take money out of the public by chicanery to rate himself higher and be rated higher by society than the one who truthfully confesses to himself and others the real ground on which property is diverted to his support.

Some of these objections apply with less force to works of agriculture and land improvement, because the danger of undue diversion of laborers into this line of industry is slight. We are suffering from a drift of population into mechanical industries. If we can keep some of this drift back, and employ it in the production of food, we have a twofold advantage. First, the product of agricultural labor will keep the producers from starvation, whether they can sell it or not. Second, the character of the work is not such as to render it attractive to any but those who really deserve relief.

§ 70. Labor colonies and similar means of furnishing permanent employment do not as a rule reach the class for which they are intended. They do not teach men to be self-supporting. They become "places of refuge for those who have suffered moral as well as physical shipwreck"; not for the industrially unfortunate, but for the chronic or vicious poor.

Proposals for an advance of state credit to laborers who could not find employment on advantageous terms were most actively urged by Lassalle some forty years ago. He would have allowed associations of laborers to pledge the future product of their labor as security for such advances, so that the workmen would be relieved from their present dependence on the capitalist, and be put in a position to exercise their powers to the best advantage. But no association of workmen is in a position to guarantee the utility of its future product to society. The very industry of its members might readily result in overproduction of things that were not wanted; nor could the agents of the government, on the basis of any statistics yet devised, be trusted to guard against this danger. If too many men made watches, the selling price of watches would not cover the advances made by the government; and, what is more important, the utility of such watches would not make good to society the waste of food and other forms of public capital consumed by those engaged in their production.

If such advances are confined to agricultural laborers, the danger is, for the reasons already given, much less. Several schemes have been proposed for this end. The one most under discussion at present is the allotment system, which plays a somewhat important part in Eng-lish social policy. Under this system the public authori-ties buy land for the use of actual cultivators in small plots, borrowing the money for that purpose at a low rate of interest. It is confidently expected that the occupiers can pay the government a sufficiently large sum to make the experiment financially self-supporting, and that they will thus be relieved without great public cost from most of their present dependence on the fluctuations of trade. This plan has much to recommend it; but it has not been tried long enough for decisive judgment as to its success.

§ 71. Less radical in their aims, but perhaps quite as promising in their operation, are the attempts to help people to find work for themselves instead of trying to make it for them. In Germany, bureaus of information have accomplished much in this way; and the German police system is so efficient that it has been found pos-sible to provide food and lodging for those who were actually in search of work without great danger that such relief would be misused. But in the absence of such effective police control this system would certainly in-crease the number of tramps who make the seeking of work a pretext instead of an object of their journey, and might readily result in a condition like that which pre-vailed in the worst days of the English poor-law.

Systematic effort to give the unemployed a chance to find work often sets in its true light a form of pauperism which is widespread, and shifts the responsibility for many cases of destitution from society as a whole to the indi-vidual with whom it belongs. There is a large number of people in times of commercial crisis who really want work but who want it in cities, and who are absolutely unwilling to engage in those lines of food production which require them to live in the country. The number of people who ask relief and are willing to take even light farm-work as a means of earning it is exceedingly small. They insist on their right to live, and in many instances are prepared to maintain that right by a readiness to work in certain trades in the city, but they absolutely refuse to engage in the production of food, which alone can keep the community alive.

§ 72. Another means by which it is proposed to reduce the burdens of pauperism is compulsory insurance. This can be utilized in some measure for the incapable as well as for the unfortunate, if they have been compelled to contribute to the insurance funds before they have become incapacitated for work.

The system of compulsory insurance has been more completely carried out in the German Empire than anywhere else. Small contributions are levied from the workmen or from their employers to create a fund for the support of the workman and his family when he becomes ill or superannuated. There are many reformers who are anxious that other countries should follow the example of Germany. But the experiment has not progressed far enough to pass judgment on its success. In many respects the gain to the public from a system of this kind is more apparent than real. The payments to the insurance funds must chiefly, if not wholly, come out of wages. Even though they be nominally levied on the employer, he is compelled by competition with other employers who are not subject to this levy to reduce in corresponding degree the wages which he pays. If the workman receives less wages, he must either consume less or save less. So far as he economizes on useless items of consumption the insurance fund thus created represents a positive gain to the community, providing for the workman's support in the future without causing any corresponding general loss or burden in the present. But if he economizes on articles that are necessary or useful to his well-being and that of his family, he lessens his own labor power and that of his children and diminishes rather than increases the general ability of the community for maintaining the necessary burdens of poor-relief. If, finally, he makes these payments out of money that he otherwise would have saved, he transfers the provision for his support from his own shoulders to that of the public organization. He becomes less self-supporting, and more dependent on society.

§ 73. The opposition of friendly societies to schemes of government insurance is something quite rational. These societies are in their nature agencies for the promotion of voluntary saving as a means of mutual insurance. If the government uses compulsory saving as a means to the same end, it takes away the ground for the existence of these societies and substitutes a system which secures the same material results to the workman but fails to secure the same educational and moral ones. To those who regard these educational and moral results as a chief advantage in voluntary saving, the change to a compulsory system looks like a step backward.

§ 74. There is also a positive danger that the amount of accident and sickness may increase under the operation of compulsory insurance. The accident insurance law, in its early application to the German railroad service, had a distinct effect of this kind. The number of disabling accidents was increased. The individual, being freed from responsibility for his own loss of time, put himself in a position where more aggregate time was lost. Whether this was due to increased carelessness or to slackness in returning to work is a matter of comparatively slight consequence. In either event, the diminution of individual responsibility and assumption of such responsibility by public organizations lessened the incentives to continuous work and to the care which makes such continuous work possible. In factory insurance this difficulty can perhaps be avoided by localizing its management in such a way that the people who have to pay the cost of unnecessary accidents can see them and guard against their recurrence.  Accident insurance works much better in Germany, where it is locally administered, than in Austria, where it is a national matter.

§ 75.  Finally, there is a danger that the apparent advantages of an insurance system of this kind may blind public opinion to the more real advantages of better forms of insurance.  A certain section of the public is so dazzled by the prospect of pensions that it overlooks the true ground on which pensions are justified.  It comes to regard the pension as an end in itself rather than as a means of relieving the general funds of the government of a burden.  Schemes are already proposed in England for giving a pension to every one above a certain age, independent of any contribution which he may have made. People are impressed with the advantages of a pension and with the difficulties of every special system of contribution for securing it.  They therefore propose to transfer the burden of such payments to the general tax account. They do not see that three quarters of the arguments for pensions are based upon their usefulness in lightening the claims upon this general account, and that a system which increases these claims undermines the very grounds on which it is advocated.  It is sometimes argued that the total amount of these claims is not really much increased by the adoption of a liberal pension policy : because, pensions or no pensions, society must in the last resort support the aged who have worked out their usefulness, and no harm can be done by recognizing as a right on the part of the individual what society already recognizes as a duty.  But this is an unsound position.  There are certain things which society must do in justice to itself, which it cannot safely allow individuals to demand in justice to themselves.  If you give every man a right to a pension when he is incapable of self-support, you tacitly approve his failure to provide for himself and his children. That the necessary degree of production and of economy by the community as a whole would be maintained if such a point of view were adopted, seems highly improbable. We need measures which shall increase individual responsibility rather than diminish it ; measures which shall give us more self-reliance and less reliance on society as a whole. We cannot afford to countenance a system of morals or law which justifies the individual in looking to the community rather than to himself for support in age or infirmity.

# CHAPTER III.

## COMPETITION.

Freedom of Exchange—Bargaining—Mercantile Competition—Market Price
—Effects of Competition—Normal Price—Value—Socialistic Theory of
Value.

J. E. Cairnes : " Some Leading Principles of Political Economy, Newly
Expounded." London (and New York), 1874.

A. Marshall : " Principles of Economics." Vol. i. 3d ed. London and
New York, 1895.

W. S. Jevons : " Theory of Political Economy." 3d ed. London and
New York, 1888.

F. v. Wieser : " Natural Value." (Trans. by Malloch.) London and
New York, 1893.

§ 76. In mediæval times separate families and communities supplied their own needs to a degree which it is now hardly possible to realize ; although the plantation life in the Southern States a generation ago furnished in some respects an approximation to the feudal type. In such a condition of society the laborer has not, as a rule, any large surplus above the bare necessaries of life. The excess of his production over his consumption goes into the hands of the lord of the manor or plantation. It is the ruling class alone which has goods to exchange for outside products. Within the plantation or manor everything is done by the inhabitants for one another, under a system of labor wholly or partly compulsory, and on terms rigidly fixed by custom or by superior authority. Each individual, from master to slave, finds his consumption no less than his production closely restricted. A man's labor and his enjoyments both form part of the status into which he was born and from which his most strenuous exertions can hardly free him. He may be bound by caste regulations as in India, by positive law as was the case in many parts of Europe, or by the mere force of custom, which often needs no formulated law to give it effect.

In such stages of society trade plays a relatively unimportant part. The fundamental characteristic of the manorial group in England in the thirteenth century, says Ashley, was its self-sufficiency. The village included men who carried on all the occupations and crafts necessary for every-day life. There was little room for anything like freedom of exchange. The few things that were purchased were paid for at prices fixed by custom. The value of an estate was measured by the physical resources which its owner possessed. The difference between the measurement of public and private wealth, noted in the first chapter, had not yet come into play.

§ 77. But when the nation became sufficiently advanced to carry on commerce a different state of things developed. Its members produced more than they needed for their own requirements and sold the surplus to others. The country obtained much of what it used from the towns. The people in the towns lived on food provided by the country. Markets and fairs were held at stated times, to which men of different occupations could resort as a means of buying what they needed and selling what they produced. In such a market, prices were never wholly fixed by custom, but, in some measure at least, by the relative number of buyers and sellers. The rate of exchange was not based upon the number of days' labor involved in the product, but upon the amount which the consumers were ready to give in exchange for it. The more remote the point of origin of the goods purchased, the less dominant was the influence of custom in fixing the price which should be charged.

5

§ 78. As labor became freer and more diversified, people produced more and more for one another and less exclusively for themselves. The advantages of division of labor made themselves felt. If a man attempted to supply himself and his family with everything, he was obliged to spend a great deal of time for a comparatively small product. The many occupations, which he was forced to pursue by turns, prevented the attainment of a high degree of dexterity in any one of them. The waste of time in passing from one to another meant a corresponding loss of efficiency. When regular means of sale were assured, each man found it more profitable to devote himself to some one thing in which he had special advantages, and to exchange the surplus product which he could not use for the goods which others were ready to offer. In this way it was possible for the community to combine the advantages of specialized production and of diversified consumption. Each man could contribute the largest share to the public wealth by confining his production to one line. He could obtain the largest use and enjoyment from the public wealth by spreading his consumption over a great variety of lines. As hand labor was gradually supplemented and rendered more efficient by machinery the specialization of work became more and more marked. In the industrial civilization of the present day there are few who produce all that they need for their own requirements. The most prosperous man is usually one who consumes only a small portion of his own product and has a large surplus to sell to others.

§ 79. Freedom of production and of trade are accompanied by increased freedom in consumption. With the adoption of a system which gives a great many individuals property to exchange, there has been a gradual abandonment of legal enactments which were intended to restrict exchange and limit expenditure. Sumptuary laws, which prescribe the dress and food which individuals may use, have for the most part become a thing of the past. We have ceased to pass statutes to prevent men from ruining themselves in their own way, if they see fit to do so. Only in those cases where the individual, by exercising rights of trade, will injure others as well as himself, do we continue to prohibit sales and purchases.

The clearest case for prohibiting such transactions is connected with the abolition of slavery. Formerly a man could buy and sell slaves, and in a great many communities he could sell himself or his children into slavery. To-day it is recognized that such a transaction is a public wrong, not a private one. The man who sells himself or his children into slavery harms not only the parties immediately interested, but the industrial future of the nation as a whole. Such dealings are therefore absolutely forbidden. But the corresponding evil and wrong of prostitution is allowed to go on unheeded. It is only where public sentiment is practically unanimous as to the existence of a public necessity that prohibitory laws can be enforced. The case of the liquor traffic furnishes a marked illustration of this truth. No one denies that a great deal of harm is done by the sale of intoxicating drinks ; but in the majority of communities society finds it extremely difficult to enforce any effective restrictions upon such traffic. The doctrine of individual freedom has made such progress that most communities tolerate the exercise of such freedom in many transactions which their moral sense distinctly condemns.

§ 80. When we try to make positive laws as to what people shall buy and sell, instead of negative ones as to what they shall not buy or sell, we are confronted with even greater obstacles. The enforcement of sanitary regulations, however necessary for the public health, is attended with extreme difficulty. There is a universal consensus of opinion that tenement houses should conform to certain requirements with regard to light, air, and drainage, but the difficulty of giving effect to these requirements is enormous. If the demand for bad tenement houses is such that people find it profitable to build them and to let them, it is nearly impossible to stop such traffic. The erection of model dwellings enables that class of the community which appreciates the advantage of such improvements to enjoy them. But it does not prevent the rest of the people from living as they did before, nor does it stop the tenement-house owner from making his profit out of public squalor. Even if some of the worst tenements are condemned by the exercise of municipal authority and better ones are built in their places, the result is too often merely an overcrowding at some other point. Public knowledge of the laws of health and public responsibility as to the evils of overcrowding are needed in order to give effect to any statute or ordinance.

A striking instance of the difficulties connected with the effort to avoid overcrowding was furnished by the experience of Mühlhausen. This city, which formed the centre of the cotton industry of upper Alsace, was long noted for the model dwellings in which its operatives lived. But the direct personal and unofficial investigations of Herkner disclosed the fact that these supposed advantages were in large measure illusory, and that any slight gain at some points was offset by increased pressure and more shameless overcrowding at others.

§ 81. A certain amount of positive legislation is always necessary for public health and public enlightenment. We cannot allow the ignorant man to exercise his freedom in cultivating bacteria or in leaving his children without education. The one is dangerous to the health of the whole community, the other to its future intelligence and morals. In neither case will a let-alone policy cure itself by the elimination of the unfit. Wise and unwise together are bound to suffer in very considerable measure from the pestilence engendered by public filth or the corruption attendant on public ignorance. In cases where such positive legislation is found necessary, it is generally best for the government to take the transaction wholly out of the realm of sale and purchase, and to provide means by which sanitation and education can be had at the expense of the tax-payers. Compulsory education involves public schools ; compulsory drainage involves public sewers ; compulsory vaccination involves public medical service. Only in those cases where violations of the statute are done in public sight, under the authority of parties who can be held responsible—as in the case of unhealthful and dangerous appliances in factories—do we find important exceptions to this rule.

§ 82. Although laws prescribing what a man may buy or sell have fallen into disuse, it must not be supposed that every man exercises his intelligence and pleasure to buy what will give him the most happiness. People are bound by custom where they have ceased to submit to law. A large part of the expense of most people is regulated, not by their own desires and demands, but by the demands of the public sentiment of the community about them. The standard of life of every family is fixed in large measure by social conventions. Few are intelligent enough to break away from those conventions, even where they are manifestly foolish. Although we have made much progress in the direction of economic freedom, it is a mistake to assume that the authority of custom in these matters is a thing of the past. With most men, custom regulates their economic action more potently than any calculation of utility which they are able to make. Nor can we assume, as some writers are prone to do, that such custom represents the average judgment of the community as to the things needed for the comfort and happiness of its members. It represents an average absence of judgment—a survival of habits which doubtless proved useful in times past, but which in many instances have entirely outlived their usefulness.

The success of advertising shows how little intelligence is habitually exercised in these matters. A man does not generally use his nominal freedom to buy what he wants until some one comes and tells him in stentorian tones what he wants to buy. The authority of custom and tradition can only be overcome by the authority of drums and trumpets. It is a mistake to draw too fine-spun deduction as to the motives which guide buyers in their choice, when three quarters of the buyers exercise no choice at all. It is not merely that people want things which hurt them, or which fail to do them the maximum good—a point well developed in the writings of Patten— but that they buy things without knowing whether they want them or not, through sheer *vis inertiæ.*

§ 83. Where consumption has become diversified and the division of labor has established itself, the determination of the rate of exchange of goods between different producers becomes a matter of cardinal importance. In undeveloped societies a man's wealth is measured in the physical things which he has at command. He is rich or poor according to the extent of his lands, the number of his dependents, the herds and the crops which he can raise for their support. But when property has taken the place of slavery as an economic force, and when people have begun to exchange their property more or less freely with one another, a man's personal wealth is estimated in money. The goods which he makes are valued, not as a source of enjoyment to the producer himself, but as a means of commanding the goods and services of others in the open market. The measure of his wealth is found in the exchangeability of his product and its power to command a price.

A *price*, in the broadest sense of the word, is the quantity of one thing which is exchanged for another.

§ 84. Where two persons exchange their goods or services, without the intervention of money, the transaction is known as *barter*. I may barter a ton of coal for a pair of shoes, or an hour's labor for a breakfast. Under a system of barter, either man's contribution may be regarded as the price of the other. We may consider the breakfast as the price of the labor, or the labor as the price of the breakfast.

Barter flourishes chiefly among uncivilized communities, or those reduced to severe straits by the operation of a destructive war; though survivals of this method, as well as of many other uncivilized ones, may be seen in the dealings of children with one another. Barter is not available in any complicated system of trade. If *A* makes shoes and wants cloth, while *B* makes cloth and wants shoes, the two can resort to barter; but if *B*, who makes cloth, wants flour, while *C* makes flour and wants shoes, the attempt to provide for the needs of all three men by a system of barter becomes very perplexing. The difficulty is met by a resort to *money;* that is, to some medium of exchange which *A*, *B*, and *C* are all ready to accept. If *A* sells a pair of shoes to *C* for five dollars, he does not need to inquire whether *C* makes cloth; he can take the five dollars and buy cloth of *B*. *B* can then take the five dollars and buy flour of *C*. Through the intervention of money each producer has sold his product to the man who wanted it, and obtained what he wanted from the man who produced it, in a way which would have been almost impossible under a system of barter.

§ 85. Just what constitutes money is a question which can best be answered at a later stage of our inquiry. For the present it is enough to say that it must be *universally acceptable* throughout the community, so that it can be used for the purchase of goods or services of every kind; and that it must be sufficiently *homogeneous* in character for p·ople to desire a given *quantity* of it, rather than a

particular *piece* of it.[1] Anything which possesses these two
characteristics may serve as money. The actual money
of any civilized nation usually consists of gold, silver, and
paper, accredited with the stamp of the government. The
international money of the world, acceptable by weight
without the stamp of any government, is gold.

Under the modern commercial system, prices are measured in money. A price, in the commercial sense of the
word, may be defined as the quantity of money for which
the right to an article or service is exchanged. The man
who furnishes the article or service is known as the seller;
the man who furnishes the money is known as the buyer.

§ 86. If the transaction is an isolated one, and not one
of a series of similar transactions, the price is usually
fixed by *bargaining*. Suppose *A* wishes to sell a house
unlike other houses in situation or construction, and *B* is
the only man who, for the moment at any rate, wishes to
buy it. It may happen that the maximum price which *B*
is willing to pay is less than the minimum which *A* is willing to accept. In that case there will be no sale. Or it
may happen that *B*'s maximum exactly coincides with *A*'s
minimum. In that case there will be a sale at exactly this
price. But it may also happen that *B*'s maximum is somewhat higher than *A*'s minimum; and in view of this possibility, *A* is unwilling to name the lowest price at which
he will sell until he sees whether *B* may not be induced to
pay more, while *B* is equally unwilling to name his highest
price until he sees whether *A* may be induced to sell for
less. So it will probably happen that *A* names a price
somewhat higher than the minimum which he would accept, and that *B* replies by offering a price somewhat less

---

[1] Whenever certain pieces of money, be they few or many, are decidedly
preferred to the general stock, they are rapidly withdrawn from circulation.
They may find their way into the collections of numismatists, into the strong
boxes of bankers, or even into the mints of foreign countries, according as
one cause or another has produced the preference in question.

than the maximum which he is prepared to give. Thus *A* might ask a nominal price of $15,000 when he would be ready to take $12,000 rather than lose the chance of selling the house; while *B* might make a first offer of $11,000, though he would be prepared to pay $13,000 rather than lose the chance of buying it. Successive offers bring *A* and *B* nearer together, and finally the house is sold at some price not less than $12,000 nor more than $13,000; the exact figure depending on the relative skill in bargaining shown by *A* and *B*.

§ 87. But if there are other house owners in the same situation as *A*, or other buyers in the same situation as *B*, the matter assumes a different aspect. *A* is afraid to ask an exorbitant price for fear *B* may go and buy of some one else; *B* is unwilling to begin with an unduly low figure, for fear that *A* may break off negotiations with him and deal with some other buyer. The moment there are other sellers who can enter into competition with *A*, or other buyers who can enter into competition with *B*, the chance for bargaining is greatly restricted, if not altogether abolished.

*Competition* may be defined as the effort of rival sellers to dispose of their goods and services, or of rival buyers to secure the goods and services which they require; an effort limited by the desire of the seller to secure as high a price as possible, and by the desire of the buyer to pay as low a price as possible.[1] Its existence shows that people are guided in their dealings by individual self-interest. Its action may be totally suspended by combination, where sellers or buyers act in concert and not in rivalry. An effective combination of sellers is known as a monopoly. It may also be greatly modified by custom or by sentiment. Custom, with or without the authority of law, often causes the seller to accept a price lower than

---

[1] It may be briefly but pertinently defined in the vernacular as the effort not to get left.

that which he could otherwise obtain. Sentiment, on the part of an individual or of the public as a whole, occasionally leads the buyer to pay a larger price for goods or services than that which would be absolutely necessary for securing them.

§ 88. A place where prices are determined by competition is known as a *market*. It makes no difference whether the goods are actually exposed for sale, as in the mediæval markets, or largely bought and sold on the basis of warrants or telegraphic orders, as in the produce exchanges of to-day. The essential thing is that different buyers and sellers shall know something about one another's transactions, so that the individual buyer need not pay more than the prevailing rate, nor the individual seller be forced to sell for less than the prevailing rate.

There may be different markets for the same article in the same place. The prices in the wholesale market are determined by one set of conditions, and those in the retail market by another. Though not wholly independent, they can often move separately.

It is doubtful whether we should apply the term market to places or groups of transactions where there is competition on one side only, and monopoly or combination on the other; where the buyers compete and the sellers do not.

§ 89. In any given market, the *supply* of an article, in its technical sense, is the amount offered at a given price. It tends to increase as the price increases. It must be distinguished from the *stock*, which is an absolute amount independent of price.

In any given market the *demand* for an article is the amount which will be taken at any given price.[1] It tends

---

[1] There is another sense of the word demand, occasionally used by nearly all the older economists, and emphasized by Cairnes. In Cairnes' use of the word, it means, not the quantity of a particular article demanded, but the quantity of money, or other things representing general purchasing power,

to diminish as the price increases. It must be distinguished from desire, which is a feeling, while demand is a concrete quantity. Desire is the cause of demand, but the two terms are different in kind and can never be used interchangeably.

§ 90. The market price of an article, under the modern commercial system, is the price at which the demand is equal to the supply. For, if the supply at any given price is greater than the demand, the several sellers will be driven to make special efforts and concessions in order to dispose of their goods; while conversely, if the demand at any given price is greater than the supply, the buyers will be led to offer special inducements in order to get the goods which they want. Suppose that cotton of a certain grade is selling in the New York market at eight cents a pound. If the amount of cotton brought to New York from week to week to be sold is exactly equal to the amount taken out of the New York market by the consumers, the price is likely to remain at eight cents. But if the amount brought is in excess of the amount taken away, the sellers will see that the stocks are increasing, and each will be afraid of being left with unsold cotton on his hands which he may be unable to dispose of, except at a great sacrifice. Competition among sellers now becomes active. Each seller strives to get rid of his cotton,—at eight cents if possible, but if that price cannot be had, at seven and a half cents, or perhaps even at seven cents, rather than be left with unsold and unsalable cotton. As this process goes on, the lower prices induce the buyers to take more cotton, and discourage the pro-

which buyers stand ready to give in exchange for it. The word is used by the commercial world in both senses with about equal frequency. It makes comparatively little difference which meaning we adopt, as long as we adhere to the one selected. While Cairnes' definition is for some purposes better than that given in the text, there are many other purposes for which it is not so good. There appears to be no sufficient reason for departing from the prevalent usage of modern economists.

ducers from sending so much to New York; in other words, they increase the demand and diminish the supply, until a new point of equilibrium is established. How far the actual price goes down depends for the moment chiefly upon the amount of additional use of cotton which is caused by a fall in price. If a difference of half a cent a pound greatly stimulates the manufacture of cotton, the price in the case supposed is not likely to fall below seven and a half cents. If, on the other hand, the difference of half a cent has no great effect on consumption, the price for the time being is likely to fall to seven cents or even lower.

Now take the opposite case. Suppose that at eight cents the demand is greater than the supply. We shall have competition of buyers instead of sellers. There is not going to be enough cotton for everybody at eight cents. A cotton merchant or broker sees that the stock of cotton is being gradually reduced. If this process goes on, it means that there will be a scarcity in the immediate future. He therefore refuses to part with his cotton at eight cents, hoping to be able to command higher prices a week hence. Others follow his example. The buyers can no longer get the amount of cotton they need for eight cents a pound. Some are unwilling to give more than eight cents and drop out of the market; others are prepared to pay eight and a half cents; still others will go as high as nine cents rather than do without the cotton. Whether the actual price goes up to eight and a half cents, or to nine cents, or even higher, depends largely on the number of buyers who withdraw from the market at successive changes in the price. If a large proportion of the buyers will not pay more than eight cents, the merchants can increase the price but little. The man who holds his cotton at a price which drives the buyers out of market cuts off his own head. But if a large proportion of the buyers are prepared to pay nine cents, the merchant will probably do well to refuse to sell for less than this figure. If he is wise, he will continue to hold back his cotton as long as the stock in the market continues to diminish; that is, as long as the amount taken by consumers at existing prices exceeds the amount sent to market by producers. When this state of things is on the point of being reversed, he will sell. No further rise in prices is probable. He is much more likely to see a fall, and cannot afford in such an event to be left with unsold goods on his hands. The self-interest of each merchant leads him to refuse to sell as long as the demand exceeds the supply, and to sell when the two things become equal to one another.

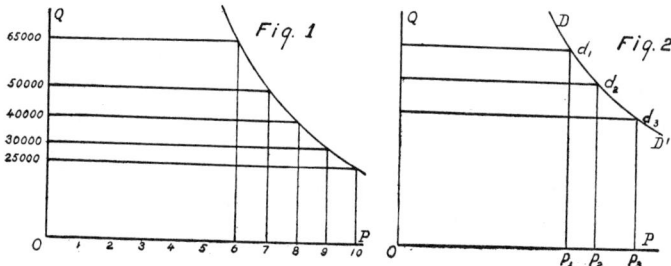

§ 91. Beginning at the point *O* (Figure 1), lay off in the horizontal line *OP* a series of points whose distances from *O* shall represent successive *prices* of cotton per pound. From these successive points, representing price, let vertical lines be raised representing *quantities* of cotton which will be taken by the purchasers at those prices in the course of a week. These quantities tend to fall as the price rises. If the purchases at eight cents are 40,000 bales per week, we may assume for the sake of illustration that only 30,000 bales would be taken at nine cents, and only 25,000 at ten cents; but that a fall in price to seven cents would call out a demand for 50,000 bales a week, and a fall to six cents a demand for 65,000 bales. A fractional price, like seven and a half cents, would call forth a demand intermediate between that at eight cents and that at seven. If we establish a number of points in this way and connect them by a line, we shall have what is known as a demand curve, representing the whole series of relations between price and quantity demanded.

If, in Figure 2 $DD'$ is the demand curve for a given article in any given market, then at any assumed price $Op_1$, the demand will be represented by the line $p_1d_1$; similarly at the prices $Op_2$, $Op_3$, the demand will be represented respectively by the lines $p_2d_2$, $p_3d_3$.[1]

§ 92. The shape of the demand curve is different for different commodities,[2] and even for the same commodity in different markets. But its form is limited by one general law; the quantity demanded tends to increase as the price diminishes, and to diminish as the price increases. This is readily established by observation of commercial facts. It can also be proved theoretically, as a deduction from observed principles of human nature.

It is a well known law of psychology that the same stimulus, if repeated more and more rapidly, produces a constantly diminishing sense of added pleasure or pain. As an economic consequence of this, rapidly increasing supplies of the same class of goods do not proportionately increase the happiness of their possessor, but are all the time diminishing in their utility[3] to him. The first slice of

[1] In these figures the horizontal lines represent prices, and the vertical lines quantities of the commodity. Horizontal lines must therefore be compared with one another, and vertical lines with one another ; we must not attempt to take the ratio between a horizontal and a vertical line, since the two represent quantities of different kind, with different units of measurement.

[2] This point is further developed in chapter x.

[3] Utility, as the word has been used by writers on economics, means the power of satisfying a temporary desire rather than the power of doing a permanent good. In this sense, whiskey would be regarded as having a high degree of utility to many to whom it is by no means beneficial in the long run.

bread received in the course of a day has almost infinite utility as a means of preserving life. The second has great utility as a means of avoiding hunger, but not so great as the first ; the third makes less difference than the second ; and when we come to the tenth, the added gratification is perhaps hardly appreciable. So it is to a greater or less degree with all other commodities. Additional increments in quantity do not bring proportionate increase of enjoyment or utility. The *total* utility of the larger amount is greater than that of the smaller, but the *marginal*[1] utility of *additions* to the supply available for any individual keeps diminishing.

§ 93. If there is only a small amount of a commodity in the market the buyers are often extremely anxious to add to their consumption, and are willing to pay high prices. If the amount available becomes larger, and the most urgent needs of the buyers have already been satisfied, the holders must offer inducements to those whose need is less urgent ; that is, they must lower prices to create a larger demand. The demand for cotton at ten cents a pound comes from those to whom the utility of adding to their stocks of cotton is greater than the sacrifice involved in earning ten cents, or in giving up something else which the ten cents might purchase.[2] The demand for cotton

---

[1] Also called *final* utility.

[2] Desire alone cannot create demand. A man must have the means of payment ; and these means usually come from the supply of goods or services which he has previously sold. If producers and consumers come in personal contact with one another each man's supply of commodities which he sells becomes a demand for the commodities of others which he wants to buy. He will sell his goods, and increase their supply, as long as the utility of what he can buy at the market rates of exchange is greater than that which he sacrifices in parting with his own products. This double aspect of his goods as supply and demand forms the basis of the theory of *reciprocal demand* which was developed by Cairnes in popular form and by Walras with scientific accuracy.

But if an interval elapses between the time when a man makes prices for the goods which he sells and spends the money thus obtained in the purchase

at nine cents comes from those to whom its utility is greater than the sacrifice measured by nine cents. Each reduction in price increases the amount of goods whose utility to the buyers is greater than that which is measured by the price charged ; that is, it increases the demand. It may, however, happen that the stock of an extremely useful article is so great that no reduction in price will serve to create a commercial demand for the whole. Water, except in cities, is an example of this. The total utility of water is enormous; but if there are already a million gallons available, the marginal utility of an additional gallon is so small that no one is likely to pay anything for it, and there is no commercial demand in the proper sense of the word.

This is, in substance, the theory of demand set forth by Jevons, and carried out in detail by the Austrian school of economists. It is of great importance as showing the direct connection between utility and price under the existing commercial system. It explains more clearly than previous theories have done the psychological motives which determine the relations between price and demand. Much of the work of this school, however, seems to belong rather to the domain of psychology than of economics, and to have a very remote application to the practical problems of business and of legislation.

§ 94. The demand for an article thus depends upon its utility as estimated by the consumers, and can be increased by lowering the price. To dispose of any given supply the holders must make the price low enough to create a corresponding demand.

In the case of perishable goods, the conditions deter-

of other goods, the theory of reciprocal demand ceases to work smoothly. We can no longer say without much reserve that "a market for products is products in market." The intervention of the speculator and the varying success with which he performs his work, make such a difference in the rapidity of exchange that they cannot be ignored in the discussion of price variations.

mining the supply are comparatively simple. The supply of such goods is substantially the same as the stock brought to market. If a thousand quarts of strawberries come into the hands of the retailers of a certain city to day and cannot be kept till to morrow, the price must be made low enough to create a demand for the thousand quarts, even though such a price be wholly unremunerative.

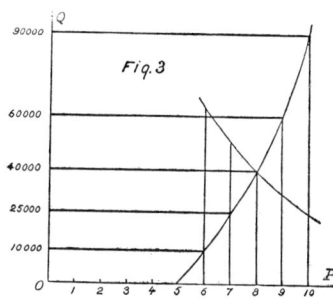 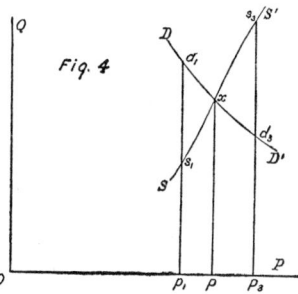

But if an article be of a more permanent character and less liable to deterioration, it will not be necessary to sell the whole stock. If the price goes too low, the merchants may hold back a part of the stock in the hope of realizing higher prices in the future. At a price like ten cents the merchants would try to sell every available pound of cotton ; at nine cents they would not wish to leave themselves wholly bare, but would reserve a little for future contingencies; at eight cents they would reserve more; while at seven cents or six cents, increasingly large shares of the product would be held back. If we assume the stock of unsold cotton in New York to be 100,000 bales, the supply might be 0 at five cents, 10,000 at six cents, 25,000 at seven cents, 40,000 at eight cents, 60,000 at nine cents, and 90,000 at ten cents. On this basis we can construct supply curves, similar to the demand curves in Figures 1 and 2 ; and can then combine the two curves into one figure as in Figure 3 or Figure 4.

§ 95. The market price of an article is determined by the intersection of the supply and demand curves.[1] The price for cotton in Figure 3 will be eight cents a pound, at which price 40,000 bales will be offered and taken. Any price lower than this will produce an excess of demand over supply, and the competition of buyers will tend to force prices upward ; any price higher than eight cents will produce an excess of supply over demand, and the competition of sellers will tend to force prices downward. Had the price been seven cents we should have had buyers for 50,000 bales and sellers for only 25,000 ; had it been nine cents, we should have had sellers for 60,000 bales and buyers for only 30,000. But a price of eight cents will just clear the market. There will be no one left who wants to sell except at a higher figure, or to buy except at a lower figure. In the general illustration (Fig. 4) the price $Op$ is determined by the intersection $x$ of the curves $DD'$ and $SS'$. This is the point at which the quantities demanded and supplied are equal, both being represented by the line $px$. At any lower price, $Op_{_{,}}$, the demand, $p_{,}d_{,}$, exceeds the supply, $p_{,}s_{,}$, and produces competition of buyers; at any higher price, $Op_3$, the supply, $p_3 s_3$, exceeds the demand, $p_3 d_3$, and produces competition of sellers.

In some markets, like the Berlin Stock Exchange, this equalization of supply and demand, instead of being left to individual intelligence in competition, is performed by a committee, which, after revising all the bids and offerings for the day, at their various prices, establishes a settling price which will secure the *maximum* number of transactions ; a price, that is to say, which leaves the smallest difference between the amounts wanted by buyers and offered by sellers.

§ 96. A market price, as thus explained, is a price fixed

---

[1] The case of a perishable article may be represented by a horizontal supply curve, the supply being a fixed quantity whatever the price offered.

by the self-interest of buyers and sellers, each acting independently—that is, with *free competition* on both sides.
The price thus fixed is generally an advantageous one for
society. This proposition may best be proved by considering the various causes which may defeat the action
of competition and observing the evils which result from
them.

The action of free competition may be defeated by
ignorance, by custom (either with or without the authority
of law to enforce it), and by combination.

The bad effects of ignorance hardly need proof. An
ignorant buyer, unfamiliar with the market rate, is liable
to be charged a higher price on account of that un-
familiarity. This results in uncertainty with regard to
prices, and redounds chiefly to the advantage of the more
unscrupulous sellers, who will make money by deceiving
those who deal with them. A one-price system, which is
a most important element in commercial honesty, is
secured by intelligent competition and defeated by
ignorance.

The disadvantage of relying on custom or combination
as a means of fixing prices may easily be proved in
detail.

§ 97. Suppose that, at the old price, the supply is less
than the demand, but that custom prevents the buyers
from competing with one another to force prices up. The
low price continues as long as the stock lasts. The buyers
get what there is at the old price, and use it freely. There
is no apparent motive for them to lessen their consumption, nor is there any motive for producers to send a
larger supply to market. After a time the stock of goods
is used up, and we have distressing scarcity or famine.
The temporary gain which resulted from the low price is
more than offset by the suffering due to the total absence
of the commodity in question. But if the buyers are
allowed to compete and to force prices up at the very

beginning of the scarcity, the advancing price at once operates as a warning to use the article economically. This of itself causes the stock to hold out longer. It will also generally happen that the advancing prices lead the producers to send more goods to the market where higher prices prevail ; and that long before the advent of actual famine new sources of supply are developed by which the severest scarcity is avoided. If this result can be secured by a moderate advance in price it is worth many times what it costs. For it must be remembered that high prices are not so much an evil in themselves, as an indication of an evil. If they exist in an open market, it shows that certain needs of the community are inadequately supplied. It often happens that the higher prices serve as a natural cure for the underlying evil, and that the effort to force those prices down by custom or law prevents the evil from curing itself. If custom or law prevents buyers from paying a competitive price, it soon means that some buyers must go without things they very much want.

Where for any reason competition cannot or will not act, it is sometimes much better to fix prices by custom or law than to leave them to the results of special bargaining. Each city has its rates of carriage hire established by public ordinance. The medical practitioners of any given locality have their customary scale of charges, from which professional etiquette forbids them to depart. In the case of monopolies, complete or partial, like docks, water-works, or railroads, the fees for their use are not infrequently fixed by legislative authority. But while a system of established rates is better than one of special bargains, it is worse than one of free competition because it does not ensure an adaptation of the quantity of service to the needs of the community. The effort to fix railroad charges by law results in low rates for those who can get the needed transportation facilities ; but it often curtails the construction of new roads and the development of train service on old ones to such a degree that the loss to those who cannot get their goods to market overbalances the gain to those who can.

§ 98. Suppose, on the other hand, that at the old price the supply is in excess of the demand, but that the sellers are enabled, either by custom or combination, to avoid the effect of competition in forcing prices down. The sellers get the old price for what is actually bought : but the purchases continue smaller than the supplies, and the visible stock increases up to the limit of the merchants' carrying capacity. One of two things must happen. Either a part of the accumulated goods will deteriorate, and a useful article be wholly lost to the community ; or there will come a time when there is such a glut in the market that enormous stocks are sold at a sacrifice which causes widespread commercial failure. The acts of the French Copper Syndicate of 1888 furnish a good example of this effect of non-competitive prices. This syndicate succeeded in controlling so large a part of the copper of the world that it could apparently fix its charges to suit itself; but the high prices interfered decidedly with the use of copper, and although the increasing stocks of metal could be carried without deterioration, the financial burden ultimately became too great for the largest business concerns to bear, and the accumulations had to be sold at panic figures.

Receding prices are, as a rule, the effect of increased supply. If they are allowed to work out their natural results, they bring about increased use of the article, and prevent the large supply from being wasted or allowed to deteriorate ; while they also act as a warning to producers not to increase the supplies of an article where low prices prevail. They may seem like a temporary evil to merchants and to producers; but it has been proved over and over again that the attempt to stave off this evil by interfering with the action of competition makes the disaster worse in the end.

§ 99. Not only does competition tend to utilize the aggregate product of the community to advantage, as shown in the previous paragraphs; it also tends, on the whole, to make the prices of different articles proportionate to the expense of producing them.

Suppose that the market price of iron, as fixed by supply and demand, is insufficient to cover the expense of producing it. No investor seeking a business opening is likely to go into the production of iron, nor will those already engaged in the business increase their plant or even renew it when it wears out. If at the same time there is another article, for instance copper, whose market price, as fixed by supply and demand, affords a large excess over the expense of production, new investors will seek to produce copper, while those already engaged in the business will extend their plant and keep it up to the highest standard of efficiency. We shall see a diminution of the output of iron and an increase of the output of copper, by a process which, though not generally involving actual transfer of capital from one industry to another, amounts to the same thing in its effect on the community. The permanent supply of iron being diminished, while the conditions of demand remain the same, the producers will be able to charge a higher price and yet dispose of the total product; while, conversely, the permanent supply of copper being increased, the producers will be forced to charge a lower price in order to call forth a corresponding demand. This process will go on until the profit in the production of copper is no greater than that in the production of iron.

§ 100. This adjustment actually takes place among the industries of the country as a whole. There is a constant supply of free capital and labor seeking investment in localities and industries where the higher profits are to be obtained, and not entering those where the profits are lower. This process tends to force down the prices of products in lines where they have been unfairly high, and to maintain or increase them in those where they have been disproportionately low. When this equalizing process has taken place, the price is said to be *normal.* A normal price is reached when the product has so adjusted itself to the demands of consumers, that the market price affords the current rate of profit to the producer who enjoys no extraordinary advantage. We may contrast market and normal price by saying that a market price is one at which, for the moment, the supply is equal to the demand ; while a normal price is one at which, as long as the existing stage of the arts continues, the production is likely to be equal to the consumption.

Under the modern industrial system there is first a temporary adjustment of the demand to the supply by the *commercial* competition of merchants, which lowers (or in the converse case raises) the price to make it correspond to the marginal utility. This temporary adjustment results in market price. Then there is a more permanent, though less accurate and universal, adjustment of the supply to the demand, by the *industrial* competition of investors which lowers (or in the converse case raises) the price (and the marginal utility) until it becomes proportionate to expense of production. This permanent adjustment, as far as it is carried out, results in an approximation to normal price.

§ 101. The adjustment of market price to normal price, by changes in the direction of business activity, is a fact of cardinal importance. But it should be understood, from the very outset, that the process is a rough and not an accurate one. The causes which prevent it from being completely carried out may be grouped as follows :

(1) Some articles are absolutely fixed in quantity, so that the price received has little or no effect on the

supply.   Historic autographs, old coins, or rare postage
stamps cannot be said to have any normal price, since
no amount of labor and capital can honestly duplicate
them.

(2)   A larger number of articles and services are under
the control of monopolies which strive to limit the supply
in such a way as to maintain high profits.   A railroad may
charge high rates for a long time without calling a competitor into being; for business which gives unusual profit
to one road may afford very inadequate remuneration to
more than one.   As a rule, however, the effect of such
monopolies is only to retard and not to destroy the forces
of industrial competition which check exorbitant profits.
More will be said of this when we come to examine in
detail the results of modern industrial combination.

(3)   A more universal difficulty in applying the theory
of normal price arises from the uncertainty attaching to
the phrase " expense of production " in any given line of
business.   This expense varies with different men, different locations, and different processes.   Are we to take the
average expense of production as the standard of normal
price, or the expense of the most skilful and well-situated
producer, or that of the least skilful and well-situated ?
This will depend upon the line of business.   In agriculture or mining, where the best lands can only meet a part
of the demand, the community must habitually pay a
price high enough to induce owners of other lands or
mines to enter the market ; a price which affords the
owners of the better lands or mines a surplus profit
known as *rent*.   In manufacturing, on the other hand,
when the best plants can increase their output with little
restriction, so as to be able to supply the whole market, it
is often the better concerns that fix the price and the worse
ones have to get on as they can.   In general, it involves
no great error to say that the normal price of any article
is measured by the expense of producing *additional* sup-

plies on the part of those who go into business without either the advantage of old locations or the disadvantage of old methods.

(4) Another case where the relation between cost and price is obscured is seen in *bye-products*—incidental results of industrial processes which have been established for some other purpose. If a furnace is engaged in reducing pyrites for the sake of the metal which it contains, its owners find themselves left in possession of a quantity of sulphur from which the metal has been separated. This sulphur is a bye-product, not a main object of the business; its owners are ready to sell it for what they can get without attempting to figure the cost. In the manufacture of illuminating gas, coke is an important bye-product. If there is much demand for gas and little demand for coke, the latter will be sold by the gas company for almost anything it can get. If the demand for coke becomes greater, it may come to be treated as a main product of the business; and the effort to determine the normal price either of gas or of coke becomes a matter of serious doubt.[1] When a large concern like a railroad performs many kinds of service at the same time, it is often quite impossible to say which of its services is to be considered as the main object of its existence, and which are to be treated as bye-products. Under such circumstances the determination of the expense and the normal price of any individual piece of work becomes quite an arbitrary matter.

(5) Another difficulty in applying the theory of normal price arises from the fact that the process of investment is so slow that new inventions may often create a new normal price before the original adjustment is complete. This is especially the case in industries involving large capital. If a factory or a railroad charges too high a price, it may be some years before a competitor is found

[1] Mill: "Political Economy," Book iii., ch. xvi.

to reduce it ; if, on the other hand, too many competitors come in, it will be a number of years before they can drop out again. Under these circumstances, the price may easily remain for a long time either unfairly high or unfairly low, without effective remedy from free competition.

§ 102. In spite of all these hindrances, the adjustment of market price to normal price, though a rough and slow process, is a most important one ; and the efforts to ignore it, whether on the part of combinations for keeping prices too high or legislation for keeping them too low, have generally resulted in signal failure.

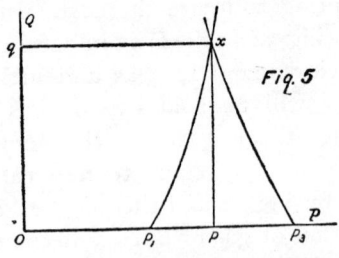

*Fig. 5*

§ 103. Let *Op* (Fig. 5) represent the normal price of an article, and *px* the quantity which will ordinarily be produced and consumed at that price. Let *Op₃* represent the maximum price which any buyer is willing to pay, so that above this price all permanent demand ceases. Let *Op₁* represent the minimum expense of production to the most advantageously situated producer, so that below this price all permanent supply ceases. The total demand for the article will be made up by consumers to whom its utility ranges from the price represented by *Op₃* down to that represented by *Op*. The total supply of the article is made up by producers to whom its cost ranges from *Op₁* up to *Op*. At the normal price the amounts of this production and consumption will be equal. If the normal price of wheat is seventy-five cents, it shows that the number of consumers to whom the utility of the wheat is such that they can afford to give seventy-five cents or more just takes up the supply which the producers can afford to furnish at seventy-five cents or less.

Competition by making a one-price system enables the consumers whose necessities are greatest to get the article for less than they would be willing to pay in an emergency ; it also enables the producers whose advantages are greatest to charge more than they would be able to accept if hard pushed. The gain to the consumers by this process is represented by $pxp_3$; the gain to the producers by $pxp_1$. The former corresponds in a very rough way to the excess of utility over price ; the latter corresponds in an equally rough way to the excess of price over cost.[1]

§ 104. A price is a fact. A value is an estimate of what a price *ought* to be.

The word value is used in a number of wholly different meanings, but this idea of a permanent standard or cause of price, as distinguished from a temporary or accidental phenomenon, lies at the basis of them all. Sometimes value is used in the sense of utility—for instance, when I say that an article has a value to me out of all proportion to the amount for which I could sell it.[2] Sometimes it

---

[1] While these curves of normal supply and demand are useful for purposes of illustration, they are often misleading, because they are based on assumptions rather than on observations. The use of the supply curve is specially open to danger. There is a tendency to identify the area $pxp_1$, with economic rent (ch. ix.). This is an error. Rent is the excess of price received over the *actual* expense of the several producers. The area $pxp_1$, represents an excess of price received over the *hypothetical* expense which the better producers would incur if the worse ones went out of business. The reduction of wages incident to the withdrawal of weaker competitors would make the expense in the second case much lower than in the first.

In the more complicated cases under (2), (4), and (5) in § 101, a normal supply curve can hardly be said to exist.

[2] An estimate of this kind is sometimes called *subjective* value. But it is better to use the term utility to avoid the confusion which would otherwise arise.

means purchasing power in the abstract, as distinct from concrete measures of this power ; for instance, when I say that an article has value, though I do not know just what its price may be. Sometimes it means purchasing power measured in commodities instead of in money. In countries with a paper currency there is frequent occasion for using the word in this sense. If the currency is doubled by act of the legislature, the prices of goods measured in this currency will tend to double also ; but we are justified in saying that there is no increase of real value corresponding to this change in nominal price. Sometimes the term value means average probable price. If I say that a certain railroad stock is selling below its true value, I simply mean that in the long run it is, in my opinion, likely to command a higher price than it does now. Finally the word value often means a *proper and legitimate* price, as distinct from an unfair or extortionate one. The last is much the commonest and most important sense of the word in commercial usage, and there seems to be no good reason against our adopting it. In this sense, the substantive value corresponds exactly to the adjective worth. If we say that a man is charging a higher price for an article than it is worth, we mean that he is putting the buyer at an unfair disadvantage.

The price of an article or service, in the ordinary commercial sense, is the amount of money which is paid, asked, or offered for it. The value of an article or service is the amount of money which may properly be paid, asked, or offered for it. A theory of price puts us in a position to explain the transactions of commercial life. A theory of value undertakes to pass judgment upon their advisability or their morality.

§ 105. Value being essentially an ethical term, we may have as many different theories of value as there are different views of business ethics. But these views fall under two main heads : the commercial or competitive theory, which bases value upon what the buyer is willing and able to offer for an article; and the socialistic theory, which bases it upon what the article has cost the seller in the way of toil and sacrifice. When we have grasped this ethical character of the controversy between the commercial and socialistic theories, we seize more clearly upon the points which are essential to the adjudication of that controversy. The question between the two parties is not primarily one of fact, but of advisability; not what necessarily determines value, but what kind of a price we shall stamp with our approval by calling it a value. The commercial theory is that the value of an article is the price which it would command under a system of free and open competition, as distinct from one which is the result of special bargaining or fraudulent concealment.[1] In this sense, the market price represents the temporary value of an article, and the normal price represents its permanent value. The advocates of the commercial theory hold that the competitive system serves the economic interests of society so well, that the first rule of business morals is to conform thereto; and that the demands of commercial justice are generally satisfied by a schedule of prices made under the influence of fair and open competition, as allowed and encouraged by the common law of England and America.

§ 106. From this view of commercial justice the socialistic theory dissents. The advocates of the socialistic theory say that, whatever the effects of competition may be upon society as a whole, its relative effects upon different members of society are extremely unfair. Many of those who do the most disagreeable work have the least enjoyment to show for it. This the socialists hold to be contrary to the principles of popular government, or of enlightened government of any kind. In criticising the results of free competition, they emphasize the fact that the adjustment of price to expense of production is

---

[1] The "Austrian" theory of value is nothing more than the commercial theory carried out to its logical conclusion.

extremely imperfect; and they add that the expense of production, as measured in money, is a very different thing from the *cost* of production, measured in the labors and sacrifices of the producer. They think that the increased extent of modern competition intensifies this divergence between cost and expense, because it brings in labor of different grades of efficiency to supply the same market, and forces men to accept the same price under increasingly different conditions of supply. They hold that the rendering of labor constitutes the only just ground for charging prices and the only just basis for estimating values. This basis they believe to be habitually ignored or defied in the processes of modern trade. They think that trade involves an effort to buy goods for less than their value and to sell them for more than their value; that the profits of traders and capitalists of every kind represent money unfairly extorted from consumers or withheld from producers; and that society must employ some organized means to prevent this extortion, and not let the trader take advantage of his power to fix prices to suit himself.

§ 107. That there is an obvious inequality in the returns under the existing commercial system of payment may readily be granted. None but the blindest optimist will deny that many of the men who do the most disagreeable work have the least comfort to show for it. The socialists are justified in asserting that there is an inconsistency between our political doctrine of equal rights to the pursuit of happiness for everybody, and the facts of the industrial world, as we see them about us. But when they come to formulate a positive theory or standard of value, they give us something which, if carried into practice, would be inconsistent, to a far greater degree than is the existing system, with the political doctrines of a free commonwealth and with the chances of happiness for its citizens.

If we attempt to reward every one according to his labor, we are at once brought face to face with the danger that people will make the wrong things. Give free choice of occupation under this system, and we should at once have an overplus of painters and musicians, with a deficiency of farmers and mechanics. It would be necessary for the government authorities to regulate the number who should engage in each occupation—a method which would be subject to the gravest industrial and political dangers.

The free choice of employment under the modern competitive system, while it doubtless increases the inequalities of return within the same trade, diminishes the inequalities of return between different trades, and gives able men in underpaid industries or localities a chance to better their condition by a change. If the numbers employed in different trades were regulated by public authority, the chances for such movement would be much reduced. The possibilities which, under the commercial system, are open to a man of real ability, even under unfavorable circumstances, would under the socialistic system be confined to those who could command exceptional political influence.

§ 108. There is another even greater danger inherent in the socialistic theory of value. It takes away the premium for efficiency. It makes a man's claims for reward depend not upon what he has done for others, but upon how he has occupied himself. Time wasted counts for as much as time spent. This is a difficulty which the leaders of socialistic thought have in vain tried to meet. To say, as Marx does, that value depends on the quantity of socially necessary labor represented by an article, introduces two conflicting standards. Social necessity is a quality which varies in degree—a fact whose consequences Marx fails to take into account. How shall we rate an article which embodies a little labor with a great degree of social necessity, as compared with one which embodies a great deal of labor with a less degree of social necessity? If we deem the producers of the former article worthy of the higher award, we reintroduce the commercial standard of value under a new guise. But if we reward the producers of the article which represents much labor and little social necessity, we take away all inducement for the efficient or wise application of labor and capital. The commercial theory of value has the inestimable advantage of giving a man a motive for efficient work by the best methods. Success and power are made dependent on doing as much as you can, with the least possible waste. It is by this process that capital is accumulated and fortunes made. The socialists are wrong in regarding trade as robbery. Individual instances there may be which lend color to this idea; but those instances are far from being the rule. If a man obtains a large income, in nine cases out of ten it is because he furnishes something which society wants; if this income leaves him a large margin of profit, it is because he has known how to economize social force in doing the work. The theory of value and of commercial justice which puts a premium on work of this kind is far better for the community than that which, in its pursuit of distributive equity, is ready to sacrifice collective efficiency and economy.

# CHAPTER IV.

## SPECULATION.

§ 109. WE have thus far studied some of the principles which regulate compensation for goods and services. We have now to deal with those which regulate compensation for risk.

The first case to be considered is that of gambling. If *A* agrees to pay *B* a dollar in the event that a coin, tossed into the air, turns up heads, and *B* agrees to pay *A* the same amount in the other event, we have a transaction which gives each party an equitable compensation for the risk involved. Yet the moral sense of the community disapproves of dealings of this kind, and the law does what it can to discourage them. The courts will not enforce such contracts, and the public authorities usually try to stop people who make a living in this way. The more enlightened the community, the more decided is the moral disapproval, and the more persistent are the attempts to enforce legal prohibitions of lotteries, policy shops, and book-making establishments.

§ 110. We saw in the last chapter that successive expenditures on the part of any individual were accompanied by diminishing additions to his enjoyment. The first hundred dollars of a man's income represents a difference between life and death. The second hundred is a matter of less absolute necessity. The third represents an in-

crease of comfort which is still great, but not equally indispensable. When it comes to the tenth hundred it is a
question of enhanced enjoyment; at the twentieth, it perhaps becomes a matter of luxuries only. In general, we
have a diminishing scale of utility for each additional
hundred dollars as the income itself gets larger and
larger.

If a man with an income of $1000 a year bets $500 on
an event which is in equal degree likely to happen or not
to happen, and then wins, he finds himself with $1500 in-
stead of $1000. If he loses, he has $500 instead of $1000.
His loss of comfort and efficiency in the latter case far
outweighs his gain in the former. A risk which appears
equitable when measured in dollars and cents, is very in-
equitable when measured in the comforts which that man
can command for himself and his family. He is risking
the loss of a larger amount of comfort, for an even chance
of gaining a smaller amount.

When a man stakes a large percentage of his income in
this way, it is easy to see that gaming is folly. The apol-
ogists for gambling say that they risk such small proportions of their income, that the difference in utility between
equal money gains or losses is very slight, and that the
pleasure of the excitement in the hazard outweighs any
such trifling difference. This is in many instances true;
but it is also true that in a large number of instances
people do not know when to stop; that under the stress
of excitement they risk very considerable proportions of
their money (not to speak of cases where they risk other
people's money also); that the losses represent losses of
comfort and self-respect, while the gains are spent in
luxury or carousal. Under these circumstances, the public is fully warranted in holding that gambling contracts
are against public policy. It is a public misfortune to
have people hazard their fortunes in this way; and the
man who makes a living by persuading other men to take

such risks on terms advantageous to himself, whether in gaming, horse-racing, or lotteries, is worse than a parasite on society.

§ 111. Let us now contrast the workings of insurance. In this case also the contract is a wager. A house owner pays an insurance company fifty dollars, in return for which he is to receive five thousand dollars in case his house burns down within a specified time; just as he might pay a bookmaker fifty dollars and receive five thousand in case a specified horse wins a race. But the motives and effects in the two cases are wholly different. The man who wins in betting on horses secures an addition to his income which means increased luxury; the man who has insured a house that burns down prevents the distress to his family consequent upon the loss of a home.[1] In like manner, the man who has insured his life makes small annual payments at a time when he can do so without encroaching on the comfort of his family; thereby assuring to that family, in the event of his death, a payment of money at a time when the loss of the earning power of its head might otherwise mean want and destitution. Insurance puts money where it is needed, instead of putting it where it is not needed; where it has the highest utility to the individual and to society, instead of the lowest; where the possibility of securing it, instead of being a means of demoralizing excitement, becomes a source of security and of industrial efficiency. Hence the insurance company in protecting the individual insurer against losses to himself and his family from fire, accident, or death, is rendering a public service; and the profits of such a company, unlike those of the bookmaker or the

---

[1] If a man insures a house in which he has no interest, or insures his own house beyond its real value, the transaction comes very close to gambling and is discountenanced both by the insurance companies and the law; not simply or primarily because it is a gambling transaction, but because it leads to fraud and arson.

lottery, are honestly earned by an actual contribution to the public wealth.

§ 112. Commercial speculation is sometimes analogous to insurance, and sometimes to gambling. In the former case it is said to be legitimate, in the latter it is said to be illegitimate. But the legitimate and illegitimate transactions are so much alike in their form, and so inextricably mingled in practice, that it is often extremely hard to draw the line between them.

§ 113. A large speculative element is involved in trade of every kind. The trader seeks to buy articles at as low a price as he can and to sell them at a higher price. He may do this either by buying them in a market where they are cheap and selling them in a market where they are dearer; or by buying them at a time when they are cheap and selling them at a time when they are dearer. The difference between his buying and selling prices represents his profit on the transaction. The uncertainty attaching to the amount of such profit makes the operation a speculative one. There is a serious risk of loss, which the trader assumes for the sake of a possible gain. Unless we can prove that the gains are honestly earned by some service to society, we shall be forced to regard them as little better than book-makers' profits.

Those who hold the socialistic theory of value regard trade as a dangerous occupation, which affords almost irresistible temptations to dishonesty. Believing, as they do, that the value or just price of an article depends on the labor embodied in it, they see in trade a constant effort to buy articles for less than their value and to sell them for more than their value; an effort in which the trader's superior shrewdness often enables him to cheat both producer and consumer. In that form of trade where articles are bought in one *place* and sold in another, they admit that the trader may do a necessary work of distribution which increases the value or just price of the goods in question, so that a part of the profit of this form of trade is legitimate. But in that form of trade where articles are bought at one *time* and sold at another, they deny that there is any service rendered which increases the value of the goods, and they hold that all profit obtained by this means is unjust and extortionate. In mediæval times, when the socialistic theory of value was generally accepted, all trade was regarded with a suspicious eye : and the attempt to buy an article when it was cheap, with a view to selling it when it became dear, was visited with the severest penalties.

§ 114. But those who hold the commercial theory of value believe that trade renders a service to society, independent of the labor of distribution ; and that this service is of essentially the same character, whether the sale be made in a different market or in the same market. They hold that the work of the trader, in acquiring goods when they are cheap and parting with them when they are dear, results in an increase of their utility to the public. If an article is unusually cheap, it means that the supply is unusually great and the utility of additions to the supply less than it ordinarily is. If it is unusually dear, it means that the supply is unusually small, and the utility of additions to the supply greater than it ordinarily is. If wheat stands at 50 cents a bushel, the need for additional wheat is small; if it stands at $1.00 a bushel, the need for additional wheat is great. The man who withdraws wheat from the market in the former case and is thus enabled to add it to the supply in the latter, serves the wants of society. Nor is it true, as might at first sight appear, that he is enabled to appropriate to himself by the higher price the whole benefit of the increased utility. If any considerable quantity of wheat is bought by the traders at the lower figure for future sale, it will increase the demand and make the present price higher than 50 cents ; while the supply thus made available when wheat

becomes scarce will prevent the future price from reaching $1.00.

§ 115. Let *DD'* (Fig. 6.) be the demand curve for

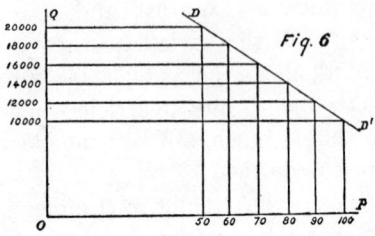

Fig. 6

wheat in a certain market where 10,000 bushels a week
would be taken at a dollar a bushel, but where 20,000
bushels a week could not be disposed of except by reducing the price to fifty cents. If a single trader stores away
a few bushels of wheat when it is plenty, and sells it when
it is scarce, he hardly affects the price to the producer or
the consumer, and can in that case realize nearly the
whole gain for himself. But his success will teach others
to follow his example. Now if he and other traders store
away 2,000 bushels a week in time of plenty, they so reduce the amount for immediate consumption that the
ruling price at that time is sixty cents instead of fifty;
while by selling this same wheat in time of scarcity, they
increase the supply so that the ruling price only goes up
to about ninety cents. If the traders withdraw 4,000
bushels a week in times of plenty, and thus provide an
increased supply for times of scarcity, it is probable that
they will have to pay seventy cents for what they buy,
and only get eighty cents when they sell it—a difference
which may little more than pay them for the cost of
carrying the wheat. The more fully the traders seek to
take advantage of differences in price, the narrower is the

margin they can realize for themselves. In general, if a supply $Oq_1$ (Fig. 7) will only command a price $Op_1$, while

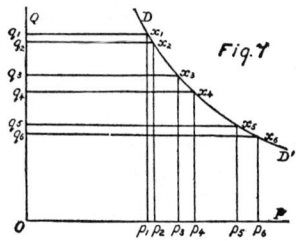

a supply $Oq_6$ will command a price $Op_6$, it means that the need of increased supplies in the latter case is greater than in the former, and that any man supplying that need renders society a corresponding service. If a trader withdraws a small quantity $q_1q_2$ in time of plenty and sells it in time of scarcity, the extremes of price variation are $Op_2$ and $Op_5$, and the trader is able to realize the difference $p_2p_5$. But if the traders reserve a larger quantity $q_1q_3$ and correspondingly increase the supply from $Oq_6$ to $Oq_4$ in time of scarcity, the extremes of price will be $Op_3$ and $Op_4$. This leaves only a small margin $p_3p_4$ per bushel for the traders (instead of $p_2p_5$, as in the former case), and leaves a much larger part of the gain to society for the benefit of producers and consumers. Anything which tends to prevent fluctuation in price renders a service in putting goods where they are needed—a service which has an effect on the public wealth far greater than can be measured by any of its effects on the private wealth of individuals.

§ 116. If the traders can compare accurately the relations of supply and demand in different markets, they will all try to put the supply where it is most needed, as long as the difference in price is likely to cover the cost

of transfer.  The profits from trade of this kind are small,
and relatively sure.  But if no such accurate comparison
can be made, the trader's possible profits are much larger,
while the risks and uncertainties are at the same time
greater.  The transaction in this case becomes a more
speculative one.

§ 117.  Down to the present century, a large part of the
speculative profits were made by taking advantage of differences of price in different places—chiefly in connection
with foreign trade.  The means of communication and
transport were so defective that there was often a great
scarcity of an article in one region and an abundance of
the same article in another.  The shipowners who moved
the article from the latter place to the former had a chance
of enormous profits.  But the business was also attended
with great risks.  Transportation was far less safe, either
from the elements or from human violence, than it is to-
day.  There was no telegraph, no good postal service, no
efficient protection from pirates by sea or highway rob-
bers by land.  All these causes combined to render the
arrival of goods so uncertain that the very wages of the
seamen were made contingent upon the safe delivery of
the cargo, and the whole body of sailors thus became
participants in the speculation.

The nineteenth century has witnessed a change in these
respects.  Improved means of communication have greatly
lessened the differences in price in different markets.  It
is no longer possible to have a glut of wheat in Chicago
and a scarcity in Liverpool.  The modern post-office and
the telegraph furnish prompt information of what is going
on all over the world, and enable merchants to know where
goods are most needed.  The steamship and the railroad
furnish a quick and safe means of placing the goods where
they will meet such needs as may arise.  The difference
of price of any staple article in two large wholesale
markets will not generally be much greater than the cost

of transportation from one to the other. So moderate have the profits from this source become, that the business of those who try to secure them is now known as *arbitrage* rather than speculation. Only in the trade with barbarous or half-civilized races does foreign commerce retain its character as an extra-hazardous business.

§ 118. The speculator of to-day makes his money chiefly by taking advantage of differences of price between different *times*, rather than between different markets. It is not so much the difference in the price of wheat in Chicago and in Liverpool which furnishes the source of his profits, as the difference between its price in Chicago this month and next month. If the speculator foresees a rise, he buys wheat to-day with the hope of selling at an advance. If he foresees a fall, he contracts to make future deliveries at to-day's prices, in the hope that he can secure the means of filling those contracts at rates low enough to leave him a profit. This is the type of transaction which forms the bulk of the business on all the leading exchanges of the world.

§ 119. When such speculation anticipates an actual demand, it is of great service to the community, The long time which elapses between production and consumption, between contracts and their fulfilment, makes it extremely important to have responsible men to anticipate the wants of the market and take the risks on their own shoulders. If I wish to build a house, I ask a builder to give me an estimate of the cost. He in turn goes to dealers in lumber and other materials and asks them to tell at what price they will deliver him the goods when he wants them. In this way he knows approximately what it will cost to build the house. The lumber dealer probably contracts to deliver lumber which is not now in his possession. But if he understands his business he knows more accurately than any one else what its future price is likely to be. He habitually makes a profit by his superior knowledge; but this profit is far less than the loss which would be involved if every builder, at the time of making a contract, had to buy all the lumber he was going to want six months hence, leaving his capital (and the community's capital) unproductive for that length of time, besides being subject to the dangers of loss by fire.

Nor does this case illustrate the full measure of service which legitimate speculation is able to render the community. Suppose that the cotton crop of this year is an unusually small one. The price will go up, the amount of manufacture lessen. But the cotton brokers foresee that next year's crop will be larger. They therefore contract to make future deliveries at lower rates. The manufacturers do not need to buy raw material in advance of their actual wants. They use up the whole old stock just as the new crop comes in ; and the mercantile community gradually accumulates other reserves from this large crop which may become available for use in a year of scarcity. The effect of such speculation is to equalize the supply of cotton in different years, and to render its price comparatively steady. More steady price makes larger consumption and manufacture for consumption; it therefore tends to increase the total quantity demanded and to benefit producers also. If we compare the prices of the present day with those prior to the development of speculative activity, we find that the margin between amounts paid to producers and those charged to consumers is much narrower now than it was before. Part of this difference is due to cheap transportation; but a part is due to the action of speculators in minimizing the effect of variations in production upon prices paid to the producer.

§ 120. This is the effect of legitimate speculation—anticipating movements of supply and demand and taking fair risks. Unfortunately there is a mass of speculation which is not legitimate—which is either pure gambling or something worse. If a man goes into the purchase of grain or cotton, not because he foresees that it will be wanted, but for the excitement of the wager, he is doing the same kind of business as the man who bets on a horse-race or on cards. The amount of these gambling transactions veiled under the forms of commerce has become very large. In many cases it has assumed the proportions of a public evil.

The sales of certain commercial staples, such as wheat, cotton, or petroleum, in the New York market are in some years fifty times as great as the actual deliveries. Of the transactions in stocks, perhaps an equally small proportion represent purchases for investment. A large part of such sales and purchases are made on *margins ;* the buyer not paying or intending to pay the full amount, but depositing with his broker a sufficient sum to secure the latter from loss, and receiving or paying at the completion of the transaction an amount corresponding to the change in price of the commodity purchased. The narrower the margin, the greater is the chance of gain or loss in proportion to the capital invested, and the higher are the stakes to the gambler on either side.

Here, as elsewhere, high stakes constitute a temptation to unfair play. If the outside public, as frequently happens, has bought securities or produce in the ill-grounded hope of a rise in price, the professional operators will speculate for a fall and try to ensure its advent by spreading false reports of every kind. If, on the other hand, a large number of operators have made contracts to deliver securities or produce which they do not possess, a few men with large capital will often try to lock up the whole available supply of such commodities, and compel those who have made the contracts to purchase the means of filling them at an exorbitant figure. Such an operation is known as a corner ; and its success is made possible by the number of speculative contracts which must be filled within a limited period of time. The man who thus attempts to manipulate the market, lowering prices by false reports or raising them by factitious scarcity, is doing the same kind of business as a man who "pulls" horses or stacks cards. In fact, he is doing worse; for the men who suffer from false running or from card sharping are those who voluntarily go into the business of betting; while the knavish speculator may hurt to some degree not only other speculators, but also producers and consumers—the producers by his deceit, the consumers by his combinations to raise prices. The direct harm done to producers and consumers by these means is very likely much less than is generally supposed; in the first place, because successful corners are relatively few, and, in the second place, because the profits of one group of speculators are for the most part made at the expense of other groups. But the indirect harm to business methods and business morals is incalculable.

§ 121. So great has been the extent of this evil that many have desired to see an entire prohibition of contracts for future delivery of things which a man does not possess at the time; but this is obviously out of the question. It would prevent operations like those of the cotton broker or the lumber merchant, which economize the capital of the community and have become a necessary feature in modern business life. It would be attended by great and disastrous irregularity in prices. Any legislation of this kind, in order to be successful, must be so contrived as to affect the gambling transactions and leave the legitimate ones comparatively untouched.

§ 122. It is extremely difficult to make this distinction by law. It cannot be based on the subject-matter of the transaction. The illegitimate speculations deal with the same articles as the legitimate ones. Sometimes when public indignation has been roused by the operation of brokers in certain lines there have been attempts made to stop all transactions in those lines ; but they have usually proved disastrous. In the year 1864, the large issue of paper currency had driven gold out of circulation and caused it to be bought and sold as a commodity. Much of it was in the hands of speculators. When its price rose more than one hundred per cent. it was supposed by the public that a part of this increase was due to the operations of these speculators. All gold speculation was therefore prohibited by statute. Under the excitement of public opinion in time of war this statute was enforced to a far greater degree than could have been done in peace. The effect was precisely the opposite of what had been anticipated. Every man who was engaged in foreign trade had to provide security for being able to make gold payments in the immediate future, if called upon to do so. Being prevented from dealing with speculators, he now had to accumulate a reserve of his own. This caused an increased demand for gold at a time when it was unusually difficult to maintain an adequate supply. Under two weeks' operation of the act, the price of a hundred gold dollars rose from about two hundred paper dollars to very nearly three hundred. So obvious was its evil effect that it was hurriedly re-pealed as a means of preventing further commercial dis-asters. Again, in the early part of 1866 there was a rise in the price of gold, which was attributed by public opinion to the speculators. Their machinations were defeated, not by legislation, but by the issue to the market of a part of the gold lying in the Treasury of the United States. For the moment the price of gold fell, and people rejoiced that the plans of the speculators had been defeated. But a short time later, when the war between Prussia and Austria caused a demand for gold in Europe, there were large exports of the metal, and its price rose by natural causes. The United States was

obliged to buy back, at a decided loss, a part of the gold
which the Treasury had so unwisely issued.   It turned out
in the end that the operations of the speculators in anticipating the wants of the future would have prevented a
loss to the country, and that the attempt of the Treasury
to defeat those operations was attended with expense
both to the government and to the mercantile community.

§ 123.  Nor can the distinction be based on the form of
the transaction.   In England the law attempts to enforce
a requirement of actual delivery.   But in the majority of
speculative commodities delivery is made, not by turning
over the product itself, but by a warehouse receipt.   The
physical delivery of a thousand bales of cotton every time
the right to that cotton changed hands would involve an
absurd waste of power.   A warrant is all which can be
delivered.   But a warrant for delivery can be passed as
many times as the exigencies of the law require.   Instances are on record where such warrants have changed
hands fifty times before reaching the actual consumer.
The spirit of the law requiring delivery can thus be
evaded.   It is almost as easy to evade laws which prohibit the settlement of transactions by the payment of
margins—transactions where there is no delivery of
goods, but a payment of money from one party to the
other, based on a change in value of the goods.   Where it
can be proved that this was the original intent of the
transaction it is easy to stamp it as gambling ; but a very
slight change in form is sufficient to enable such operations to be continued under a nominal compliance with
the letter of the law and in open opposition to its spirit.

§ 124.  The difference between legitimate speculation
and gambling lies neither in the subject-matter nor in the
form of the transaction, but in its intent and purpose.
Legitimate speculation involves anticipation of the needs
of the market and a power to assume risks in making con-

tracts to meet these needs. A failure to fulfil either of these requirements makes the operation an undesirable one for the public to tolerate. If a man, instead of anticipating the needs of the market, attempts to manipulate that market by combinations and corners, any gain that he makes is usually at the expense of the public. A stricter enforcement of laws with regard to conspiracy, and, what is more to the purpose, a better understanding by the business community of the distinction between what is good and bad public policy in this matter, would do a great deal to remedy some of the worst evils with which speculation is attended. Of even more importance is the requirement that a speculator should actually take the risks which he pretends to take. He should speculate with his own capital, and not with other people's. If a man speculates with his own capital the transaction is apt to be a legitimate one ; if he speculates with the capital of the community it is almost always pure gambling, whether he intends it to be so or not. In the first place, a requirement that a man should speculate with his own capital makes him more cautious. He is not likely to take risks unless there is a reasonable chance of winning. Moreover, the man who has the capital is likely to be a fairly good judge of such risks. If he has saved it by his own exertions it shows that he possesses industry and prudence. If he has inherited it, there is some probability that he has inherited these same qualities, and an even higher probability that he has had the advantages of a commercial education. If in spite of these advantages he makes mistakes and fails to provide the public with what it actually needs, he is unable to repeat his experiments. His bad judgment has eliminated him from the ranks of speculators, while his successful rival, by the very fact of his success, is able to repeat his operations on a larger scale in the immediate future. As long as the requirement that a man should speculate with his own capital is rigidly enforced, there is a progressive elimination of the unfit and selection of the competent. The longer this process goes on the greater is the probability that the wants of the market will be anticipated and that the work of speculation will prove one of equalization : putting products where they are needed, increasing their utility to the community, and insuring it against fluctuations in their supply.

§ 125. But if a man can speculate on borrowed capital and have the credit of the community placed at his disposal for this purpose, the result is likely to be quite different. The chance of using other people's money puts a premium on reckless gambling operations. It allows the speculator to take indefinite chances in risking what does not belong to him, with the assurance of increasing his own power and influence if such gambling is successful and losing nothing if it fails. We expose ourselves to this danger by loose systems of credit, by loose bankruptcy laws, and above all, by loose commercial ethics, under which the public opinion of the business community not only tolerates but admires success in operations of this kind. Instead of treating speculation on borrowed capital as a fraud on the community and denouncing it as such, we offer mild criticism in case of failure and unqualified admiration in case of success. There is no more serious danger to the present commercial system than that which arises from the easy-going tolerance of abuses like this. As long as this state of mind continues no law to check the abuses of speculation can be made effective. With a reform in public sentiment, little or no law would be needed.

§ 126. It is not only in commercial matters, but also in industrial ones that the speculator exercises a dominant influence. He controls production as well as trade. What the merchant does when he buys products in the hope of selling them at an advanced price, the manufac-

turer is doing when he buys labor in the hope of selling the
results of that labor at a profit. The whole wage system
is one under which the employers of the country part
with property rights to-day in the hope of securing larger
property rights in the future. Part of their prosperity
arises from skill in organizing labor; part, and usually a
larger part, arises from skill in foreseeing the wants of the
market. The success or failure of a man engaged in
manufacturing, in transportation, or in agriculture depends
more upon his skill as a prophet than upon his industry
as a producer. When Henry George says, "It is never
as an employer of labor that any producer needs capital.
When he does need capital it is because he is not only an
employer of labor, but a merchant or speculator in or an
accumulator of the products of labor," he has described a
salient feature of the modern industrial system. But
when he goes on to assume that this state of things is an
unnecessary and arbitrary one, he fails to take the facts
of industrial history into account. We have put the employment of labor into the hands of those who are able
and ready to speculate in the products of labor, because
this method has on the whole proved the best for the
community. The industrial development of the last three
or four hundred years, rightly interpreted, is an account
of the reasons which have led society to put the control
of its industry into the hands of a body of speculative
investors.

§ 127. All productive industry involves a certain amount
of risk. Whenever time elapses between the application
of labor and the completion of the product of labor in a
form available for actual enjoyment, there is an advance
of capital to the producers for the sake of a remote and
generally somewhat unknown result. In the building of
a factory or a railroad a great deal of food is consumed.
Whether the product of the labor thus applied will be as
useful to the community as the food which was consumed

by those who have produced it, is always somewhat uncertain. The more remote the result, the greater is the
uncertainty. George's own chosen illustration refutes his
assumption that labor necessarily replaces the capital
which it consumes. " Here is a blacksmith at his forge
making picks ; clearly he is making capital—adding picks
to his employer's capital, before he draws money from it
in wages. Here is a machinist or boiler-maker working
on the keel-plates of a Great Eastern. Is he not also just
as clearly creating value—making capital ? " No. The
men who worked on the keel-plates of the Great Eastern
were clearly *not* creating value. The Great Eastern was
an ill-designed boat that never rendered the services expected. It was a case of misdirected labor. Had the
machinists and boiler-makers who worked on the Great
Eastern been compelled to content themselves with the
price which the result of their labor ultimately commanded, they would have starved before it was half done.
In the simple processes like those of the blacksmith the
result is so near at hand and the needs of the consumers
so well known, that the chance of conspicuous failure to
replace the public capital consumed is very small indeed ;
in processes like those of steamship or railroad building
the danger is indefinitely larger. The more remote the
consumers in time or place, the greater is the uncertainty
and the more speculative the whole transaction.

§ 128. Especially prominent does this uncertainty become in the application of any new process or the development of any new locality. Under old conditions,
experience has proved what products are wanted and how
labor can be economically applied ; but every new invention or new settlement involves a multitude of new and
unknown conditions. Scientific experts cannot predict
the success or failure of a commercial enterprise ; it requires the test of actual experience. Every business man
will tell you of many projects that look well on paper

but fail to work in practice. A large proportion of the capital embarked in such enterprises is lost. A large proportion of the food consumed by the laborers engaged in such undertakings is virtually wasted.

§ 129. Are we then to forego all chance of such progress? No. The gain to the community as a whole, from one successful experiment, may outweigh the loss from ten unsuccessful ones. The conservative nation that never changes its methods avoids a great many losses, but it fails to make the conspicuous gains which constitute modern industrial civilization. The problem of industrial growth can be solved only by encouraging enough experiments to secure progress without encouraging so many as to destroy the whole accumulated capital of the community. We have tried to accomplish the former object by giving individual possessors of capital the chance of realizing large profits in case of success; and to protect ourselves against the latter danger by insisting, at least in theory, that a man shall make these experiments at his own expense. If everybody were free to undertake them, whether he had proved his fitness by accumulating private capital or not, the food supply of the community would probably soon run short. If nobody were allowed to make them until the whole community was ready to vote for their adoption, they would be indefinitely delayed. By leaving it to the option of the individual property holder to undertake them or not as he pleases, society secures most of the gain and avoids most of the loss. It allows him to waste part of the capital of the community in unsuccessful experiments, believing that his example will be a warning to prevent others from following in his track, and that the immediate loss to the community may become a means of future gain. It guarantees him the good results from the successful experiments, trusting that competition will subsequently prevent his profits from being too large.

§ 130. Where this view prevails, a new motive is given for the acquisition of property. It is no longer desired simply as a means of enjoyment, but as a means of controlling the industrial actions of other men. The pursuit of wealth beyond a man's present necessities is no longer a matter of avarice but of ambition. Such wealth gives its owner a power in no wise inferior to that of the successful general or politician.

§ 131. The introduction of this new motive for amassing wealth produces the following effects :

1. A great increase of accumulations. Under the stimulus of ambition many men are led to increase their production and diminish their consumption far more than any intelligent consideration of their own comfort would dictate. In this way we have a great increase in the amount of public wealth available for enterprises whose return is remote and involves long waiting. The rights to such wealth may not always remain in the hands of those who have done the most work or practised the most abstinence ; but it remains none the less true that private motives for work and abstinence are the most effective means of accumulating public capital.

2. A process of natural selection of men who have ability to manage capital. If the property owner has shown foresight in investment he reaps a rich reward for his services in rendering a new process or locality available for supplying the wants of the community. If he has been over-sanguine, he loses his own capital and that of those who have trusted him, and becomes once more dependent on his labor. Under this system we have not simply a selection of the strong and an elimination of the weak, nor a selection of the industrious and an elimination of the lazy ; but a selection of the prudent and intellectual with an elimination of the reckless or emotional. The moral character of the employers thus developed presents a mixture of good and

bad qualities. The control is placed in the hands of men who are enterprising and efficient, but often narrow and unscrupulous. They possess sagacity which enables them to deal with the market ; they often fail to possess that broader sagacity which would enable them to deal equally well with those in their employ. The danger of this deficiency is greatly intensified by the possibility of speculating with borrowed capital, and gaining control of industrial enterprise by transactions which are virtually gambling.

3. An increased intensity of competition among those who handle the large accumulations of capital. This is contrary to the popular view. It is commonly assumed that the more competitors you have, the greater will be the intensity of competition. But in actual experience there is no competition in the world so intense as that which prevails between two highly organized bodies that stand opposed to one another. In the old days of small concerns there was much more slackness of management, and much larger profit per unit of product, than we find to-day. It is proverbial that the largest houses can make the closest calculations in selling goods at a slight margin above expense ; and competition is generally strong enough to force them to make these calculations closer than would have been deemed possible a half-century ago—in other words, to keep down profits.

§ 132. In comparing our large factories of to-day with the smaller ones of two generations past, we find, on the whole, that the ratio of wage payments to interest and dividends is larger now than it was then. The margin of profit has been narrowing more conspicuously than the piece-price for labor has been diminishing. The large capital and its earnings make a greater impression on the public mind than did the numerous small capitals of independent producers ; but it is not probable that the aggregate valuation or remuneration of the capital of to-day has increased proportionately with the increase of demand for labor. We are not warranted in assuming, as so many of the socialists do, that profits are growing enormously and are to be regarded as sums withheld from labor. They are in most cases not disproportionate to the chances of loss. A very slight change in efficiency of management may readily convert the capitalist's surplus into a deficit. The charge made by the capitalist classes, for their services in industrial speculation, cannot be regarded as immoderate, *if the work is well done.*

§ 133. But how far is this condition fulfilled? Does the existing system secure progress and avoid loss? To the first half of this question we may unhesitatingly give an affirmative answer. Whatever else the speculative system may do or fail to do, it gives us industrial progress. It was for this reason that it displaced the traditional methods of agriculture and manufactures which had preceded it. The feudal system and the gild system were both too conservative; the system of private capital proved its superiority in being progressive. Nor has this merit outworn itself with age. The superior flexibility of the speculative system makes itself conspicuous not only in contrast with feudal industry, but also with modern state-owned industry. Though half the railroads and nine-tenths of the telegraphs of the world are in government hands, all the large improvements of method in these lines have been made under private enterprise.

The work of avoiding losses has not been so well done. It is the theory of the modern system that the accumulated capital of speculators should act as an insurance fund to secure a steady supply of products and an unimpaired reserve of national resources. This general reserve is fairly well maintained; but it is not always well utilized. The supply of capital is steadier and surer than the employment of labor. Mistakes and wrongs of large speculators frequently result in commercial crises from which the whole community suffers. The occurrence of these crises constitutes the severest possible indictment against the modern speculative methods.

§ 134. It will not do for capitalists to try to minimize this indictment, or to evade the responsibility for the evils attendant upon industrial depressions. Society gives its great financiers a trust compared with which all other trusts sink into insignificance. It gives them the power of directing the labor and capital of the country. If they can do this well, they will deserve the power and retain the trust. But in order that it shall be well done, the control must be in competent hands.

To secure this result, the process of natural selection of employers must be what it purports to be—a survival of those who have proved their power to serve the public and an elimination of those who have failed to do so. The contest for commercial supremacy must be settled by success in organizing production and foreseeing consumption, not by success in gambling. If the industrial and financial struggle actually brings the best men forward, they show their ability in such a manner that we have little to fear from socialism. If a man's personal advantage is identified with the success of his business ; if his position in the financial world is dependent on his competence in the industrial world; if, in short, he arranges to stand or fall with the success or failure of his management, then we have a process of natural selection under which men who serve the public inevitably come to the front, while their less competent rivals are pushed into the background. If, on the other hand, the question of control is settled by gambling instead of by legitimate business transactions, if the possession of financial authority is made to depend on success in stock operations, rather than on success in organizing producers and meeting the wants of consumers, then we have a process of selection by which the wrong leaders come to the front driving out competitors who might serve the public better, though they have not known how to serve themselves quite so well. When the wrong men are brought forward, the speculative system is in real danger, because it does not do what the public has a right to demand of it.

§ 135. We cannot rely upon legislation to protect us from this danger, because, as we have already seen, gambling transactions and legitimate transactions are indistinguishable in form. We must look to the public sentiment of the business community ; we must see that it recognizes the difference between legitimate and illegitimate speculation, and condemns the latter as a breach of trust. Such it is under existing conditions. The man who gambles away his money is not simply parting with his own enjoyment, but with his control of the industrial forces of the community. It is not like selling his labor : it is like selling his vote.

If business men are not to be controlled by commercial ethics—ethics fitting the economic conditions of today, rather than those of five centuries ago,—they must expect to be controlled by something else. If they will not accept the full measure of responsibility which goes with their industrial power, they must expect to be deprived of responsibility and power together, by a popular movement in the direction of socialism. Such a movement is being aided and countenanced by every financier whose interests in the stock market lead him to forget the interests of his properties, by every lawyer who teaches his clients to evade the responsibilities attaching to wealth, by every man who in the excitement of speculation loses sight of those responsibilities—by every one, in short, who forgets that under the existing system the possession of money involves a public trust, with whose fulfilment or non-fulfilment that system must stand or fall.

# CHAPTER V.

## INVESTMENT OF CAPITAL.

The Wage System—Private Land Ownership—Patent Right—The Payment of Interest—Limited Liability.

W. J. Ashley : " English Economic History." London and New York, 1891, 1893.

K. Marx : " Das Kapital." This book (which has been translated by S. Moore and E. Aveling), in the closing sections of the first volume, gives the socialistic view of the events and processes described in this chapter.

§ 136. IT is characteristic of the modern industrial system that a laborer who owns no capital, though nominally free to do what he pleases, must actually find some property owner who will give him enough to keep him alive during the period which must elapse between the rendering of the labor and the sale of the finished product. Under such circumstances, the laborer almost inevitably submits to the direction of the property owner in deciding how his labor shall be applied. Laborers without capital must necessarily work on this basis; even those who have small amounts of capital habitually do so. Such advances of capital are known as wages. Many writers of good standing give broader definitions than this, but in the actual usage of ordinary life wages designate the sums paid by property owners, or their representatives, to laborers for work done under the direction of the property owners.[1]

[1] If the degree of education required is such that the laborer must be in large measure *self-directing*, these payments are known as *salaries* or *fees ;* the former term being applied to payments for continuous employment, the latter to payments for irregular or varying employment. Salaries correspond to time wages (ch. x.), fees to piece wages.

§ 137. Whatever be the details of the contract by which wages are determined, the employer must be in a position to guarantee the fulfilment of his part of the agreement and to relieve the workman of any risk which may arise from failure to sell the product of his work at the expected profit.    This is essential to the idea of wages, and to the principles on which modern industrial society is organized. This is the reason why the employer must be a property owner, or must at any rate act as the agent or representative of property owners.    If he is not in this position, he cannot guarantee the payment of the wages he has agreed to give.    The certainty that wages shall be paid is so important to society that the law strains every point to secure this end.    The employer should pay his hands in money, or in checks which are as good as money, not in orders upon stores or other forms of "truck."    In many states he is compelled to make his payments as often as once a week.    The workman not infrequently enjoys a "mechanic's lien" upon the results of his work; for instance, if a builder for any reason cannot pay his journeymen the wages agreed upon, the journeymen can attach the building upon which they have been employed, and compel its owner to pay the wages due them.    On the other hand the wages themselves are in many states exempt from attachment; that is to say, if the laborer owes money to an outside party, that party cannot have recourse to the employer, and divert from the workmen wages earned but not yet paid.    The wage contract, in such states, must be fulfilled with the workman directly, and not with the workman's creditor.    Wherever society tolerates any failure on the part of the employer to meet such contracts fully and directly, it indicates a low stage of industrial development.[1]

[1] An exception to the stringency of this requirement is found in the law concerning seamen's wages.    In times past the shipowner has not generally been held liable for such wages unless the voyage was successfully completed. This was because marine enterprise was attended with such risks from shipwreck or piracy that an effective guarantee was impossible.    In recent years,

§ 138. The great bulk of the wage payments in any community is made by those who expect to sell the result of the labor to others instead of enjoying it themselves. Such a payment is a speculative investment of capital. Looking at the transaction from the private standpoint the property owner transfers a certain amount of money to the laborer, in the hope of obtaining a larger amount of money in the future by the sale of the product of that labor. Looking at the transaction from the public standpoint, the laborer is enabled to consume a certain part of the public wealth, in the expectation that the products of his labor will more than replace the amount thus consumed. He receives as income the right to enjoy a part of the capital already existing[1]; his employer hopes and believes that any destruction of public capital will be made good, and is prepared to bear the loss, in his own property, in case this expectation is not fulfilled.

§ 139. The amount of capital thus sacrificed in the hope of its replacement and increase is known as *cost of production*. In its private sense, the cost of an article to any individual speculator is the amount of capital which he has advanced to secure it. This may have been paid either to the laborers in the form of wages, or to other speculators as a means of controlling the results of past labor. Private cost is better designated as expense.[2] In its public sense the cost of an article to the community is

as the industry has developed and become more secure by better navigation and by the development of marine insurance, there has been an increasing tendency to treat seamen's wages just like other wages ; that is, to guarantee their payment even in the event of shipwreck.

[1] The money which he receives is known as nominal wages ; the enjoyment which he can command is called real wages. (See ch. x.)

[2] Some writers prefer to measure cost in terms of pain (total and marginal " disutility ") rather than in terms of waste. The practical difference resulting from the use of the two methods is not very great, for an increase or diminution of pain is usually accompanied by a corresponding increase or diminution in waste ; but waste is a better standard, because it is a more measurable thing than pain, and because the reduction of waste furnishes a more tangible goal of public policy than the reduction of pain.

the amount of public capital which has been consumed or rendered unavailable in connection with the production of that article.

The excess of return above cost is known as *profit.* The profit of an individual is the difference between money advanced in production and money received from the sale of the product. The profit of a community is the difference between old products consumed and new ones produced. Individual profit is tolerably easy to measure ; the profit of a community, extremely difficult.[1]

Under the modern wage system society gives the employer the right to realize individual profit from the sale of the products of labor in the belief that his effort to do this will conduce to public profit.

§ 140. Profits are neither more nor less than the excess of the selling price of the products of industry above the amount advanced as wages. It is true that some of the investments of an individual capitalist are not made in the form of wages, but in payments for materials and machinery which other capitalists have made ready for use. But if we look at the relation between capitalists as a class and laborers as a class, we shall find that the capitalists as a body advance wages, and appropriate the difference between the price paid to the laborers and that received from the consumers. The expectation of this difference or profit gives them a motive to utilize their capital, and to make it more available as a means of public income.

---

[1] While the effort of the speculator to reduce his expense and increase his profit tends on the whole to reduce public cost and increase public profit, it must not be assumed that expense corresponds at all accurately to cost, or private profit to public profit ; any more than the selling prices of articles correspond to their total utility. The producer's surplus described in chapter ix. represents in large measure an excess of expense above cost ; an amount transferred from the capitalists to the laborers in excess of the necessary consumption of the latter.

If the process of production is a brief one, this motive is enough to make people invest their capital. If a man has more property than he needs for immediate use, he is glad to apply it in such a way as to give him control of the labor of others. If the chance of gain is greater than the chance of loss most men would rather invest their capital than store it up. There is good ground for such expectation of gain from investment of capital when an intelligent man takes control of a process whose duration is short. Any skill that he may show redounds to his own advantage. But in a long process of production the case is different. The instant it has proved a success, other competitors come into the field and reduce profits by their competition. The pioneer in any industrial method which involves remote returns, takes all the chances of failure, and may receive but a small part of the rewards of success. Naturally there is great reluctance to take the initiative on terms like this. It is not enough to give the speculator direction of his labor and the right to dispose of his products, in order to induce him to invest his capital for such remote objects. He must receive a guarantee of permanent profit in case of success, sufficient to make him hazard the risk of permanent loss in case of failure.

§ 141. Capital thus invested for the sake of a remote return, whether in the form of agricultural improvements, buildings, or machinery, is said to be *fixed*. It can rarely be withdrawn from its original use and applied in any other place or for any other purpose, without great loss to the owner and to the public. But in spite of this danger of loss the economy to the public, attendant upon the use of fixed capital, is very great, and constantly increases as population becomes denser.

The first farms cultivated are not as a rule the best ones, but those which require the least original outlay. The first industries practised are those which require the fewest tools. The first roads are made with the least possible amount of surfacing and drainage. The minimum of fixed capital is used in every instance because of the small market and the need of immediate returns. But as the community grows it adopts a different system. It resorts to farms which are less accessible, and to methods of cultivation which are less obvious, but which, when once brought into use, are more productive. It applies processes of manufacture whose dominant principle is not to reduce the outlay, but to increase the output. It adopts means of transportation which cost much more to establish, but much less to use. The permanent investment of fixed capital keeps growing larger; the current expenses per unit of product grow correspondingly smaller.

The original outlay connected with an old-fashioned shoemaker's establishment was very small. A few benches and tools were sufficient means for conducting the business. But the labor of sewing each pair of shoes was very large. When hand work gave place to factory work, it necessitated an original investment of many thousands of dollars; but when a factory was once established, the direct expense of making each pair of shoes was very small. The larger the market for shoes, the greater was the comparative economy of factory labor. The cost of an old-fashioned country road is next to nothing; the cost of carriage upon such a road may amount to a dollar a ton a mile. Substitute a modern macadamized road, and you increase the original cost, but diminish the cost of carriage. Spend $30,000 a mile on a railroad, and the direct cost of carrying freight will be less than a cent for each ton carried. Increase the investment in the railroad by reducing grades and making more solid structures, and you will treble the possible train loads, with a corresponding diminution in cost per ton.

To realize this economy a large market is necessary. If there are only a hundred people to wear the shoes or to use the road, old-fashioned methods are more economical than modern ones. But with increase of population we find the opportunity for increasing use of fixed capital and the necessity for such economic institutions as shall encourage its investment.

§ 142. The first and in some respects the most important of these institutions was private property in land.

The feudal land tenure, whose development was described in chapter ii., was based upon force. The dependants of the mediaeval lord paid him rent, either in labor or in money, as a price for the security of possession which he could give them. These feudal burdens were far more analogous to modern taxes than to modern ground-rents. They represent a price paid to the sovereign for his protection, rather than an economic equivalent paid to the property owner for the productive capability of the land. But when this security was once so thoroughly established that the strong arm of a military chieftain was no longer needed to protect his vassals, tenure of land gradually passed out of the hands of soldiers and into the hands of capitalists. It was found more profitable by the tenant to cultivate improved land which produced a great deal, and pay a substantial rent for it, than to get a bare living from unimproved and unproductive land, even though the rental of such land was merely nominal. This change was not only better for the tenant but better for the community. If a new system of cultivation enabled more food to be raised from a given area with the same amount of labor, it was of great advantage to the community to have that system adopted. When processes of agriculture were discovered which promised an increased permanent productiveness of the land, it became necessary to guarantee to men who had the capital for applying these processes a sufficiently long and complete tenure to give them the motive to make the experiment. No one would be willing to incur the outlay involved in draining or in artificial fertilizing unless he was guaranteed the occupancy of the land thus improved for a sufficiently long time to make the change remunerative to him, as well as to the community in general. For no new process is an assured success until it has been actually tried. Successful investment of capital in the improvement of real estate has been a means of making large fortunes ; but these fortunes were not certainties from the outset. If they had been, the community could and would have made the improvements from the public funds at public expense. The profits of the successful, in land speculation and land improvement, have been offset by the losses of the unsuccessful. The monopoly of an advantageous location or of a fertile piece of ground which the real-estate owner enjoys is a premium which has been offered to him because of the skill of capitalists in developing land at the points and in the ways where such development was needed.

In view of the public necessity for improvement of real estate the laws which prohibited the alienation of land from the families of the nobles were gradually modified ; and the farms passed from the hands of soldiers who only knew how to spend money into the hands of property owners who understood how to invest it.

§ 143. This change in the system of tenure was by no means confined to agricultural lands. The same course of development is seen in mining. Mining law has its hunting stage, where a man wanders up and down the bed of a creek in the hope of finding nuggets of gold. It has its pastoral stage, where the miner has his movable property, perhaps a mule and a wheelbarrow, and uses them as best he can in collecting natural deposits. In this state of society rights to the instruments of production are clearly recognized, and the stealing of a mule is punished with the utmost severity. But rights to real estate are as yet chaotic. A man must be prepared to defend them by his own arm. The wanderer has a claim to the bed of a stream only as long as he is actually in possession and can maintain his right for himself. But as population becomes more dense and these superficial sources of supply are exhausted, a new system of mining property becomes recognized in usage and in law, whereby the man who invests capital in a location obtains permanent rights to this location. Whether he makes his arrangements for washing down large alluvial deposits far away from an existing stream, or for tunnelling into the quartz rock for the sake of the veins of metal which it contains, the real estate which he has developed becomes his own. This permanent right of property, with the attendant monopoly which it gives, is an absolute necessity if the community wishes a man to invest large capital in mining; for the whole investment may prove a failure, and no man is willing to take the chance of failure unless assured of special and permanent advantages in case of success. If the community has reached a point where it needs to have much capital used in mining, it must give the capitalist rights of control and chances of possible gain, to offset the great chances of total loss.

§ 144. The conditions under which private ownership of land has developed are strikingly illustrated by a comparatively new form of landed property,—submarine rights to oyster-beds. Of all waters in the United States, those of the Chesapeake are perhaps best fitted for the production of oysters. But the system of tenure recognized by the state of Maryland was not well adapted to their development. Certain ill-defined parts of the Chesapeake and other oyster grounds were set apart for dredging, certain other parts for "tonging." There was also a right given to individuals to take up five acres of oyster land under

9

water.  But this right or license was revocable at the pleasure of the state, so that the licensee had not the assurance of permanent holding which would make far-sighted
policy in the use of these oyster-beds profitable or even safe.
The oyster law of Maryland was almost exactly analogous
to the land law of the mediæval village community, with
its ill-defined common, its ill-defined forest land, and its
extremely precarious rights of use of individual strips of
the soil.  The result was the same in either case.  Proper
utilization of the land was impossible.  The Maryland
oyster-beds were so rapidly exhausted as to threaten the
extinction of the industry in spite of all natural advantages for its prosecution.  Meanwhile there was a great
increase in the production of oysters in the waters controlled by some other states, where rights of permanent
tenure were allowed that were closely analogous to ordinary property in land.  The oyster-beds thus held formed
a large source of income to their owners, but it was not
an income amassed at the expense of the state.  The
oyster growers of Long Island Sound have paid in taxes
an amount far exceeding the total rental value of the
oyster-beds which the state of Maryland leased for short
terms under licenses revocable at will.

§ 145.  The good effects of the system of private land
tenure are most conspicuously seen when the owner and
the occupier of the land are one and the same person.
Under these conditions, land ownership serves at once as
a motive to zeal in labor and to liberality in investment.
Where one man owns the land and another occupies it,
the right of the owner to the benefit of all improvements
not infrequently acts as a discouragement to the occupier
and prevents him from laboring with the zeal or the skill
which he would otherwise use.  The loss in efficiency of
labor under such circumstances may be greater than the
public gain from the capital invested.  Large tenant
farms are sometimes less well developed than the peasant

properties on the continent of Europe,—in spite of the disadvantages, inseparable from small husbandry and scant capital, under which the latter suffer. Systems which recognize the right of the tenant to compensation for improvements, or which guarantee him fixity of tenure at a stated rent, have often proved salutary. They help the public by encouraging the tenant more than they hurt it by discouraging the owner—unless the owner was far-sighted enough to give the tenant these privileges without compulsion. Even so crude a device as the metayer system (§ 40) often works better, on account of the permanence of tenure which it gives the occupier, than a system of tenancy at will under a capitalist landlord.

If for any reason the landlords do not properly develop the real estate which they own, and try to get money out of the land without putting money into it, the system of private ownership proves itself a thoroughly bad one. The land tenure of a body of foreign conquerors represents a drain on the community rather than an addition to its resources. The case of Ireland is an instance in point. The right to receive rent from Irish land has habitually served, not as a motive to improve the land, but as a means to degrade the laborer. When this result takes place to a marked degree, modern society often so far modifies the principle of private property in land as to introduce *judicial* rents instead of competitive ones; substituting public arbitration between landlord and tenant for a system of competition which is so short-sighted or imperfect as not to subserve the public needs.[1]

§ 146. When the habit of land speculation becomes

---

[1] Another conspicuous case where private land ownership fails to serve the public interests is connected with the destruction of forests. In this case the governments have tried to remedy the evil by encouraging the right use of the land rather than by prohibiting its wrong use. The point involved in public or quasi-public forestry is treated in the chapter on co-operation.

prevalent, there is always danger that the system of private land ownership will be made a means of hurting the public instead of helping it.

It will not do to go to the extreme of condemning *all* land speculation as hurtful. A man who sees that a large business block will be wanted in a certain spot at the end of ten years may serve the public by keeping the lot unoccupied during that time. For the gain which the owner and the public would reap from the use of inferior buildings during those ten years would not compensate the loss which would be involved in tearing them down before they had paid for themselves, or in waiting until they had paid for themselves before erecting the new block. In such a case a land speculator will contribute to the best utilization of the public wealth by a far-sighted calculation of the time when investments of capital will be most profitable. But it is needless to add that a great deal of land speculation is of a totally different character from this, and is a mere effort to get money out of the land without putting money into it. Such irresponsible speculation is greatly increased by the mistaken practice of assessors in rating unimproved land at relatively low figures on account of its lack of productivity and consequent inability to bear high taxes. No man should be encouraged to keep land out of use by a remission of burdens which necessarily puts heavier taxes on those who have put adjoining land into use. He is holding his property in a shape where it does the public no present good in the hope that the work done by others will make this a profitable policy in the long run. He may be right; but for the present he is causing public inconvenience, and cannot complain if he is taxed on the basis of his own estimate of the value of the land rather than on that of its immediate productiveness. If he cannot pay taxes he can sell it to some one else. Great as are the mistakes of the single-tax agitators it is to be hoped that they may have a salutary effect in leading assessors to put heavier burdens on ground values and lighter ones on improvements. For after all that can be said in behalf of land speculation, it remains practically true that the men who have done conspicuous public service with their land are as a class those who have been prompt rather than tardy in its development.

§ 147. While agriculture was helped by giving the capitalists ownership of the land, the development of manufactures was stimulated by grants of monopoly. At first these grants were made quite recklessly. In the early history of England we find frequent records of permanent privileges assured to an individual citizen in consideration of his services in introducing some new industry. Such a system afforded grave opportunities for abuse. Privileges were often granted to court favorites as a reward of personal or political services. The introduction of a new manufacture was made a pretext for oppressive taxation of the people who had to use its products. Special grants of this kind, however plausibly worded, were generally unpopular, and formed a frequent source of public complaint against the sovereigns of mediæval Europe.

§ 148. In modern times the grant of monopoly privileges is hedged about with precautions against such abuse. The system of patents confers a monopoly on the man who introduces a new invention. But the government takes pains to insist that such an invention shall be really new, and the monopoly granted is only a temporary one. A patent system, if properly guarded, seems to be thoroughly justified by its results. In the absence of such protection few new inventions would be developed. The risk attending the introduction of a new process is always great. Even when it works thoroughly well in the laboratary or model room, it may not work well in public. The man who first develops a new invention loses his whole capital if it fails. If he is immediately exposed to free competition in case of success, he can enjoy exceptional profits for a short time only. The risk of loss, under such circumstances, outweighs the possibility of gain. No man, as has already been said, will take the lead in a hazardous experiment when those who follow him have practically equal chance of gain and almost no chance of loss. The patent, by making the gain a permanent one, makes it safe for a capitalist to develop a new process. This is the real justification of the system. The American theory that the patent is a reward for invention, and the English theory that it is a reward for disclosure of the invention to the public, both fail to touch the true grounds on which patent right has grown up. It has established itself, not primarily as a stimulus for invention or for disclosure, but. for utilization and development of new methods requiring the investment of capital and the guarantees which shall make such investment possible.

The monopoly of the patentee is in one respect much more complete than that of the landowner. The exclusive right to use a certain process may shut out all competition; while the exclusive right to use a certain piece of land rarely prevents other landowners from competing with the most favored individual. It puts them at a slight disadvantage, but not often at a prohibitory one. The monopoly conferred by a valuable patent while it lasts is thus much more absolute. To offset this, it is limited in duration. After a comparatively short term of years the patent expires, leaving its owner no advantage except what he has derived from possessing an established business; while the land monopoly may continue to give an increasing advantage for an indefinite length of time.

§ 149. The monopoly conferred by copyright is closely analogous, both in its form and in its justification, to that of patent right. It is of comparatively little importance for the community to decide whether an idea is or is not a fit subject of property; but it is of great importance to have the law in such a shape that a publisher can safely risk his capital in making that idea accessible to the reading public. A new book may prove a failure, just as much as a new process. For the sake of profits possible under a copyright law, the publisher can afford to take the risks of failure which he cannot do in the absence of such protection.

§ 150. Another form of monopoly, less complete than those just described, is exemplified by protective tariffs and navigation acts. The benefit of such monopoly is not given to one individual to the exclusion of other individuals, but to the home producers to the exclusion of foreign competitors. The underlying motive for such protective legislation, when framed with a public purpose in view, has been like that of private land ownership or patent right; to give the home country the benefits accruing from investment of capital under its own immediate control. The case of a protective tariff differs from that of a patent in that the private risks in case of failure and the public gains in case of success attendant upon the *transplantation* of a process which is already in use elsewhere are far less than those which attend the *development* of one which has been as yet totally untried.[1]

§ 151. Where for any reason grants of monopoly have been impossible, or inadequate to secure their purpose, governments have often resorted to subsidies; as in bounties for the production of sugar, municipal subscription to railroad securities, or, most frequent of all, payments to shipbuilders and shipowners.[2] How far such

---

[1] The arguments concerning the protective tariff system are so complicated and depend so much upon the theory of wages that their discussion must be reserved for a later chapter.

[2] Exemption from taxes, such as is frequently granted by our western cities for the purpose of attracting manufacturing capital, is to all intents and purposes a subsidy. The same thing of course can be said of the grants of public lands which have been used by the United States to encourge transportation enterprises. From a very early period we have had important

subsidies are justified is a question which must be reserved for further discussion in connection with matters of international policy.

When debts were chiefly created for the sake of personal expenditure, the taking of interest or usury was deservedly condemned. The men who borrowed money and spent it did not, as a rule, increase their productive capacity. They relieved a present need ; but they generally did nothing but put off a day of reckoning and make it heavier when it actually did come. In cases like this, it was fair enough to say that money did not produce money and to condemn interest on this ground. Mediæval loans were generally unproductive loans. The lender did no service to society which would entitle him to claim encouragement. So far as the prohibition of interest prevented borrowing for personal expenditure, it was a good thing.

But when a considerable part of the loans were made for productive purposes, the case was altered ; and it was not long before the law and public sentiment were altered correspondingly. We have not space to follow out in detail the various subtleties by which this change was justified to the legal mind.[1] The traditional excuse for interest, as a penalty for delay in payment,[2] was made to cover

gifts to encourage the building of roads and canals. In the years from 1850 to 1856 more than 25,000,000 acres of land in various states were given to railroads. During the war and the period immediately following it territorial lands were given away on a yet larger scale, the grants in aid of Pacific roads alone amounting to over 150,000,000 acres. The result of these gifts has been far from proving an unmixed good. They stimulated unsound railroad schemes and caused railroad building to be misdirected. Provisions intended to protect the interests of the government were disregarded. Settlers were induced to move too far west, to points where they were at the mercy of railroad agents. In many instances the only gainers were land speculators and financiers of the worst sort.

[1] The reader is referred to Ashley, " English Economic History," vol. i., ch. iii. ; vol. ii., ch. vi.

[2] Hence the derivation of the word *interest—i.e.,* a difference made by time.

cases where the delay was purely nominal. The theory of compensation for loss (*damnum emergens*) was stretched to cover cases where the only loss was loss of opportunity for profit (*lucrum cessans*). Of yet wider importance was the recognition of the right of one associate in an enterprise to insure a fixed return to another instead of a variable one. This contract of assurance (*contractus trinus*) really stands at the foundation of the modern interest system. The lender of capital is an investor who commutes his chance of a large profit for the assurance of a smaller one. Society allows this commutation, because it is a public advantage to have the capital of these investors used in enterprises which they cannot themselves supervise, and whose risks they must therefore leave to others. The justice of interest is not based primarily on equities between borrower and lender, but on the public advantage of encouraging guaranteed investments.[1]

§ 153. The use of capital as a means of ensuring its owners a fixed return derived additional recognition and sanction from another quarter as the *purchase of rent charges* became more frequent. Whenever a piece of property was economically productive, its selling price was pretty sure to bear a fixed relation to its rental.

---

[1] Most of the popular justifications of interest try to reach their end by too short a route. Bastiat uses the illustration of a man who has made a plane which so increases the efficiency of labor that some one who wants to borrow it will promise to give back, at the end of the year, not only a new plane to replace the old one which has worn out, but a plank in addition. George criticises this as inconclusive, since the only way in which the owner of the plane could have obtained a plank was by working with it ; but says that if one person lends another a calf, the productive powers of nature will put him in a position to return a cow at the end of the year [without working : a curious conception of farm life], and that this justifies interest, because capital gives control of the productive forces of nature. In point of fact there is no essential difference between the two cases. We allow interest because it is for the advantage of the community to encourage a man to save capital which will support people in making more planes than he himself can use, or in bringing up more animals than he himself can watch.

What this relation was depended partly on the number of persons who needed ready money and were prepared to sell future income for that purpose, and partly on the security felt by the buyers that their tenure and income would be undisturbed. The ratio of the selling price to the income is known as the rate of *capitalization*. Where there was a well-defined rate of capitalization it amounted to almost the same thing as an interest rate to the investor. Instead of loaning money at five per cent he could buy a piece of rented land at twenty times the annual rental. Even where the fee of the land was not actually sold, it often happened that fictitious rent charges were created and the right to receive these charges forever was sold for a lump sum; which amounted virtually to an interminable loan at interest secured by the productivity of the land. The German word for interest (*Zins*) is derived from the *census* or rent charge thus capitalized.

§ 154. When interest was once recognized as a legitimate thing, the authorities were not slow to profit by it; sometimes in questionable ways. Governments were enabled, by the promise of interest, to obtain in the form of voluntary contributions sums which they could not have secured by taxation without danger of revolt. Privileged classes or individuals were allowed to establish pawn-brokers' shops and other doubtful agencies as a means of making profits by loaning money. All these things, in spite of the evils connected with them, taught the statesmen and the public the usefulness of a fund of capital and the power of a small fixed return to lead people to save and invest such capital. The modern savings bank, which offers depositors a low rate of interest and then invests the money thus obtained in channels which the depositors could not have used by themselves, either because their individual savings were too small or their business experience inadequate, is an example of what can be done in this way. The life insurance company, when properly managed, is an almost equally effective—indeed, in some respects a more effective—means to the same end.[1] Both these institutions give a stimulus to save and avoid the necessity of hoarding. They thus cause the public capital to be increased and to be effectively utilized.

§ 155. It is one thing to recognize the usefulness of the *system* of interest; it is quite another thing to leave borrowers and lenders at liberty to fix the *rate* of interest by mutual agreement. To a large section of the public it seems as if the lender had every advantage over the borrower in settling the terms of such a transaction, and were likely to make an unfair use of this advantage. He has capital and can wait, while the borrower cannot; he has intelligence to see what other people are doing, while the borrower's vision is often much more restricted. Under the influence of these ideas nearly every nation has passed *usury laws*, fixing a legal rate of interest, stigmatizing any charge above that rate as usury, declaring contracts at higher rates void, and often visiting the lender with the severest penalties.

Where a large part of the borrowers are so ignorant that there is no effective competition among capitalists, and no market rate of interest, such prohibitions appear to be justified; especially if the legal rate is placed high enough

---

[1] The life insurance company has the advantage over a savings bank in knowing when it will receive payments and (by the law of averages) when it must make them. It can thus keep smaller reserves and utilize more fully the capital entrusted to its charge. It also makes its payments at the time when the need for them is supposed to be greatest. It is further claimed, as a public advantage, that it compels a certain amount of saving on the part of the policy holders every year. But this is quite as likely to prove a burden as an advantage. While such compulsion is of use to the improvident, it may prove a severe load to the unfortunate, enhancing instead of lightening the weight of his misfortune. To such a man, and indeed to the provident investor as a rule, the elasticity of his relations with a savings bank, where he deposits money when he can and withdraws it when he must, is an inestimable advantage.

to cover the risks on all ordinary loans.[1] A usury law of this character may prevent cases of shameless extortion, where the creditor so presumes on the debtor's ignorance as to charge rates far above those which ordinarily prevail. Among non-commercial peoples there is serious danger of just this thing. The Russian peasantry is now suffering severely from loans unintelligently contracted, whose charges have become a burden too heavy to be borne. Anything which can prevent the imposition of such burdens is likely to be good for the community. A law fixing a maximum rate of interest which can be collected from such borrowers may cause temporary hardship by making some men unable to borrow ; but even this is much better than an assumption of obligations which purchases temporary relief at the expense of future independence.

§ 156. In commercial communities the case is quite different. Where each borrower knows to some extent what the others are doing, the competition of different lenders produces a market rate which is fair to both sides. Even if the borrower in a particular case be weak and the lender strong, the latter cannot charge a high rate of interest, because other lenders stand ready to underbid him. The rate of interest for any given class of risks will fall until the supply and demand of capital become equal. If the attempt is made to reduce the market rate still further by usury laws, the effect is analogous to that of laws regulating price (§ 97) ; but there are complications, due to the ease with which usury laws can be evaded, which make the attempt to reduce interest by statute even more conspicuously futile than the attempt to reduce prices.

---

[1] The German usury law names no specific maximum rate, but leaves it to the judicial authorities to determine whether, in view of the special circumstances of each case, the lender has taken advantage of the borrower's ignorance or distress to charge more than a fair amount. This seems a wise method of procedure.

If the legal rate of interest is made lower than the competitive rate which equalizes supply and demand, and if the law is obeyed, the demand for loans will tend to increase in consequence of the lowness of the rate, and the supply of capital to loan will tend to diminish. There will then be an excess of demand over supply. A part of those who want loans will get them at low rates; a part will not get them at all.

If we could be sure that the people who did not get the loans were the ones who did not need them, and that their willingness to pay higher rates was the result of self-destroying recklessness, we might be well content with the effects of a usury law. But this is not ordinarily the case. In an intelligent community the men who are willing to pay high rates are quite generally the ones who can make productive use of capital. So far as they are prevented from borrowing, the active use of capital is lessened, and the industrial progress of the locality hindered. If a state makes a law fixing interest at six per cent when a number of men are willing to pay eight, it simply means that those men, if they obey the law, cannot get the capital they want.

§ 157. In point of fact, they do not obey the law. If a borrower is really desirous to get a loan and cannot have it at low rates, there are many indirect ways of making the interest charge higher than appears on the face of the contract. On an ordinary industrial loan, the borrower may pay a large commission to the man who negotiates it, part of which can go to the lender; or he may tacitly content himself with the receipt of a sum smaller than the nominal amount of the loan. If a note is given for $1,000, payable at the end of five years, bearing six per cent interest per annum, and the borrower tacitly accepts a payment of $950 instead of $1,000 as a consideration for this note, the actual rate paid is about seven per cent annually instead of six. On short-time loans from

banks, the means of evasion are yet more numerous and
more difficult to detect.   The bank may insist on the
maintenance of a large deposit account in its hands,
which virtually reduces the sum lent ; or it may make a
fictitious charge for collection of the note at maturity,
which, on a short-time loan, adds a great deal to the rate
of interest.  If a bank discounts a sixty day note at six
per cent, the total interest charge is one per cent; if to
this figure it adds one quarter of one per cent for collection, it greatly increases the interest rate without
directly conflicting with the letter of the usury law.

   If intelligent borrowers want loans and can get them by
using these means, they will use them.   The borrower
runs little or no risk in these operations ; it is not against
him that the provisions of the law are directed, and he
does not regard himself as a lawbreaker.   The case of the
lenders is different.   They run a slight risk ; and even if
the act cannot be brought home to them, they know that
they are breaking the law.   Some are deterred from these
transactions by their risk ; more, by their crookedness and
virtual illegality.   Thus while the demand for such loans
is not much checked, their supply, even at the old competitive rate, is considerably diminished.   Therefore,
while the more scrupulous lenders are kept out of the
market by a usury law, the less scrupulous ones are able
to take advantage of the reduced competition to charge a
higher rate of interest, which serves as a more or less adequate compensation for the risk to their pockets and
the strain on their consciences.   Meantime the borrowers
are suffering both from the scrupulousness of the honest,
who refuse them capital, and from the unscrupulousness
of the dishonest, who charge them extra high rates ; and
even if some borrowers get their loans a little cheaper
from the operation of the law, the gain at this point is
dearly purchased by the loss at others.

   § 158. While the system of interest on loans has won its

way to recognition, imprisonment for debt and other personal means of enforcing payment have been gradually falling into disuse. Increased control over the terms of the loan has gone hand in hand with diminished power over the person of the debtor. Both of these changes arise from the same cause. Each is a virtual recognition of the fact that a loan is justified by the productiveness of the *thing* for which it is used, rather than by the wants of the *person* by whom it is borrowed. Once having grasped this fact, we can draw two conclusions from it. (1) If a loan will result in a really productive thing, we should give the borrower every chance to attract capital for its creation. (2) If a loan will not result in a really productive thing, we should give the lender no inducement to advance the money except the motive of personal kindness, and no right to impose future burdens on the debtor which will belie or conflict with the motive of kindness. Both of these results are in large measure accomplished by making the creditor look to the investment rather than to the borrower for his security. We have abolished imprisonment for debt, not so much on account of the hardship to the debtor, who may be a very worthless person, as on account of the disadvantage to society in having money lent on personal security. It is not that we love the debtor more, but the creditor less. It is for like reasons that civilized communities have so frequently abolished or mitigated laws concerning attachment of wages. If a store has given a workman credit, it seems at first sight fair that the owner of the store should have a legal claim on the workman's wages when they become due. Yet the evils connected with store credit are so considerable, and the unwisdom of encouraging workmen to get into debt is so manifest, that society discountenances the creation of such debts by removing or restricting the facilities for their collection.

§ 159. Another phase of the limitation of personal liability, and one which has stimulated productive speculation in the very highest degree, is exemplified by the position of the shareholders in a modern industrial corporation or joint stock company. The old theory was that if a man went into business of any kind he should be held personally responsible for all debts incurred in connection with it. In case of an individual who has matters under his immediate control this is perfectly right. In the case of a partnership it may work injustice, when one man is held responsible for debts incurred by the unwisdom or wrong doing of his partner; but as long as the number of partners is small, each can be presumed to know if the other is doing wrong and can be held accountable for any failure to protect himself and the public. But as a concern becomes larger and larger, it grows more difficult for a number of individual owners to see how it is managed. If a hundred men unite their capital in an industry they must necessarily put the control in the hands of a board of directors, and can only know by occasional reports how their business is conducted. Under these circumstances it is manifestly unjust to hold them all responsible to the extent of their whole private fortunes for mismanagement on the part of a director. The investors know less about the actions of the director than do those who have commercial dealings with him. Under such circumstances it is quite fair to transfer a part of the responsibility for loss from the shoulders of the investor to those of the outside public. It is not only equitable, it is necessary. Without such limitation of responsibility it is practically impossible to get the necessary capital subscribed for undertakings where the investors cannot exercise personal supervision. One of the earliest attempts to meet this need was by the partnership *in commenda*, where a comparatively small number of persons assumed the active management and the responsibilities of the enterprise, while others simply furnished capital for the sake of a share in the profits. A better form is the modern joint stock company, in which all shareholders stand on a common basis of limited liability, and choose a few representatives to exercise active supervision of the business. The system of limited liability distinguishes such a corporation from a partnership. If a man puts a thousand dollars into a partnership, and the firm contracts debts in excess of its resources, he may be called upon to pay many thousands more to satisfy the claims of creditors. But if he puts his thousand dollars into railroad stock, he is quit of all further responsibility. His liability is limited to the amount of his original investment. If the company is well managed he will get his dividends. If it is badly managed he will probably lose his money. But his loss will be confined to the amount of his stock subscription. If the liabilities of the company exceed its resources, that is the affair of the creditors. They can take possession of the concern and run it to suit themselves; but they have no further claims against the individual stockholders. What is true of railroad stock is generally true of manufacturing stock, and partially true of the stock of banks and of trading corporations. The liability of the individual shareholders is in each case accurately defined by statute.

§ 160. It was with much reluctance that the system of limited liability was admitted as an integral part of corporation law. It seemed like an attempt of the investors to secure large profits from an enterprise without assuming corresponding liabilities. But the experience of countries like Great Britain or states like Massachusetts, which strove to restrict the introduction of limited liability, proved that this conservatism was either unwise or unjust : unwise, so far as it prevented investments of capital on a scale which the community required in order to utilize modern improvements in the arts; unjust, because in the dealings of large concerns the creditors were in a better position to prevent the creation of bad debts than were the individual shareholders. The experiences in the City of Glasgow Bank failure in 1878, which reduced to penury a number of small investors who had no possible control over the affairs of the bank or moral responsibility for its management, were sufficient to prove to the most conservative how ill adapted was the old system to the conditions of modern investment.

As the need of permanent improvements gave shape to the system of land tenure, so the need of concentration of capital gave shape to corporation law. When a hundred men putting their capital together could do much more for society than if they kept it separate, it was necessary to devise some system which should make it easy and safe for them to unite. The modern corporation, combining as it does the principles of perpetual succession, representative government, and limited liability, has met the industrial needs of the case. The feature of perpetual succession prevents any loss of continuity in operation when one of the shareholders dies or transfers his interest. The feature of representative government allows the different shareholders to choose a board of directors small enough in number to secure efficiency of control and operation. The feature of limited liability, whereby each shareholder is responsible for the debts of the concern only to the extent of his original holding, protects him from losses due to the misconduct of other shareholders, which the large size of the corporate body makes him unable to control. The union of all these features allows the public to secure the economy resulting from large accumulations of capital limited neither by the lifetime of a few individuals nor by the extent of their private fortunes.

§ 161. These institutions and the motives connected with them have served their purpose so fully that in modern times we are quite as apt to find an excess in the saving and investment of capital as to find a deficiency.

In the beginnings of civilization scarcity of capital is a most serious and imminent economic danger. Under such conditions anything which will lead people to save and use their savings productively is good for society. But in more modern times, there is a temptation to invest capital in machinery to such a degree as to reduce the demand for the products of machinery. If one man tries to save, and convert his capital into permanent investments, he can do so ; but if every one tries to save, a great many people will fail to realize their expected profit because of an over-production of machinery. It is in this way, rather than by a fall in the rate of interest, that the effect of over-accumulation of capital shows itself most conspicuously. This mistaken investment proves a loss to society as well as to the individuals immediately concerned. In a given stage of the arts, and with given habits of consumption, a certain amount of machinery can be advantageously utilized ; a larger amount than this is a waste. We have for generations been cultivating motives which should make individuals reduce their consumption and increase their investment until we could obtain the required amount ; and we have apparently overdone the matter. It is certain that the increased utilization of existing capital which follows any stimulus to consumption is apt to be more conducive to general prosperity, than a corresponding increase in the amount of investment without such stimulus. A superficial observation of this fact leads many people to adopt means of stimulating consumption which are transient in their nature, and which provoke a reaction which makes matters worse in the end than they were at the beginning Currency inflation may serve as a type of such means. The danger of measures like this is greatly increased if the economist shuts his eyes to the small fraction of truth hidden amid larger fractions of error in the arguments of

their advocates. The modern civilized world is in perpetual danger of under-consumption. Too many of its
members use their supplies of products, not to purchase
the consumable products of others, but to duplicate machinery and other permanent investments. Under the
operation of the credit system the danger in the process
remains unseen, until masses of such machinery come into
use ; then its comparative worthlessness becomes apparent. The men who own it find themselves poor
instead of rich. The laborers who have been trained
to produce it are thrown out of employment, and the
community is plunged into a commercial crisis (ch. ix).

§ 162. The historical study of the origin and development of capital in its various forms may guard us against
several rather prevalent fallacies.

In the first place we must beware of treating rights to
land, or to the management of corporate property, as
"absolute" or "natural" ones. This danger is not so
great now as it was a century ago, for political science
makes far less of natural rights than it once did. But
enough of the old view remains [1] to make it worth while
to emphasize the fact that the various institutions under
which capital is invested have been sanctioned by society

---

[1] A curious aftermath of the old theories of natural right is seen in some
of the modern theories of natural value. Labor, land, and capital are regarded as co-operating in production, and an attempt is made to determine the natural share of the product which each factor obtains by free
competition, under the assumption of a certain normal degree of intelligence
in the investment of capital and development of land. But this is a thing
which we cannot assume ; and it is precisely *because* we cannot assume it,
that the various institutions described in the foregoing chapter are tolerated.
Interest and rent and the different forms of monopoly gain have grown up as
means of enabling the community to make progress by the elimination of
investors of lower degrees of intelligence and the substitution of better ones.
The habits of mind which determine the relative value of present and future
goods are so bound up with these institutions and these differences of intelligence, that reasonings based upon the continuance of present methods of
valuation apart from existing institutions and their historical causes, seem at
once hazardous and unprofitable.

for the sake of their effect on the public well-being ; and that they derive their efficacy from this sanction. When they stand in the way of progress, society does not 'hesitate to modify or limit them. The power of expropriation, based on the right of " eminent domain " inherent in the people, furnishes a conspicuous instance of such limitation. If a man uses his land tenure to stand in the way of public improvement, the government arranges a process by which his land can be taken from him, whether he will or no; saying that the community has rights to such property which, in case of necessity, override the individual will. In like manner, if a corporation uses its authority to harm the community which depends on its services, the government brings its " reserved police power " into play to check such abuses of authority. It is perfectly clear that in case of public necessity private property may be taken by the state, always providing that " due process of law " is used and compensation given to the owners.

§ 163. A little study of this idea of compensation will show us how much less absolute (if such a phrase may be permitted) are the rights of capital than the more general right of property. Any considerable impairment of the right of property would involve a change in the whole industrial system, and even in the moral system on which society is organized. Property-right is the chief modern motive to labor, to care, and to avoidance of waste and destruction. Rights of capital, however important or beneficial in their effects, are much narrower in their scope. They affect the methods of management of industry, rather than the motives on which all industry is based. They can be seriously modified without changing the general substructure of society. There can be no reasonable doubt that they will be thus modified as better methods are found to take their place.

§ 164. But it is a much more serious error to go to

the other extreme, and assume that they can be modified at will by the action of organized force. The fact that the present organization of capital is the result of historical development, and that present forms have survived while others failed, is the strongest proof of their vitality. George's argument that collective property in land is perfectly practicable because so many races have tried it and given it up, is but the *reductio ad absurdum* of many attacks on the present industrial system. While it is undoubtedly true that the various rights of the capitalist depend upon the existence of a civilized society which maintains them, it seems equally true that the existence of a civilized society in the stress of the struggle for existence among different members of the human race depends, for the present at any rate, upon maintaining the rights of the capitalist.

# CHAPTER VI.

## COMBINATION OF CAPITAL.

Modern Tendencies toward Monopoly—Their Effect on Prices—Limitation
of Profits—Laws Fixing Rates—Enforcement of Responsibility.

T. H. Farrer : " The State in its Relation to Trade." London, 1883.
The general subject of monopoly is not adequately dealt with in economic
literature—especially in book form. On railroads and railroad charges,
mention may be made of C. F. Adams, " Railroads, their Origin and
Problems," New York, 1878; A. T. Hadley, " Railroad Transportation,
its History and its Laws," New York, 1885 ; W. D. Dabney, " The
Public Regulation of Railways," New York, 1889 ; W. M. Acworth, " The
Railways and the Traders," London, 1891 ; and, above all, of G. Cohn,
" Untersuchungen über die Englische Eisenbahnpolitik," Leipzig, 1874,
1875, 1883. The third volume of Cohn gives the best general investigation
of the principles regulating monopoly price. Compare also the fifth book
of A. Marshall, " Principles of Economics," 3d ed., London, 1895.
For further references on closely allied subjects see chapter xi.

§ 165. THE investment of fixed capital described in the
preceding chapter has wrought much more radical changes
in manufactures and transportation than in agriculture.

There are several reasons for this difference. In the
first place, the productiveness of factories has increased
faster than that of farms. No means has been found for
indefinitely enlarging the amount of food which can be
obtained from a given area. We can perhaps double it or
treble it ; but no investment of capital, wise or unwise, is
likely to increase it a hundred-fold. Therefore no one
farm, however large, is likely to supply more than a very
small fraction of the world's consumption. Until there
is some radical change in the art of food production, we

shall continue to have competition between different
producers. Nor has the investment of fixed capital in
agriculture gone so far that its interest and maintenance
constitute the chief elements in the cost of food products. They form an important, but not a dominant
factor. Under these circumstances, the theory of normal
price, though hindered in its operation, is by no means
rendered inapplicable. There is a slight delay in the
adjustment between price and cost ; there is a certain
margin between the price which will induce new competitors to enter the field, and that which will drive out
the old ones. But, in the majority of cases, we can still
rely on competition to protect the consumers and do no
gross injustice to the producers.

§ 166. In manufactures the case is different. The units
of capital are much larger. Each producer can extend
his output with a gain rather than a loss in economy. If
he can increase his sales, there will be only a slight increase—perhaps none at all—in the expense for wages
and materials and a decided decrease in the share of the
charges on fixed capital, which each unit of product must
pay. There is no fixed standard of cost which we can
treat as the normal price ; for the cost per unit of product
depends on the quantity sold, falling as sales increase.

The price which will induce new competitors to enter
the field is also much higher than that which will lead
old ones to withdraw. No concern will quit competition
as long as it can pay an appreciable part of its interest
charges. It is better to lose part of your interest on
every piece of goods you sell, than to lose the whole of
it on every piece you do not sell. As long as the price
received more than covers the expense for wages and materials each of the old factories will continue to compete.
Even if it changes ownership by foreclosure it will remain
in operation. But, on the other hand, no new competitor
will be called into being unless the price is high enough

to afford a liberal profit, after paying interest, maintenance, and other charges on fixed capital invested under modern methods. Thus prices, instead of constantly tending to gravitate toward an equitable figure, oscillate between two extremes. The rate of production, at figures which give a fair profit, is usually either much larger than the rate of consumption, or much smaller. In the former case, prices are unremunerative and unjust to the producer; in the latter case, they are oppressive to the consumer. The average price resulting from such fluctuations may perhaps be a fair one; but the wide changes of price are disastrous to all parties concerned.

§ 167. The failure of competition to secure fair or stable rates gives additional force to the pressure toward combination which always exists among certain classes of business men.

Many writers on combination treat it as a new thing, peculiar to the present stage of commercial and industrial development. This is a mistake. Efforts at trade combination have always been made, and have not infrequently been successful. The more we study the past history of any line of business, the more we are impressed with the extent of such efforts at combination. The distinctive feature of the present age lies in the existence of certain added causes peculiar to this stage of commercial development, which work in favor of those who advocate combination, and make it harder for independent competitors to resist it, or for the law to prohibit it on grounds of public policy.

§ 168. The economy, to the public as well as to the individual, of concentrating capital as much as possible, always furnishes a pretext, and sometimes a real reason, for substituting combination for competition. In some cases the industrial units which are necessary for proper utilization of labor have become so large as to produce actual monopoly. This is especially true of distributive services, like water, gas, telegraphs, or railroads. The attempt to have two independent agencies perform any of these services for a single community is apt to result in loss to the producer and inconvenience to the consumer. So much of the expense of delivery of water or gas is connected with the laying of mains, that a system which duplicates these mains is a public burden. So much of the advantage of the telephone service to each subscriber lies in the power of reaching all the other subscribers, that the existence of two competing exchanges in the same city destroys the usefulness of both. In railroad transportation a single organized company can put lines just where they are needed, and run trains at the time when the public wants them. If the same service is performed by two companies, there will be unnecessary duplication of lines in some places, and failure to build needful ones in others; while the train times and train connections will be arranged, not with regard to the maximum convenience of the public, but with a view to increase the business of one competitor at the expense of the other. Even in cases where the necessity for concentrated management is not quite so marked as in those just described, the competition of different concerns always involves a loss, from the need of maintaining too many selling agencies, the expense of unnecessary advertising, and the lack of proper utilization of fixed capital.[1]

---

[1] The increasing profit when we enlarge the output of a factory is often contrasted with the diminishing profit when we attempt to do the same thing on a farm; and some writers say that industries with large fixed capital are subject to a "law of increasing return" which contrasts with the law of diminishing return that prevails in agriculture. This statement hardly goes to the root of the matter. The distinction is not so much between kinds of industry as between kinds of capital. With a given amount of fixed capital, whether invested in agriculture or in manufactures, any increase of output diminishes the charges on such capital per unit of product. The *current* expenses per unit of product do not thus tend to diminish as the output increases; in fact, when a certain relation has been established between out-

§ 169. The simplest form of combination is an agreement to maintain rates, where the several competitors promise not to reduce their prices below a scale fixed by common consent, with a view to giving producers a fair profit. But such an arrangement rarely proves effective. Each company is at the mercy of its agents. They will try to steal business from rival concerns by cutting rates. If they are allowed a commission on sales, they will divide it with the buyer; if they are not allowed such a commission, they will find a hundred different ways, less obvious but hardly less effective, of rendering a rate agreement nugatory. It is so profitable for one concern to steal business from another, and so disastrous to its rival to lose the business, that the latter will always suspect the former of bad faith when any irregularities of its agents are discovered or surmised. A contest will be inaugurated which tends to drive prices far below the normal rate ; usually to the advantage of those who least need and least deserve such reductions. The honest and straightforward business man is content with the one-price system. He is not seeking to gain an unfair advantage over his neighbor, but to be treated squarely. Fluctuating and uncertain rates are not what he desires, for he knows that his less scrupulous rival will be the first to gain the benefit of such changes. It is better for *A* to be paying 30 cents and be sure that

---

put and fixed capital, the current expenses per unit of product increase very rapidly. Whether, with an increase of output, the gain from fuller use of fixed capital offsets the loss from increased current expenses, depends partly on the amount of the fixed capital, but chiefly on the degree to which it was previously utilized. If it was not fully utilized we shall see the phenomena of increasing return ; if it was already fully utilized, we shall see those of diminishing return. The apparent contrast between agriculture and manufacturing in this respect is chiefly due to the fact that population habitually approaches a limit set by the arts of food production, so that its agricultural improvements are always employed nearly to the limit of profitable output ; while in manufactures there is no such increase of demand, and fixed capital is often quite inadequately employed.

his competitor *B* is also paying 30 cents, than for *A* to pay 25 cents when *B* pays 20. Wars of rates, though they produce very low prices, generally work to the disadvantage of the honest purchasing public and to the advantage of the shrewder speculators.

§ 170. A single instance will serve to illustrate the difficulty of maintaining rates by agreement. Twenty-five years ago a fair rate for cattle from Chicago to New York was about $110 a carload. If the large shippers of cattle wished to break this rate, they would drive all their steers to one of the competing lines and would spread a rumor in the commercial columns of the newspapers that this line was not maintaining rates. This rumor, combined with the fact that the line in question was getting all the shipments, would make the other lines think there was foul play, and lead them to order a reduction in rates to meet the supposed cut. As soon as any such reduction was announced the shippers would all divert their cattle to the lines that had made it. The road that was carrying everything yesterday received nothing to-day ; and indignant at the bad faith on the part of its rivals it would meet their reduction by a yet larger reduction. To this process there was no limit as long as the price paid for the carriage of cattle more than covered the expenses of loading and hauling. Under the excitement of the contest the railroad agents sometimes went even lower than this, and carried cattle at an actual loss in order to prevent rivals from making a profit.

§ 171. When competing concerns are thus at the mercy of their agents or of outsiders, a resort to closer forms of combination is inevitable. If it proves that an agreement to maintain rates is not enough, they will arrange a pool or division of traffic. Pools take three distinct forms. Sometimes rival concerns divide the field ; as when competing gas companies agree to serve different streets in the same city, or when competing railroads agree not to build branch lines into one another's territory. Sometimes they divide the traffic itself. If three railroads find that each has done an approximately equal amount of business during the year preceding, they may arrange to divide the competitive business equally, and let each company take one-third. If more than one-third of the shippers desire to use one of the three lines during the coming month, that line agrees to turn over a part of its business to one of its rivals. If the different railroads are not of equal importance, the traffic can be divided on the basis of the percentages actually carried during the previous period of competition. Sometimes the railroad which is less favorably situated has to make concessions in rates in order to secure any traffic at all. In this case it is allowed to charge a lower price than its rivals, and receives a percentage of traffic at this lower rate. Such a concession is called a differential rate in favor of the weaker line, and is used as a means of inducing it not to enter into cutthroat competition. Sometimes, instead of dividing the traffic, the competing concerns may divide the earnings from that traffic, having a common accounting office and perhaps a system of joint agencies connected with it.

These divisions of traffic or earnings are far harder to arrange than agreements as to rates, but, when once established, they are much more effective. For when such a division exists, any irregularities of the agents in the matter of rates hurt the company which they represent far more than its rivals. This arrangement, therefore, substitutes mutual confidence for mutual suspicion.

§ 172. Pools have not been regarded with favor by the law.[1] In the United States they are treated as contracts

---

[1] In England the legal decisions are much more favorable to pools than in the United States ; while in most parts of Continental Europe they are accepted as matters of course ; the governments themselves entering into pooling contracts with private companies with which they find themselves brought into competition in the management of state railroads or other industrial enterprises.

in restraint of trade, and therefore void as a gambling contract would be void.  The courts say that they are against public policy and will not aid in their enforcement.

In certain kinds of business, notably railroad transportation, such pools or combinations are treated as misdemeanors, and attempts are made to punish their promoters by fine or imprisonment.  But these efforts to do away with pools have conspicuously failed of their object. There are many ways of evading them.  A joint accounting office may take the form of a clearing house established for the convenience of the public, and yet may serve all the purposes of a pool.  If competing companies are forbidden to divide traffic by contract, they may secure a permanent understanding by putting a majority of their stock into the hands of a common board of trustees.  Such an arrangement is known as a trust.  The stockholders, in thus putting their securities in trust, part with the voting power,—that is to say, the power of directing the policy of the concern,—retaining the right to receive whatever may be earned on their stock, while it is held in trust by a board that secures harmony of management between the different companies engaged. If trusts are prohibited, it is always possible to resort to actual consolidation ; the only serious difficulty being that a large consolidated company is liable to be taxed on the whole of its capital stock in a number of different states.  It was this difficulty which the trust agreement was primarily designed to evade.  As tax legislation becomes more systematic, the trouble from this source becomes less, and the possibility of consolidation is decidedly increased.

§ 173.  The attempt to prohibit combination has proved futile, and has simply driven the competing concerns into closer consolidation.  Had it been successful, it must either have retarded the development of modern business and the utilization of modern methods requiring concentrated management of capital, or it must have subjected all of our large industries to constant fluctuations in their scale of prices, which would have been hardly less disastrous to the consumer than to the investor.

But the advantages of industrial combination, when it comes to include all competitors, are frequently balanced by the evils of commercial combination. The economy connected with the use of concentrated capital is in some measure offset by the loss of that stimulus which competition alone seems able to give ; and the resulting monopoly makes it uncertain whether the consumers will get the benefit of the economy which is actually obtained.

§ 174. If a monopoly is managed by inexperienced hands the effort to put prices up is usually more noticeable than the effort to put expenses down. It seems so easy to make a profit at the expense of society, that managers are apt to neglect the more laborious method of making a profit by service to society. When business men have been all their lives accustomed to face immediate competition, they think that the combination of all competitors removes the only effective restriction upon charges. But this is a short-sighted view of the matter which has wrecked most of the enterprises run on such a basis, and has made the average trade combination a means of hindering rather that helping its members.

If the managers of a combination make it their chief concern to suppress competition rather than to realize economies in production, their policy toward trade rivals results in violation of commercial morality, if not of commercial law. Not content with obtaining unfair advantages in the way of discriminating rates for transportation of its goods, the combination tries to exclude its rivals from their accustomed markets by methods of boycotting and intimidation, which, when they are used by trades-unions, provoke fierce denunciation from the same men who have been ready to practise them for their own advantage.[1]

Even among those combinations which, like the Standard Oil Company, have realized economies and reduced rates for their product, this unscrupulous policy toward competitors has been carried to such an extent as to create a just prejudice against them ; a prejudice which is enough to explain, and in one sense to justify, the tendency on the part of the public to ignore or depreciate the industrial services which they have actually rendered.

§ 175. There is one case, and one only, where a monopoly has almost unlimited power to make high charges. If a number of contracts must be fulfilled within a specified time, a combination which controls the matter which is made the subject of these contracts can fix prices to suit itself, limited only by the danger of driving the contracting parties into bankruptcy.[2]

If operators have sold for future delivery stock which they did not own, or have contracted to deliver wheat during a certain month without assuring themselves of their sources of supply, the owners of the stock or of the wheat can, by a sufficiently extensive combination, force the operators to pay what price they please. Such a combination is known as a *corner*. Its managers have a great advantage in not being compelled to control the supply for more than a limited period, and of being assured of a fixed demand during that time. But the number of successful corners is less than is commonly supposed. Though the apparent profits of such an operation are often large, the expenses of securing control of the whole supply, and the difficulty of selling it to advan-

---

[1] It is interesting to see how combinations of capital and combinations of labor are subject to the same possibilities of abuse or mismanagement ; and how the same violation of commercial right looks excusable to the party benefited, but monstrous to the party injured.

[2] Or by special rules of particular exchanges framed to avoid such a result.

tage upon the expiration of the corner, make the real gains less than the apparent ones.

§ 176. If the article is to be sold to consumers instead of to speculators who have made fixed contracts, the chance for financial success by a policy of exorbitant prices is very small indeed. We have seen in chapter iii that the demand for an article falls as the price rises. In the case of almost everything except necessary food supplies, this fall in demand is very rapid, so that the gross receipts of the sellers under a high charge are less than those which they obtain with the lower scale of prices. Under these circumstances the maximum gross income is obtained by making rates low enough to develop a good volume of traffic, instead of by raising them so high as to reduce that traffic to a small amount. If a concern uses a large amount of fixed capital, it will rarely happen that the most money can be made by a policy of high charges with small volume of business. Experience has shown that the opposite method is the one which has proved permanently profitable, even to the concerns whose monopoly seemed most assured. It pays in the long run to bring rates down very near to the limits of actual cost, if such reductions are followed by a large development of traffic.

§ 177. Where a monopoly is of such precarious character that it may be subjected to direct competition at almost any moment, this truth is sufficiently obvious. If a concern in this situation attempts to do a small business at high rates and make large temporary profits by such a policy, new capital will come into the business in the hope of securing the good-will and custom of the community by lower rates. High charges invite duplication of plant in all cases where such duplication is possible. If, on the other hand, the original concern adopts a policy of doing a large business at low rates, the promoters of a rival enterprise will soon see that they

11

cannot hope either to do the business cheaper, or to make a satisfactory profit on that moderate fraction of the existing business which it is possible for a new competitor to secure without special concessions in rates.

§ 178. Even where a monopoly does not fear direct competition, there are many cases where it is subjected to similar restraints in an indirect manner. If there is but one railroad in a certain section of country, and this has a monopoly of available routes for reaching the market which the producers of the district naturally seek, the shippers are apparently at the mercy of that company and its agents. But if there is another railroad line which supplies the same market with goods from another section, it is all but inevitable that the competition of the two districts with one another should regulate the price which the railroads can charge.[1] We cannot have two different prices for similar goods in the same market. If the supply and demand of wheat at Liverpool fixes the price of wheat in the Liverpool market at a certain rate per bushel, the railroad and steamship lines in every direction must make their charges such that the wheat producers, in the sections which they can serve, can ship their supplies at a profit. Some of the transportation agents may disregard this necessity for a year or two, but not permanently. The penalty for such disregard is the destruction of the traffic on which the transportation route makes its living. The railroads of the United States, of Russia, and of British India feel one another's competition in determining the prices which they can charge on their international traffic.

§ 179. There are a few cases where the monopoly of the sources of supply is so complete that even this possi-

---

[1] When permanent monopoly rights are guaranteed by law in *all* the competing districts, as on French railroads, we are apt to find a system of high charges which no nominal powers of public supervision prove adequate to control.

bility of indirect competition is absent. A private company may thus control all the available water within reach of a large city. A great industrial combination like the Standard Oil Company may become the sole means of supplying certain grades of oil to the United States, or even to the world. Here it might seem as though the power to make high charges were absolutely unlimited. Yet, even in these cases, the self-interest of the producers dictates the adoption of a relatively low scale of prices. Such monopolies can, as a rule, only be secured by very large investments of capital. Adequate profit on these investments involves correspondingly large public consumption. A man whose facilities are so rude that he makes only a few articles in the course of a year and supplies but a small part of the public demand, is interested in having the price of those articles as high as possible. But the man who makes a great many articles in the course of a year and meets a large part of the public demand is primarily interested, not in getting a maximum price for a few things, but in getting the public to take a great many things. Among those trusts and other combinations that have had apparently a complete monopoly, a large number have made conspicuous failures, simply because they thought of high prices rather than large sales, and did not see that such a policy was suicidal.

§ 180. Perhaps the most striking illustration of this truth is furnished by the history of the French copper syndicate of 1888. By a series of brilliant financial operations, this syndicate obtained control of the copper product of all the best mines of the world. It attempted to raise the price of copper from nine cents a pound to sixteen cents. Everything was apparently favorable to the success of these operations. Copper was a necessity for use in the arts ; the sources of supply where copper could be produced cheaply were few in number, and the syndicate had exclusive contracts with them all. The demand for copper was constantly tending to increase, owing to the new uses of electricity. The syndicate itself had very large capital, and was supported by many of the strongest financial houses of Europe. Yet with all these things in its favor it failed disastrously, because the consumption of copper at the advanced prices shrunk to such a degree that all the calculations of the syndicate were deranged and its financial resources put to a strain which they could not stand. Even the strongest of monopolies must make its price low enough to cause the public to buy its goods or services to a sufficient extent to utilize its capital, and this price will usually be found to be nearly the same as that which would have been fixed by free competition.

§ 181. If a large industrial combination uses the advantages given by concentration of capital to render labor more efficient and obtain a good profit at low rates, it has excellent chances of success. But if it makes such economy of labor a pretext instead of an object, and uses its monopoly to put prices up, the danger of failure is wholly disproportionate to the chances of success. Such a policy may succeed for a few years, but sooner or later it seems bound to ruin those who adopt it.

Can we trust the managers of our large industrial enterprises to see this for themselves? Can we treat their mistakes as a self-correcting evil, and wait quietly for the time when they shall learn that their own permanent interests are best served by doing good public service? To this question it is impossible to return a general answer. Our decision in any particular case will depend partly upon the character of the business involved, partly upon the intelligence of those who manage it, and most of all, perhaps, on our own habits of mind.

§ 182. If we are in the habit of looking at direct consequences, and disregarding indirect ones, we shall see grounds for active public interference in almost all cases of industrial combination.  The managers of a monopoly have it in their power to do a great deal of harm before they begin to feel the loss to themselves which arises from the adoption of a short-sighted policy.  Even if the trouble corrects itself in the long run, a great many legitimate interests are sacrificed in the process.  A railroad ultimately finds it suicidal to kill the local shippers who are its best permanent customers; but it is small comfort to the shippers to know that their deaths are to be slowly avenged by the operation of economic laws.  The shippers demand some immediate control over the railroad agent ; something which will prevent the evil in the beginning, instead of simply sufficing to prevent its indefinite repetition.  They will be prone to adopt the socialistic solution of the problem, and insist that the government should own the railroad, as the surest means of avoiding such abuses.

But the man who is in the habit of looking at indirect consequences will see that the undiscriminating attempt to prevent evil often results in preventing an even greater amount of good.  He will be prone to take the individualistic view of the matter.  He will be disinclined, except as a last resort, to put the business into the hands of a government whose agents are almost always chosen on other grounds than those of industrial efficiency, and whose methods are much less flexible than those of a private corporation.  He will be indisposed to see stringent regulations put in force until he is convinced that milder remedies are inadequate to protect the interests of the public as a whole.

§ 183.  The industrial and political conditions which determine whether the conduct of a business may advantageously be entrusted to the government instead of being delegated to the property owners, are discussed at length in chapter xii.  We have here to consider the merits of various methods of regulation of such industries, where government ownership proves undesirable or impracticable. These may be grouped under three heads :

1. Limitation of profits.
2. Fixing of rates by public authority.
3. Enforcement of far-sighted methods of management.

§ 184. The first of these methods looks much better than it really is. It is a favorite remedy with people who have had no practical experience of its working. They say that it is very unjust for a monopoly to obtain a much higher dividend than would be possible under free competition ; and they think that if we limit the dividend we shall remove the motive for extortion. In practice the matter does not work in this way. Laws limiting profits, if obeyed, tend to keep rates high instead of low ; if evaded, they substitute a crooked method of distribution for a straight one.

If a company is selling gas at $1.50 a thousand feet, it indicates that this is the price which furnishes the maximum profit. A higher rate would lessen this profit by limiting consumption ; a lower rate would lessen it by making the margin above expenses too narrow. If the cost of making the gas is $1.00 a thousand feet, and the consumption will be 10,000,000 at $1.75, 20,000,000 at $1.50, and 30,000,000 at $1.25, the profit at $1.75 would be $75,000, at $1.50 it would be $100,000, and at $1.25 it would be $75,000. If the company were forbidden to divide $100,000, the price would be quite as likely to be kept up at $1.75 as to be reduced to $1.25. In fact, the higher figure would be very much the more probable one ; first, because it is on the whole easier for the officials of a company to handle a small business on a liberal margin of profit than a large business on a close one ; and second, because the actual rates charged almost always represent the result of a process of reduction which has been going on for years, for the very purpose of obtaining a maximum profit. If our large corporations were trying to raise their charges, limitation of profits might readily remove the temptation to such a policy. But this is not what they are habitually doing. They are lowering their charges for the sake of possible profits. Take away the chance for increased profit and we destroy the motive for reductions in charge. We invite corporations to pursue a conservative policy when a progressive one means better public service at cheaper rates.

Lord Farrer, whose long experience as secretary of the Board of Trade gave him unique opportunities for observing the effects of various methods of regulation practised in England, says that limitation of profits does *not* cause reduction in rates; and that in trying to apply this principle Parliament has gone on a wrong tack and involved the country in a " maze of absurdities."

§ 185. Besides hindering reductions of rates, limitation of profits also prevents the increased investment of capital which is the best guarantee of efficient public service. If it is impossible for a concern to make more than an ordinary rate of profit, there is no adequate motive offered to the investor to develop new facilities and introduce new methods. These experiments may turn out badly and involve loss. If the company is to be deprived of the special profit in case they turn out well, the motive for their introduction is taken away, and the public fails to secure the service which it might otherwise enjoy.

§ 186. If laws limiting profits are evaded instead of being obeyed, the effects, though different in kind, are equally undesirable. It is easy to reduce profits by extravagance in management, or by giving officials large salaries. This does no good to the consumer, and positive harm to the investor. Such laws may also be evaded by inflating the company's capital account: a practice known as stock-watering. If a corporation is allowed to divide all the money that it makes, there is no temptation to honest managers to create a fictitious capital account. But if the dividends are arbitrarily limited to eight per cent when the company is really earning twelve, the directors are tempted to pretend that there has been an investment of capital one and one half times as great as has actually been expended. On the basis of this supposed investment they issue a stock dividend of fifty per cent. This is in common language, "water." It does not represent money actually paid in. By dividing eight per cent on the watered stock, they can put the real earnings of the company into the hands of the investors without direct conflict with the law, and sometimes without public knowledge of the actual nature of the transaction.

The worst of the matter is that when the practice of stock-watering once becomes tolerated, it is indefinitely abused by those who are in a position to do so. If companies begin to issue fictitious capital, there is no limit to such issues. A false capital account gives opportunity for every kind of stock-speculation and for all sorts of illegitimate methods of control by financial operators. Many attempts have been made to prohibit stock-watering; but as long as limitation of profits is attempted, there are enough honest men who are interested in the more defensible forms of stock-watering to render it almost impossible to detect and punish the indefensible ones. The evil from this source alone far outweighs any good that has ever been obtained by trying to limit dividends.[1]

§ 187. By limiting rates instead of profits we have a somewhat more effective means of control. It has the

---

[1] Some charters, especially in England, try to combine limitation of profits with limitation of rates by providing that whenever the profit exceeds a specified percentage, the charges for services shall be correspondingly reduced. Others (like those of the French railroads) provide that all dividends above a certain figure shall be shared with the government. Neither of these systems has won its way into general recognition.

merit of aiming at the right target, whether it hits it or not. Its chief difficulties are connected with the complexity of the conditions affecting modern traffic. It is seldom possible to say what any specific piece of work really costs a large concern. The cost depends upon the amount of work done. The larger the investment of capital, the more complete is this dependence of cost upon quantity.

Under the old system of hand labor it was possible to know with approximate accuracy the cost of a single pair of boots. It could be estimated by finding the commercial price of the material, and the time involved in sewing the boots. But under the modern system, when the boots are produced in a large factory, it is impossible to tell how much they cost, unless we know how many pairs the owners of that factory sell in the course of a year. If the annual charges of the factory for interest and maintenance are $10,000 a year, and 10,000 pairs of boots are manufactured in that time, every pair costs $1 over and above the price of the labor and materials involved. But if only 5,000 pairs of boots are made, the proper charge under this head is $2 a pair ; while if 20,000 pairs are made, the charge may be reduced to 50 cents a pair. In fact, the chief means which a manufacturer possesses for reducing cost is to increase the number of his sales so as to make it possible to lower this item of expense. This is the really critical element in price determination in all cases where large amounts of capital are involved ; and it is precisely this which public authorities are unable to determine in advance, because it is essentially speculative in its character. Of course, the business men themselves have the same difficulty ; but they are experimenting with their own capital, at their own risk, and in lines where they have the maximum technical knowledge ; while the government authorities, dealing with the capital of others and the results of others' experience, find themselves sorely perplexed.

§ 188. Among industrial monopolies, the case where these difficulties are least is probably that of water companies. The capital invested is known with a fair degree of accuracy. If the engineering work has been properly performed at the outset, it is comparatively easy to decide on the amount of annual repairs required. The water consumption can be predicted on the basis of population served. In the case of gas works the matter is rather more complicated. Fluctuations in the cost and quality of coal make a great difference in profits. New processes may be invented which will either increase possible economy, or render a part of the old investment valueless. Other methods of lighting may conceivably be introduced, which will so far lessen the demand for gas as to deprive the shareholders of a large part of the permanent value of their property. In order to know the real profit we must deduct from the apparent profit a considerable sum to allow for the *depreciation* of the fixed capital; a sum which in cases like this is not calculable with certainty. Under such circumstances the whole business becomes more speculative, and the possibility of prescribing fair rates less satisfactory.

§ 189. These difficulties are yet more conspicuous in the matter of electric lighting, and in fact in all the commercial applications of electricity. With the possible exception of the telegraph, there is no electrical industry in which we have even an approximate means of estimating the real profits from year to year. We have not had long enough experience to know what is a proper allowance to be made for depreciation. In some cases—notably that of the telephone—we do not as yet know the proper basis for the arrangement of charges. Shall telephone charges be based on the message, as in long-distance business, or on the instrument, as in the ordinary local business? The former is the more logical basis, but it involves decided difficulties. The public, in local telephone exchanges, distinctly prefers the latter method. But if a company charges by the instrument and not by the message, we are brought face to face with the remarkable fact that the expenses per unit increase with an increase in the volume of business done. In a town with only 100 telephones in operation, the expense to the company per instrument and the rate which can be profitably charged is far less than in a city with 1000 instruments. In the one case, it need only be prepared to make ninety-nine connections for each subscriber ; in the other, it must arrange for nine hundred and ninety-nine. This will serve to illustrate the highly experimental character of the problem of rate-making in the newer forms of industry. It is difficult enough for the investors to find agents who can be trusted to experiment with property under these conditions. Still more diffcult is it to find public officials who can be trusted to experiment with other people's property.

§ 190. It is in transportation service that the regulation of charges is most perplexing, because transportation agencies do a great many different kinds of work, and no rule has been found to decide how much of the expense of maintenance and interest may justly be charged to one kind rather than to another (§ 101). A railroad carries both freight and passengers. How are we to decide how large a part of the expense of maintaining the road in efficient condition shall be charged to passengers, and how much to freight ? If we attempt to apportion these charges on the basis of the number of trains of each class, we seem at first sight to obtain a fair basis of distribution. But if we make passenger rates high enough to pay their share of the general expenses of the road on this basis, it may happen that a great deal of passenger traffic will be lost. In that case such an adjustment of charges, however great the apparent equity, will hurt the road, the travellers who live on its line, and even the shippers of freight themselves ; for if passenger rates kill passenger traffic, transportation can only be had when the shippers of freight are prepared to bear the whole expense of maintaining the line instead of a part only. There is the same difficulty in making the further apportionment of charges between short-distance and long-distance traffic of the same kind, or between different consignments of freight that have the same weight but different commercial value.[1]

§ 191. A private company solves the problem of apportionment by charging what the traffic will bear. If the maximum revenue can be obtained by fixing a high rate on cloth and a low rate on coal, the company adopts this policy. It argues, with much justice, that its own interests in this matter are substantially identical with those of the public. If cloth gives the maximum revenue at high rates, it shows that such rates do not burden the traffic. If coal gives the largest net revenue under a schedule which allows the company very little profit per ton, but very large tonnage, it shows that a low coal rate is needed in order to meet the public requirements. Rates are based on value of service not only in the tariffs of well managed private companies but in all effective schemes of public regulation. A turnpike company has been allowed to charge a pleasure wagon more than a freight wagon, not because the former involves greater cost of maintenance to the turnpike company, but because it could be compelled to pay more without destroying travel. But a public official has not at command the

---

[1] The proposal to solve this difficulty by leaving different carriers free to run their trains over the track of any railroad company, if they will pay tolls to cover the interest and maintenance of the capital invested in the roadbed, ignores the chief difficulty of the case. The perplexing problems about regulation of rates would be felt in the apportionment of tolls. The assumption that the matter of tolls for the use of the track will be simple and can be easily dealt with, if separated from loading and movement expenses, is quite unwarranted. It is just because of the difficulty connected with compensation for interest and maintenance of permanent way that a railroad problem exists at all.

means which a railroad agent can use in order to decide what the traffic will really bear. The agent can try experiments and see whether the column of business grows enough to justify reductions of rates. The legislature or commission can only guess at such a result in advance, without the chance of feeling its way by experiment.[1]

§ 192. Of the means of transportation now controlled by private companies, street railroads offer the fewest difficulties to the legislator. Their rates of fare are almost always regulated either by custom or by law. This can usually be done without much injustice. If rates are fixed so low as to be unprofitable, the company can crowd its cars a little more. By putting enough persons on a car at almost any rate, however low, it is possible to meet the running expenses of that car, and the fixed charges attaching to the track as a whole are comparatively slight, because the city, in the great majority of instances, has given the right of way for nothing. Even in cable, electric, or elevated railroads, the conditions of traffic are far simpler than in a steam railroad. built for general purposes ; the chief difficulty of fixing rates in all these cases being connected with

[1] The price charged by a railroad for any service really consists of two parts—a fee and a tax. The former covers the *direct* or immediate expense of doing the particular service in question—expenses of billing, loading, hauling, etc. The latter contributes to the general expenses attaching to the road itself as a mass of fixed capital—interest, maintenance, and other costs which are not greatly affected by additions to the volume of business done. The railroad agent endeavors to make the aggregate amount of these contributions to the general expenses as large as possible ; for any excess of this total above such expenses constitutes the net profit of the road. If a reduction in rates increases gross earnings faster than it increases expenses, it shows that the old tax was too high, and was defeating its own purpose by destroying traffic. The most profitable rate on any class of goods is the one where the product obtained by multiplying the amount of traffic secured into the profit per unit of traffic—*i. e.*, the excess of price received above direct expense—is a maximum. The same rule which applies to railroad rates of course holds good of any other concern which has a monopoly of any species of traffic.

the uncertainty attaching to the depreciation account.
(§ 188.)

§ 193. In the case of steam railroads, the theoretical
difficulties attaching to a just apportionment of rates are
almost insuperable.  If a government commission wishes
to prescribe a schedule of rates, it must find what system
of charge is adopted on other roads similarly situated,
and whether those charges pay or do not pay a fair profit
on the investment.  But no two roads are just alike, and
any commission is liable to make its schedule too high or
too low, according to its personal bias.  In countries like
England, where the railroads are owned at home, and
where their promoters have great influence with the legislature, such maxima are placed so high as to be inoperative.  Where, on the contrary, a large part of the railroad
stock is owned at a distance from the road itself, the
legislature is tempted to fix the maximum rates too low
and to leave the owners no opportunity for profitable
work.  The evil resulting from the latter alternative is
worse than from the former.  It was seen in the operation of the Potter law in Wisconsin in 1874, where the
maxima were placed at a figure that prevented the roads
from earning interest or even maintenance.  They were
compelled to contract their service to such a degree that
the development of the state was checked, and after two
years' trial the very men who had been most anxious to
pass the law were equally pressing in favor of its repeal.
While few instances of railroad legislation have had as
bad an effect as this, the temptation to exercise a short-
sighted policy is always present when the legislature feels
the urgent pressure of shippers for a reduction in rates
and does not feel the claims of absentee owners for a fair
return on their property.

§ 194. Where state ownership is impracticable, and
private enterprise short-sighted and extortionate, laws
fixing rates may be the best available resource for the

protection of the public ; but their operation is in almost all cases rather unsatisfactory. They subject the community to the evils resulting from inequality of supply and demand, as described in chapter iii; and the burden consequent upon these evils is apt to outweigh the good actually accomplished by the statute.

§ 195. Less ambitious in their aims, but more successful in their practical results, have been the attempts to secure fair rates by insisting on far-sighted management in the affairs of monopolies.

It cannot be too often repeated that it is not so much the character of a particular industry which creates an apparent conflict of interests between the investors and the public, as the want of foresight in the management of that industry. The principle of charging what the traffic will bear, adopted by our large corporations, is a good one; it is only when it is made a pretext for charging what the traffic will *not* bear, that it gives rise to abuses. It depends largely upon the intelligence of the management whether it is used as a principle or abused as a pretence ; and intelligence in management is often a matter of slow growth. In the Middle Ages people thought it necessary to regulate by public authority the rates that bakers might charge for their services in making bread. They said that in the absence of such regulation the public baker had the rest of the community at his mercy. He could take advantage of the necessities of his customers to exact starvation prices. We have passed beyond this industrial stage. Our business men can look a week or a month ahead ; the baker can see that other bakers will take away his business unless he is guided by considerations of public policy. But we have not learned to look ten or twenty years ahead. The managers of our largest enterprises still invite competition by high rates instead of forestalling it by low ones, and still handicap their best customers by discrimination instead of developing their trade by equality of charges. The newer the industry, the greater is the danger of unnecessary conflicts between producers and consumers, and the need of applying every agency to quicken public intelligence.

§ 196. The power of the government may be so exercised as either to hasten or to retard this educational process. Attempts to prescribe rates have a tendency to retard it; and this is probably the severest positive evil connected with them. If, as so often happens, the results of such attempts prove unsatisfactory, the managers will impute all their own shortcomings to the existence of a control which hampers them, and will not take to heart the lessons which they might otherwise learn from mistakes.

On the other hand, the educational process may be stimulated by measures which secure greater publicity in the affairs of monopolies. Much of the apparent conflict of interest between producers and consumers is due to misunderstanding on the part of each side as to the real needs of the other. This misunderstanding can be lessened, if not wholly avoided, by clear judicial opinions. A great deal of the influence exercised by English and American courts has been due to the fact that they placed economic principles before both sides in a non-partisan version and in an absolutely clear light. There is some danger that the bench will lose this influence, partly because of the increasing complication of modern industry, which renders it difficult for a lawyer to understand the indirect economic effects of his decisions; partly on account of a somewhat dangerous doctrine of sovereignty, which is leading our courts to lay too much stress on precedent and statute and too little on the common sense of the people. The authority of the court depends, not on the acts of the legislature, not even on uninterrupted tradition, but on the fact that it knows more than the parties between whom it is deciding and can see the consequences of different lines of action more clearly, as well as more impartially, than they can.

§ 197. To meet the deficiency of technical knowledge, recourse is often had to special commissions of experts for impartial investigation of disputes. The Massachusetts Railroad Commission is perhaps the best known example of this kind. In the days of its most successful operation it had practically no power except the power to report; but its reports showed such a clear understanding of the points at issue that they were accepted as authority by impartial men on both sides. The Interstate Commerce Commission was in some respects modelled upon the Massachusetts commission, and such success as it has enjoyed has been based on its power of applying sound economic principles to difficult cases. It is true, though it sounds paradoxical, that the power of these commissions is lessened by increasing their powers. They are engaged in building up new laws, new traditions, and new methods of business where it is absolutely essential that their reasoning should command the assent of clear-headed men on both sides. When they cease to rely on their reason and fall back on authority, they lose the educational power which is the source of their dominant influence.

Another useful form of advisory commission is composed of local business men, or representatives of commercial and industrial organizations, who can give advice as to the probable effect of changes in rates. Without such advice a railroad agent (or a tariff committee composed exclusively of railroad men) is in danger of making reductions, not where they are most needed, but where they are most clamorously called for. The system of local advisory boards has been most consistently applied in the German Empire; and, though a little slow in its operation, seems to have much to recommend it.

§ 198. The legislation which is most serviceable in giving

12

force to the decisions of such commissions and advisory boards is that which prescribes publicity of rates. The most serious evils in connection with arbitrary management of monopolies have taken the form, not of attempts to oppress the public as a whole, but of attempts to make differences between different sections of the public and to charge the poor man more than the rich man. When these differences are brought prominently before the public eye, they often stop of themselves ; and the courts find comparatively little difficulty in dealing with those which persist. It may at times seem necessary to supplement these provisions with special statutes to secure equality, such as the "long and short haul" clause of the Interstate Commerce Act, which prohibits railroad companies from charging local business a higher aggregate rate than through business of the same sort ; but the good done by such acts is usually much less than their promoters have anticipated. Effective control must be sought in the application of general legal principles, rather than in special statutes.

§ 199. Another means of securing far-sighted management is the enforcement of directors' responsibility. If those who are engaged in the actual management are striving to make the largest immediate income out of a concern, they will pursue an extremely short-sighted policy, destructive alike to customers and to investors. If, on the other hand, their interests are identified with the permanent profits of the company instead of the temporary ones, they will be almost certain to do well by the public. Anything which so increases the borrowing power of corporations or diminishes the liabilities of directors as to make it possible for them to speculate with other people's money, causes short-sighted and unintelligent use of monopoly powers. Whatever makes the director responsible to the investor, tends to make the whole corporation serve the public better in the long run.

§ 200. If the managers of an enterprise are allowed to use other people's money while they risk comparatively little of their own, a number of serious evils will inevitably follow. They will persuade the public to engage in enterprises which are doomed to failure in advance, in the hope that they may themselves make a temporary profit out of their management, either in the form of large salaries or of lucrative personal contracts. Or they may so manipulate the finances of the companies which they control, as to make a personal profit out of fluctuations in the value of their securities. These possibilities form a temptation to waste the investors' private capital and, what is far worse, to misuse an appreciable part of the public capital. The former causes loss to the individual investors directly concerned ; the latter affects the whole community, consumers as well as investors, by preventing the national resources from being properly utilized. This danger is most inadequately met in the United States. There are few localities where either law or public sentiment does much to check it. In this respect America is far behind other countries. In most parts of Europe, these evils are avoided or mitigated by holding the promoters of new concerns responsible for the correctness of their indications, and by making it a crime for them to divert the money of investors to their own uses by lucrative private contracts. In England these laws are backed by a public sentiment which looks on the position of a director or an official of a corporation as one of trust, and which unsparingly condemns every attempt to use such a place for personal aggrandizement at the expense of the investor. But in the United States the legal responsibility is inadequate, and the public sentiment even more so. Perhaps the most serious among all the evils under which American business suffers is the lack of clear understanding as to directors' responsibility.

# CHAPTER VII.

## MONEY.

Its Functions and Forms—Seigniorage—Depreciation—The General Level of Prices—Conflicts between Debtor and Creditor—Bimetallism in Theory and in History—Irredeemable Paper Money.

Of the abundant literature on this subject, perhaps the best short work for general use is W. S. Jevons : "Money and the Mechanism of Exchange." 4th ed. London and New York, 1878. This may be supplemented by H. White: "Money and Banking." Boston, 1895.

The general theory of money and credit is admirably developed in the third book of John Stuart Mill's "Political Economy."

J. L. Laughlin, "History of Bimetallism in the United States," New York, 1886, deals with the subject of silver coinage from the monometallist standpoint. The best presentation of the bimetallist argument is perhaps given in J. S. Nicholson: "A Treatise on Money and Essays on Monetary Problems. 2d ed. London, 1893.

The annual reports of the U. S. Treasury Department furnish much statistical matter which is of great value.

§ 201. NEARLY all business contracts and agreements —sales, leases, wages, loans, insurance, etc.—call for payments of *money* from at least one party. Money is best defined as a thing which, by common consent of the business community, is used as a *basis of commercial obligations.* Whatever may be chosen for this purpose, becomes, by the very fact of being thus used, a convenient standard for measuring private wealth—a value denominator, as it is sometimes called—by means of which the power and advantage attaching to the ownership of different kinds of saleable property can be compared.

§ 202. There are two quite distinct purposes for which

supplies of money are needed by the business community and its individual members.

(1) A certain amount of capital *must* be held in this form as a cash *reserve* to secure solvency.

(2) A large amount of income *may* be received in this form as a convenient *medium of exchange*.

The latter function seems at first sight much more important than the former. The volume of transactions settled by payments of money as a medium of exchange in the course of a year is far greater than the whole amount of cash reserve in existence at any one time. In spite of this disparity, the function of money as capital is of more fundamental consequence. If we have a proper cash reserve of money, we can use other things as media of exchange. We can make our payments by bank checks or other instruments of credit. If we have not an adequate reserve of capital in the form of money, no credit or banking system, however well devised, will act as a substitute. The individual or the community that wishes to do a successful business must keep an adequate stock of cash—not necessarily as a means of payment, but as a guarantee of solvency. The ease with which other means of exchange can be substituted for money, does not prove that money is unnecessary; it proves that its function as a means of exchange is not the sole or even the principal object for which it is needed.

§ 203. It sometimes happens that there are two different standards of contract in common use at the same time. In that case we really have two independent forms of money in the same community. It may be that one article is used for the settlement of debts and other long time contracts because of the stability in the conditions which affect its supply and demand, while another is used for sales and wages because of its superior convenience as a means of exchange. This state of things has been exemplified in English history in cases where rents were

calculated in wheat [1] or in days' labor, while payments
were made in coin.  The standards which served as units
for hiring land, were absolutely unavailable as a means of
exchange in ordinary life.

A basis of contracts which does not serve as a medium
of exchange is known as *money of account*.

§ 204. The concurrent use of different kinds of money
for different purposes may result from the attempt of the
government to force the nation to use money of a kind
which some of its members dislike or distrust.  This state
of things has seemed imminent in the United States, when
the agitation for free silver coinage has been most active.
A large number of the more permanent contracts have
been made payable specifically in gold.  If silver became
the medium of exchange and unit of reckoning for ordinary transactions, we should see the concurrent use of
two different kinds of money side by side.  Such a state
of things is extremely undesirable.  It is of great importance to the commercial world that the money which a
man receives for the goods which he sells should be available for the settlement of debts ; and conversely that the
money which the creditor receives from those who are
indebted to him should be serviceable for the purchase of
current supplies. [2]

[1] Adam Smith has discussed the advantages and disadvantages of " corn
rents."  In the long run, wheat is probably a more equitable standard of
payment than either gold or silver, because the number of people tends to
adjust itself to the food supply, so that there will be a rough correspondence
between the value of a bushel of wheat and that of a day's labor.  But from
year to year wheat fluctuates more than gold or silver, because of variations
in its production, and still more because of the absence of an accumulated
stock large enough to reduce the effect of these variations to a minimum.
In ordinary contracts the danger from momentary fluctuations outweighs the
gain from permanent steadiness, because sudden changes involve worse violations of commercial equity than slow ones.

[2] Menger has observed that the essential characteristic of money is its
saleableness.  If the same thing serves at once as a medium of exchange
and a basis of contracts, it combines present and permanent saleableness in
the highest degree.

§ 205. Any commodity can serve as money where the public accepts it without question as a unit of reckoning and a means of settlement of debts. To this end it is only necessary that it should be universally desired, so that no man need fear having it left on his hands ; and that it should be homogeneous, so that people demand a certain quantity of it rather than a specified piece of it. Articles of the most diverse sort, like the salt of Abyssinia, the tobacco cakes of the Virginia colonists, or the shells which formed the wampum of the North American Indians, have been used as money by communities in different stages of civilization. Among pastoral peoples cattle serve as a unit of reckoning, and not infrequently as a medium of exchange. The Latin name for money, *pecunia*, is derived from *pecus*, a flock ; and it is probable that the English word " fee " is connected etymologically with the German *Vieh*, cattle.

§ 206. Metals have some advantages over all other commodities for use as money. In the first place, they are more permanent. They are not liable to destruction by fire nor to quick consumption in emergencies. There is thus a large permanent stock of metal carried over from year to year, which makes the available supply less dependent upon fluctuations in current production. The world's stock of gold coin and bars probably amounts to nearly four thousand million dollars—many times the annual production or consumption. Under such circumstances, the amount produced in any one year might be greatly increased or diminished without causing more than a slight effect on the total volume in use. If this state of things continued for a series of years, we should have a gradual expansion or contraction of the world's gold currency ; but the large permanent stock would make the percentage of annual increase or diminution so small as to allow contracts to adjust themselves to the change in conditions.

The metals are also, as a rule, more homogeneous than any other commodities in use, and offer great mechanical advantages as means of exchange. They can be cut into pieces of whatever size is wanted, and these pieces can pass from hand to hand; being accepted either by account or by weight, as the importance of the transaction demands.

§ 207. The choice of a metal for use as money has depended mainly on its cost of production. If the cost was too low as compared with the purchases of daily life, the pieces of money became so large as to be inconvenient to handle. If the cost was too high as compared with that of articles to be exchanged, the pieces of money became so small as to be incapable of the necessary subdivision without great danger of loss. As the knowledge of mining and metallurgy has increased there is a tendency to substitute more costly metals for less costly ones, on the basis of convenience alone. Iron, which was in occasional use in ancient times for coins of low value, has been displaced by copper and nickel. Copper, which was first used for transactions of considerable moment (the Roman *as* being originally a pound of copper), has been gradually relegated to a position of trifling importance. Silver, which was formerly a medium of exchange for very large transactions, has now on the whole given place to gold for these purposes.

On the other hand, a metal may be too rare to command universal acceptability. The experiments of Russia in coining platinum did not prove a success. Even gold has a relatively low value among less civilized nations, which have but slight experience of large transactions. There was a time when an ounce of gold in Europe would purchase thirteen or fourteen ounces of silver, but could be bought for three or four ounces of silver in the far East.

§ 208. When the government or some accredited agent

of the government places a stamp upon a piece of metal certifying its weight and fineness, the process is known as *coinage.* When the genuineness of a coin is undoubted, it has a great advantage over uncoined metal as a medium of exchange. People will then accept it by tale or count instead of by weight. Such acceptance furnishes a temptation to the counterfeiter, who attempts to place a stamp like that of the government on baser metal or on a piece of inferior size, and to the clipper or sweater, who attempts to abstract part of the metal from the coin by processes which will not so greatly change its appearance as to prevent its acceptance in ordinary transactions. To meet the danger of counterfeiting there has been a constant improvement in the art of coinage. The oldest coins have a stamp on but one side. A little later the stamp was put on both sides, so that the thickness of the metal could not be reduced without defacing the stamp itself. To prevent clipping, the edges were milled by mechanical devices. To defeat the art of the sweater, provision was made for the retirement and recoinage of pieces that began to show the effects of natural wear; thus rendering artificially worn coin an object of public distrust.

§ 209. Where a system of coinage has become established it is customary for the government to declare its coins *legal tender* for all debts. A seller, laborer or creditor, if he has agreed to receive a certain amount of money in settlement of what is due him, is obliged to accept such coins as money. They are a " legal tender," which he has no right to refuse unless his contract has been made in terms of some commodity other than money. Where the coin is really acceptable, and the function of government is only that of certification, the legal tender feature simply gives effect to the public will, and prevents annoyance and uncertainty. Where for any reason the money is not thus universally acceptable, and

the government attempts to create by legislation a demand and a purchasing power which does not otherwise
exist, the opportunity to declare a coin legal tender is apt
to be abused. Such abuse is most common and flagrant
in communities which are about three-fourths civilized.
Before they have reached this stage, people make contracts payable by weight, because they have not yet
learned the uses of coinage; after they have passed this
stage, they have recourse to the same means, because
they have learned the abuses of coinage and the methods
of protecting themselves against them. The authority of
the government in making money acceptable seems quite
unlimited as long as it is used to give expression to the
will of the property-holders; but when once it attempts
to act independently of that will, it is found to be very
shadowy.

§ 210. When the government agrees to put its stamp of
weight and fineness, and thus bestow the legal tender
character, on any piece of metal of the required size and
quality, we are said to have *free coinage* of that metal.
This does not mean that it is done for nothing, but that it
is done for every one who desires it, and at a price not
disproportionate to the actual cost of the operation. The
work of coinage involves certain expenses to the government for assaying and minting, amounting in the case of
modern standard coin to about one-fifth of one per cent.
If a private person brings gold to the mint to have its
weight and fineness certified, most governments retain an
amount of metal sufficient to defray this expense. A
few nations, like England, have made no such deduction,
believing that it is an advantage to the country to allow
people to convert their gold into coin with the utmost
freedom, and that the government for the sake of this
public advantage can well bear the small loss which is
involved. The balance of opinion is on the whole against
this view. Countries like the United States or France

which make a small charge for coinage, in order to cover the expense of the process, have habitually performed the work better than those which have done it for nothing. The advantage to the public in the superior execution of the coinage has been of more consequence than the slight gain in the elasticity of the currency which the English business world may have enjoyed.

§ 211. In some cases the government retains, for the profit of the exchequer, an amount larger than the actual cost of coinage. A charge of this kind is known as *seigniorage*.[1] The word is derived from the fact that rights of coinage in mediæval times were often made a most valuable prerogative of the " seignior " or feudal lord.

Almost every civilized nation deducts a considerable seigniorage from its smaller coins; that is, it puts less metal into these coins than they can purchase in the open market. The object of this practice is to prevent them from being melted down for use in the arts or for export. A certain amount of small currency is always needed as a medium of exchange. If any of it is withdrawn for use in the arts the remainder becomes inadequate for monetary transactions, which causes great inconvenience, if not hardship. Now if the metal in a half dollar is worth less than half as much as the amount of metal in a dollar, people will choose the large coin to melt down, and the small coin will remain in circulation. When the fractional currency is made of a different material from the larger currency, this principle is equally applicable. If a hundred cents contained a dollar's worth of nickel and other metals combined with it, not only would the cents be of inconvenient bulk, but we should be in constant danger of having them withdrawn from circulation and

---

[1] The name " seigniorage " is sometimes, though less properly, applied to the small charge described in the previous paragraph. This is better designated by the French term *brassage*.

melted if the price of nickel went up while that of gold remained stationary. In order to maintain this currency in daily use at a value higher than that of the bullion which it contains, the government limits the quantity of such issues to the actual wants of the people. Two half dollars are worth as much as one dollar, because half dollars are needed for current purposes of exchange. As a rule, governments do not give this fractional currency the attribute of legal tender, except in small amounts. Limited issues of small currency containing less than its market value of metal are known as *subsidiary coin.*

Where a seigniorage is abstracted not only from the subsidiary coin, but from the legal tender money, the process is known as *debasement.*

§ 212. If a relatively small amount of debased currency is issued, its chief effect is to drive a nearly corresponding amount of better money out of circulation.

If the people of a country have been in the habit of using a thousand million dollars of standard weight, it shows that this amount is needed as a reserve for carrying on the business of the country at the old price level. The loss of productive power due to any attempt to transact business with a smaller cash capital is greater than the gain from the use of a little more metal in the arts, or from the purchase of foreign products with that metal. But if the government adds one hundred million light-weight dollars to the money of the country, this equilibrium will be destroyed. The increase in the number of dollars in the country will tend to make each dollar worth less, and given sums of money will purchase fewer goods. Under these circumstances, some dollars will be melted down for use in the arts, and some will be exported to buy foreign products, until the supply of dollars is reduced to approximately its old amount.

The dollars chosen for melting or for export will be the ones which contain the largest weight of metal. For if

two coins are equal in debt-paying power, but unequal in
utility in other respects, a man will reserve the worse coin
for paying his debts, and use the better coin for purposes
where its advantage is felt. This tendency of bad money
to drive out good money was noted by so ancient an
observer as Aristophanes. It was brought prominently
to the notice of the English-speaking world by Sir
Thomas Gresham, Chancellor of the Exchequer under
Elizabeth, and is commonly referred to as *Gresham's
Law.*

§ 213. When the amount of debased currency has become so great as to afford the necessary reserve for all
transactions in which the government can compel the
creditor to accept this form of payment,[1] the limit of displacement is reached. For when *all* the current circulation of the country is debased, there is none left which can
be advantageously used in the arts or for export. Any
further issue will produce a redundant stock of money,
and a fall in the value of each piece of money, which

---

[1] As the amount of debased money grows larger, its sphere of usefulness
grows smaller. Importers and others engaged in foreign trade have to provide themselves with a certain amount of cash reserve which derives its value
from something more wide-reaching in its effects than a legal tender act.
Farsighted capitalists, who fear the future fiscal policy of the government,
insert stipulations in their loans or in their leases, requiring payment of dues
in some specific commodity rather than in the general currency of the country.
Even as a medium of exchange in domestic transactions, the debased money
may be discredited by the action of the people. D'Avenel has collected
some curious facts which show that the arbitrary changes in coinage made
by the French crown were to a large extent rendered inoperative in this way.
The same result was seen in California, during the Civil War, when the
public was able to nullify the legal tender act and prevent the use of paper
currency as money throughout the state. A man might pay one debt in
paper, but he was thereby cut off from the chance of doing a credit business
afterward. In the rest of the country paper money was available for general
business purposes, but a certain amount of gold had to be retained by those
engaged in the foreign trade, for the adjustment of their purchases abroad
and for payments of any customs duties to the United States at home. The
interest payments of the United States Government on the great bulk of its
loans also involved the use of gold coin, and correspondingly restricted the

manifests itself in the form of rising prices.  If the government persists in putting debased coin into circulation, this increase in the amount of currency and diminution in its value can go on until the purchasing power of the coin falls so low as to allow it to be melted down or exported in spite of the seigniorage.

Such an increase in debased currency beyond the displacement limit, is known as *inflation ;* the resulting loss in purchasing power is known as *depreciation.*

Debasement usually results in depreciation, because the fiscal motive to expand the amount of a debased currency is very great.  If the government abstracts a certain amount of bullion and coins the remainder, the bullion as bullion is relatively useless.  The temptation to coin the seigniorage as a means of paying current expenses, or of meeting some unexpected emergency, is enormous.  This motive, seconded as it habitually is by the interest, real or supposed, which many voters have in seeing an increased abundance of money, has proved well-nigh irre-

---

field of circulation of paper.  In later years, in connection with the agitation for silver coinage, the number of obligations which specifically promised payment in gold was gradually increased.  It is obvious that if the United States should change from a gold to a silver standard, a large part of the transactions of the country must still be fulfilled in gold, unless the courts should legalize a direct violation of specific promises.

The parity of gold and silver dollars is to-day jeopardized, not because the supply of silver money has become nearly equal to the *total* demand of the United States for currency, but because it has become nearly equal to that part of the currency demand over which the legal tender act exercises effective control.  There is no reason to apprehend that the country will lose all its gold.  But there is a great deal of apprehension that people will cease to treat gold and silver dollars as equivalent.  To keep them at equal value the government has been compelled not only to stop the coinage of silver dollars, but to pay gold on demand for any of its coin obligations.  The equivalence between the two forms of currency is thus made dependent, not on the large stock of gold in the country, but on the small stock of gold in the treasury ; not on the solvency of the United States as a nation, but on the sufficiency of the current receipts of the United States Government—a far more precarious matter.

sistible. The world's monetary history shows that very few governments have been able to resist the temptation which the existence of a seigniorage involves.

§ 214. Paper money is a convenient substitute for gold or silver on account of its lack of weight, and has therefore come into increasing use as transactions have grown larger. It has three forms, governed by different laws and to be judged on wholly different principles.

1. *Coin or bullion certificates.* These certificates simply state than an amount of coin or bullion corresponding to the face of the note has been deposited with the government and is held as a fund to redeem that note, not to be used for any other purpose whatsoever. The amount of coin or bullion thus specially reserved always corresponds exactly to the amount of coin certificates. These, therefore, have exactly the same purchasing power as the coin or metal for which they call. They are more convenient to handle than metal and do not involve any danger except that of absolutely reckless dishonesty and violation of pledges on the part of the government; a violation which is not likely to occur with deposits thus specifically appropriated. The gold and silver certificates in the United States, and (to all intents and purposes) the notes of the Bank of England (see chapter viii), are of this description.

2. *Redeemable paper.* Like the coin certificate, this is a promise on the part of the government to pay coin; but, unlike the coin certificate, it is secured only by the general solvency of the treasury department, and not by a specific deposit, dollar for dollar. Experience proves that this is not nearly so safe a reliance as that on which the coin certificate is based. The government, in issuing notes which are secured by the general assets of the treasury, is really doing a banking business, whose safety depends upon the degree in which the administration and the legislature understand the methods of banking. At the very best,

there is danger that the assets on which the government relies for the payment of such notes will fail in an emergency. The treasury department is not well constituted for doing a general banking business. The assets of the government are, for the most part, permanent investments of a kind which it is not easy to sell at short notice. When a fiscal emergency arises the dangerous power, possessed by the legislature, of declaring such notes a legal tender even if they are not redeemed, is a constant menace to financial stability.

3. *Irredeemable paper.* This is neither more nor less than money on which the government has charged a seigniorage of approximately one hundred per cent. It is subject in an exaggerated degree to all the dangers arising from debased coin. If a coin is debased twenty per cent there is a limit to the issue of such coins by the government. When that issue has gone so far that prices have risen twenty-five per cent,[1] the profit to the government on further issue stops, and the danger from this source reaches its natural limit. But in the case of irredeemable paper such issues may go on indefinitely, until legal tender provisions are nullified by the refusal of the people to accept the discredited paper.

§ 215. Besides these various forms of government paper, the banks of most countries issue notes which are intended to circulate from hand to hand. Except in those comparatively rare instances where bank-notes are made a legal tender, they do not properly come within the definition of money. They are only promises to pay money, which are made by responsible corporations. But the note of a bank is apt to be quite as good as that of the government which charters the bank; and we find both kinds of paper in circulation side by side.

The sum total of instruments of circulation which pass

[1] If the value of $1 falls to $0.80, things which formerly sold for $1 will now sell for about $1.25.

from hand to hand—coin, government notes, and bank-notes—is known as the *currency*.

Of equal importance as means of exchange are certain instruments, like bank checks, which do not circulate from hand to hand, but which are cancelled when they have served to settle one transaction, or at most a short series of transactions. The conditions which govern the use of these instruments as substitutes for money are described in the next chapter.

§ 216. The *value of money* is measured by the quantity of other things which a unit of money will purchase. It varies inversely as the general level of prices. If general prices are high, a given amount of products or services will cost a great many dollars. This of course means that a given number of dollars will buy comparatively few products or services. The purchasing power or value of money is therefore low when the price level is high, and *vice versa*.

If the prices of different commodities rose or fell simultaneously, it would be easy to ascertain the amount of change in the general price level and in the value of money. But the price of each article is subject to independent variations of its own. Some articles rise while others fall. Under these circumstances the problem of determining the general price level becomes an extremely difficult one. Several different methods have been proposed for its solution. Under the method first used, which has the advantage of simplicity, we take the recorded prices of a number of articles in a market where statistics have been accurately kept for a series of years. We select some one year for a basis of comparison, and call the price of each article in that year 100. We then compare the price of each article in the next year with its price in the year which we have chosen for our basis of comparison, and take the average of the percentages thus obtained to constitute what is known as the *index number*

for the year in question.  For instance, if we choose 1860
as our base, and are considering four articles whose prices
in 1861 were respectively 98 per cent, 101 per cent, 104
per cent, and 109 per cent of those in 1860, the average
recorded price of these four articles in 1861 would be 103
per cent of the average for 1860.  If the level of prices in
1860 were represented by the index number 100, that in
1861 would be represented by the index number 103.

The results obtained by this method are somewhat
arbitrary, because they depend upon the articles selected
for observation.  This difficulty may be partly met by
dealing with as wide a range of articles as possible.[1]  But
even when we apply it with the utmost completeness this
method is defective, in that it fails to take account of
differences in importance between different commodities.
It is unfair to let a rise in the price of pepper offset a corresponding fall in the price of wheat, because the total
expenditure for the one is so much less than for the other.
To avoid this difficulty Palgrave has urged the use of a
*weighted* average of prices where each article is given an
importance proportionate to the quantity marketed, as
recorded in trade statistics.  Falkner, working for the
United States Senate Committee on Wages and Prices,
has adopted a modification of Palgrave's method, in
which he assigns commodities their relative importance
not on the basis of total amounts sold in wholesale markets but on the basis of quantities used by the typical
workingman's family.[2]  In point of fact, the results
obtained by an unprejudiced application of the three
methods are substantially alike.  They all indicate that
gold prices in different countries rose from 1850 to 1873,

[1] The tables of the *Economist* and of Soetbeer are perhaps the best and
most widely known.

[2] The method of the United States Senate Committee is open to criticism
from the fact that it applies *wholesale* prices to quantities which are purchased at retail.

and have fallen since that time; so that the index numbers which represent the general price level in 1890 stand not far from the level of 1850. Since the crisis of 1893 there has been a further fall, so that the general price level of 1895 is exceptionally low.

§ 217. If we regard our index numbers not as records of wholesale prices but as indications of the enjoyment obtained in spending money or the sacrifice involved in earning it, all the methods which have been employed make the figures for recent years lower than they ought to be.

1. They deal with payments for products and not for services. The former have fallen in price, owing to labor-saving improvements; the latter have risen quite as often as they have fallen. A budget of family expenses should include house rent and services as well as supplies, in order to indicate the actual expense of living.

2. They deal with wholesale prices instead of retail ones. The work of the retailer is one of those services which have been least affected by modern improvements; and therefore retail prices have fallen relatively less than wholesale prices.

3. As a rule, the index numbers are based on prices in the wholesale markets nearest the point of consumption. If a *producer* is obtaining the *same* price for an article in 1895 that he did in 1875, while the cost of railroad and steamship transportation has fallen, the *recorded* price of the article falls. This tends to reduce the index number correspondingly, and to show an apparent loss to the producer where there is no real loss to any one except the transportation companies.

All these causes combine to make the gain to the consumer and the loss to the producer from the observed fall in prices much less than a superficial view of the index numbers would lead us to infer.

§ 218. The problem of explaining variations in general

prices is even more complex than the problem of determining the amount of those variations.

If the total amount of business transactions in the United States is $100,000,000,000 in 1895 and $110,000,-000,000 in 1896, this change indicates, from the standpoint of the sellers, either an increase in the extent of the transactions themselves or in the general price level on which those transactions are conducted. From the standpoint of the buyers it indicates an increase either in the number of dollars in use or in their rapidity of circulation—in the amount of exchange work which a dollar can perform in the course of a year. The $110,000,000,000 paid by the buyers may be regarded as the product of the amount of money in the country multiplied by its average rapidity of circulation. If there are 1,000,000,000 dollars in use, a volume of business of $110,000,000,000 indicates that each dollar on an average changes hands 110 times in the course of the year. The $110,000,000,000 received by the sellers may in like manner be treated as the product of the physical volume of business multiplied by the general price level. If the price level of 1896 is to that of 1895 as 102 : 100, and the volume of business has increased from $100,000,000,000 to $110,000,000,000, it indicates that the transactions of 1896 at the prices of 1895 would have amounted to very nearly 108,000,000,000 ; in other words that about eight per cent of the increase in the monetary transactions is due to changes in the amount of transfers of goods and securities rather than to changes in the scale of prices paid.

Let the amount of money in the country be represented by $M$ and its rapidity of circulation by $R$. Let the price level of 1896 be represented by $P$ (that of 1895 being treated as unity). Let the transactions of 1896, estimated at the prices of 1895, be represented by $T$. Then $R \times M$ will represent the total of prices paid by buyers and $P \times T$ the total of prices received by sellers. The two products obviously represent opposite aspects of exactly the same series of transactions ; so that as a matter of necessity,

$$R \times M = P \times T$$

If we can treat the rapidity of circulation and the extent of business transactions as constant,[1] the *quantity of money and the general level of prices will be proportionate to one another.*

§ 219. This proposition simply states a fact. It does not show the method by which this fact is brought about, nor does it indicate which of the things under discussion is cause and which is effect. When the amount of money is regulated by the discretion of the government, as in the case of irredeemable paper, the changes in quantity of money are the cause, and the variations in price level are the effect. Whatever may be the quantity issued, the prices will tend to adjust themselves to it with great rapidity. If the government inflates the currency ten per cent it is forced to make most of its purchases with that money at a ten per cent advance because active business men know enough of commercial history to be sure that an increase in the number of dollars means a proportionate fall in the purchasing power of each dollar. Among persons of less commercial intelligence, prices will not adjust themselves to the new conditions quite so rapidly, and there will be a time when their more astute neighbors make a profit by paying them in an inflated currency at the old scale of prices. But this state of things is quite transient, and the general price level soon adjusts itself to the volume of government paper in circulation.

When the amount of money is regulated by the discretion of individuals, under a system of free coinage, the case is more complicated. Changes in the quantity of money under this system are *at once a cause and an effect*

---

[1] Or as rising and falling together. The study of the conditions which affect rapidity of circulation must be reserved for the next chapter.

of changes in general price level. If we have to choose between the two ways of looking at the matter there is in the majority of cases less error in treating them as an effect than as a cause. The amount of production and coinage of gold is so far affected by changes in the general price level that it tends to adapt the supply of money to the demand and mitigates changes in general prices far oftener than it causes them.

§ 220. Under a free coinage system, the amount of money is not fixed by action of the government, but is allowed to adjust itself to the wants of trade. If the marginal utility (§ 92) of an ounce of gold in the arts is less than the marginal utility of the products for which it can be exchanged when used as money, there will be a tendency to withdraw gold from the arts and convert it into money. If the utility of gold in the arts is greater than the utility of the things which it will purchase when used as money, the process is reversed; coin is melted down, and used in gold manufactures. Equilibrium is reached when the marginal utility of an ounce of gold employed in the arts is equal to the marginal utility of the things which that ounce will buy if it is converted into money.

This is sometimes treated as a solution of the problem of the value of money. It is far from being a full one. It indicates certain conditions which prevail when the adjustment between quantity and price is complete; but it does not adequately describe or explain the processes by which this adjustment is brought about.

§ 221. The average amount of gold coin held in a country as a reserve during the year will be the sum of the average reserves held by individual citizens or corporations. If a nation uses no banking system, each individual must hold a relatively great reserve of coin.[1] If it

---

[1] Equal to his average payments per day multiplied by the average time that elapses between his receipts and payments—*plus* a slight margin for contingencies.

uses bank checks as means of making large payments,
the individual can avail himself of a bank account instead
of a cash reserve for such payments, and the amount
of coin which the nation needs as a reserve to secure
prompt settlement of these transactions will be greatly
reduced (§ 269). If the nation uses bank notes as well as
bank checks, thus making small payments as well as large
ones on the basis of bank credit, the reserve necessary
to secure the smaller transactions can be similarly reduced (§ 275). But whether the amount needed be larger
or smaller, whether it be held directly in the cash drawer
or indirectly in the bank, a certain amount of capital must
be kept in the form of money. If an individual tries to
reduce his cash capital to a figure lower than this, the
loss from doing business with inadequate money is
greater than the gain from having more capital to put
into machinery or other things which are more obviously
productive than money. If a man invests $10,000 in
machinery, and keeps a cash reserve of $2000, it is be-
cause the loss of profit from reducing his cash reserve to
$1000 more than balances the gain in profit which would
result from increasing his investment in machinery to
$11,000. For the sake of the profit to be derived from
holding a money reserve, he causes gold to be treated as
productive capital instead of being used in the arts; just
as he withdraws a certain amount of iron or copper from
uses which give immediate enjoyment, to those which
promise future profit.[1] The fact that the gold appro-

---

[1] The great apparent difference between permanent investments of gold
in money and permanent investments of iron in machines, or copper in wires,
is due to two facts. 1. The investments of gold as capital can be converted
back into means of direct enjoyment with little or no loss, while those of
iron or copper cannot. 2. The laws governing the utility of the total investment of gold are much more uniform than those which govern the utility
of the total investment of iron or copper. But after making allowance for
both these differences, the process of using gold as money is far more
closely analogous to that of using other commodities as productive capital
than most writers have assumed.

priated as capital consists of individual pieces which circulate from hand to hand, obscures the relation between investments in money and investments in machinery, but does not essentially alter it.

The nation's demand for money, measured as capital—and this is our only practicable way of measuring the quantities of money—is the sum of the cash reserves which the individual members of the nation deem necessary for their maximum profit. The higher the general price level, the greater will be the amount of money which it is necessary to hold as a reserve; for with a high price level a given amount of money will settle a smaller number of transactions.

§ 222. If there is a temporary deficiency of the money reserve, those who have not provided themselves with adequate means of making payments will try to make use of the gold of individuals or nations who have provided themselves with a slight margin above their immediate wants. This they will do by offers of more than the usual rate of interest on short time loans. If this high rate of interest on short time loans lasts so long as to neutralize the profit obtained from holding capital in other forms, people will try to sell their goods and securities in order to get gold. This will diminish the price of goods and increase the purchasing power of gold. This change will usually cause some gold to be imported from other countries, and some to be withdrawn from the arts for conversion into coin. Under a free coinage system this process will continue until the stock of gold available for use in the arts has become so reduced and the stock of coin so increased that the marginal utility of an ounce of gold used in the arts is as large as the marginal utility of the things which an ounce of coined gold will purchase.

The converse case of excess in money reserve shows corresponding effects. If it is temporary, the rate of commercial interest on short time loans falls lower than that on industrial investments. If it is local, it operates to send gold coin away from the place where it is redundant, for the sake of obtaining higher prices somewhere else. If it becomes universal, it causes gold coin to be melted down for use in the arts, until the diminishing utility of an ounce of gold bullion and the increasing utility of the things purchased by an ounce of gold coin reach a common level.

§ 223. The supply and demand of gold money are in equilibrium when the amount of gold which the individual members of the commercial world find it profitable to hold in the form of productive capital—*i. e.* money—at a given price level, leaves the remaining supply of gold, available for the consumers, of such a size that the marginal utility of an ounce of gold used in the arts is exactly equal to the marginal utility of the goods which it will purchase at current prices when used as money.

§ 224. This conception of marginal utility in its relation to money requires further illustration.

If no gold were used as money, the relative prices of gold and wheat would be determined by the enjoyment attending their use and the cost involved in their production. Some of the supplies of gold could be produced at a cost of 1 bushel of wheat per ounce[1] of gold, some would cost 1.1, some 1.2, some 1.3, some 1.4, some 1.5 bushels. On the other hand, there would be different degrees of utility or enjoyment furnished by different parts of the gold which might be purchased in the market. Some of the gold would give its possessors an enjoyment for which they would be willing to sacrifice 1.5 bushels of wheat, or more ; for increased quantities they would be willing to give but 1.4 bushels, 1.3, 1.2, 1.1, or 1 bushel only. At a ratio of one ounce of gold to 1.5 bushels of wheat, the supply of gold would probably be greater than the demand ; at one ounce to 1 bushel of wheat, it would be less than the demand. If the demand and supply are equal at

[1] In §§ 224–226 for "ounce" read "gramme."

a ratio of one ounce to 1.3 bushels, it means that the
number of people who make a gain in utility by exchang-
ing wheat for gold at this ratio have a supply of wheat
corresponding exactly to the demand of those who make
a gain by selling gold for wheat on these terms. When
this condition is fulfilled, the market price will be 1.3
bushels. If this is the normal price (§ 100) as well as the
market price, *i.e.*, if the rates of supply and demand are
*permanently* equal at this ratio, it indicates that the cost
of producing the last ounces of gold is 1.3 of the cost of
producing the last bushels of wheat supplied to such a
market. For if the cost of producing an ounce of gold
were greater than that of 1.3 bushels of wheat, some of the
producers would gradually cease to mine gold and devote
their capital to wheat raising; and conversely, if the cost
of producing one ounce of gold were less than that of producing 1.3 bushels of wheat which are exchanged for it,
some of the producers would cease to grow wheat and
gradually devote their capital to gold mining.

§ 225. Now suppose that to the uses of gold in the arts
is added a new use as capital. A part of the gold which
was formerly used for ornament or manufacture will now
be used for monetary purposes. The part which is given up
to these new purposes will be that for which the purchasers
were formerly willing to give the lowest rate; in the case
supposed, 1.3 bushels of wheat. When this part has been
coined, none of the users of gold will part with his stock
at less than the rate of 1.4 bushels of wheat to the ounce;
nor will he convert it into money unless the scale of prices
is such that the coin made from an ounce of his gold will
buy 1.4 bushels of wheat. A new equilibrium is established, not between the demands of those who offer
gold in exchange for wheat and those who offer wheat
in exchange for gold, but between those who use gold for
enjoyment and those who use it as capital. The purchasing power of an ounce of gold will go up to the point where

its marginal utility as gold bullion to the consumers is equal
to the marginal utility of any of the various articles which
the money coined from such bullion would purchase.

§ 226. In this example we have supposed the rate of
production of gold to remain unchanged. In point of
fact, it would almost certainly increase. As a result of
the withdrawal of gold from use in the arts, it would exchange at the rate of 1.4 bushels of wheat for an ounce,
instead of 1.3, and there would be a similar alteration
in its ratio of exchange for all other commodities. But
this change of ratio would soon increase the production of
gold. For there would be some persons who could more
profitably grow wheat than mine gold if the ratio of exchange were an ounce to 1.3 bushels, but who could more
profitably mine gold than grow wheat if the ratio were
one ounce to 1.4 bushels. And a number of other men,
engaged in the production of other commodities besides
wheat, would find themselves similarly situated. There
would thus be a diversion of capital from agriculture and
manufactures to gold mining, and an increased supply of
gold which would prevent the change in the relative
prices of gold and wheat from being so great as it otherwise would be. In the case supposed, it might readily
happen that the production would increase until one ounce
of gold exchanged for 1.35 bushels of wheat.

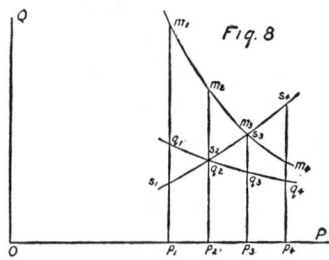

In Figure 8, let $Op_1$, $Op_2$, $Op_3$, $Op_4$ represent prices of
gold expressed in wheat, *i. e.*, the number of bushels of

wheat for which an ounce of gold will exchange ; and let $p_1q_1$, $p_2q_2$, $p_3q_3$, $p_4q_4$ represent the quantity annually used in the arts at these ratios. Let $q_1m_1$, $q_2m_2$, $q_3m_3$, $q_4m_4$ represent the part of the annual product which will be needed for use as money at successive prices.[1] Finally, let the cost of mining be such that, at the successive prices, the quantities normally produced will be represented by $p_1s_1$, $p_2s_2$, $p_3s_3$, $p_4s_4$. Then if the gold is used in the arts alone, the normal price will be fixed by the intersection of the curves $s_1s_4$ and $q_1q_4$; but if to this there be superadded a use as money, we shall have a new point of intersection with the supply curve at a higher price and larger quantity. The difference in marginal cost of production (at the limit to which it is profitable to extend mining operations) will be represented by $p_2p_3$; the total quantity produced will increase from $p_2s_2$ to $p_3s_3$. Of this increased product there will be withdrawn from use as money an amount $s_3q_3$; leaving the amount used in the arts $p_3q_3$.

§ 227. In point of fact, the scarcity of gold, so severely felt in recent years, is adjusting itself by an increase in supply. The gold production of the world, which for a number of years (1875–1885) did not vary much from five million ounces, had risen in the year 1891 to six million, and in the year 1893 to more than seven million. As long as the men who wanted to invest in mines thought that the users of money could be compelled to take the metal that the producers desired to offer, there was a tendency to mine silver rather than gold ; but when it became evident that mining was to stand on the same footing as other industries, and that the producers must consult the consumers' convenience in order to dispose of

---

[1] This may take the form of a negative quantity ; that is, the need for gold in the arts may rise so high that some will be taken from the stock of money left over from past years. In this case the direction of many of the changes described in this paragraph is reversed.

their product, the public soon began to get what it wanted in surprisingly large amounts. If this process continues the present very low price level can be only temporary.

§ 228. In the case of gold bullion or any other form of money of which increasing supplies can be obtained only at increased cost, we thus have a double equilibrium :

1. Between the marginal utility of the bullion to the man who can just afford to use it in the arts, and the marginal utility of the amount of commodities purchased by a coin of corresponding weight.

2. Between the cost of production of such bullion and the cost of the production of the articles for which the corresponding amount of coined money is exchanged.

If the utility of the bullion is temporarily greater than the utility of the articles for which it is exchanged, coin will be melted down and converted into bullion. If it is temporarily less than that of the articles for which it is exchanged, bullion will be taken to the mint for conversion into coin. If for a series of years the utility of the bullion is greater than that of the articles for which the corresponding weight of coin can be exchanged, capital will be diverted from the production of those articles and used in mining gold. In the converse case, capital will be withdrawn from gold mining and devoted to other industrial purposes.

This adjustment, which is simply an application of the general laws of normal price (§ 100) to the special case of gold, furnishes a guarantee against sudden changes of ratio between gold and other commodities. If the general level of prices goes up so that fewer commodities can be bought for a given weight of gold, the resulting conversion of coin into bullion will diminish the quantity of money and will put prices down. If, on the other hand, the general level of prices goes down, and more commodities can be bought for a given weight of gold, the resulting conversion of bullion into coin will increase the quantity of money and tend to put prices up. If either of these processes continues for any considerable length of time, until the reserve stocks of coin have been melted into bullion or until the reserve stocks of bullion have been converted into coin, the effect of cost of production will begin to come into play. If prices continue high, so that a given amount of gold exchanges for a small quantity of other useful things, people will abandon gold mining and produce more of those other things. If, on the other hand, prices remain low, so that a small quantity of gold purchases a large number of useful things, people will increase their production of gold and divert capital from the production of other things for that purpose. These movements will make the change in the relative value of gold and of the articles which gold purchases a slow one, and will give time for contracts to be adjusted to any slow changes which may take place.

That which holds true of gold in this respect holds true of silver or copper or any other relatively indestructible commodity which is subject to the law of diminishing return and has been continuously used as money under a free coinage system.

§ 229. In spite of these adjustments, there is always considerable fluctuation in the purchasing power of coin. Enlarged volume of business, or new uses for the metal in the arts, may increase the demand for the metal and make its value go up; improved methods of doing business on credit (chapter viii) or new developments in mining will tend to increase the available supply of the metal and make its value go down. In the former case we shall see a fall in the general price level; in the latter case, a rise.

Such fluctuations in value alter the relative positions of debtors and creditors. If prices rise, a man who has a debt to pay can accomplish his object with less labor; while the man who receives the payment cannot purchase so many things with the money which he has received. If prices fall, both of these results are reversed. In the former case, injustice may be done to the creditor; in the latter case, to the debtor.

§ 230. Some writers propose to obviate this injustice by a plan known as the *tabular standard*. They would have contracts payable in coin, as they now are; but the amount of such coin for which the creditor might call would under this plan depend upon the price level at the time when the payments became due. When the index number rose (*i. e.* when the purchasing power of money fell) the amount paid should be larger; in the reverse case, it should be smaller. It is argued that in this case all the demands of equity would be fulfilled; and that we could use our present money as a medium of exchange without subjecting ourselves to its disadvantages as a basis of contracts.

The execution of this plan would involve considerable machinery. In the first place we should have to obtain common consent as to the table of commodities which would form the basis of the standard; and in the next place we should have to find an authority that could be trusted to apply it with intelligence and fairness in order to say just what had been the change in purchasing power on the basis of this table. This is extremely difficult to do. The only group of officials which has the technical knowledge necessary for dealing with the problem is connected with the treasury department. But the treasury department is itself habitually a very large debtor, and its awards would, justly or unjustly, be made the objects of suspicion and criticism. In emergencies it would be difficult to trust to their impartiality. Under these circumstances, the uncertainty attaching to the tabular standard makes its practical usefulness seem doubtful.

§ 231. If the tabular standard is considered to be impracticable, there is often an apparent conflict of interest between debtors and creditors in the choice of a metal to be used for coinage. The creditors believe it to be for their advantage to insist on payment in the dearer metal. The debtors believe that it is for their interest to compel the creditor to accept payment in the cheaper metal at a ratio fixed by the authority of law; and they claim that the interest of the community in these matters coincides with that of the debtor classes.

§ 232. A policy which by allowing free coinage of more than one metal gives the debtor the chance of using the cheaper metal, and which at the same time undertakes to protect the creditor by keeping both metals in concurrent or at any rate in alternating use, is known as *bimetallism.*

Some of the agitation in favor of bimetallism is the result of the efforts of silver mine owners who seek a market for their product on more favorable terms than they can command at present; and some is connected with an unintelligent demand for increase in quantity of money irrespective of its quality. But there are several serious arguments for the attempt to maintain the two metals in concurrent circulation which must be carefully examined in detail.[1]

§ 233. It is urged in favor of such a policy, that it diminishes the chance of fluctuations in the value of money. Its advocates say that if the commercial world uses but one metal as money, anything which greatly affects the

[1] The reader who wishes to pursue the subject of bimetallism more fully than it is treated in the general references given at the beginning of the chapter will find a mine of information in the report of the "Gold and Silver Commission" of 1888 (Royal Commission appointed to inquire into Changes in the Relative Value of the Precious Metals 1887–88) with accompanying documents.

The popular discussions of the silver question from each side contain so many overstatements and even mistakes of fact that they are generally of little use.

production of that metal will cause a large proportionate increase in the volume of coin and a corresponding rise in prices ; and that conversely, if its use in the arts is increased without a change in the conditions of production, there will be a very decided scarcity and a corresponding fall in prices. If, on the other hand, two metals are simultaneously used as money, a change in the production or use of one metal alone will make less proportionate difference. At the time of the California gold discoveries there was a large stock of coin added to the currency of the world, and an appreciable rise in prices. How much greater would this increase have been had the new supplies of money been added, not to an existing stock of gold and silver coin, but to the relatively small stock of gold alone ? The comparatively slight effect of the gold discoveries in California and Australia is cited by the advocates of bimetallism as an instance of the salutary action of their principle. Only in the rather improbable contingency of a simultaneous change in the conditions of production and use of the two metals should we have a disturbance comparable in magnitude with that to which a monometallic world is daily subject.[1]

§ 234. The bimetallists further emphasize their position by pointing out the evils which have arisen since the abandonment of the policy of bimetallism by several of the leading nations of the world, in the years immediately succeeding 1870. They say that the attempt to use only a

---

[1] A few years ago when the world was pretty equally divided into gold and silver using countries, a nation which maintained both metals in concurrent circulation gave its business men the advantage of whatever stability in value is due to bimetallism, in a very tangible form. Being able to export and import currency freely to or from all parts of the world with which it had dealings, such a country not only protected itself against fluctuations in price, but protected those of its members who were engaged in foreign trade from the more obvious danger of fluctuations in exchange (chapter viii). But so few countries now have free coinage of silver that this argument for bimetallism has lost much of its force.

single metal has caused an actual contraction of the currency; that the use of gold in the arts is so great that the additions to the world's stock of coin are inadequate to maintain the old price level and properly meet the wants of existing business. They attribute the series of severe industrial depressions during the last twenty-five years to a decline in prices directly consequent upon the abandonment of bimetallism. They show that many of the staple commodities have fallen in price concurrently with the fall in silver. They claim that the gold currency, which is now the only available basis of contracts, has *appreciated;* that each unit of money will purchase more commodities; and conversely, that an increased amount of commodities is required in order to fulfil an agreement which has been made in terms of money. A contract which calls for the payment of a hundred dollars or a hundred pounds sterling in return for past services, puts the man who pays the money in a worse position, and the man who receives it in a better position, than was contemplated at the time those services were rendered. Every man who borrowed money with the expectation of producing commodities as a means of paying his debts finds himself in worse financial circumstances than he had any reason to expect. The result has been a loss to the debtor and a gain to the creditor, a loss to the active business man and a gain to the one who sits quietly at home and receives interest. The bimetallists urge that this loss is at once unjust and destructive; unjust as between man and man, destructive to the active prosecution of business enterprise throughout the community.

§ 235. They also urge—and this is in some respects their strongest argument—that a slowly depreciating currency is better than a slowly appreciating one. We have seen how, in the present tendency toward under-consumption, the contraction of expenditure for the sake of profits which are expected but not always realized forms a source of danger to the community ; and how, for the moment at any rate, an inflation of the currency may contribute to the better utilization of national capital by increasing national consumption. The bimetallist claims that a slowly depreciating currency maintains this healthful process without the reaction which follows reckless inflation ; and that an appreciating currency, such as gold appears to be, intensifies all the evils incident to the modern passion for over-investment.[1]

§ 236. To these charges the monometallist replies, in the first place, by denying most of the allegations of the bimetallist concerning the amount of appreciation of gold. He can show that the fall in prices chiefly affects those articles where new processes have economized the labor of production and distribution. He can point out many commodities which have fallen but little and a number that have actually risen. The articles which have most conspicuously fallen in price belong to two classes : (1)

---

[1] Besides these arguments there are two sentiments working in favor of bimetallism, which it will not do to leave unnoticed. One is the feeling that the debtor is more deserving of sympathy and assistance than the creditor. The creditor is pictured as a rich financier living on the income which he draws from the struggling debtor. In point of fact, the financiers are apt to be debtors quite as much as creditors. They hold relatively large quantities of stock, as compared with bonds ; their advocacy of the gold standard arises from the fact that it enables them to borrow money at lower rates of interest and in larger quantities. The chief creditor classes of the community are the people who live upon past savings—not usually in very large amounts,—the holders of life insurance, and above all the receivers of salaries and wages. To deem the debtors worthy of encouragement at the expense of these classes is to put a premium on economic recklessness.

The other sentiment is connected with the feeling that silver mining is an industry which has not been very profitable and that it ought to be helped. The claim is gravely made that 371 grains of silver really costs as much as 23.2 grains of gold and that therefore we ought to pay as much for it. But if consumers do not want an article, the high cost is a reason against stimulating its production, and the theory that a man may use the power of the government to compel people to buy a thing they do not want at the price which it has cost him, is socialism of the extremest type.

Products like steel or sugar, in whose preparation there have been marked improvements during the period in question, enabling a given number of producers to increase their output and compelling as well as justifying a fall in price. (2) Products like wheat, whose improved transportation facilities have greatly widened the area from which trade centres could draw their supplies, and have increased the intensity of competition between different producers. Where one or the other of these causes has not been conspicuously present, prices have been quite as apt to rise as to fall. We see this exemplified in goods which are mostly consumed at home, like eggs; in goods in which there is little international competition, like corn; and even in goods which form the subject of international trade, like india-rubber, in case there have been no new sources of supply or methods of economizing labor.

§ 237. He can also show that the recent years of falling prices were preceded by a corresponding period of rising prices, and can claim that the injustice to debtor classes for twenty years succeeding 1873 was but an offset to a corresponding injustice to creditors before that time. In point of fact, the amount of such injustice either way is very much less than would appear from looking at the figures of the prices alone. For in times of advancing prices a part of the loss to the creditor was offset by an increase in the interest rate. As prices rose, interest rose. Most of the contracts for the payment of interest were terminable at short enough periods for the creditor to indemnify himself by increased interest charges for any probable depreciation of his principal. Conversely, when prices began to fall, interest fell also. The burden upon the debtor due to the realization of lower prices for his product was in very considerable measure offset by the possibility of borrowing capital at lower interest rates.

§ 238. The monometallist further claims that even if the

prices of many important staples have moved concurrently
with that of silver, the price of labor has maintained
a more nearly constant ratio to that of gold. He urges
that the demands of justice are better satisfied if the dis-
charge of a debt requires a fixed amount of labor than if it
requires a fixed amount of commodities. The question
of equity in his mind resolves itself into this: Must a
man do more work to pay a debt than he would have had
to do at the time when that debt was contracted? If
this is the case, there is a hardship to the debtor; if this
is not the case, he suffers no hardship. The debtor was
not borrowing a certain amount of comfort from the
creditor. He was borrowing a certain amount of control
of labor. Of that labor and its products he has had the
use during the period stipulated. Even if he is compelled
to sell the commodities which are the results of that labor
at lower rates than he expected, because of the increased
efficiency in production which the rest of the producing
world enjoys in common with him, this was a risk which
he might have foreseen and expected when he contracted
the debt. The over-production of goods at unremunerative prices was the very thing which he as a business man
should have taken care to avoid. That he failed to foresee it and to avoid it indicates, not a defect in the monetary system, but an over-sanguine temperament on the
part of the individual speculator or group of speculators.

§ 239. The monometallist rejects the theory that two
metals will necessarily be more stable than one. All
depends upon the metal in question. There is at most a
slight *a priori* probability in favor of the concurrent use
of two metals if it can be proved practicable. But the
gold monometallist urges that any argument based upon
this *a priori* probability is completely overthrown by the
facts concerning silver mining in recent years. Even
admitting what may be plausibly claimed as to the
appreciation of gold, the monometallist urges that this is

far less conspicuous than the depreciation of silver. The marginal cost of gold has gone up a little: that of silver has gone down a great deal. The attempt to maintain bimetallism would have resulted in a rapidly depreciating standard with all the evils of over-speculation incident thereto; and this would have been a far worse state than that in which the commercial world at present finds itself.

§ 240. He denies that the evil secondary results which follow quick inflation are avoided by a slow and continuous process of depreciation. They do not come so soon; but in his opinion they come just as surely. For while prices are gradually advancing, the more reckless speculators come into control of business by offering high rates of interest which they cannot pay unless the depreciation of the currency is still further continued. There is then sure to be a gradual over-production of machinery under circumstances which make its permanent usefulness out of the question. Such a condition was reached, the whole world over, in 1873, when the depreciation of gold reached its extreme. The monometallist claims that the severity of the depression that followed was not so much a direct result of contraction, as an inevitable secondary effect of the expansion which had preceded; one which the demonetization of silver may at most have intensified, but for which it cannot be held responsible as the cause.

§ 241. But the monometallist has a stronger argument than any of these. He claims that the maintenance of bimetallism is impracticable under any of the plans proposed by its advocates, and extremely doubtful under any plan whatsoever; so much so that the uncertainty attaching to the future of a bimetallic currency would make it an extremely bad one to adopt.

We may make three distinct suppositions as to the conditions under which bimetallism is attempted:

1. When the ratio chosen for the coinage of two metals

is exactly the market ratio of the price of the two metals at the time. If an ounce of gold sells at the same rate as a pound of silver, the nation which coins each of these two metals, putting sixteen times as many grains of silver into the silver dollar as it puts grains of gold into the gold dollar, will probably have a considerable amount of both metals brought to its mint. But it is improbable that this exact ratio of bullion value, independent of the operation of coinage laws, will be maintained for a long time ; since anything which affects the conditions of production or consumption of either metal is liable in some degree to disturb it.

2. If the ratio adopted is near the market ratio of the bullion price of the two metals, though not absolutely coincident with it, their concurrent circulation may still be maintained. If, apart from any attempt at bimetallism an ounce of gold would exchange for 16½ ounces of silver instead of 16, it might readily happen that the opening of the mints of a large nation or group of nations to the free coinage of silver at a ratio of 1 to 16 would so change the conditions of demand and supply of the two metals as to make their bullion value conform to the coinage ratio. For if twenty million dollars of silver were coined yearly under the operations of such an act, twenty million dollars' worth of gold which would otherwise have been needed for coinage would be set free for use in the arts. To call forth a demand for this additional twenty million dollars of gold buillion, some people must be induced to use it under the new conditions who would not have done so under the old ; a result which can only be accomplished by a slight fall in the ratio at which it is exchanged for other commodities. On the other hand, the increased monetary demand for silver would at first cause withdrawals of silver from use in the arts. This would mean that those who now wanted the silver would have to pay a little higher price to get it. This price

would stimulate an increased production, but additions to the product being subject to the law of the diminishing return could only be obtained at an expenditure of a little more labor per unit of product. If the labor, and other elements of expense, needed for the units of added product were appreciably greater than that by which the old demand for silver had been supplied, this disadvantage would soon put a stop to increased production from the mines, and the price of silver would be permanently raised by the additional demand for coinage purposes. Meantime, the increased supplies of gold set free for use would have made gold mining less profitable, would have thrown some gold mines out of use, and would have left in operation only those where the cost per unit of product was less. Under those circumstances we should have a new ratio between silver and gold, where more silver was demanded and produced at slightly higher marginal cost, where less gold was demanded and produced at slightly lower marginal cost, and where the final ratio of such cost would be 16 to 1 instead of $16\frac{1}{2}$ to 1.

The effective operation of this process depends upon the power of the nations which adopt bimetallism to take a sufficient quantity of silver, year after year, to raise the marginal cost of production without driving gold wholly out of use as money. If the annual demand of such nations for currency is small, or if the amount of additional silver which can be produced at a slight advance in price is large, the experiment fails. The greater the quantity of silver which the nations that strive to maintain bimetallism can absorb annually, the better are the prospects of success. The greater the amount which miners stand ready to produce at a moderate advance in price, the larger are the chances of failure.

The power of legislation to influence the demand for the precious metals is on the whole surprisingly small. People will demand a metal for coinage whose bulk makes it convenient to handle. If their transactions are small they may use copper as a standard. As they buy and sell more they will use silver. When their business is very large, they will prefer gold. Consequently the relative value of the cheaper metals tends to fall as the amount of coin in use becomes larger.[1] In eastern countries the ratio of value of gold to silver has been as low as four to one. In Europe in the middle ages it was in the neighborhood of twelve to one. For the greater part of the nineteenth century it was fifteen and a half to one. With the development of new mines and new processes since 1870 it has risen as high as thirty-two to one. This change of ratio has been accentuated by the action of a number of governments in abandoning the attempt to keep gold and silver in concurrent circulation. But there is no proof—in fact, there is a decided absence of probability—that the various governments could have succeeded in maintaining the old ratio if they had tried to do so.[2]

3. Where the ratio chosen for coinage is far from the market ratio of the bullion the failure of any attempt to maintain bimetallism is certain. The difference between this case and the preceding one may be made clear by a

[1] If two metals are in concurrent use, an increase in the supply of the dearer metal, by increasing the amount of coin, lessens the monetary utility of the cheaper metal, and makes but a slight change in the ratio of value—witness the trifling effect of the periods of large gold discovery. On the other hand, an increase in the supply of the cheaper metal increases the monetary utility of the dearer metal and makes a great change in the ratio—witness the great effect of the silver discoveries in the seventeenth century, when there was no legislative discrimination against that metal. An increased supply of gold means diminished demand for silver, and a parallel movement of value of the two metals. An increased supply of silver means increased demand for gold, and a divergent movement of value of the two metals.

[2] The quantity of silver coined in some of the recent years has been greater than at any previous time in the world's history, but has not sufficed to create a demand for the product of the mines at anything like the old prices.

concrete illustration. If it takes $15\frac{1}{2}$ days' labor to produce a pound of silver and $16\frac{1}{2}$ days' labor to produce
an ounce of gold, a country which has several hundred
millions of gold and proceeds to make purchases of silver
at 16 to 1 can so increase the quantity of silver demanded
and diminish the quantity of gold demanded, that the
marginal cost of the pound of silver and the ounce of
gold will soon become equal; but if it takes 12 days' labor
to produce a pound of silver and 20 days' labor to produce an ounce of gold, no amount of regulation is likely
to make the 12 days' labor command a price equal to that
of the 20 days' labor. The most that can be expected is
that a supplementary demand for the products of the 12
days' labor should increase their selling price to a point
represented by 13 or possibly 14 days' labor, and that a
reduction of demand for the products of the 20 days'
labor should lower their selling price to a point represented by 19 or 18 days' labor. But we should still be
far from reaching an equality of value or concurrent use
of the two metals as coin at the ratio of 16 to 1. Even if
the whole world should adopt a ratio of 16 to 1 under
those conditions of production, the chance of a successful
issue of such a policy would be extremely problematical.
It is more than likely that the whole gold product of the
world could be used in the arts, leaving silver alone to perform the functions of money, without so far lowering the
demand for gold and increasing that for silver as to make
their price ratio as low as 16 to 1.

§ 242. When the coinage ratio for one or more countries is fixed so far from the commercial ratio as to prevent the use of more than one metal, we have nominal
and not real bimetallism. Gresham's Law comes into
operation. The less valuable metal is brought to the
mint to be coined and used in paying debts; the more
valuable one is exported or used in the arts for the sake
of its bullion value.

§ 243. The most important case where free coinage of
two metals was successfully maintained was in France
in the first half of the present century.  The conditions
were favorable for such an experiment.  Production of
both gold and silver was slow and equable.  There was no
likelihood of sudden changes, either in demand or in supply.  The French financiers saw that the normal commercial ratio of the two metals under the conditions of use
then existing was such that 15½ ounces of silver exchanged
for one ounce of gold.  In 1803 this was adopted as the
ratio at which the French mint would coin either metal.[1]
For nearly fifty years this policy was successfully maintained.  If for a time the price of silver rose, gold
was taken to the French mint ; if the price of gold rose,
silver was taken to the French mint.  The causes for
such fluctuations were so slight that a moderate amount
of coinage of one or the other metal was sufficient to
exercise a very decided compensating action.  But in
1850, when the California gold discoveries came into
effect, there was a distinct fall in the price of gold, due to
its increased production.  Silver ceased to be coined by the
French mint, not on account of any change in the law,
but from a change in the commercial conditions.  In
order to preserve its stock of fractional silver unimpaired, (§ 211), the French Government had to reduce the
amount of metal in its smaller coins, which it did by increasing the proportion of alloy, the weight of the coins
remaining the same.  At about this time (1865) Belgium,
Switzerland, and Italy, whose coinage systems resembled
that of France, joined with her in forming the Latin Union,
which has been cited as a most conspicuous example of
successful bimetallism.  As a matter of fact, the success of
the bimetallic experiment was ended before the Latin
Union was formed.  The bimetallism of the Latin Union

[1] This was only the re-adoption of a ratio which had been established
in 1785.

was nominal, and not actual. The great bulk of the free coinage under the Latin Union has consisted of gold ; the silver coined under its auspices has almost all been subsidiary.

Had the cheapness of gold continued, it is highly probable that the nominal bimetallism of the Latin Union might have been indefinitely maintained ; but as the Californian and Australian gold fields became somewhat exhausted and new sources of supply of silver came into play, the relative price of gold rose, and that of silver fell correspondingly. People began to take silver to the mints instead of gold. This change was not regarded with the equanimity with which the authorities had seen the substitution of gold for silver. It was in fact a change from a metal which was convenient for use in large transactions to one which was extremely inconvenient. Just as France in 1864 had taken measures to preserve her silver for use in small transactions, she now took pains to preserve her gold for use in large transactions, not of course by diminishing the number of grammes of gold in a twenty-franc piece, but by limiting the amount of silver which she was prepared to coin. The example of France was followed with more or less hesitation by other states in the Latin Union, and in 1876 the principle of bimetallism was abandoned in name as it had been twenty years earlier in fact.

§ 244. The other great series of experiments in bimetallism was made in the United States. By the coinage act of 1792 the United States offered to coin both silver and gold. Our financiers were, however, less successful in their judgment of the probable commercial value of the two metals than the French authorities, and fixed the ratio at 15 to 1, making the dollars contain either 371.25 grains of pure silver or 24.75 grains of pure gold. But 24¾ grains of gold bullion was worth more in the world's markets than 371 grains of silver bullion. Where the two things had the same debt-paying power, it was advantageous to use the 371 grains of silver for paying debts and to sell the gold for export or for use in the arts. We had practically nothing but silver in use as coin. This state of things continued until 1834, when the desirability of using gold for large transactions was felt, and the coinage law was so amended as to make the ratio 16 to 1 instead of 15 to 1, by changing the weight of gold in a dollar from $24\frac{3}{4}$ grains to $23\frac{2}{10}$. This overdid the matter. While $24\frac{3}{4}$ grains of gold had been worth more than 371 grains of silver, $23\frac{2}{10}$ grains of gold was worth less than 371 grains of silver. It was far preferable to take gold to be coined and sell the silver either for use in the arts or for export. This took place to such a degree that in order to preserve its subsidiary currency the United States was compelled to do what France did some years later. It reduced the amount of silver in its fractional coins in order to prevent export, and maintained their value by limiting their issue. From 1853 to 1873 we had nominal bimetallism, but in fact the silver was so over-valued that few silver dollars were coined, and practically none went into actual circulation in the United States.

§ 245. In 1873 the free coinage of silver was abolished. This action seemed to have little importance at the time, particularly as the United States was using neither silver nor gold dollars, but paper ones; these being worth much less than coined dollars of either kind. But in the years immediately following, the increased production of silver made the price of silver bullion fall until 371 grains of silver were cheaper than a paper dollar. Under such circumstances there was a loud demand for the reënactment of the law permitting people to take their silver to the mint and have it coined. This demand was urged both by the silver producers, who wished a market for their product, and by the debtors, who wished an inflation of the currency. They were not strong enough to put their wishes into effect, but succeeded (1878) in securing the passage of a measure known as the Bland Act, by which the United States purchased and coined two million dollars' worth of silver per month, the seigniorage on the transaction accruing to the advantage of the government. There was a discretionary power given to the Secretary of the Treasury to purchase twice this amount, but it was never exercised.

The Bland Act disappointed the expectations both of its advocates and of its opponents. It did not create a sufficient demand for silver to keep the price from falling, as its advocates had hoped. On the other hand, it did not prevent the use of gold currency, as its opponents had feared. The United States was in a strong financial position, both as a people and as a government. It demanded, for use in its expanding trade, an increase in currency of more than two million or even three million dollars a month, so that it was able to absorb into its circulation the whole amount of silver coined under the Bland Act, without in the least crowding gold out of use. The government also had so large a surplus that it was able to make the necessary purchases without impairment of its gold reserves.

§ 246. Twelve years later the silver men were strong enough to secure the passage of a more sweeping act than the Bland law. This was known as the Sherman Act of 1890. It provided for the purchase of four and one-half million ounces of silver a month, by an issue of treasury notes equal in amount to the bullion value of the silver thus purchased. It was hoped by the friends of the measure that the increased amount of silver purchased would send the price of the product up, and that notes based on the bullion value of the silver at the time of the purchase would be secured by a reserve sufficient to protect the government against loss and the currency against depreciation. Had silver not fallen in price these expectations would perhaps have been fulfilled. But the actual working of the measure was far from being satisfactory to any one. A temporary rise in the price of silver brought new mines into use and caused a speculative over-production of silver, which made the price fall lower than it had ever done before. When the Sherman Act was passed the selling price of an ounce of silver was $\frac{1}{22}$ of that of an ounce of gold. Three years later it had fallen to $\frac{1}{25}$. Meantime, the additional purchases were a burden both to the country and to the government. The country had been able to absorb two million dollars' worth of silver coin monthly without crowding out gold. It was not able to absorb a much larger amount, especially under the adverse financial conditions that followed. Nor were the revenues of the government adequate to make the purchases out of surplus income. Extravagant appropriations had so completely destroyed the disposable funds that the payments under the Sherman Act were accompanied by a reduction of the gold reserves in the treasury. In 1893 the supply of silver currency in the country had nearly reached the limit of the demand for such currency ; partly because of the increase in the supply itself, partly because the people began to distrust it to such a degree that they were making gold contracts and using gold reserves for many of the needs of commercial life. Nor was the government in a position to maintain, by force of the treasury reserve, an equilibrium which had become so precarious. Relief was barely obtained by the repeal of the Sherman Act and a return to gold monometallism.

The experience under the Sherman Act is extremely valuable as showing how little is the chance of increasing the market price of silver by its forced use as currency. During recent years the world's coinage of silver has been large, but the increased production has been so great as to outrun the monetary demand. The Sherman Act proved beyond a doubt that the United States would be wholly unable to maintain bimetallism at 16 to 1, or any ratio approximating to this figure.[1]

§ 247. Those who see the impracticability of bimetallism at a fixed ratio, on account of uncertainty in the volume of silver production, but who at the same time deplore the contraction of the currency which they believe to be incident to the adoption of gold monometallism, have several plans to propose :

1. Free coinage at shifting ratios, to be determined from time to time as the conditions of the market may change.

The practical difficulties connected with the execution of this plan are very great. It would make a complicated currency system instead of a simple one, and would offer government authorities a constant temptation to meddle with the currency to their own advantage and to the disadvantage of others. If an attempt were made to regulate these matters by international agreement, the friction attendant upon the operation of such agreements would inevitably be very great.

2. Large coinage of silver by a number of nations to supplement any deficiency in the gold supply, the issue of such silver being limited by statute to an amount which would not drive gold wholly out of circulation.

This was practically the position of the United States from 1878 to 1893. Every nation does this to some extent by the use of subsidiary silver. The attempt to carry out the policy on a larger scale, as a means of keeping the volume of the world's currency large, subjects the nations that undertake it to dangers like those suffered by the United States under the Sherman Act. A commercial crisis may make an amount of silver coin which it is easy for a nation to carry during one year exceed-

---

[1] Besides the references at the beginning of the chapter, see F. W. Taussig's excellent little book on " The Silver Situation in the United States," New York, 1893.

ingly difficult to carry during the next. This liability is intensified by the creation of a number of contracts in which the commercial world nullifies the action of the government and uses the metal it wants, independently of legal tender clauses.

3. *Symmetallism,* under which the unit of currency would consist not of a certain weight of either metal, but of a certain weight of both metals combined. Instead of saying that a dollar should consist of 23.2 grains of gold *or* 371.25 grains of silver, we might say that it should consist of 11.6 grains of gold *and* 185.625 grains of silver. Of course the ratio of weight and valuation of the two metals might be wholly different from what it is in this illustration without altering the principle.

The advocates of this system, which has been independently suggested from several quarters, urge that it offers all the advantages of bimetallism while reducing its dangers to a minimum. The reply of the gold monometallist is that these advantages of bimetallism are not so great as to warrant us in exposing ourselves to even a fraction of its dangers ; that the artificial character of the system opens the door for abuse of government powers ; and that unless it were adopted by concurrent action of all the commercial nations of the world, it would give rise to fluctuations in exchange and complications in the fulfilment of international contracts which would more than neutralize any benefits which we might expect from it.

4. Free coinage of silver at the old ratio of 16 to 1, or even $15\frac{1}{2}$ to 1, regardless of what becomes of gold.

This is the policy urged by those who see the evils of contracted currency so clearly that they have no vision left for the much worse evils which would follow the adoption of some other plans. They attempt to correct a comparatively slight ill by an indefinitely worse one.

§ 248. If free silver coinage were adopted we should find ourselves using a currency different from that of the other

15

nations with which we deal. The currency of the United
States would be exposed to the full stress of any future
changes in the conditions of silver production. If its supplies were stopped, we alone should have to bear the contraction; if its supplies were increased the whole inflation
would come upon our markets.[1] As matters stand at
present, an increase of a supply of gold in one country
causes a momentarily higher price level in that country,
but this high price level makes it a good market to sell
in and a bad market to buy in. People bring goods from
abroad and take away gold. Prices adjust themselves
nearly to their normal level. If the world's increase in
gold coin has been so large that the whole effect cannot
be neutralized in this way, the change, such as it is, is
shared by the different trading countries alike, and does
not affect their commercial relations one with another,
either in the matter of imports and exports or in the more
important matter of interest payments. But if we used
a different currency from that which was accepted by the
nations of Europe, we could not dispose of a surplus except with great delay and inconvenience and after fluctuations in prices almost if not quite as great as those
to which we were liable in our time of irredeemable
paper money.

§ 249. Moreover, such a currency would not be universally acceptable even in our own country; and the contraction of credit which would result from its use would
outweigh any apparent gain from increase in the currency. No man can be compelled to lend against his will;
and if he is liable to be paid in unacceptable coin, he will
either refuse to lend or charge a high rate of interest.
Those who lay most stress on the injustice of the demonetization of silver overlook the fact that the saving on
interest payments to the borrowers of this country since

---

[1] We should have nominal help from a few silver-using countries, but their
demand for additional currency is so small as to be scarcely worth counting.

1873 has done much to counterbalance their loss on the appreciation of the principal. The borrowers have taken with one hand and given with the other; the low borrowing rate has been dependent on the acceptability of the terms of the loan.

§ 250. In the third place, the change would create a sudden alteration of the relative positions of debtor and creditor which would involve a disastrous violation of equity and give the future credit of the country a blow from which it would require years to recover. Its adoption would at once scale down all debts to much less than their present value. Our experience under the Sherman Act shows that free coinage on the part of the United States, or any single nation, could hardly be expected to raise the cost of a silver dollar to a point much higher than two-thirds of the cost of the present gold dollar. The resulting depreciation of the dollar would from its suddenness be infinitely worse than any gradual appreciation which has taken place during the last twenty years.

It is not a question whether it would have been more equitable to have had continuous free coinage of silver and let people adjust their contracts and interest rates accordingly, but whether we can properly scale down to a silver basis contracts which were made under the expectation that the country would be on a gold basis. Such a change once made would create a liability of similar changes in the future, and would make the negotiation of loans or of long-time contracts enormously difficult. Any apparent gain to the debtors would be much more than offset by the difficulty of borrowing capital in the future; a difficulty which could be avoided only by abandoning the use of a discredited currency and employing some other standard than the legal tender fixed by statute.

§ 251. Even greater dangers than those connected with

the free coinage of silver are involved in the proposal that
the government should undertake to furnish the people
the quantity of money that may be needed by the issue
of paper which is a legal tender.  Some of the plans for
this purpose arrange for the assumption of banking functions by the government; these are discussed in the next
chapter.   Others contemplate the direct issue of legal
tender notes without the pretense of a banking reserve.
Under each and every plan the existence of a currency
whose volume and purchasing power are regulated by
the discretion of the government exposes the people to
the most serious dangers.

Three motives combine to cause unwise and spasmodic
inflation of paper money of this kind :

1. A fiscal motive which leads governments to issue
such money as a means of paying expenses without taxation.

2. A constant pressure from the debtor classes, which
form a large and frequently a most influential element in
the body politic, for an increased volume of legal tender
money.

3. A general popularity of such issues among those who
look only at surface effects, and who observe a certain
temporary prosperity to which they give rise, without
foreseeing the inevitable reaction, or tracing it back to
its proper cause when it finally comes.

§ 252. Whatever momentary ease may be derived from
inflation proves to be dearly purchased.  If a government
resorts to this method as a ready means of settling current accounts, all persons who have dealings with the
government will make charges for future supplies at
prices high enough to cover the risk; or they may go so
far as to insist on payment in coin, which can only be
obtained by borrowing at a rate of interest much higher
than would have prevailed in the absence of inflation.
The history of the United States in the Civil War shows

how great was the real increase of debt due to the use of paper money. Such instances might be indefinitely multiplied. Events take the same course in the transactions of private debtors. To many of these debtors inflation may give momentary ease. If a man has commodities to sell and debts to pay, anything which increases the price of his goods makes it possible for him to pay a larger amount of debts with a given amount of products. But if he has no such products to sell, he is neither better nor worse off than he was before ; and if he wishes to contract new debts he suffers exceedingly from the change.

§ 253. The reason for this is not always apparent to a superficial observer. He thinks that he wants to borrow money, and that therefore if there is more money he will find it easier to get. In point of fact, he does not want to borrow money, but capital.[1] If he has land to improve, he wishes to invest a certain amount of capital in its development. If he has a factory to build, he wishes to buy bricks and mortar and machinery and put them into use. If the currency is inflated and the number of dollars increased, he will have to borrow more dollars in order to obtain the same amount of capital. If the currency of the country has increased fifty per cent, and the general level of prices has correspondingly risen, making it easier for the old debtors to pay their debts, the borrower who needs $1000 on the old basis will now have to borrow $1500. The demand for money will thus keep pace with the artificial increase of the supply. Meantime, the risk attendant upon lending money will have become very great, since a government which has once begun to inflate the currency will be liable to do it again. Some men will be unwilling to lend money at all and will insist on using it themselves; others will demand additional

---

[1] There is an exception in a panic or other similar emergency where people are seeking means of payment rather than means of investment. In such cases, issues of money may, for the moment, prevent interest from rising.

rates of interest as a means of insurance against possible loss from further depreciation of the currency. The timidity of those capitalists who are afraid to invest at all will enable those who actually do invest to demand and receive these high rates of interest. Instead of lightening the future burdens of the debtor classes, it will tend to increase them; for capitalists, if they lend at all in a country with "political money," will almost certainly over-insure themselves by demanding exorbitant interest rates. No usury law can stop this process without still further lessening the amount of capital available for borrowers, thereby hindering the development of the country in question.

§ 254. Meantime, any general stimulus to business, which shows itself as an immediate result of inflation, is rapidly exhausted. During the period when prices are rising, there is often great business activity, and products change hands rapidly. Everybody can make so much money by his sales that he does not enquire too closely into the purchasing power of the money thus received. Consequently the products on hand are quickly disposed of, and labor is actively employed to make new ones. The public enjoyment is large in proportion to the public capital because people spend freely and content themselves with a small real profit under the guise of a large apparent one. But when prices have ceased to rise, the illusory character of these profits makes itself felt. People find that their investments are not worth what was supposed. A reaction sets in which diminishes the utilization of the national capital even more conspicuously than the inflation increased it. An attempt may be made to stave off this reaction by further issues of currency; but there soon comes a time when these issues are discredited and when the reaction becomes more severe from the efforts which have been made to postpone it. The stimulus of inflation is like that of alcohol or opium ; the ensuing depression can be temporarily averted by increasing the dose, but at the expense of making the final collapse more ruinous.

§ 255. Under these circumstances, the proportion of legitimate transactions is diminished, and the amount of speculative or gambling transactions largely increased. Business becomes less of a certainty and more of a game. The whole country becomes poorer under conditions which prevent conservative borrowing and safe investment. Perhaps the greatest sufferers of all are the working classes. They accept gladly an increase in money wages, not noticing that the purchasing power of that money has decreased faster than its nominal amount has increased. An examination of statistics during the Civil War shows that under inconvertible paper currency, though the nominal wages of the workmen increased considerably, the amount they could purchase with a day's wages was decidedly reduced. And if the speculative activity under these circumstances sometimes causes the working force of the community to be more fully employed than it was before, it is followed by a reaction and a period of unemployment whose burdens more than counterbalance the transient gain.

Of all the scientific students of currency questions, there is no one who emphasizes the needs of the debtor classes as vigorously as General Walker ; and Walker does not hesitate to say that the man who, having reference exclusively to economic interests, advocates the scaling down of debts for the sake of encouraging trade and production, shows himself so ignorant of history as to be a wholly unfit adviser as to the present and the future.

# CHAPTER VIII.

## CREDIT.

C. F. Dunbar : "Chapters on the History and Theory of Banking." New York, 1892.

W. Bagehot : "Lombard Street, a Description of the Money Market." 7th ed., London, 1878.

G. J. Goschen : "The Theory of the Foreign Exchanges." 14th ed., London, 1890.

Those who wish to study the subject more thoroughly should acquaint themselves with the writings of Ricardo and with those of H. D. Macleod. Still more detailed are the six volumes of Tooke and Newmarch : " A History of Prices and of the State of the Circulation, 1792–1856." London, 1838–57.

§ 256. THE money which an individual uses in his business, though a necessary part of his capital, often seems like an unproductive one. If he can employ credit instead of cash as a means of making his payments, he has a correspondingly larger amount to spend in machinery and other permanent investments whose direct productive power is more obvious than that of money. What is true of an individual is at least equally true of a community. If capital is scarce, the community makes every effort to use credit instead of money, so as to avoid the necessity of employing any part of its capital for conducting exchanges. If the property of a certain town amounts to $100,000 and $20,000 of this must be used as a cash reserve in order to transact the business of the place securely, the inhabitants often try to avoid the use of the $20,000 in every way possible, so as to have the whole $100,000 to spend for things directly serviceable in production and consumption, instead of $80,000 only. In other words, they try to get along with just as little actual money as possible.

§ 257. It is sometimes thought that this is a sign of advancing civilization. We are told that people first pass through a *regime* of barter, where goods are exchanged for goods; then follows the use of money as a means of transfer; and this in turn, in the highest stages of industrial evolution, gives place to credit. This last statement is hardly warranted by the facts. The tendency of recent times seems to be pretty clearly in the direction of an increased use of cash in mercantile transactions. It is in semi-civilized countries like Turkey that we see the fullest operation of the credit system. It is doubtless true that highly organized communities do some things on credit which less advanced communities cannot do at all. But when such operations have once become established, the tendency is toward an increasing use of cash in their consummation; a practice which saves time, saves waste, and saves middlemen's profits. Experience shows that the apparent advantages from the use of credit are often outweighed by less obvious but more real advantages from not using it.

§ 258. The pressure to use little money and much credit makes itself felt in two distinct cases:

1. In very poor communities, where the obvious needs for consumption are great, money in the cash drawer seems an unnecessary luxury. People are apt to spend all they have, and trust to getting more when more is needed. In this way they overreach themselves. They leave too little for effective use as a medium of exchange. By spending every cent they possess, they hamper

production and exchange by constantly keeping their cash reserves at too low a figure; somewhat as the improvident operative, who spends every dollar before he has earned it, keeps himself constantly in the power of credit stores which charge him an unfairly high rate for his accommodation. In a community of this kind we find an inadequate supply of money, a very low level of prices for cash, a much higher level of credit prices, and a commercial system so uncertain and cumbersome as to prevent people from serving one another most effectively and from selling their products in outside markets at the best advantage.

2. Another cause of scant money supply is exemplified in communities of active producers. Such people spend their money, not for immediate personal consumption, but for various forms of capital which will tend to increase their wealth in the future. It is not because they are poor that they keep themselves scantily supplied with money, but because they hope to be rich by means of its investment. Where farms, railroads, factories, and other forms of productive enterprise seem to insure their owners a return of ten per cent, the temptation to use too much money in purchasing means of production and leave too little to serve as a medium of exchange is at times quite overwhelming. In such communities there is always an active attempt to develop a credit system which shall serve the place of money.

§ 259. The simplest means of accomplishing this result is the use of account books and offsets. If A purchases stoves of B, and B purchases coal of A, each transaction creates a debt. If A's purchases in the course of a year amount to $100 and B's purchases to $90, the debt can be settled by the payment of $10, and the use of money thus greatly lessened. But such a process is only available where two people are dealing with one another. If A sells to B, B to C, and C to A, a comparison of the

books and a system of offsets connected with it would involve so much time and uncertainty that it would probably be easier to pay in cash.

§ 260. The system of bank credits has been utilized
to meet this difficulty. Suppose that *A*, *B*, and *C* all have
deposits in the same bank. *A* owes *B* $100, *B* owes *C*
$90, *C* owes *A* $80. Instead of paying one another the
money, each gives his creditor an order or draft on the
bank for the amount of the debt. Such an order is known
as a check. When *B* receives *A*'s check he takes it to the
bank; and instead of collecting the money he has the
sum credited to his account. Against this credit of $100
we have to offset a debit of $90, which *B* has drawn from
his account to pay *C*, leaving him $10 better off than he
was before. *C* in like manner has a credit of $90 and a
debit of $80; while *A* has a credit of $80 against a debit
of $100, representing a net reduction of $20 in the value
of his deposits. All of these transactions can be settled
or " cleared " if the bank collects $20 from *A* and pays
$10 each to *B* and *C*. Transactions to the amount of
$270 would thus be effected by the use of $20 actual cash.
In many instances, even this small amount can be reduced.
*B* and *C* will leave their money on deposit instead of
calling for the cash from the bank; while *A* will make
good his deficit, not by an actual deposit of cash, but by
an excess of credits over drafts in the immediate future.
A balance against him to-day will be offset by a similar
balance in his favor to-morrow. The necessity for actual
payments of cash to or from the bank will be diminished,
if the accounts of different depositors are left to run from
month to month.

§ 261. If *A*, *B*, and *C* deal with different banks, the same
process of settling debts without the use of money is
effected through the agency of a clearing house. If *A*
has a deposit in the First National Bank, while *B* has a
deposit in the Second National Bank of the same place,

*A* pays *B* by giving him an order on the First National Bank, but *B* does not take it to that bank for collection ; he takes it to his own bank, and transfers to that bank by endorsement his title to the check, the bank meantime crediting him with a corresponding sum on his deposit account. This check, which was formerly an order from *A* to the First National Bank to pay $100 to *B*, is by this endorsement made an order to the First National Bank to pay $100 to the Second National Bank. In the course of the day each bank thus accumulates a large number of orders in its favor against other banks in the same place. These orders or credits are all sent to a clearing house, which does for the different banks the same work that the bank did for its individual customers in the case previously supposed. Any bank that has an excess of orders in its favor over the orders presented against it is credited with the surplus ; while any bank that has a balance in the other direction is debited with the deficiency. By paying these small differences to the clearing house the banks can settle their obligations to one another with very little use of actual cash. If the accounts, instead of being settled every day, are allowed to go on for a week or month, the proportion of cash payments to checks cleared becomes exceedingly small.

§ 262. For the successful operation of this system it is not necessary that the different banks should all be situated in the same place. Every large city acts as a clearing centre for the country banks in the districts around it. New York, in like manner, acts as a clearing centre for the whole of the United States, and London for the whole of England. If *X* in Albany wishes to pay a debt of $100 to *Y* in St. Paul, he sends a check on his own bank in Albany. This check is an order to the Albany Bank to pay $100 to *Y*. *Y* takes it to his bank in St. Paul, endorses it payable to the order of that bank, and receives the corresponding sum to the credit of his deposit account.

The St. Paul bank sends it for collection to a bank in New York with which it maintains a deposit, endorsing it to the order of the New York bank, and is credited with a corresponding sum on its deposit account in New York City. The New York bank sends it to the clearing house for collection from some other New York bank which acts as agent for the Albany bank on which the check is drawn, and with which the Albany bank is presumed to have a deposit account. In the New York clearing house it now appears in the form of an obligation from one New York bank to another. It is credited by the New York clearing house to the agent or depositary of the St. Paul bank, and debited to the agent or depositary of the Albany bank. The New York bank which is thus debited with the check deducts it from the deposit account of the bank in Albany; which, in its turn, on receipt of the check, deducts it from the account of its customer who originally signed it. In the New York clearing house, meantime, this check has gone in with a mass of other checks drawn in all parts of the country, and sent to all parts of the country, which in time reach New York in the form of claims of one New York bank on another. These claims are thus settled by the payment, to or from the New York clearing house, of insignificantly small sums of money representing the difference between the credits and debits of individual banks.

§ 263. It is assumed in describing this transaction that the right to receive a given sum of money commands the same price, whether the payment be made in St. Paul, in New York, or in Albany. This assumption is not always fulfilled. If a great many people want money in the West, while comparatively few want it in the East, there will be an excess of checks calling for payments in one direction, and a deficiency in the other. Some money will have to be shipped westward; and rights to receive money in St. Paul will be worth more than rights to corresponding sums in New York or Albany, by a difference which may equal the cost of such shipment. These differences show themselves in the quotations for " domestic exchange." The bank which makes a payment in St. Paul, where money is scarce, and receives a claim on New York, where money is plenty, must either deduct this difference or pocket the loss. If it is dealing with a regular depositor it will probably do the latter. A loss at one season is likely to be made up by a corresponding gain at another; and in any event the amount of such loss in domestic exchange is small as compared with the profit which the bank can make from a steady deposit account.

§ 264. In foreign exchange the case is different. The cost of shipment is greater, giving a wider margin of profit and loss; and the remittances are managed by houses which make them a direct source of income, instead of doing the work for nothing as a means of attracting deposit accounts.

The bullion value of a pound sterling is $4.86⅔; but the right to receive a pound sterling in London cannot always be bought or sold for that sum in New York. This will happen only when the payments which Americans wish to make in London are approximately equal in amount to those which Englishmen wish to make in New York. In that case the foreign exchange houses which have branches in both cities will sell drafts in each place payable by their branch in the other; and the money received from the sale of the drafts in one direction will furnish the sums needed for paying those in the other direction as fast as they are presented. The competition of different houses with one another will prevent them from doing much more than this; the profits of such remittances are made on a very narrow margin.

§ 265. If there are more payments to be made in London than in New York, the London houses will find that they are called on for much money, and will find it hard to sell drafts on New York with which to obtain the means of payment. Their cash reserves diminish just when they need them most. On the other hand, the New York houses find everybody desirous to buy drafts, which may prove a source of embarrassment at the London end of the transaction. They therefore raise the price of such drafts to $4.89 or thereabouts. It cannot go much higher than this, because two cents and a half covers the various items in the cost of shipping the gold— freight, insurance, etc.,—and a man desiring to pay a debt in London will therefore ship the specie rather than pay a rate much above $4.89.

If, on the other hand, there are more payments to be made in New York than in London, the New York houses are anxious to sell as many drafts as possible ; for they can thus obtain the means of fulfilling commercial engagements which their London houses can make with profit. To save the necessity of actual shipment of gold from London to New York, the New York houses will sell drafts as low as $4.83 ; the difference between this and $4.86⅔ representing the expense for freight, insurance, and loss of interest which they would incur by shipping the money. Exchange cannot go lower than this, for any further reduction would make it cheaper for the banking houses to meet their obligations by importing specie.

§ 266. The limits of variation in foreign exchange are largely affected by the rate of discount (interest on short-time commercial loans) [1] in the two countries. If the rate in New York is higher than in London, there will be a tendency to keep gold in New York for the sake of profit-

---

[1] If the interest on industrial investments (as distinct from commercial loans) is enough higher in New York than in London to overcome the disinclination of English capital to emigrate, we shall see a movement of goods from England to America which is paid for by securities—commercial bills in one direction being balanced by financial transactions which offset them.

able investment in short-time or demand loans instead of shipping it to London. Such a difference of interest rate will retard the movement of gold from New York to London when exchange is high, and accelerate the movement from London to New York when exchange is low. When a movement of gold from London seems imminent, an increase of the Bank of England rate of discount is sometimes made for the purpose of checking the anticipated outflow, and is usually successful in accomplishing its end.

§ 267. Besides selling drafts, the houses engaged in the business also *buy* exchange, advancing money in New York on bills that are to fall due in London sixty days hence, and *vice versa*, at a discount corresponding to the period which must elapse before collection. Besides the profit due to this discount, the foreign exchange houses may reap an advantage from foresight in predicting movements in exchange. For it may happen that the abundance of bills on London in New York to-day which causes them to be sold at a low rate will be followed by a reverse condition two months hence. In that case the collection of the sixty-day bill in London will give the banking house the money at just the right time and place, and put its resources where they are needed. Such anticipations of future wants, when correctly made, lessen the necessity for gold shipments and result in public convenience as well as in private profit. For, unless a country is a large producer of gold, an outflow of the metal at one season is very apt to be balanced by an inflow at another. The withdrawal of a large supply of money would tend to make prices lower than they were the year before. This would make the country a good market to sell in and a bad market to buy in. It would increase the exports and diminish the imports far more effectively than any tariff ever devised. People would take away goods and leave gold in their place until the old price level was reached.

If a foreign exchange house can foresee this prospective return of the metal and content itself with sending rights to money by mail instead of shipping the metal itself, it can save the public the loss involved in the double movement of money back and forth.

§ 268. It is not necessary that we should receive the money back from the same country to which we send it. If we ship gold to England and England ships it to Brazil, Brazil may ship it back to the United States. And similarly, if we remain indebted to England and England remains indebted to Brazil on the current exchange account, the whole affair will settle itself without movement of money if Brazil becomes indebted to the United States. The competition of arbitrage brokers (§ 117) with one another enables the most roundabout transactions to be adjusted (usually through the medium of London as a clearing house) at a very small margin of expense, and with comparatively little shipment of specie.

§ 269. The credit system as thus developed affords two quite distinct advantages to the public. In the first place it furnishes a convenient method of payment, which avoids the risk attendant on remittances of specie or even of government notes. In the second place it saves the wear and tear incident to the use of metallic money; and more important still, it saves the interest on the capital which would be represented by a large mass of unnecessary coin. It is also attended with profit to the bankers, independent of the commissions which they may charge on exchange. A bank knows that all the people who have the right to draw checks upon it will not do so in a single day, and that even if checks are drawn by a great many of them, others will make deposits which will balance the losses. If every bank had to keep a reserve of coin equal to the total amount of checks that might be drawn upon it, the check and clearing-house system would save the public the trouble of handling money,

16

but would not save interest on idle capital or give any profit to the bank. But no bank finds it necessary to keep a reserve of one hundred per cent of all its liabilities. Experience proves that a bank which keeps a cash reserve equal to one-third, or even to one-fourth of its deposits, is prepared for all contingencies that are likely to arise.[1]

§ 270. The proper amount of this reserve will vary according to the circumstances of the bank. A savings bank (§ 154) can work with a very small amount of cash. It does not encourage its depositors to draw drafts upon it and use them as means of remittance. In fact, most savings banks expressly reserve the right to refuse payment of such drafts for a considerable length of time. The savings bank is essentially a means of investment rather than of convenience in payment or economy of currency. It attracts funds from depositors by the offer of interest. It invests a large proportion of those funds in long-time loans, chiefly on real estate, and it keeps on hand only a sufficient amount of cash or easily collectible assets to meet a few drafts from those persons who wish to reduce their deposit accounts. But a commercial bank of the modern type encourages its depositors to draw checks upon it, and gives them every conceivable facility for using such checks as a means of remittance of money. It must therefore hold a larger reserve of cash to meet such drafts; and its investments, instead of being of a permanent character like those of a savings bank, are put into assets that will mature quickly, so that in case of any sudden call on its funds in excess of the ordinary cash reserve it can at once secure the means to meet all demands. There is no standard proportion between reserves

---

[1] The theory of modern banking was apparently first formulated by Alexander Hamilton. It is most fully developed in the works of H. D. MacLeod, especially his "Theory and Practice of Banking," London, 1856.

and liabilities. Everything depends on the situation of the bank and the kind of business that it is doing. City banks, as a rule, need a larger reserve than country banks. Account is taken of this difference in the United States National Banking Law, which requires the banks of the larger cities to keep a reserve of twenty-five per cent on all liabilities, while those in the rest of the country are only required to keep one of fifteen per cent. In places where a large reserve is kept, the banks as a rule do not pay interest on deposits. They cannot afford to do it. Besides, the very existence of a large reserve shows that they are constantly called upon to furnish facilities to their depositors in the payment of debts by check. This consideration is sufficient to attract depositors without the offer of interest. The country banks, on the other hand, and the loan and trust companies—which are something intermediate between true banks and savings banks [1] —frequently offer a small rate of interest on deposits of any considerable amount and duration.

§ 271. In any good banking system, most of the deposits used as a means of payment by check are founded on the transactions which create the necessity for such payment; so that the credit given is made proportionate to the occasion for its use. A bank invests its capital to a very great extent in *commercial paper*. If a retailer wishes to deal in stoves and has not at the moment the money with which to buy those stoves from the manufacturer, he can pay for them by accepting a bill due at ninety days from the date of the purchase. The manufacturer takes the bill to the bank, where he endorses it— that is to say, guarantees that he will make it good to

---

[1] In the original conception, a trust company should not receive deposits subject to check, but should chiefly occupy itself with handling trust funds, in which case it can make long-time investments like those of a savings bank; but most of the large American companies of this kind hold deposits subject to check, discount a considerable amount of commercial paper, and perform all the important functions of a bank except that of note issue.

the bank if the dealer does not—and then has it *discounted.* [1] In this transaction the bank credits him with the face value of the bill less ninety days' interest. If the discount rate is six per cent and the bill is accepted for $1,000, the bank deducts three months' interest at six per cent, $15, and credits the manufacturer with $985. Theoretically, the manufacturer can have this money given to him in cash at once; but if he did this without some exceptional reason the bank would not be likely to discount bills for him in the future. He leaves it on deposit, drawing checks against his account as he has need of funds. The bank is reasonably sure that the total amount of checks drawn in a single day will form but a small fraction of its whole deposits. It therefore keeps but $200 of the $985 as reserve, and can use the balance as a means of discounting other bills. In due time the manufacturer's account is exhausted; but at the end of three months when the bill matures, the bank will receive $1,000. This gives the bank a profit on the transaction which compensates it for the trouble and risk involved, and for the loss of interest on the comparatively small reserve which it has been compelled to maintain.

§ 272. Accepted bills are not the only kind of security on which a bank makes advances; but it is desirable that the bulk of the paper discounted should be of this nature, if not of this form. It should represent a need of money for current transactions on which the profit is to be realized in a comparatively short space of time. Whenever there is a pretense of this without the reality there is a decided danger to the bank. When parties are found to be drawing what is known as accommodation paper,—

---

[1] This process is sometimes accomplished through the agency of a *bill broker*, who borrows a large part of his capital from the banks and buys bills created by transactions which he watches more closely than the board of bank directors finds it possible to do. By charging his customers a slightly higher rate of discount than the bank charges him, he can make a small margin of profit on such operations.

accepted bills on the basis of fictitious transactions instead of actual ones,—well managed banks generally refuse to have further dealings with them.

§ 273. The public service rendered by the banking system bears some analogy to that of the ordinary commercial speculator. The speculator sells products which he does not now have, on the carefully considered expectation of obtaining them in the future. He thus enables the existing stock of such products in the community to be more effectively utilized (§ 119). In like manner the banker agrees to deliver more money than he has in hand, with the expectation of obtaining such money to advantage when he needs it. He thus allows the stock of money in the community to be more fully utilized, and makes it unnecessary to carry so large an idle reserve. The bank also performs a work of insurance, though of somewhat different character from that done by the speculator. It may be said to insure credit. If it discounts a three months' note and allows the maker to draw checks upon the sum with which it credits him, it protects the public, which accepts such checks, from the risk of subsequent insolvency on the part of the maker. It is because this insurance is effective that the public will accept checks where it will not accept promissory notes.

The use of bank deposits as means of current payment gives *elasticity* to the currency. To see what this means, let us consider the case of a nation doing its business without bank checks. If progress in the arts, or immigration, or an unusually good harvest creates a necessity for an increased number of transactions, a scarcity of specie will probably ensue. A larger volume of business cannot readily be done with the old amount of money, unless means are devised to make it circulate more rapidly. In default of such means prices will fall ; and although this fall in prices will probably work its own cure by bringing in specie from other communities (§ 222), the process will be attended with some hardship. But if these additional transactions furnish a basis for the discount of bills and increase of bank deposits, they can be settled by drawing checks with comparatively little use of money. The price level will thus remain stable, the need for additional gold will be reduced to a minimum, and the industrial growth of the community can go on unhindered.

§ 274. In looking at the advantages of this method of payment, we must not lose sight of its dangers. The discounts of the banks may not merely keep pace with the growth of business, but exceed it. Credit may be employed, not as a supplement to money, but as a substitute for it.[1] If it becomes easy to obtain the accommodation

---

[1] The view here advanced is intermediate between those of Walker and of Mill. Walker holds that checks have very little effect on the general price level; Mill thinks that they have substantially the same effect as money and exactly the same effect as bank notes.

Walker's position is as follows : The general level of prices is determined by the supply and demand of the *medium of exchange*—either coin or notes which circulate from hand to hand. On the price level thus created, there are a number of credit payments which cancel obligations without the use of money ; but the credit instruments used for this purpose originate in the transactions to be settled, and disappear when the business which occasions their use is finished. Therefore checks are supplementary instruments of trade, which do not affect the money supply or demand and can have no influence on prices. (Walker counts bank *notes* as actual money.)

Walker seems to overlook the fact that there are a great many transactions for which money or checks can be used indiscriminately ; transactions which people will settle by coin if they cannot use bank credit, but which will be paid by checks when public confidence is good and bank accommodation ample. The use of credit for this purpose has the effect of diminishing the demand for money.

Mill apparently goes too far in the other direction. Instead of treating checks as a partial substitute for money, he reasons as though they were a *universal* substitute. Because an individual can use cash or credit indiscriminately, he argues that a nation can do the same. This inference is not fairly warranted. The individual can convert his credit into cash, with little or no loss, because commercial credit is backed by a considerable cash reserve in the banks, and no single depositor or noteholder has large enough credits to reduce that cash reserve very seriously by his personal demands upon it. He can therefore treat cash and credit as equivalent. But if too

at the banks, a large number of transactions will be made on credit. The checks which result from the creation of such bank credit furnish a medium of exchange almost as efficient as money. The over-abundance of a medium of exchange in this form will make it easier to get money than it was before. This will tend to raise prices. Where this process is once begun it goes on by its own momentum. When stoves are worth $10 apiece, a bill for one hundred stoves can be made the basis of a bank credit of only $1,000. But if the use of bank credit raises the general price level, stoves may soon be sold for $12 instead of $10; in which case the next lot of stoves will be made the basis for a credit of $1,200 instead of $1,000. This concurrent increase of credits and prices may continue until the liabilities of the banks become disproportionate to their reserves. When the public perceives this there is a sudden shock to confidence and a withdrawal of accommodation which causes far greater distress than would have resulted had the facilities of payment by credit been less elastic at the outset.

§ 275. This danger is very much greater when bank credit takes the form of notes instead of checks.

We have thus far assumed that when a bank discounts a bill it gives as consideration a credit or deposit account against which checks can be drawn. The bank may, however, with equal advantage to itself, pay out over its counter a corresponding amount of notes. In these notes the bank agrees to pay to the bearer on demand a sum of money corresponding to the face value of the note. From the standpoint of the bank, a note is exactly like a

many individuals try to do this at the same time, the conversion is often attended with difficulty and loss. The domain within which the two things can be used interchangeably is after all a rather narrow one ; and an enlargement of this domain can be effected only by a rather slow change of commercial habits. Therefore, while bank credits have the same *kind* of effect on prices as do additional issues of money, it will hardly do to assert that they have the *same* effect.

deposit account. $985 of notes imposes on the bank precisely the same obligation as $985 of deposits; namely, the obligation to pay that amount of coin whenever the evidence of the right to receive it is presented. But upon the public the note may have a very different effect from the deposit account. Credit given in the form of a deposit account is exhausted in a short time, because the checks drawn against it soon come back to a bank for redemption. But credit in the form of notes may remain outstanding for an indefinite period. These notes may change hands a thousand times before returning to the bank. Where a check settles a single transaction, a bank note of the same value may settle a very large number.

There are also practical limitations to the undue expansion of credit in the form of deposits which are by no means equally effective in case of notes. If a bank is tempted to increase its deposit accounts more than the business of the community warrants, and tries proportionately to augment its coin reserve, this process soon finds a natural limit from the difficulty of getting coin. The people themselves, outside of the banks, need to use a certain amount of coin. If the banks try to encroach on this amount for their own purposes, a stringency makes itself felt. But if the banks are increasing their note issues instead of their deposit accounts the people will use these notes as a reserve in their pocket-books and let the banks withdraw coin from actual circulation without observation on the part of the public. All of these things make bank notes a more dangerous medium of inflation than bank checks, even if a proper reserve is maintained. This danger is greatly enhanced by the probability, almost amounting to a certainty, that in the absence of special legislation the proper reserve will *not* be maintained. In a new country, where money is wanted, the issuing of notes is regarded as a patriotic function, which promotes the growth of the region and renders it independent of the money lenders of older communities. The presentation of bank notes for redemption, which would compel the banks to keep a proper reserve, is condemned by an unwise public sentiment as tending to injure the growth of local trade. The bank officials are thus actively encouraged to do business with an inadequate supply of cash. The worst abuses of the bank note system have been made with the connivance, if not with the active participation, of the communities in which they were carried out.

§ 276. If prices begin to increase, from any cause whatsoever, this increase furnishes a ground for an enlarged issue of notes on the same physical volume of business. This goes on until prices and currency both become so inflated that people see the danger, and suddenly refuse to accept the notes as the equivalent of money. If the note issue is very large in proportion to the coin available, such a change of sentiment may come at almost any moment. A bank failure is sure to precipitate it; a large commercial failure not infrequently has the same result. When prices have risen on the basis of an artificially increased amount of the medium of exchange, a great many people make contracts which can only be fulfilled, and plans which can only be successfully carried out, on the assumption of continued public confidence— not to say over-confidence. Under such circumstances, the whole industrial community lives in daily peril from every kind of event which can shake this confidence. Even a slight shock to credit may result in a severe commercial crisis, with a long list of failures, and a long period of industrial prostration.

§ 277. Of course, bank note inflation does not always lead to such serious disaster. It may be stopped before the crisis is reached. If it is purely local in its extent, it is almost certain to work its own cure. If the banks of a single locality put out an unusually large number of notes in proportion to the wants of trade, coin is driven to other localities so rapidly that people take warning at once. Even if a whole country is flooded with increased bank note issues, the automatic movement of money to other countries, described in the last chapter, may give the alarm in time to prevent more serious evils. But where there is no such outlet, and where, as not infrequently happens, the whole world is more or less involved in simultaneous inflation, there is no marked change in the movement of coin from one country to another, and no warning is given until it is too late to profit by it. We find that the great commercial crises of the present century have been preceded by periods of inflation which have simultaneously involved a large part of the civilized world.

§ 278. No method of organization of the banking system has been devised which will avoid these evils. Local banks and centralized banks have alike been subject to them. It is urged by the advocates of local banks that they will know what are the needs of their customers ; that they will issue just enough currency to meet these needs ; that this currency will only circulate in a region for which it is specially destined ; and that when money becomes redundant in that region, the evil will work its own cure. This argument depends for its force upon the assumption that the local banks of different regions will choose different times for increasing their issues. As a matter of fact, there is every probability that they will do it at the same time in a large number of regions. Under such circumstances each community will be able to float an increasing volume of money as long as confidence continues. The local character of the currency may prove an actual disadvantage in more ways than one. As it does not go far from home, it will circulate altogether too freely among people who have a patriotic pride in not presenting it for redemption. In the old days of state bank issues, the customer who tested the solvency of a bank by presenting its notes for redemption was looked upon in the light of a public enemy. If he wanted coin for foreign travel or any purpose for which the local bank issues were unavailable, he was obliged to explain his reasons in order not to become an object of suspicion. These disadvantages, combined with those which arise from the absence of any power of control on the part of the central government, usually outweigh the merits claimed for local banks of issue.

§ 279. Centralized control of banking and bank note issues has worked somewhat better; yet it has by no means avoided the evils and dangers which have been described. The United States banks of 1791 and 1816 had a checkered career, and did much to heighten speculative activity at the very times when restriction of such activity was most needed. Even the Bank of England has more than once been open to a similar criticism. Experience proves that the mere existence of centralized organization is not enough to prevent abuse unless strict legislative limits are placed on the issue of bank notes.

§ 280. The actual choice between local and centralized banking has usually been determined by political considerations rather than by economic ones. When a government has needed the help of a strong banking house, in order to borrow money or perform other necessary financial operations, it has given special privileges to any bank or group of banks that would help it in this matter, and has correspondingly restricted all bankers outside of such an association. When, however, the immediate financial need is over and the local demands for increased banking privileges prove strong, the government has usually been unable to resist the pressure of such local demands, and has annulled or modified the exclusive privileges given in times of financial stress. Only after long experience of the evils of both systems have nations learned to develop

well defined lines of legislative policy which are guided
by far-sighted commercial intelligence rather than by the
pressure of political influence.

§ 281. The Bank of England was established in 1694.
It grew out of the necessity of the English government
for a loan of £1,200,000. In 1708 it was given an important monopoly by an act prohibiting companies of more
than six persons, with the exception of the Bank of England, from issuing notes or bills of credit. This restriction,
however, did not extend to Scotland or Ireland. In the
latter country especially, bank note issues of large amount
were put forth by irresponsible parties. Nor did the
restriction of 1708 suffice to prevent the issue of notes by
country banks in England. At the close of the last century, the English bank note currency was so inflated that
a crisis took place in 1792 and 1793, and a suspension of
specie payments in 1797 which lasted for twenty-four
years. In spite of the experience of this period, the
directors of the Bank of England made no efficient
attempts to check the speculation of the years 1824
and 1825. In September of the latter year there was
a severe commercial crisis, which at one time threatened
to reduce the country to a state of barter. Amid the
efforts to prevent the recurrence of such evils there was a
temporary movement in favor of decentralized banking;
but it accomplished very little. No radical reform was
effected until Sir Robert Peel's Act of 1844. By this
Act discretionary power over the issues of paper money
was taken out of the hands of English bank authorities. The country banks were absolutely forbidden to
increase the small circulation which they had outstanding at the time of the passage of the Act. The Bank
of England was allowed to issue £14,000,000 (afterwards
increased to £16,000,000 to take the place of circulation
surrendered by some of the country banks), on the basis
of securities, chiefly British Public Funds, which it held

in its coffers. Every note beyond this was to be based on an equal amount of coin or bullion placed in the hands of the bank. If the Bank of England has £28,000,000 of notes outstanding, it indicates that there are £12,000,000 of coin or bullion on deposit in the bank. It is not allowed to vary its note issue on the basis of the wants of trade, real or supposed. Changes in the amount of notes outstanding are based on equivalent changes in the amount of coin deposited. To all intents and purposes the Bank of England notes are of the nature of gold certificates (§ 214). The Act of 1844 makes the volume of currency in Great Britain depend on movements of coin or bullion, and not on the discretion of bank authorities in issuing notes.

This Act was vehemently criticised at the time of its passage. Its opponents urged that a currency which was secured by proper banking reserves [1] would be equally convertible with that contemplated by Peel's Act and much more elastic. This criticism found considerable confirmation in England's experience during the crises of 1847, 1857, and 1866. On two of these occasions the restriction on the note issues of the Bank of England was suspended by authority of Parliament, and a discretionary power was given which it had been the purpose of the Act of 1844 to take away. In the third, measures were taken by bank authorities which were based on the probability of such parliamentary action. In all these cases the bank issued notes more freely than was consistent with the operation of the Act of 1844, thereby relieving commercial stringency and preventing great public calamities. Yet this fact, as we shall presently see, does not prove that the Act was useless or undesirable.

§ 282. In Scotland there was no such monopoly of note

---

[1] Notes thus protected are said to be secured on the "banking principle," while notes which can only be issued on an actual deposit of coin are protected by what is known as the "currency principle."

issue. Banks were allowed discretion to advance notes to individual borrowers. The convertibility of the note and the solvency of the bank were thought sufficient safeguards to prevent the danger of over-issue. The system seems to have worked well; but the Act of 1844 was applied to Scotland as well as to England and took away the rights of the banks to make uncovered issues beyond the amount then outstanding. The principle of the old Scotch system is carried out in Canada at the present day. The Canadian banks are allowed to issue notes up to the limit of their capital. Every facility is afforded the note holder to present his notes for redemption; and it is believed that this facility of redemption furnishes an adequate safeguard against inflation.

§ 283. The Bank of France was established at the beginning of this century. Down to 1848 it shared the right of note issue with certain departmental banks. By laws passed in that year these banks were consolidated with the Bank of France, which has since had a monopoly of the note issues in that country; a power which it has on the whole exercised with great wisdom. During much of its history there has been no statutory limit to its note issue; the existing limit is about $800,000,000.[1]

§ 284. Prior to the consolidation of the German Empire, the banks of that country were necessarily local, and their issues could circulate in comparatively small districts only. The establishment of an imperial bank in 1875 was dictated by considerations of national policy. The local bank note issues were not stopped, but are subjected to strict control, and the imperial bank has charge of nearly two-thirds of the note circulation of the empire. One-third of the note issue must be protected by a coin reserve. If the difference between the issue and the reserve exceeds $70,000,000,[2] an annual tax of five per cent is levied upon the excess. More reliance seems to be placed

---

[1] 4,000,000,000 francs.  [2] 296,000,000 marks.

on general supervision of the management of the affairs of the bank, and less on specific restrictions affecting the reserve or the note issue, than is the case in England or the United States.

§ 285. The first United States bank was established in 1791, chiefly for the purpose of assisting the government in its financial operations. Its charter expired in 1811; but in 1816 a second bank was organized on a similar plan and with the same general objects. The formation of the United States bank simply established an accredited fiscal agent of the government; it did not prevent note issues by state banks. These issues were large in amount and badly secured. The charter of the second United States bank, owing to the opposition of President Jackson, expired in 1836, but it continued business under the laws of the State of Pennsylvania, and took an unenviable part in the speculations which led to the commercial crisis immediately following. No United States bank was afterward established; but the issue of state bank notes, usually with inadequate supervision, continued until the Civil War.

§ 286. The first improvement in the state bank system originated in Massachusetts, where a number of banks established a common agency for the redemption of notes, with a view to the prevention of irresponsible issues. A further reform was made in New York in 1838, by a law which compelled the banks to hold United States or state securities, or real-estate mortgages, of an amount equal to the value of the notes issued, and to deposit them with the State Treasurer as a pledge for the ultimate redemption of those notes.[1] As long as the securities

---

[1] This feature of the New York law, which also lies at the basis of the National Bank law, is known as the the "safety-fund system." The plan of redemption used in Massachusetts is commonly designated as the "Suffolk system" from the name of the bank which acted as a general redemption agency.

thus deposited were worth what they purported to be, the ultimate soundness of the notes was secured.

§ 287. In the years 1863 and 1864, under stress of the Civil War, it became desirable to place large government loans upon the market. With this end in view, special facilities for note issue under national authority were offered to banks that would subscribe to United States bonds; and in 1865 all note issues under any other authority were virtually prohibited by a tax of ten per cent on the use of State bank notes. To avoid the imposition of this tax upon their note issues, banks were compelled to surrender their state charters and accept in their place charters under the National Bank Act of 1864. Under this Act they were to invest one-third of their capital in United States bonds, to be deposited in the Treasury. Besides receiving interest on these bonds as it became due, they were given the right to issue notes to the amount of 90 per cent of the face value of the bonds —unless the bonds should depreciate, in which case the amount of notes was to be correspondingly reduced. Provision was also made for the redemption of national bank notes by the agents of the government, in conformity with the Massachusetts system already described.

This plan made it certain that the national bank notes would be fully as good as the United States bonds on which they were based. Inasmuch as these bonds have always commanded a premium, there has never been any doubt as to the soundness of the currency issued under this system. With regard to its volume there have been many complaints. For some years the banks were anxious to increase their circulation, and a limitation on the total amount which they were allowed to keep outstanding was considered a hardship. After 1880, on the other hand, the price of the United States bonds became so high as to render the maintenance of the circulation unprofitable, and a large amount was surrendered, reducing the total volume of the bank note issues to a figure less than half of that which the law would have allowed.[1]

§ 288. It is urged, both against the English and American systems, that they are based on no philosophical or economic principle. Each of them limits the issue of bank notes by a somewhat arbitrary line. Instead of furnishing an elastic currency that will expand or contract with the demands of business, they furnish a highly inelastic one. In England there is no available means of increasing the circulation except by suspending the Act of 1844. It has been pointedly said that the English Bank Act is of use only when it is rendered inoperative. What is done in England by suspension of the Bank Act is done in America by the issue of clearing house loan certificates[2] in virtual disregard of the National Banking Law. Each of these things represents a breach of the statutory principle, justified only by a public emergency.

§ 289. Yet the necessity of thus suspending limitations in an emergency does not prove that the limitations themselves are unwise. The most important function of bank note issues, in a country which enjoys the benefits of the check and clearing house system, is to provide a reserve for emergencies. If we limit note issues in ordinary times we have a reserve power upon which we can fall back in extraordinary times. The objection to unlimited bank note issues is that they leave us no such reserve to fall back

---

[1] The effect of this reduction was to leave room for other forms of currency to take the place of bank note issues thus withdrawn from circulation.

[2] In times of great stringency the New York Clearing House Association has allowed its members to deposit securities with its loan committee and receive in return "Clearing House Loan Certificates" for 75 per cent. of their par value. These certificates are accepted in lieu of cash in payment of balances at the Clearing House, and set a corresponding amount of actual cash free for general business purposes. In the crisis of 1893 other clearing houses resorted to this measure. The whole subject is admirably handled by Horace White, *Money and Banking*, pp. 244-248.

upon. If the currency is made thoroughly elastic in years of confidence, there is no power of stretching it further in days of doubt. If the check system alone has been over-strained, a bank that has the power to issue additional notes can ease public confidence. But if the public demand for the use of notes as well as checks has been supplied to the utmost, we have no further reserve at our disposal. For this reason an unphilosophical limit to note issues is far better than no limit at all. People may complain that the currency does not adapt itself to the need of a certain place or a certain time ; but on ordinary occasions this defect may be made up by an extension of the use of checks. At such times the receiver of a check can readily satisfy himself whether the man who makes payments in this form is financially solvent or not. If he is in danger of failure, there will be special reasons which make such danger imminent, and against whose operation the commercial community can protect itself. But in extraordinary times of stringency, any man is liable to fail ; no man can be sure that his checks will be received. It is in such emergencies that notes must be substituted for checks in order to prevent an unlimited stringency and a disastrous panic. On these occasions additional issues of bank notes are not merely a public convenience, but a public necessity. The advantages of having such a reserve power at command during one month out of every fifty far outweighs the very slight disadvantage of being unable to substitute notes for checks during the other forty-nine. To prevent the recurrence of experiences like those of 1825 in England or 1857 in the United States, the important thing is to have a limit on note issue, even if it be an arbitrary one, and to have it low enough. Whether it should be as stringently drawn as in England, where to all intents and purposes a bank note is simply a certificate of deposit of gold, or whether we should allow the somewhat wider liberty in use in the United States, is open to question. Probably it does not make so much difference with business as might appear on the surface. England has fewer bank notes, but this does not cause a less proportion of her business to be done on credit. Checks are substituted for notes, and the proportion of transactions settled by handling of actual coin or coin certificates is even smaller in England that in the United States. Paradoxical as it may appear, the all-important thing is that the bank note currency should *not* meet the wants of business in ordinary times; that it should not be sufficiently elastic at such times as to be unable to take additional strain in times of emergency.[1]

§ 290. If, as experience shows, the right of note issue is a dangerous power to place in private hands, some people think that the best way to avoid this danger is by having the government take that power, instead of trying to restrict somebody else in its exercise.

Those who urge this view of the matter say that the government by making its own note issues would combine protection to the people with profit to the treasury. A bank, by keeping a reserve of thirty per cent of its outstanding notes, earns interest on the other seventy per cent without furnishing any corresponding amount of capital. Why should not the government avail itself of this chance of getting something for nothing? *A fortiori,* if the bank has been allowed to secure its note issues by the purchase and deposit of government bonds and thus

---

[1] Political reasons may sometimes make it wise to allow freer issues of bank notes than can be defended on strictly economic grounds. The advantages of bank issues over government issues are so great that it may become advisable to increase the volume of the former as a means of forestalling a demand for the latter. In these circumstances there is much to be said in favor of any well-considered plan by which the banks can issue, under public supervision, notes based on securities of unquestioned value ; paying a tax on their circulation sufficient to furnish a fund which will protect the community against loss to the note-holders from the mismanagement of any individual bank.

earn double interest on the securities and on the notes outstanding, why should not the government appropriate this profit to itself instead of giving such a premium to the banks?

§ 291. To these points it may be answered, first, that much of the profit to the banks from such transactions is apparent rather than real. The best proof of this is found in the fact that so many of the national banks of the United States have surrendered their circulation, finding that they could employ their capital more profitably in discount and deposit business than in the purchase of government securities and the issue of notes. The expense of the operations connected with the business of note issue is apt to eat up the alleged double profits. In the second place, if the government should take this business out of the hands of the banks, the apparent profit that it would derive from such transactions would be outweighed by certain indirect losses. The existence of a large body of outstanding notes, guaranteed by the government and secured only by a fractional reserve, involves a loss to the credit of the government and an increase in the rate of interest which it must pay on all other parts of its national debt. If the government took two hundred million dollars of circulation out of the hands of the national banks and held a reserve of sixty million to protect it, it would earn interest at (say) five per cent on one hundred and forty million dollars, or seven million a year. If, however, as a result of this operation, the rate of interest on the national debt in general were one per cent. higher than would otherwise be the case (and this is not an improbable supposition), there would be a loss of one per cent on a thousand million dollars. This loss of ten million would outweigh the gain of seven million connected with the assumption of the banking business by the government, and leave a deficit of three million. The exceedingly low rate of interest on the loans to the English government is largely connected with the fact that that government does not guarantee any paper currency on the banking principle, directly or indirectly. England's gain from this source almost certainly outweighs any loss of possible interest which might be earned by floating the currency on a fractional reserve. If this is true at ordinary times, it is most conspicuously true in emergencies. When the revenues of the government are deficient in amount, the existence of a circulation guaranteed by the treasury and protected only by a fractional reserve constitutes a public danger. This is the time when people will want coin instead of notes, and it is just the time when the government cannot give them the coin in exchange for the notes without resorting to a loan on more or less unfavorable terms. If the government finds itself face to face with a war instead of a commercial crisis, these difficulties are multiplied. Every dollar of notes over and above the stock of coin or bullion available for their redemption is under such circumstances a source of weakness to the government when it most needs strengthening. If it has an accumulated supply of cash assets, it can tide over the initial stages of the war, until advantageous arrangements have been made for placing loans and obtaining other means of meeting the extraordinary expenses. But if instead of such a reserve there is an absolute deficiency and an excess of liabilities over assets, the finances are embarrassed from the very outset, and the war burdens indefinitely increased.

§ 292. Side by side with the fiscal reasons why the government should not attempt to carry on the work of bank note issue for itself, there are equally important commercial ones. The treasury department is not well situated for doing a banking business. It has no means of getting currency into circulation where it is wanted, or of retiring it when it is no longer wanted. A bank every day handles commercial bills and other evidences of the need of money. Its assets are of such a kind that they can be used either for putting currency into circulation or withdrawing it from circulation. The assets of the government are of a totally different character. They furnish no indication of the volume of currency needed. If the government attempts to issue notes on the basis of its own property or the property of the country, quick inflation is the result. The limit of power of the treasury to maintain specie payment for such notes is soon reached. When the government comes to that limit, the temptation to suspend specie payments and declare the notes legal tender is enormous. If this is once done there is no limit to the issue of more notes, but a very speedy restriction of their commercial utility. The *assignats* of the French revolutionary government were avowedly secured by the value of confiscated lands which it held. But this set no limit to their inflation. To avoid over-issues of notes, they must be based, not on some form of property whose value is measured in money, but on something which can be used as money itself and which will at once be taken out of the hands of the government when people begin to distrust the value of government promises.

§ 293. Proposals are occasionally made that the United States government should issue notes on the basis of products entrusted to its hands ; the notes to be retired as soon as the products are withdrawn, and the proportion of such notes to the value of the product deposited to be kept low enough to ensure the government against loss and stimulate the owner to dispose of his goods as soon as he conveniently can. The Farmers' Alliance lays great stress on a project of this kind. Such a plan, if carefully carried out, would do very little good or harm. But the chance of its being carefully carried out is not one in a thousand. The motive which lies back of its advocacy is the desire to raise prices, coupled with the belief that prices are being unduly depressed by combinations of capitalists who hold money back. It is not the temporary difficulty of getting money, but the permanent difficulty of getting more money than consumers are willing to pay, which constitutes the chief cause of demand for government intervention. If safe action on the part of the government does not make the currency larger than it is with safe action on the part of the banks, the whole reason for the scheme will fall to the ground. In itself, it would be neither good nor bad. But it would involve the existence of a system of governmental machinery which with slight changes in the law could be made to inflate the currency under the guise of promoting credit; and this would be a perpetual menace to the commercial stability of a country which adopted it.

# CHAPTER IX.

## PROFITS.

Competition among Investors—The Rate of Interest—Causes of Variation
—Economic Rent—Net Profits and Losses—Commercial Crises.

E. v. Boehm-Bawerk : "Capital and Interest," "The Positive Theory of
Capital." (Innsbruck, 1884, 1889.) Translated by W. Smart. London,
1890, 1891.

§ 294. IF only one capitalist is engaged in the production of an article, any labor-saving improvement which he
may apply will give him an obvious advantage. He will
sell his product at a high rate, and pay for his labor at a
low rate. The difference between the two, which constitutes his gross profit, may be very large.

But the amount of this profit invites other competitors
to enter the field. They will increase the supply of the
product, and thereby drive prices down ; they will increase
the demand for labor, and thus tend to force wages up.
This process will continue as long as the excess of price
above wages furnishes a sufficient motive to attract capital ; in other words, as long as the market price is above
the normal price.

§ 295. Let *Oa* represent the minimum price [1] which any

---

[1] This figure differs from those in chapters iii and iv, in having the axes
reversed, so that horizontal lines represent quantities and vertical lines represent prices. This has been done because it is customary in mathematical
diagrams to represent causes by horizontal lines and effects by vertical ones.
In chapter iii we treated price variations as the causes and showed their
effects on quantities produced and consumed. Here we treat the quantities
produced and consumed as the causes which determine the price that can be
charged. Hence the reversal of axes.

laborer is willing to accept for his services in producing an article, and *Ob* the maximum price which any consumer is willing to pay for this article. If only one such thing is pro-

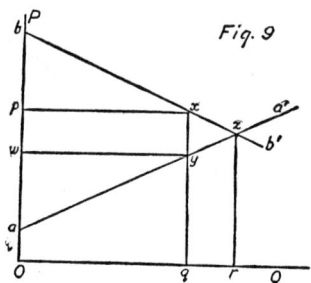

Fig. 9

duced the capitalist will make a very large profit—no less than the whole difference between the minimum cost *Oa* and the maximum price *Ob*. But, with industrial as with commercial speculation, the success of one operation paves the way for others (§ 115) ; and as these operations become more numerous, the margin of profit becomes narrower. If *aa'* represents the supply curve of labor (§ 94), so that any desired quantity of labor *Oq* can only be obtained at a price *qy*, and *bb'* represents the demand curve for the products of this labor, so that the results of *Oq* can only be sold at the price *qx*, it is obvious that the margin *yx* becomes narrower as the quantity of production increases. When the amount of productive labor reaches *Or*, the selling price of the product only equals the amount of wages paid, and there is no possible inducement for capitalists to extend their operations. In fact, they will not wish to go as far as this point; for at *Or* they simply recover what they advance, with no compensation for the risks which are always involved. To assume these risks, they must have some adequate motive. They will not care to employ labor unless they expect it to yield them a margin of profit *xy* after replacing the capital advanced. If this margin attracts possessors of capital enough to employ an amount of labor $Oq$ at a price $qy$, the product will be furnished to the consumers at a price $qx$. The competition of different sellers will create a market price for products which will render it unnecessary for any buyer to pay more than $qx$; the competition of different employers will create, though in less perfect fashion,[1] a market rate of wages, which will render it unnecessary for any laborer to accept less than $qy$.

Under these circumstances we have

(1) The area $Oqya$ representing the amount which different laborers would be prepared to accept.

(2) The area $Oqyw$ representing the amount which competition enables them to get.

(3) The area $Oqxb$ representing the amount which different consumers would be prepared to pay.

(4) The area $Oqxp$ which competition allows them to pay.

The difference $pxb$ between what consumers are prepared to pay and what they actually do pay may be treated without great error as illustrating the consumers' gain or surplus from the process of production.[2] The difference $ayw$ between what laborers are prepared to receive and what they actually do receive, may in like manner be treated as the laborers' gain or surplus. The area $wxyp$ represents the total profit of the capitalists who have brought the operation to a successful conclusion. The ratio of $xy$ (profit) to $yq$ (capital advanced)[3] is the percentage of profit on the transaction. If the time which elapses between the rendering of labor and the sale of the product is one year, this percentage represents the

---

[1] This incompleteness of competition for labor is due chiefly to the fact that different producers apply their labor under very different conditions. For purposes of illustration, we have for the moment ignored these differences.

[2] These illustrations find their chief practical use when we study the incidence of taxation (chapter xiv).

[3] Note that the amount advanced by capitalists *as a class* is neither more nor less than the sum of wage-payments (§ 139).

rate of profit, as it is ordinarily expressed. If the time be longer or shorter than one year, the ratio must be correspondingly reduced or increased to bring it down or up to the year's time unit as a basis of measurement.

§ 296. It rarely happens that the case is so simple as this illustration assumes. Different units of product do not as a rule involve the same amounts of labor. In some cases the amount paid in wages is far less than the selling price; in others, the margin is very narrow. Part of these differences may be explained by the difference in time which elapses between the application of labor and the sale of the product. If one capitalist waits twice as long as another and by so doing obtains double the amount of profit, the rate of profit of the two men is approximately the same. But after making all proper allowances for differences in time, there remain other differences, due to superior foresight in investment or skill in management, which make the profits on capital, in its different applications, take a very wide range. Instead of a fixed rate of profit, as the result of competition, we find an extremely variable one.

§ 297. Wherever the system of interest prevails, it is customary to explain these differences by analyzing profits into several parts, each governed by laws of its own. If the prevailing rate of interest on good security in a certain market is five per cent, and a concern with an invested capital of a hundred thousand dollars shows a gross profit of eight thousand dollars in the course of a year, we consider five thousand dollars as interest on the capital invested, and the other three thousand as surplus gain. If this surplus is due to excellence of location we call it *economic rent ;* if it is due to superiority of management we call it *net profit.* We thus separate the gross profits into three elements :

(1) A payment for *capital* known as *interest.*

(2) A payment for *location* known as *rent.*

(3) A payment for *skill* known as *net profit*.

These distinctions are clear and important ; but there has been a tendency among students of economics to exaggerate their importance and their clearness. In dealing with these various elements of profit we have to guard ourselves against several prevalent fallacies with regard to interest.

§ 298. We must note, in the first place, that interest is not a " natural " return for capital independent of skill. The power of capital to yield interest is dependent upon the skill with which it is managed. A borrower offers interest because he thinks that he has the ability to earn it. The rate which capital commands will depend primarily upon the *borrowers' estimates* of their skill in this respect, rather than upon any natural or inherent qualities in the capital itself. Of course there is a certain conformity between the borrowers' estimates for the future and the actual experience of the past ; but this is by no means so close as some writers seem to assume.

§ 299. In the next place, we must beware of confounding the causes which have established the *system* of interest with those that determine the *rate* of interest. It is partly with the object of avoiding this confusion that the writer has chosen to explain the development of the system in one chapter (§§ 132–157) and to discuss the determination of the rate in another. The system of interest was approved by jurists, because the accumulation and use of capital was advantageous to society as a whole, and increased the public wealth (§ 3). With this end in view, society was willing to offer rewards to those who would abstain from destroying wealth and would use it productively. But it is an unwarranted statement that the amount of the reward corresponds or ought to correspond to the sacrifice involved in the abstinence or to the increased utility of the product. The idea that the increase of *public* wealth will enable anybody to pay interest is justly characterized by

Boehm-Bawerk as a " naïve " theory. This naïve theory furnishes us a true explanation of the cause of the *system* of interest; but it does not touch the questions involved in the determination of the *rate*. Society is anxious to have a great deal of capital invested for the sake of the resulting gain to the public wealth. It does not undertake to pay a corresponding price, or in fact any specified price whatever, for the capital used for this purpose. It leaves to the skill of the investors the problem of determining what rate they shall pay for the use of one another's capital.

§ 300. For we must constantly note that interest is not paid by society to the capitalists, but *by one group of capitalists to another*. It is not paid for capital, but for the *control* of capital. The rate depends upon the relative number of capitalists who desire such control and of those who are willing to part with it for a fixed consideration guaranteed by some other capitalist.

In any large industrial enterprise there are usually two classes of investors, represented by the stockholders and bondholders of a railroad. The former class is willing to take large risks for the chance of contingent profits. The latter class wants security of return and is quite willing to abandon possible chances of large gain. The modern system of interest is nothing more than the recognition of these two classes of investors and their mutual relations; the rate of interest is the outcome of a bargain between them. Interest results from a contract between two capitalists uniting in a common enterprise. It is a sum paid by one investor to another investor—out of capital, if necessity shall require. If the borrower has not capital enough to cover such contingent necessity, what is called interest really is compensation for risk, and is apt to be made far too small in comparison with the chances of loss on the principal.

Interest, from the standpoint of the borrower, is the

price paid for the control of industry. Capital gives its possessors the right to direct the productive forces of society if they will take the speculative risks connected with the uncertainty as to the value of the product. When some of those who unite in an investment are anxious to do this and others are not, the former stand ready to offer the latter a price for such rights of control. Interest from the standpoint of the lender is the price for which he is ready to forego the chances of control which, under the present social system, the ownership of unconsumed wealth gives him. It represents commuted profits.

§ 301. The rate of interest, in its industrial aspect, is neither more nor less than a *competitive rate of commutation.* It is fixed like any other competitive price, by the self-interest of individuals, in such a way that the demand for loans becomes equal to the supply.

Nearly all loans are made with the immediate or ultimate purpose of investing the borrowed capital in such a way as to enable the borrower to secure a profit—as in undertaking a business enterprise—or to avoid an expense —as in becoming the owner of a home which will save the necessity of paying rent.[1] The demand for produc-

---

[1] There are three other less important sources of demand for loans which require mention at this point :

(1) A few people desire loans for the pleasure of consumption rather than for their utility in production. They will borrow money to-day which it may be ten times harder to repay to-morrow, because abstinence to-day seems to their imprudent minds a far more serious matter than abstinence to-morrow. The demand for accommodation of this kind is so unintelligent that its amount is but slightly affected by the rate charged.

(2) A somewhat larger number of people desire loans as a means of meeting contracts which they have previously made, and which they cannot otherwise fulfil without selling some of their property at a sacrifice. These loans are sought for the purpose of avoiding a loss rather than of making a profit—if the two things can be said to be distinguishable. They have special importance in times of monetary stringency. The demand for such loans is more affected by changes in the rate of interest than that for consumption loans, but less so than that for industrial loans.

(3) Nations make loans for war purposes, in order to maintain an army at the expense of future taxpayers instead of present ones (chapter xiv.)

tive loans of this kind depends almost entirely upon the rate charged. If a man has intimate knowledge of the details of a business, he knows when to borrow and when to contract his borrowings. His demand for loans arises from the fact that he expects a profit from the control of the capital. As long as this expected profit is greater than the prevailing rate of interest, he will be a borrower rather than a lender. If he thinks that the profit from an enterprise will be seven per cent, and he can borrow additional capital at five per cent, he will be glad to do so. Of course he knows that he may fail to make more than four per cent, in which case his borrowing will prove to have involved a loss ; but he also knows that there is a chance of making ten per cent, in which case there is an exceptional gain. If he has confidence in his estimate of seven per cent as the probable rate of profit on a series of transactions, he will not hesitate to borrow at five per cent, or even at six ; believing that the losses on some transactions will be more than balanced by the extra gains in others.

As the rate of interest becomes higher the number of men who are ready to borrow grows less. If in the case just assumed the rate of interest had been seven per cent instead of five, the man who expected the profit to be seven per cent would have no inducement to borrow ; and if the rate rose to eight per cent he would become a lender instead of a borrower. He would find it to his advantage to commute his profits, instead of taking his chances ; to accept guarantees instead of giving them. A considerable part of the supply of loanable capital comes from business men who are so conservative in their estimates of probable profit that they content themselves with the certainty of a moderate rate which their more sanguine competitors deem inadequate. We may say, in a rough way, that the rate of interest in any business tends to a point where the demand for capital on the part of those who think their profit will exceed that rate equals the supply furnished by those who think that it will not.[1]

§ 302. In point of fact, the rate is a little lower than this. The borrower has a certain amount of trouble in the management of capital, from which the lender is at least partly free ; and this freedom from trouble makes the lender willing to commute at a slightly lower rate than he would otherwise accept, and enables the borrower to get the benefit of this margin. Moreover there is a large class of lenders to whom a sure return is a matter of positive advantage independent of the rate charged. There are a great many people to whom the certainty of five per cent is worth more than an uncertain profit which will probably be higher but which may turn out to be much lower. The positive value of this insurance is such as to make the supply of capital equal the demand at a rate lower than would otherwise be fair or probable. For the offer of a fixed interest rate attracts capital from many investors with whom insurance is a dominant motive instead of an incidental one. These people do not ask what is the average probable profit in any line, but what they can be sure of getting on their loans. They are not prepared to make active investments in industrial enter- prises if they can possibly help it. They simply stand ready to put their capital at the disposal of the borrower who will offer them the best terms consistent with full security. Banks, and particularly savings banks, belong to this class ; so in great measure do life insurance com- panies ; and so do most of the people who have retired from active business and are living on money which they have saved.

---

[1] Some of the receivers of interest, where the contract is what it pretends to be, obtain a surplus from the transaction analogous to that of the con- sumers or laborers (§ 295). They would be willing to lend capital at much lower rates than they actually receive ; but the large demands of the loan market, and the unwillingness of other possessors of capital to lend it at low rates, enable them to get a larger return than they would otherwise exact.

§ 303. We thus have two distinct sources of supply of loanable capital. A part comes from business men who might be borrowers instead of lenders, and who take the latter position only when the interest rate seems too high in proportion to the risk. The amount of capital available from this source is directly dependent on the price offered. Another part comes from people who could not take an active share in the management of industry ; people who lend money as a means of insuring themselves an income and who accept the best terms which they can get. The amount of such capital does not vary with the rate offered —at least not to anything like the degree which is often assumed. Observation does not show that a high rate of interest has very much effect on saving. Some of the motives to save are even stronger when the rate is low than when it is high. If a man wishes to provide himself with an income of $1,000 per year for his own support and that of his family when he becomes unable to work, it is enough for him to save $20,000 if he can get five per cent interest ; but if he can only get four per cent he must save $25,000 in order to secure the required result. It may safely be said of the general fund of savings, that the rate of interest adjusts itself to the amount, rather than the amount to the rate.

§ 304. The thing which is offered by the borrowers in exchange for loanable capital, and which equalizes the supply and demand of such capital, is a rate of *income* (§ 5). The interest transaction is an exchange of income for capital. The rate of interest is the amount of income per year which the owner of capital deems an adequate consideration to induce him to part with the capital. Wealth measured in one way is exchanged for wealth measured in another. If interest stands at five per cent it means that in the judgment of the mercantile community, five dollars a year is worth a hundred dollars out and out. This judgment or market valuation

18

implies that the amounts of capital which people are willing to convert into income at that rate correspond to the amounts of income which people are willing to convert into capital.[1] If the rate of interest is less than five per cent, there will be more people who offer income for the sake of capital, *i. e.*, in common parlance, more borrowers than lenders. If the rate is more than five per cent there will be an excess of people who offer capital for the sake of income, *i. e.*, more lenders than borrowers.

§ 305. The general fund of loanable capital owned by people who desire neither risk nor control tends to equalize interest rates in different lines. There are a number of people who invest part of their money in railroad bonds, and part in real estate mortgages. If railroad interest rates fall, while farm rates remain un-

---

[1] The valuation which constitutes the basis of the interest rate may be expressed either in the form of a relation between capital and income, as in the text, or in the form of a relation between present and future goods, as is done by Boehm-Bawerk. It makes little difference whether we say that one hundred dollars of capital commands an income of five dollars a year, or that one hundred and five dollars due a year hence is worth one hundred dollars to-day. The former statement regards the transaction as an investment, the latter as a discount. The distinction between them is one of form, not of substance.

There is a different view of the cause of interest which is held by so many able writers of the Austrian school (Menger, Wieser, Clark), that it demands careful notice. According to this view, the price paid for an article, which represents its marginal utility to the consumer, is distributed among laborers and capitalists on the basis of the marginal utility of the labor and capital which have contributed to its production. If the utility of capital, as represented by its efficiency in producing the article, is higher than the interest charged for its use, more capital will be employed, and longer time allowed to elapse between the rendering of labor and the realization of the product. If the utility of labor in producing additional supplies of the article is greater than the wages charged, additional labor will be employed. These writers conceive of capital and labor as administered in successive doses. As the amount increases, the marginal utility of the doses will diminish. Competition will compel all capitalists to accept rates of interest, and all laborers to accept rates of wages, based upon the productivity of the last dose, which gives an "imputed" value to the whole

changed, some of these people will direct their new investments to farms instead of railroads ; increasing the supply of farm loans and diminishing that of railroad loans. If this process were completely carried out, we should have an equalization of the rates of interest in different lines, and the establishment of one general rate of interest for capital as a whole.

§ 306. This equalizing process is never fully accomplished, partly for lack of time, but chiefly for lack of knowledge on the part of investors. It takes months, and generally years, for property owners as a body to find out where profits really are highest and transfer their investments of capital in amounts sufficient to reduce the rate of profit in those lines to the general level. When the public has found out where the opportunity

---

supply both of capital and of labor. This process adjusts the demand and price of labor and capital in such a way that the marginal utility of a dollar spent for waiting (interest) is equal to the marginal utility of a dollar spent for labor (wages).

The obvious difficulty in this theory lies in the fact that these adjustments are apt to be disturbed by the mistakes of speculators (§ 324, note). But there is a more fundamental objection to the whole analysis from the fact that it involves reasoning in a circle. If at the beginning of a productive process we decide upon using an increment of capital instead of an increment of labor, it necessarily means that we wait longer for our product. *We cannot therefore tell when the marginal productivity of labor and capital is equal unless we know the relative value of products at two different periods ; i. e., the rate of interest.* If we do not stand at the beginning of a period of production, but decide to avail ourselves of the results of past labor instead of the services of present labor—which is the case contemplated in the more popular expositions of the theory of imputation—we do not touch the question of interest at all. We pay a price for the results of past labor directly to the owners of the property, instead of giving money to our laborers to buy those results for themselves. A manufacturer uses his capital to buy coal, which represents the results of past labor ; he pays wages which enable his employees to buy flour which also represents the results of past labor. There is no more waiting in the one case than in the other.

It may be added that if we look at the matter from any but the narrowest point of view, all "doses" of capital are administered in the form of wages.

for large rates of interest has really lain, the conditions of business which gave that opportunity have generally passed away. Instead of bringing down an unduly high rate of interest, the luckless investors will find themselves competing in an over-filled industry, where the chance of profit hardly covers the risk to any of the parties concerned.

Even without such over-competition, the uninstructed capitalists who seek high rates of interest are apt to go into the wrong places. They go where interest is apparently highest, rather than where it is really highest. They do not distinguish between high rates which offer real chances of profit on good security, and those which conceal a large danger of loss. Nor is this at all surprising. In every commercial and industrial loan the element of risk is present to a greater or less degree. It requires special knowledge of the conditions of any particular business to know whether that business gives special safety or special hazard. Where the rate of interest on what appears to be good security is a little higher than that which prevails in other lines or other localities, we generally find that there are some hidden chances of loss which account for the difference. It is these chances of loss which prevent the capitalists who have direct knowledge of the business from extending their investments on terms which are apparently so favorable. If, under these conditions, the uninstructed capitalist, who has not this special knowledge, rushes in to take advantage of the high rate, he is apt to lose a considerable proportion of the principal which he has risked. Any movement of capital to these lines results in lowering the rate of interest where the margin of risk is high, and where the true interest or guaranteed profit, over and above such special risks, was perhaps unduly low from the beginning.

If a man possesses unusual sources of knowledge, he can with a fair degree of safety undertake to secure rates of interest higher than those quoted in the open market. But in the absence of such special knowledge the chances are that the equalizing process will work in the wrong directions instead of in the right ones, and that the investor who tries to get the benefit of large returns of interest will find this benefit more than counterbalanced by losses on his principal.

§ 307. Making proper allowance for the slowness or imperfection of these adjustments, we may fairly say that there is a general rate of interest at which the demand for capital equals the supply.

This general rate of interest may be influenced in three ways: by changes in the supply of money, in the supply of products, and in the degree of commercial security. The effects of the two first are trifling in importance as compared with the last.

§ 308. We have already seen (§ 253) the fatuity of most of the attempts to lower the rate of interest by increasing the supply of money. Changes in the volume of the currency are quickly followed by corresponding changes in price. The man who desires to use a certain amount of food or machinery and to control a certain amount of labor must borrow a proportionally larger sum of money in order to get the products and services required. The demand for capital increases side by side with the supply ; and the uncertainty which loose currency legislation creates with regard to the future, actually tends to force the rate of interest upward.

The one exception to this rule which is important enough to deserve notice arises when issues of money are made in such a form as to relieve a temporary stringency in the money market. In such a case the public is seeking for means of payment rather than for means of investment, and an unexpected supply of such means of payment may break what is virtually a corner (§ 175) in the stock of available money. But even in this case it is necessary that the inflated supply of money be quickly retired, in order to prevent the subsequent rise in interest due to the speculation and insecurity which such excess of currency engenders.

§ 309. The idea that the rate of interest can be lowered by increasing the supply of products involves less practical danger, because it is very hard for any mischief-maker to put it into effect; but as a theoretical fallacy it is even more subtle and dangerous than the one just exposed. When the student of economics has mastered the idea that interest is paid for capital and not for money, he infers that an increase in the supply of capital will result in diminishing the rate paid for the use of such capital. So it undoubtedly will. If there are twice as many machines in existence, the rental value of each machine will fall. But the rate of interest will not necessarily be affected thereby. The price of each machine will fall nearly as fast, and may fall quite as fast, as its rental value. Interest on a machine is expressed by the ratio between the rental and the price. The rate of interest will therefore suffer little or no change from an increased supply of machinery. A large part of the causes which are used to explain when interest will be low really show when machinery will be cheap, and nothing more.

§ 310. The case is a little less clear when we come to investigate the effect of an increased supply of food instead of an increased supply of machines. An increase of food enables the community to wait a longer time for the various products of its labor, and to get the benefit of improvements which involve this long period of waiting. It is argued by some writers that a fall in the rate of interest necessarily follows such a lengthening of time in production. But it is doubtful whether this result takes place in practice. An increase in food supply is so apt to lead to increased consumption on the part of the laborers that the surplus will be utilized in a far different way from that contemplated by this theory—not by a lengthening of production time, but by a shortening of consumption time. Under these circumstances it seems a mistake to deduce what the rate of interest will be if the habits of the laboring class remain unchanged, when in fact the habits of the laboring classes adjust themselves to the increased supply of products faster than the rate of interest does.[1]

The chief practical effect of abundance of capital upon the rate of interest is a psychological one. If goods are scarce in proportion to people's bodily necessities, the public often sets a high value on present consumption and makes relatively little account of the future. An increasing abundance of consumable products, by diminishing the pressure of immediate necessity, gives larger room for intelligent classification of risks and for accepting future enjoyments instead of present ones, on terms more nearly commensurate to the actual risk which arises from deferring the enjoyment in question.

§ 311. The prevailing rate of interest is far more affected by the degree of security than by the volume of money or of products. While people may not always judge accurately of the security in any particular case, there is no doubt that interest in general is low where property is safe and high where property is uncertain, apart from the conditions which prevail in any particular business. This

---

[1] A scarcity of food lessens the profitable use of machinery, but not through the agency of the rate of interest. If there is only food enough to last a year, and a capitalist diverts laborers from the production of food and other articles of immediate use to employments whose return is more remote, he finds at the end of a year that the supply of food and other consumable products is scanty. The men who have produced food find their private income increased by this scarcity; those who have invested capital in machines find their possible profits diminished because of the increased expense of maintenance of themselves and their laborers during the period of waiting.

Scarcity of food and high rates of interest both have the same effect in restricting the use of machinery; but this does not prove that scarcity of food in itself causes a high rate of interest.

is partly because personal security promotes accumulation of products (chapter ii), but chiefly because an assured future enjoyment is far more valuable than a doubtful one.

The best guarantee of security is given by the personal character of the capitalists in a nation ; but the clearest evidence of such security is generally to be found in con- servative government. If law is so administered as to make property rights precarious, the value of a future return will necessarily be low. If it is so administered as to make them stable, the value of future goods will more nearly correspond to that of present ones. In the former case the rate of interest will be high ; in the latter case it will be low.[1]

§ 312. It must not be supposed that a low rate of in-

[1] Security affects the rate of interest in two ways, which must be carefully distinguished from one another.

The *conscious* attempt to provide against particular risks causes differences in the nominal rate of interest. In uncivilized countries a large part of the interest payments are of this kind. The bottomry loan in old times often called for twenty per cent interest because of the chance that the ships which furnished the security would be wrecked. But as civilization ad- vances these risks come to be separated in the mind of the investors from a residual sum which they can obtain on *what they consider* absolutely good security. This rate is not looked at by the individual as a payment for risk. Yet its height is probably in large measure a result of past experience as to losses ; and this experience is a most potent factor in determin- ing the relative value which people place upon present and future goods even when they suppose those future goods to be certain. If investors have been free from unforeseen losses in the immediate past, there is at once a greater quantity of old capital in the hands of people who are ready to offer its control to others, and a greater habitual readiness to accept promises of moderate income rates as an adequate consideration for such control. If on the other hand people have suffered considerable losses of property which they have entrusted to others, there is at once a smaller supply of capital in the hands of people who are ready to part with its control, and a hesitation to accept promises of moderate income as an adequate consideration for such control, even when there appears to be no tangible risk in the particu- lar case involved. Thus the relative valuation placed upon present capital and future income is *unconsciously* influenced by the past experience of the community.

terest, due to increased security, represents an unmixed good for society. Risk is an incident of progress. As long as the human mind is not endowed with prophetic foresight, great security may be obtainable only at the price of general stagnation. So far as insecurity results from activity in industrial enterprise on the part of the capitalists of a nation, rather than from lax enforcement of the laws protecting vested rights, it is a good thing. If a low rate of interest means that people do not tamper with laws it is good ; if it means that they do not experiment with business methods it is bad. In the latter case any saving which results from a low rate of interest is from the public standpoint more than nullified by the failure to utilize new processes and new ideas as fast as they are developed.

§ 313. The tendency of profits and interest to fall as a nation advances has been much overestimated. The high rate of profit in new countries is apparent rather than real. A new country offers more fields of exceptional profit than an old one, but it also involves more dangers of exceptional losses. The statistics of railroads in different parts of the United States, show that the ratio of income to the total capital invested is much higher in the older parts of the country, and lower in those which are more newly settled. Part of this difference is doubtless due to the fictitious capitalization of railroads in the West, where the real percentage of profit to capital invested is greater than the apparent percentage. Yet after making all due allowance under this head there remains a balance in favor of investments in the East. This balance of profit is made yet more conspicuous if we take into account the generally appreciating value of railroad securities in New England or the Middle States, and contrast it with the great depreciation which has affected so many companies in the South and West. If, instead of confining our investigation to one country, we compare the rail-

roads of Europe with those of the United States, we shall
find that the European lines, which at first promised less
apparent profit, have on the average proved more remunerative to the investors than have those of the United
States.

The popular misunderstanding about profits in new
countries is due to two causes. In the first place, the
expectation of profit on the part of men who venture
their capital in a new country is generally exaggerated.
Public opinion is influenced by the glowing reports of
profits that are going to be realized, and does not stop to
inquire how far these expectations are warranted by actual
facts. In the second place, the public sees the instances
of exceptional profit, which stand out clearly because of
their success, and does not see those failures which have
sunk out of sight because they were unsuccessful.

§ 314. While profits do not perhaps decline as a nation
advances, but simply become surer and less speculative,
the rate of interest undoubtedly tends to fall; but this fall
is not so marked as most people suppose. Many cases
of high nominal interest in a new country result from contracts that are more or less fraudulent in their character.
In an undeveloped region there are always a number of
speculators who borrow money without giving adequate
security, obtaining such money by the promise of a rate
of interest which leads investors to close their eyes to the
defective character of the security offered. It is common
to speak of the high rates of interest received in such
cases as constituting insurance against risk. But the
amounts thus received in the form of interest represent so
small a fraction of the losses on the principal that the term
insurance is an arrant misnomer. Such contracts nevertheless give rise to an impression that the actual market
rate on good security is higher than is really the case.

At a time when interest rates in one of our leading
northwestern states were quoted in the eastern market at

seven per cent on first-class security, the writer took pains to inquire of conservative local bankers what were the actual rates which persons in that section who had money to lend felt that they could command. He found that such loans ran at six per cent and less. The difference of one per cent was offered the eastern investor as an insurance against risk. How miserably inadequate it was for the purpose was seen in the collapse two or three years later of the security for a large number of these seven per cent loans.

§ 315. After making proper allowance for these causes which affect the apparent or nominal rate of interest in a new country, there still remains a slight difference in the real rate. This may be explained as follows:

1. In most new communities there is an insecurity of tenure and a chance for adverse legislation regulating conditions of payment, which make future rights less valuable than they are in more conservative countries, where the probability of change is less.

2. The high rate of apparent or false interest just described attracts into illegitimate investments a certain part of the supply of the capital which would otherwise be used in legitimate ones and prevents the rate of true interest from being lowered to the point which it should normally reach. The point of equilibrium of the supply and demand of capital is forced upward by the action of speculators who are not really in a position to offer interest, but who are enabled by the blindness of certain sections of the investing public to compete in the market for industrial loans.

3. In a new country a larger proportion of people are anxious to manage their own business, instead of leaving it to others. If a given amount of capital is in the field seeking profits, the height of the interest rate will depend upon the relative numbers of those who desire control and of those who are willing to abandon such control for the

sake of a fixed return. Where nearly everybody wishes
to conduct his own business, the interest rate will almost
necessarily be higher than where most people are willing
to leave the conduct of business in the hands of others.
In the early history of New England, rates of interest
were higher than they are now, not because property was
less secure nor because capital was scarce, but because
almost every man stood ready to manage his own capital,
and required considerable inducements in order to be willing to entrust it to others.

§ 316. The process which tends to equalize the rates of
interest in different lines, operates also, but in a less
degree, to equalize the rates of profit.

If interest goes down while profit remains stationary, there is a margin of advantage to the borrowers,
which makes each of them anxious to use more capital in
his business. So far as they do this, they will increase the
supply of products, which necessarily puts prices down,
and will increase the demand for labor, which tends to
force wages up. This process will go on until the rate of
profit adjusts itself to the rate of interest; that is, until
the difference between the two is only sufficient to pay
the employer a fair compensation for his time and trouble
—such as he could earn if working for another instead of
for himself.

§ 317. But there are certain causes which make this
adjustment very incomplete. They have already been
mentioned in some detail in connection with normal price
(§ 101.) Looking at the matter from the standpoint of
the producer instead of the consumer, we may divide
them into two groups:

1. Where all the business men in an industry combine
to prevent the increase of investment and production.

2. Where they act independently and compete with one
another, but where some have advantages, either of method
or location, which others do not possess.

Both of these are commonly called cases of monopoly ; but the term applies much more properly to the first class than to the second. The superiority which one man has over his competitor when the two are actually engaged in bidding against one another for the public favor may better be called a *differential* advantage than a monopoly.

§ 318. The exceptional profits of a true monopoly are generally transient in their character. If they are due to a patent, which is the commonest case, they end with the expiration of the patent right ; frequently even earlier than this, on account of the invention of a rival process. If they are due to closeness of organization or any of the other causes described at length in chapter vi, they may last longer ; yet even in these cases they are apt to be reduced either by legislation, by fear of new competition, or even by the pressure of public opinion. The number of monopolies which might have made exorbitant profits for a term of years looks very large ; the number that have actually done so is surprisingly small.

§ 319. Differential gains are quite another matter. They generally result from causes precisely opposite to those which produce true monopolies. A true monopoly tends to arise when a large concern can increase its output without corresponding increase in expense, so that it can supply the whole public and drive smaller or weaker concerns out of the market. This case is often exemplified when a large factory competes with a number of smaller ones. But when a large farm competes with a number of smaller ones, the case is quite different. The large farmer probably has certain advantages due to the scale on which he conducts his operations. But the amount of product on which he can realize this economy is limited in quantity. A double application of labor and capital will not double his output. He cannot drive his smaller competitors out of business, because the attempt to supply a large part of the market from one farm will result in loss instead of gain. Such an industry is said to be subject to the law of the diminishing return. The two chief causes of diminishing returns are the limited fertility or capacity of land, and the limited power of human brains. No land can produce unlimited quantities of product; no brain can direct unlimited numbers of men. If the demand for the products of any industry is too large to be met by a single organized source of supply, however great its natural advantages, we shall be likely to see a system of differential gains, due to the independent competition of men who make goods for the same market at different expense.

§ 320. Where these differential gains are due to personal ability, they are almost always transient in their character, and are known as *net profits.* Where they are due to advantages of location, they are apt to be more permanent, and are then known as *economic rent.* We may define rent in its technical or economic sense, as any *permanent* excess of the rate of profit over the rate of interest.[1] Economic rent is chiefly due to foresight in investment; net profit, to skill in management.[2] But the work of separating the

---

[1] Some writers attempt to explain *all* profits, including interest itself, as arising from differential gain. In this view, which has been most ably presented by Ricca-Salerno, interest represents an advantage enjoyed by the owners of commodities which have become ready at so early a period that they can apply labor under more favorable conditions of time than some of their competitors can command ; in precisely the same way that rent represents a power of applying labor under exceptionally favorable conditions of place. If we could ignore the functions and the mistakes of the speculator (§ 324, *note*) this would apparently be a sound position. But as matters stand there is a radical difference between rent, which is a *varying actual* advantage possessed by the owners of real estate, and interest, which represents a *fixed* rate of commutation of *possible but uncertain* advantage.

[2] We can in many cases distinguish profits from rent by finding what the plant will sell for. Excess of selling price over cost is capitalized rent. Excess of actual return from the property over interest on its price represents profit. Thus if $25,000 represents the amount of capital which has been used in improving a piece of real estate, $30,000 its price in the market,

two, even in theory, is very difficult, because we can never tell which differential advantages are permanent and which are transient.

§ 321. The " economic " or " Ricardian [1] " sense of the word rent must not be confounded with its ordinary commercial sense. Commercial rent represents a price paid for the use of land *and improvements.* A large part of it is interest rather than rent. If we deduct the interest on improvements from the commercial rent, the remainder is economic rent. This is sometimes known as ground rent ; and, if contracts for the rent of land were renewed every year, ground rent and economic rent would be substantially the same. But since in practice ground rent is habitually fixed for a very long term of years, the actual divergence between the ground rent paid and the economic rent computed on a theoretical basis is apt to be very large.

It is in some respects unfortunate that the term " rent " should have been chosen to designate these permanent differential gains. Investigators are apt to identify them much more closely with actual rents than the facts of the case warrant. Thus Shearman, in a recent book on " Natural Taxation," treats the total rent of agricultural lands in England as if it were " economic " rent; whereas, in fact, the amount of capital which the landlords have invested in English farms is enormous. If interest on the capital thus invested for agricultural improvements had been deducted, as it ought to be, the conclusions which Shearman draws from his figures would have been entirely reversed.

and $2,000 a year its gross profit to the owner, the current rate of interest being five per cent, we shall have this $2,000 made up of

$1,250 economic interest
250 " rent
500 " profit.

[1] The theory of differential gain was first clearly formulated by David Ricardo in his *Principles of Political Economy and Taxation.*

§ 322. Economic rent and net profit are like the producers' and consumers' surplus described at the beginning
of the chapter in being differential gains—gains which are
due to a difference between the conditions of the stronger
and the weaker competitors. They are unlike them, first,
in being habitually measured in money and therefore
more observable; second, in being offset by differential
losses which, in some instances, more than neutralize the
gains. The number of investments of fixed capital that
have more than paid interest is perhaps balanced by the
number of those that have failed to pay interest. While
there are many farms that are worth more than the capital
invested in them, there are also many which are worth less.
In times of advancing prices the gains are more conspicuous than the losses. In times of commercial depression the case is reversed.

The existence and persistence of this negative rent
(and of the corresponding losses or negative profits in
manufacturing industry) go far to furnish the justification
for the present industrial system. If it were true, as
George alleges, that rent is simply an unearned increment,
an appropriation of a part of the public product, then
there would be neither wisdom nor equity in leaving land
under private ownership. If it were true, as Marx claims,
that profits represent a similar unearned increment, the
same conclusion would follow with regard to capital. But
in point of fact, both rent and profits are of the nature of
compensation for risk. The amount received may be
greater than the amount lost, or it may be less. This will
depend largely upon the temperament of the capitalists
as a body. But of the fact of such losses there can be no
question whatever.

§ 323. Many of the writers who treat of the relation
between business risk and business profit make the mistake of· assuming that profits are an amount paid to the
individual capitalist to cover *his* risk of loss. Far from

it. They are paid to capitalists as a class for protecting the public against *its* risk of loss. They are charges which the capitalists make, not for insuring themselves, but for insuring society against the losses incident to industrial experiment and industrial progress.

§ 324. The prevailing theory of economic rent ignores the extent of these losses. It assumes that future prices can be foreseen with a considerable degree of accuracy. It assumes that the marginal laborer and the marginal unit of capital do in fact contribute to the product an amount equal to the valuation which is placed on their services. But this is notoriously untrue. The marginal laborer is often employed at a rate of wages which exceeds the total amount that the consumer ever pays for the product of his labor. The marginal unit of capital receives a return in the form of interest which is often decidedly in excess of the advantage which the speculator derives from its use. If the product of such labor and capital were immediately available for consumption such mistakes would not be made; but as matters stand at present they are always being made on a small scale, and often on a large one. These mistakes are likely to continue as long as we have industrial progress. Society attempts to reduce them to a minimum by a system which is intended to place the control of industry in the hands of those who have proved their foresight, and to eliminate those who have made the mistakes. But in spite of this process of natural selection, which makes the judgment of speculators as a class better than that of the average man, the number of serious errors is very great indeed.[1]

[1] The various doctrines which base the rates of wages and interest upon the actual contributions of marginal laborers and capitalists to the product of industry habitually ignore the effect of these mistakes. To justify their method of reasoning, the advocates of these doctrines would be compelled to prove either (1) that the actual value of the product of labor and capital does in fact conform to the expectations of the speculators ; or (2) that an

§ 325. Ricardo of course knew about these mistakes; but he assumed that they could be quickly rectified—that no man would stay long in a business which was unprofitable. He thought that if wages in any particular line were momentarily raised too high and prices depressed too low, a speedy withdrawal of capital would almost certainly follow. Two things led him into this mistake. In the first place, the industries of Ricardo's time were for the most part conducted on a much smaller scale than they are to-day. A number of independent producers supplied the market. The most that the community had to fear under such circumstances was a slight excess or slight deficiency of the supply of products; and as independent producers were constantly entering or leaving business such an excess speedily cured itself. In the second place, Ricardo was a banker and dealt with those forms of capital which could be most quickly transferred from less profitable to more profitable lines. Although Ricardo combined the experience of a landlord with that of a banker his theory of rent represents essentially a banker's view of farming, which, like a farmer's view of banking, takes much more account of the profits than of the losses.

under-estimate of the advantage of using a process which promises remote returns is just as probable as an over-estimate, so that the mistakes of speculators may be treated as balancing one another; or (3) that such mistakes as are made will serve to teach their lesson in so short a time that no change in the habits of society will intervene to prevent them from correcting themselves.

Of these alternatives (1) is obviously untrue; (2) is so far dependent upon national character that it is inadmissible as a general assumption; while (3) is, to say the least, open to very grave doubts which the exponents of the theory of marginal contributions have made no adequate attempt to remove. For instance: if wages in a particular trade are made higher than the actual outcome of industrial processes ultimately warrants, the habits of living of the laborers may change before the mistake is discovered and render an adjustment to the old basis out of the question. The mistakes of speculators render the problem a dynamic one (§ 27) so frequently as to justify us in challenging the claims of a statical solution to be considered as any solution at all.

He assumes that there may be a permanent profit due to monopoly of location, while any permanent loss will be avoided by withdrawal of capital. But modern capital is not ordinarily invested in such forms that it can be readily withdrawn or transferred from an unprofitable use. In a large and increasing part of our investments capital is irrevocably *fixed* (§ 141). Labor has been applied in such a shape that its ultimate product cannot be obtained for a long term of years. If such labor has proved especially advantageous to society, land laws and patent laws confer special advantages on the investor. But if for any reason it has proved unremunerative, withdrawal is impossible without great sacrifice. The positive rent which Ricardo saw, and the positive profits of which his successors have made so much, are counterbalanced by losses both on real estate and on personal property which are perhaps greater than the aggregate amount of differential gains made by the more successful investors.

§ 326. Several circumstances may give rise to such loss. The most important are : 1. Technical failure, where an investment of capital does not produce the physical result that was expected. 2. Industrial progress, where an investment of capital works well for a time, but must give place to a better one before the accumulated profits have paid for its original cost. 3. Over-competition, where a useful method is applied by so many independent investors as to make the price of its products disproportionately low. 4. Contraction of credit, which reduces the general level of prices, and thus makes the investment unremunerative to the man who has made it, even though it be otherwise perfectly adapted to the needs of society.

§ 327. Of these causes of loss, technical failure, though often the most conspicuous, is probably the least important. The evils resulting from this source are so obvious that they serve as a warning for other investors, and to make the repetition of the same mistake improbable.

§ 328. The losses from industrial progress are less obvious but more widespread. The discovery of a new process may render a mass of old investments useless. The invention of the power loom represented a great loss to the owners of capital invested in hand looms. The invention of the railroad quickly rendered canal property unremunerative. Few, even among the more conservative investors, make proper allowances for the danger connected with the invention of new processes. The owner of a factory, in estimating his profits, is often content to deduct the depreciation due to the wear and tear of machinery ; and if he makes a further deduction as the patent rights which have given him an advantage over his competitors draw to a close, he deems that he is pursuing a conservative policy. A board of railroad directors is satisfied with insisting that a certain sum shall be set apart from current receipts to keep the track and equipment at a high standard of efficiency. But there is a probable source of danger which is not adequately met by depreciation accounts in a factory or by maintenance accounts in a railroad. Even when these deductions are made on a liberal basis they do not provide a reserve fund to insure the investor against the chance of total loss in case other competitors bring into use new methods. This loss is not of a kind which can readily be estimated in accounting or be deducted from the sum available for dividends, but it represents a great reduction in the profits earned by owners of fixed capital as a class.

§ 329. Nor are landowners exempt from these dangers. Much of Henry George's reasoning is based upon the assumption that land speculators make many profits and few losses. He has probably over-estimated the former, and has quite certainly under-estimated the latter. The amount of capital which has been sunk in developing real estate that proves unprofitable is something for which it is impossible to obtain accurate statistics ; but a close observation of real estate values will indicate that it is very great. The New England farm represents a large amount of capital which was rendered unremunerative by the competition of farms elsewhere.[1] A change in the current of population has often destroyed all profits from real estate in which much capital has been irrevocably fixed. The development of new means of transportation by which wheat could be shipped from a distance has played havoc with the farm values of England and of the American seaboard. It is not true, as Ricardo assumes, that the normal price of wheat just remunerates the last producer, and that any farmer for whom it fails to be remunerative can speedily withdraw from the market. In order to compete in the production of wheat large investments of capital are necessary. To bring producers into the market the price must be high enough to cover their expenses, including interest on fixed capital, or at least to make investors think that it will do so. But when once they have entered into competition they cannot withdraw without a very considerable loss of fixed capital. If the price per bushel of wheat for a group of producers is fifty cents over and above interest, or eighty cents including interest, they will not go into the business unless they expect to get eighty cents; but once in, they will not go out until the price nears fifty cents. This difference between eighty cents and fifty cents leaves room for a large margin of loss. If the price falls to the lower figure the same differences continue to exist which the Ricardian theory requires; but they are differences of disadvantage rather than differences of advantage. Moreover, as shown by Carey, there are changes of method in agriculture as well

---

[1] The beginnings of this process were clearly noted by Carey, whose objections to the Ricardian theory of rent deserve more consideration than they have received. Carey's ideas have been further developed by Patten, in his " Premises of Political Economy," Philadelphia, 1886.

as in other lines of industry. The first settlers occupy the lands which are most accessible and easily brought into use. Subsequent settlers take those which require more capital for their development, and as transportation becomes cheaper choose lands which are more remote but also more fertile. The large production of these new competitors often forces down the price of products below the amount which it costs to obtain them on the older farms, and renders the capital invested in these farms unprofitable to its owners.

§ 330. Even if a process continues to be successful for a long term of years, each capitalist is constantly in danger from over-competition on the part of other capitalists. It is impossible for different investors to know accurately what other investors are doing. If prices are high in a particular line of industry a number of capitalists will simultaneously arrange to take advantage of those prices and to secure a share of the exceptional profits which have prevailed. When a great many people try to do this prices will fall and all investments in that line, old as well as new, may be rendered unprofitable. This state of things is known as *over-production.* The use of the term over-production does not mean that more goods are produced than the community can consume, but more than the community can pay for at prices which cover the expense to the producers. The larger the fixed capital involved in an industry, the greater is the danger of such over-production. We see this danger illustrated in the history of iron and steel, of shipping, of railroads, and in most of the distinctively modern forms of manufacturing enterprise. We find alternations between periods of inadequate supply, where products are scarce and profits large, and periods of over-supply, where products are so abundant as to be sold at a sacrifice, and profits are not only destroyed but converted into losses. The factory and the railroad put their goods or services on the market at prices which fail to pay interest or even main-tenance. The owners have invested their capital in a form which they cannot readily change. If they abandon the field to other competitors it may prove a total loss. It is better to lose a dollar on every ton of traffic shipped than to lose two dollars on every ton of traffic sacrificed. The only limit to this process of cut-throat competition is found either in the absolute exhaustion of some of the competitors, or in the growth of population to a point where the demand at remunerative prices is equal to the normal productive capacity of the whole body of com-peting investments.

§ 331. Over-production is liable to take place in any line of industry involving large fixed capital. Occasionally it will occur in one line only, without involving oth-ers ; in which case it is more properly discribed as *dis-proportionate* production. The depression in American railroads in 1888, while other lines of industry were gen-erally prosperous, furnished an instance of this kind. But it will commonly happen that the phenomena of over-production are not due so much to excess of supply in one line as to contraction of demand in a number of lines simultaneously. Such a contraction is the central fact in any commercial crisis. These crises have occurred with tolerable regularity ever since the introduction of applied steam power. They have usually come once in ten or eleven years,—a fact which led some observers to connect them with sun spots which have a period of the same length. But no one could say just why the sun spots produced the crises, and this theory has been generally set aside for lack of proof. The accepted view of the phenomena of commercial crises makes them the result of contractions in credit of the kind described in chapter viii.

§ 332. The aggregate volume of pecuniary transactions which can be performed in the course of a year with a given reserve of money depends upon the efficiency of the credit system ; that is, in general, upon the freedom with which banks are able and willing to insure the payment of money in the future by people who have not the money in hand at present. If for any reason the banks are compelled, or think themselves compelled, to reduce the accommodation of this kind which they give the mercantile community, the men who wish to deliver money cannot pay so much, and of course men who wish to receive money cannot obtain so much. The decrease in the effective circulation of money causes a decrease of the volume of business. Either the physical amount of the transactions must be lessened or the average level of prices must fall. Each of these things causes commercial disaster. A fall in price prevents a great many people from fulfilling their contracts. A fall in the number of transactions prevents some of them from getting what they need as consumers and from selling their surplus as producers. We have a congestion in all the channels of trade. We find all the phenomena of over-production in a great number of different lines, not because the investments in those lines have been disproportionate to one another, but because the contraction of credit makes the general production of the community disproportionate to the means of getting it into the right hands.[1]

This is, in brief, the description of a modern commercial crisis. With varying details but with the same general features, it has been illustrated in 1825, 1837, 1847, 1857, 1873, 1884, and 1893. As exchange and transportation have developed, crises have become more and more universal in their pressure. As matters stand today, there is scarcely an industrial nation which stands apart from their evil influence. A paralysis of credit and trade in one country commonly makes itself felt in the others.

[1] Newcomb has an interesting analysis of these events, showing how a contraction in the "monetary circulation" of means of payment produces a corresponding effect on the "industrial circulation" of goods and services which consumers are anxious to receive and producers to render.

§ 333. The order of events in such a crisis is generally this :

(1) A shock to public confidence in a period of liberal, not to say inflated, credit, creates a demand for ready money. No one is sure that his neighbor will remain solvent. Each man is therefore anxious to secure himself against future loss. Every borrower seeks means of paying his obligations and increases the demand for money ; almost every capitalist tries to enlarge his cash reserves and thus lessens the available supply.

(2) This increase of demand and diminution of supply at first puts up the interest rate on short-time loans. Money is needed to tide over the immediate exigency, and every one is willing to pay large prices in order to obtain it. But this is only a temporary measure. Under the stress of need for securing money, people who have engagements to meet sell their goods at a sacrifice in order to obtain it. An unusually large supply of products and securities is thrown upon the market just at the time when many property owners feel themselves least able to invest, and when some consumers are restricting their purchases instead of expanding them. The temporary increase in the interest rate gives place to a more lasting fall in prices.

(3) Such a fall in prices lowers profits. A large number of people have made engagements with their creditors and with their employees based on the supposition that prices will continue at the old level. If there has been a period of inflation, the prevailing rate of wages and of interest have both been driven up to a high figure on account of the large profits realized by active speculators. A fall in price renders it impossible to pay interest out of current earnings. Readjustments and foreclosures follow one another in rapid succession. In cases where the lenders of money have obtained proper security the contracts are maintained at the expense of the principal of

the borrowers. If a railroad bond is really secured by stock behind it, the loss falls on the stockholders, and the bondholders, ultimately at any rate, receive all that the interest contract called for. But if, as frequently happens, the security has been a delusive one, the lenders are compelled to assent to a reduction of the interest which they believed to be safely guaranteed.

(4) When the interest contracts have been in large measure readjusted, the chief effect on wages begins to make itself felt. It might be supposed, on general grounds, that a fall in price would affect the laborer sooner than the investor, because wage contracts are made for short periods and are liable to readjustment at any moment, while interest contracts are made for a long term of years. But in the early stages of a commercial crisis the capitalist is not in a position to dictate terms to his laborers. He must make goods and sell goods at any price, in order to keep his head above water. As long as .it lasts, the cut-throat competition which lowers profits prevents the demand for labor from being very rapidly lessened. It is when readjustments of interest have been made that the laborers' condition becomes worst. After foreclosure sales have been completed and capital is reorganized on a new basis, no capitalist is necessarily compelled to work at a loss, and some probably go out of work altogether. Under these circumstances the demand for labor becomes appreciably less than it was, and the price offered falls rapidly. The first moderate changes are as a rule accepted by the laborers as inevitable, but as reductions become more sweeping they are resisted, particularly because house rents and consumers' prices, owing to the inertia of retail trade, do not fall nearly as fast as producers' prices. The workman sees his wages reduced because his employer cannot sell goods at the old figure, while the price that he pays for his supplies remains nearly the same. He thinks that something is wrong,

and strikes. This usually indicates the beginning of the end of a commercial crisis. It has become a proverb in the financial world that railroad strikes give no help to those who are trying to depress the price of securities. On the contrary, in spite of the losses attending such conflicts, it has been found in 1877, 1885, and 1894 that the price of securities in general began to go up at the very time when matters seemed to be at their worst. There are two reasons for this. First, strikes cut down production in any given line to such an extent as to enable competing producers to dispose of their products or services more readily. Second, strikes indicate that wage contracts, as well as interest contracts, have been readjusted to the price conditions which prevail, and that matters have therefore reached a point where speculators can make arrangements for the future with the assurance that the marginal price charged by labor and capital for their services does not exceed the market price which the consumers are likely to pay for the results of such service.

§ 334. Until this process is substantially complete, actual prices do not correspond to the assumptions of the marginal theory of value. The price which consumers are ready to pay for the products of industry is less than the marginal expense of those products—including in this expense, as we properly must, a return on capital invested. Some men, in trying to cover the cost, fail to sell their products; others, in trying to sell their products, fail to cover the cost. So far as producers are able to fulfil their contracts as to interest and wages— and in the theory both of economics and of law they should do so completely—the loss falls on rent and profits and may convert the expected surplus from these sources into a deficit of large amount.

§ 335. The distributive process, whose workings have been described in this chapter, may be summed up as follows:

The competition of capitalists with one another leads them to advance to the laborers a sum equal to the expected price of the product, less a compensation for waiting and the risks attendant upon it, sufficient to induce the proprietors to hazard the required amount of capital. The advances constitute wages; the excess of the product above such advances constitutes profits.

By a somewhat similar process the competition of the more active capitalists with one another leads them to guarantee to those who will lend them capital a fixed rate of income for the use of such capital. This income, guaranteed but not advanced, is known as interest; the remaining profit is known either as net profit for skill in management, or economic rent for foresight in investment. The separation of interest from net profit or rent results in a separation of the reward for waiting from the rewards for risk and foresight.

Wages are, in all ordinary cases, guaranteed and advanced by capitalists as a body. Interest is guaranteed, but not advanced, by one group of capitalists to another. The justice of the charge made for such guarantees and advances is to be defended, not because the enjoyment of interest corresponds to the sacrifice of waiting or because the amount of profit corresponds to the risk of loss, but because society finds itself best served by the system of guarantees and advances which the institutions of wages and interest serve to encourage.

# CHAPTER X.

## WAGES.

F. A. Walker : " The Wages Question : a Treatise on Wages and the Wages Class." New York, 1876.

F. W. Taussig : " Wages and Capital : an Examination of the Wages-Fund Theory." New York, 1896.

§ 336. WAGES, under the modern competitive system, are the *discounted* product of industry. They are what capitalists are ready to advance on the expectation of a future return. The competition of different employers with one another, where it is at all active, prevents them from making their rate of discount arbitrary in amount.

The expected value of the product, less the discount, gives the labor cost per unit of product, or *piece wage*. The piece wage received by any workman multiplied by the number of pieces which he makes in a day, constitutes his day's earnings or *nominal wage*. The amount of comforts which he can buy with the money received as nominal wages represent his *real wage*. If $A$ is getting $2.50 a day while $B$ is getting only $2.00, his nominal wages are one fourth higher; but if he has to make his purchases in a market where the general level of prices is fifty per cent higher than those paid by $B$, his real wages are one sixth lower than $B$'s. For the $2.00 which $B$

receives will buy as much as *A* could obtain with $3.00, and decidedly more than he obtains with $2.50.

Strictly speaking, both nominal and real wages should be estimated by the year (or even by the lifetime), rather than by the day, in order to show anything about the financial or economic condition of the laborer; because the regularity and duration of employment is so much less in some trades than in others that the same receipts per working day mean very different things in the long run. In practice, however, it is usual to quote nominal wages by the day, and then make corrections for irregularity of employment, limited duration of labor power, and other factors of this sort which affect our inferences from the apparent height of the wage figures.

§ 337. The cost of labor to the employer is naturally measured by the piece; the return for labor to the workman is naturally measured by the day or year. This does not mean that the employer will always wish to pay his laborers by the piece, or that the laborers will always prefer to be paid by the day. The choice between the two systems will depend chiefly upon the line of employment. Time wages prevail in agriculture, in trades, in personal service, and in the higher grades of mechanical work; piece wages, in mechanical work of ordinary grades.

Under the system of time wages the workman has no immediate or obvious incentive to increase his output. A large part of the time and strength of the foreman is occupied in keeping the men under his charge up to a proper standard of efficiency. To avoid this difficulty, the introduction of piece wages is the most obvious expedient. Under this system the workman is paid, not on the basis of time occupied, but on the basis of work done; not by the hour or the day, but by the yard, the pound, or some other unit of measure. If one operative turns out twice as many goods as another, he receives twice as much pay. He thus has an incentive to work rapidly. In fact, the danger is that he may work too rapidly for his own good or for that of his work. Under the piece-work system there is little need of insisting on quantity, but much need of insisting on quality. Where the latter object can readily be secured by a simple process of inspection, the employer always prefers to pay by the piece; where this is impossible, he has to pay by time. In textile weaving, where the grades of goods are simple and definite, it is easy for an inspector to say whether a certain piece of cloth should be passed or rejected. Weaving is therefore done by the piece; the inspector looks out for the quality and the operative for the quantity. But in the work of a machinist, where it is impossible to inspect the results quickly and surely, the workman must be given every incentive to do his work well rather than to do it hurriedly. He is therefore paid by the day; he looks out for the quality of his work and the foreman for its quantity.

§ 338. Differences in the rate of wages among producers of marketable goods are due far more to variations in efficiency than to variations in piece wages. If we arrange laborers of different countries in the order of their earning power, we shall find a corresponding difference in their efficiency. America stands highest, and England next, followed by other countries of western Europe; the efficiency of the laborer of eastern Europe is much lower, and that of India lowest of all.[1]

Nor is this at all surprising. Where different laborers compete in producing the same article for the same market, there are many things which tend to make the wage payments per unit of product substantially the same for

---

[1] F. A. Walker, "Political Economy," p. 56. For fuller details, excellently presented by the same author, see "The Wages Question," ch. iii. Similiar conclusions are reached by Brassey, Schoenhof, and Schulze-Gaevernitz.

all the competitors. If the piece wage for one group of employers differs greatly from that for another, competition tends either (1) to force the price of the product so low as to drive the high cost labor out of business; or (2) if the amount of low cost labor is inadequate to do this, the persistent high price produces an extra profit to the employers of low cost labor, which other capitalists are anxious to share; and the competition of new capital, bidding for the services of a restricted supply of low cost labor, forces up the rate of piece wages which the laborers can demand. For instance, if one group of laborers makes a yard of cloth for ten cents, and another group charges fifteen cents for the same service, it generally happens either that the employers of the former group flood the market with products at fourteen cents and drive the latter group out of business, or else that all sell their products at a price above fifteen cents, and that competition between different capitalists for the services of the low cost labor forces its price up to a level which leaves only the ordinary rate of profit. In the former case the general wage-level would go down to ten cents; in the latter case it would go up to fifteen cents; in either alternative we should see an equalization of piece wages among such laborers as continued to compete.

§ 339. There are only two considerable exceptions to the rule here laid down. (1) When different competitors use different methods of production, interest may take a larger share of the product in the one case than in the other, and equal prices of products, fixed by competition, may leave unequal remainders for labor. (2) When the operation of low cost labor is restricted to land of exceptional advantage, or otherwise limited by monopoly, there may not be enough competition of capital to give the low cost laborer the advantage of his superior economy. But the importance of these exceptions, especially the former, is much overestimated. One of the facts which most strongly impresses the student of industrial statistics is the comparatively small range of variation in piece prices for competing goods, even where the conditions of production are wholly dissimilar.

§ 340. On the other hand, the labor cost of *services,* as distinct from goods, shows a very wide range of variation. This is because a community must have a certain number of people engaged in personal and professional service, and must pay them wages corresponding to what their efficiency would secure *if they were engaged in the production of goods for market.* The greater the productiveness of industrial labor in any community, the higher will be the cost of those services in which the laborer has no industrial advantage over those who perform similar services elsewhere. The price of personal and professional service in America is high because the people who render it could make large products by going into industrial employments.[1] To induce them to enter the former field, they must be paid at a rate based upon their probable efficiency in the latter.

§ 341. In occupations requiring no special skill, if the rate of wages as fixed by the discounted value of the product is insufficient to keep the laborer alive, the number of laborers will be rapidly reduced. This will diminish the supply of products in any industry where it occurs, and will increase their price. This process will go on in manufacturing industries until the discounted price of the product rises high enough to enable the laborer to buy the necessary amount of food ; it will go on in agricultural industries until cultivation is restricted to more advantageous lands or systems of tillage, so that the *per capita* product is large enough to maintain the workmen in

---

[1] For the same reason we are apt to have a relatively wide margin between wholesale and retail prices ; because the American retailer charges more per day for his services than the foreign retailer, without always being able to handle a correspondingly larger amount of products in the course of a day.

20

undiminished numbers. Conversely, if the rate of wages is more than sufficient to keep the laborer alive, there is a similar tendency (though not so universally operative) to increase numbers and reduce the price of the product, until the limit of subsistence is reached.

In occupations of higher grade, there is a similar minimum of wages fixed by the cost of educating and maintaining a laborer in the manner necessary to their successful prosecution. If the remuneration of high-grade labor falls below the cost of educating and supporting it, the number of laborers must necessarily diminish and the price of products will tend to rise. If, on the other hand, the remuneration is in excess of the cost of education and maintenance, there is a tendency towards increase of number of laborers and fall in price of products.

§ 342. It might seem at first sight as though we had solved the problem of wages by thus indicating the conditions under which the supply and demand of labor of any grade are in equilibrium. But when we look closely at the relations between supply and demand for labor in any particular trade, we are confronted with a new difficulty. The demand for labor is measured by the piece; the supply of labor is measured by the day. No equation between the two is possible until we know the number of pieces produced in a day; and this is often precisely what is hardest to determine. A community stands ready to employ laborers in producing 10,000 yards of cloth at ten cents per yard, 11,000 at nine cents, 12,500 at eight cents, 15,000 at seven cents, etc. Whether the 10,000 yards of cloth be made by 1,000 men earning $1.00 per day or 500 men earning $2.00 per day is generally a matter of indifference to the buyers. On the other hand we find 1,000 men ready to work in cloth factories at $2.00 a day, 900 at $1.75, 800 at $1.50, 700 at $1.25, 600 at $1.00, etc. Whether they make the $2.00 by producing 20 yards at ten cents, or by the use of improved machinery which will enable them to produce 25 yards at eight cents, is in the majority of cases a secondary matter to the wage-earners. Instead of one solution which equalizes supply and demand we have an indefinite number of possible solutions based on the varying rate of speed of different laborers.

§ 343. When there is little competition of capitalists, there is a tendency to accept the solution which gives the laborer just enough to keep him alive, and to get what service can be obtained from a body of workers of low efficiency. In cases of this kind the position of the common laborer is very like that of a slave, and the only escape from this lot is by combinations of labor strong enough for physical as well as industrial defense. Under this system, which was substantially that of mediæval society, we find :

(1) A large body of peasants, producing food· for the whole community, and receiving enough of the bare necessaries of life to keep them in condition to work. The only thing that can raise their condition is a plague or other destructive agency which so reduces their numbers as to give a scarcity value to their services, lasting long enough to establish a customary rate of wages higher than that which they had previously received—a state of things exemplified in England from the thirteenth to the fifteenth century.

(2) A body of craftsmen, whose numbers are determined chiefly by the demand of the rich for their products, who receive enough to pay the expenses incident to their education and the maintenance of their station in life, and who are sufficiently organized to resist any attempt to reduce their wages below this figure.

(3) The privileged classes, controlling at once the property and the political power of the nation, who use the surplus food produced by the peasants, not as a means of giving employment to labor, but as a means of supporting

in idleness a number of persons corresponding to the amount of available food.

§ 344. It is the theory of most socialists that this state of things continues to the present day; that the unorganized laborer receives starvation wages; that the organized laborer is able to insist on something more by virtue of combination; but that the property owners or capitalists are the residual claimants of an enormous surplus. The use of this surplus as capital, the socialists regard as an attempt on the part of the property owners to purchase more labor at starvation rates and appropriate a new surplus to themselves. In other words, they think that the modern industrial system really applies mediæval methods of distribution to the increased number of people which the use of modern methods of production has enabled the land to support. They believe that any increase in the efficiency of labor helps the employers and not the employed. A single laborer may raise his earnings by increasing his speed; but he thereby increases the supply of labor, reducing the piece price for his fellows and for himself. The socialists (and many observers who are not socialists) think that if one group of persons has ready money, or things which can be converted into ready money, while another group has labor to sell for this money, an increase of the efficiency of labor will put the latter group at a disadvantage in all its bargains. As the labor makes more products the price of products will be cheapened. The capitalists, or people who own the money, will be in a position to get more products for the same expenditure. If they increase their consumption in proportion to the increase of efficiency of labor, they will enjoy more goods and leave the laborers neither better nor worse off than they were before. If on the other hand they do not thus increase their consumption, some of the laborers will be thrown out of employment and left to starve.

The large body of people who take this view of the

matter—often without really formulating it in detail—regard the luxury of the rich as being on the whole a means of preventing harm to the poor. They regard free expenditure of the capitalists' money as a gain to the laborers, and its saving as a loss. Industry on the part of the wealthy sometimes seems to them a greater vice than idleness; for by the exercise of industry the rich man appears to take the bread out of the poor man's mouth and to deprive some laborer of the chance for a living in order to add a few dollars to an already overgrown fortune; while if he lives in idleness and buys the labor of others, they think that he at least transfers some part of his wealth to those who need it more than he does. They often look with complacency on the actual destruction of wealth as a blessing in disguise. The broken window pane or burnt house becomes in their eyes a source of new employment to labor, transferring money from the pockets of the men who own property to those of the men who are dependent on their work for support. Not a few of them advocate inflation of the currency, by every conceivable means whether practicable or not, in the belief that whatever increases the supply of money increases the demand for labor and the advantage of the laboring classes.

§ 345. This view of the matter is justly criticised as a superficial one. It looks at temporary effects on nominal wages, and disregards permanent effects on real wages. A fire may increase wage-payments in certain trades in a particular locality; but there are two indirect consequences of the fire which generally make the apparent advantage to laborers worse than illusory. In the first place, the money used to rebuild the burnt house is almost always diverted from some other line of expenditure, so that the gain to one group of workmen is offset by a loss to other groups. In the second place, this utilization of labor to replace commodities which have been destroyed, instead of producing new ones, means that the community in the end has fewer comforts and enjoyments than it could otherwise have commanded. This scarcity shows itself in advanced prices. For a considerable time after a fire, house rents will be higher than they were before ; so that the same amount of nominal wages means less available comfort and enjoyment. The laborers are producing for one another as well as for the capitalist. They are spending money for one another's products ; as consumers they profit by an increase in the product, or suffer by its diminution. The destruction of property by the fire does not represent something taken from the capitalist and given to the laborer. It represents a loss of comfort in the community from which, as a rule, no class can wholly exempt itself.

Nor does the money which the rich man saves represent something taken from the laborers and accruing to the capitalists as a class. The man who saves money and invests it is simply spending it in a far-sighted way, and paying laborers for services which meet the future wants of many men instead of the present luxuries of one man.

The man who spends money in employing laborers on things that are really useless, causes food to be consumed by a group of workers who leave nothing permanent to show for it, and lessens the amount of useful things which the community can enjoy in the immediate future. He usually does more harm than the man who saves money and hoards it ; for while hoarding chiefly affects nominal wages, unwise expenditure affects real wages. The harm done by the miser is a negative one—he fails to make use of the opportunities which have been given him. The harm done by the spendthrift, though not equally obvious to the popular vision, is a positive one—he actually leaves fewer products for other people to enjoy.

If we look at real wages instead of nominal ones, at things instead of money, we shall see that it is not the wealth that the capitalist consumes which really goes to the laborers, but the wealth that he does not consume.[1]

§ 346. By those who have grasped this fact it is universally held that increased production due to efficiency of labor accrues very largely to the laborers themselves.

During the early part of the present century the great body of economists believed that this process was effected through the agency of what they called a *wage-fund*. This fund consisted of that part of the past product of the community which was not consumed, but set aside by the capitalists to assist future production. In the very act of directing productive industry, this product was transferred from the capitalists to the laborers in the form of a wage-payment. The total quantity of the unconsumed product thus used as capital represented the aggregate real wages of the community. It was this capital and not the desires or wants of the consumers which fixed the amount received by the laborers as wages. Desires and wants of consumers might determine the direction in which labor was applied; they did not determine the *quantity* of its aggregate remuneration, except so far as they might cause labor to be misapplied and prevent the future capital of the community from becoming as great as it otherwise might be. If a man employed laborers in trimming a lawn instead of cultivating a wheat field, he did not thereby either increase or diminish this year's wages; these were determined by last year's product. But he diminished the amount of next year's real wages, because he caused less wheat to be produced, and thereby

---

[1] This is what is really meant by the somewhat infelicitous phrase, used by many economists, that a demand for commodities is not a demand for labor. The demand for labor, using the word demand in its older sense of "aggregate price offered," rather than "quantity demanded," [(§ 89, note)] is not to be increased by increasing the price which consumers are compelled to pay for commodities, but by increasing the capital available for the maintenance of labor. The personal consumption of the property owners is no measure of the amount of comforts which will go to the support of the laborers.

lessened the amount available for the support of next year's labor. That industry was limited by capital and not by consumers' wants, constituted the cardinal point in the wage-fund theory. Whatever tended to increase or diminish public capital, tended to increase or diminish the fund from which real wages were paid, and by which they were measured. This fund could be increased by efficiency on the part of the laborers, or by saving on the part of the property owners. It could be diminished by destruction of property, by idleness, or by useless luxury. If the laborers, by combination or by favorable circumstances of any kind, got an unduly large share of the national income in one period of production, they so lessened the rate of profit that the inducement to save was diminished; and this tended to diminish capital and wages for the years following. If, on the other hand, they were deprived of a part of their share during one year, profits were so increased that there would be a greater stimulus to save; the wage-fund for the following years would thus be enlarged, and the loss to the laborers would prove only temporary.

To find the average rate of wages in any community, according to this theory, it was only necessary to divide its total wage-fund by the number of the laboring population. The general rate of wages as thus established could not be effectively raised except by an increase of the wage-fund, or a diminution of numbers. The free capital or wage-fund constituted the source of the demand for labor; the laboring population represented the supply; the average rate of wages was fixed by the ratio between the two.[1]

§ 347. The wage-fund theory, at any rate in the form in which it is presented by its more uncompromising advocates, involves several unwarranted assumptions.

---

[1] It was one of those cases where the supply of labor was synonymous with the stock, because the laborer without capital could not wait, but must sell his services at once. Compare § 94.

If we accept MacCulloch's definition of capital as comprising all those portions of the products of industry that may be directly employed either to support human exertion or to facilitate production, we shall find that the amount of real wages falls very far short of what the theory requires. Not all the things that *may* be employed for this purpose, *are* thus employed. A part is spent in charity. A part gets into the hands of criminal or semi-criminal classes, who convert it to their own uses without giving society any return. A part is destroyed by time and natural decay without reaching the consumer at all.

Nor does the amount actually used as capital bear any fixed proportion to the total product which might possibly be thus used. The proportion wasted is by no means constant. It varies from place to place and from year to year. The ability of a community to pay high wages seems to depend more upon the avoidance of waste than upon the increase of accumulations. Laborers are better off where there is a small surplus effectively utilized, than where there is a large surplus ineffectively utilized. As Newcomb well expresses it, wages are a flow and not a fund. They are a quota of the national income rather than of the national capital.

§ 349. Contrast the conditions affecting wages in old and new countries. The old countries have large amounts of capital ; not only large in the aggregate, but large in proportion to the number of laborers. New countries, settled by men of the same race, have relatively small amounts of capital. According to the wage-fund theory wages should be high in the old country and low in the new. But the facts are just the reverse. It is the new country, with small capital, that has the high wages. Nor can this difference be explained, as Cairnes ingeniously undertakes to explain it, by saying that the capital of the old country is invested in machinery, and that the supply of products constituting the wage-fund available for the use of its laborers is therefore small. Making all due allowance for the large amount of wealth represented by machinery, it still remains true that the supply of unused and disposable products in an old country is much larger in proportion to its population than is the case in a newer one. The reason for the difference in wages must be sought chiefly in the fact of the superior utilization of its small stock of capital by the new country, where business is active and idlers are few.

We find the same point illustrated by the conditions which prevail at the close of a war. At such a time the supply of unconsumed products is apt to be small; but if the war has not lasted long enough to destroy the spirit of business enterprise, nor been so disastrous as to paralyze ambition, wages will generally be high. The effort to regain lost ground, and the impossibility of supporting idlers, cause all the available resources to be used in such a way as to counterbalance the evil to the laboring classes which would otherwise result from the diminished amount of capital.

This point is even more conspicuously illustrated in the course of a commercial crisis. At the beginning of such a crisis there is a large stock of unsold commodities awaiting consumption. Statistics of the different trades will show the presence of all the conditions which, according to the wage-fund theory, should promise prosperity to the workmen and continuance of high real wages. Yet somehow the very amount of these commodities seems to form an obstacle to their utilization. People are so afraid to continue their production when there are too many unsold products on hand, that the demand for labor is lessened and wages fall. A few years later, when the stocks of goods have wasted away and the surplus on hand is small, a revival of business, stimulated by the very smallness of visible stocks of goods, results in giving the laborer large employment and a large share in the product. Under such circumstances it may happen that his wages are not limited by the amount of goods left over from past periods of production. If he receives large money payments, and does not spend all of the money thus obtained until the next period of production has become so far advanced that the goods produced during that period are placed at his disposal, he can actually obtain his real wages, not out of past accumulations, but out of current products.

§ 350. These illustrations are enough to show that there is a fallacy in the idea that industry is limited by capital. In one sense of the word " limited," this proposition is measurably true; for the amount which goes to the support of the laborers cannot, except under rare conditions, exceed the unconsumed surplus from previous periods of production. But as the word is commonly understood, it means something more than this. If we say that one thing is limited by another we imply, not only that the first cannot exceed the second, but that it habitually comes up to the bounds set by the second. If we say that the chance of aërial navigation is limited by the height of the atmosphere, we do not mean that a balloon could not go higher than the atmosphere does, which is undoubtedly true ; but that it can go as high as the atmosphere does, which is undoubtedly false. If we say that wages are limited by capital, we are naturally understood as meaning that wages go as high as the amount of accumulations will permit ; and in modern industrial society this proposition is not borne out by the facts.[1]

[1] The wage-fund theory seems to involve a certain confusion between capital as a mode of *measurement* of wealth (§ 5), and capital as a mode of *use* of wealth (§§ 7, 138). If we look at MacCulloch's view that the wealth of the community *measured* as capital furnishes an indication of the amount which will be paid in wages, we are justified in saying that the proposition is important but untrue. If we look at Ricardo's view, that it is the amount of wealth *used* as capital which furnishes the indication of the amount of wages, we have a proposition which is true, but relatively unimportant. The

§ 351. According to the theory which is held by most modern economists, wages are kept up, not by the existence of a fund of public capital which must necessarily go to the laborer, but by the competition of a number of individual capitalists, which reduces profits to a minimum and compels them to give the laborer as large a share of his product as is consistent with the continuance of industrial enterprise. The advocates of this theory claim that there is such activity in the accumulation of capital that competition secures to the laborer the chief benefit of modern improvements, and forces the capitalist to content himself with a small fraction of the gain instead of the lion's share.

The piece-price which the employer can afford to pay in the long run, is the price of the product less the interest on the capital involved in its production ; and in the long run he is also compelled to pay as much as this. For if the price of the product more than pays wages and interest, new competition sets in which drives prices down and wages up ; and if, on the other hand, the price of the product less' than pays wages and interest, the invested

error of the advocates of the wage-fund theory consists in the assumption that the logic of Ricardo can be applied to the concept of MacCulloch. They see that the payment of wages represents an investment of capital ; they proceed to assume that the amount of such investment will bear a determinate proportion to the total amount of unconsumed surplus which is physically capable of investment. But the two things are totally different ; nor does the amount of the one bear any fixed ratio to that of the other.

When John Stuart Mill defined capital as including whatever things *are destined* to supply productive labor with the various means needed for the process of production, and thus remitted to the mind of the employer the determination of the amount of the wage-fund, he had implicitly abandoned the views of his immediate predecessors. But at the time when he wrote his " Principles of Political Economy," he was far from perceiving the real bearing of this change on the doctrine of wages. It was not until Longe and Thornton, and afterwards Walker, showed how conspicuously the wage-fund theory failed to explain the facts of industry, that proper importance was given to the anticipated value of a *future* product in determining the share of the past product of industry which goes to the laborers.

capital is allowed to wear out without being replaced until prices are driven up and wages down. Neither of these processes is under modern conditions a quick one, but both are sure to come about in course of time. It is from observation of these facts that Walker has deduced his theory that wages are the *residual share* of the product of industry. If we look at any one establishment, for a short period, this statement seems palpably untrue; for the employer pays a stipulated sum in the form of wages, and takes whatever may be left. But if we look at the industry as a whole, and at the course of events in the long run, we find much to confirm General Walker's view.

§ 352. The residual theory has a great advantage over its two predecessors, in explaining accurately the facts of modern business. It shows, as the popular theory cannot, why wages are high where labor is efficient. It explains, as the wage-fund theory fails to do, why wages are high when unconsumed products are scarce. It makes wages depend on a flow of capital instead of a fund. But it is not quite free from unwarranted assumptions. In laying stress on the competition of capitalists with one another, it seems to lose sight of the corresponding competition among laborers. Increase of numbers is tending to drive wages down in the same way that increase of capital is tending to drive profits down. To be sure, the cases are not quite parallel; for a reduction in the rate of profit means increased demand for labor, while a reduction in the rate of wages means diminished demand for capital.[1]

[1] If the rate of profit falls, the laborer gets more nearly the whole amount of the product. But if the rate of wages falls we have a corresponding fall in prices and little change in the relative shares of labor and capital.

It is a common but erroneous assumption that if general wages are reduced profits will rise. A fall in real wages, the methods of industry remaining unchanged, means that less capital need be advanced in productive industry. Now this lessened demand for capital would certainly not raise the rate of profit—if anything it would probably lower it. If the amount of invested

But this only amounts to saying that while part of the gain from low profits goes to the laborer, all of the gain from low wages goes to the consumer. It is the consumer who is the residual claimant in the results of modern industrial improvements. Inactive competition on the part of any large group of producers may delay this result [1]; it cannot essentially alter it. No one group of producers can be marked as a residual claimant under the modern process of industrial competition. Most of the gain from any improvement in production ultimately goes to the consumer, whoever he may be, by enabling him to get his products cheaper.

§ 353. Here we find a grain of truth in the much despised popular theory. It is the possessors of ready money that derive the chief advantage from improved efficiency of labor. The error of the popular view of wages is not in its assumption that increased efficiency gives its main benefit to the buyers of products, but in the assumption that those buyers are necessarily the rich, the holders of accumulated wealth. A man's power of consumption is measured by the income he receives rather than by the capital which he owns. If his labor affords him an income of one thousand dollars a year and he spends it all, he never obtains any accumulated wealth, but he obtains an enormous advantage from the large amount of comforts which modern industrial processes have placed at his disposal. The gain from an improve-

capital is diminished and the rate of profit not increased, the aggregate of profit falls with a fall in wages, and the whole gain goes to the consumer.

Of course, if an individual employer can reduce wages, he thereby increases his profits; and an observation of this fact has doubtless been the source of the mistaken belief that what can happen in each particular case can happen in all simultaneously.

[1] Cases of this kind have given rise to an opinion, frequently expressed, that the benefit of improvements goes to the owners of the productive agent which increases *most slowly*, be it land, labor, or capital. This seems to be a much more sweeping generalization than is warranted either by the facts or the theoretical proofs which have been adduced to support it.

ment goes chiefly to those who consume the products cheapened by such an improvement; and these may be either laborers or capitalists. The study of distribution of wealth between different classes resolves itself into a study of the consumption of wealth by different classes. If an improvement in production is of such a character as to cheapen goods used by capitalists, and not to affect those used by laborers, the popular theory of wages is the true one. The gain in such a case goes entirely to the rich. If, on the other hand, the improvement is such as to cheapen products used by the laborer, and not by the capitalist, the gain goes entirely to the laborer, and the wage-fund theory is the more correct one. The popular theory tacitly assumes that every improvement is of the former class. In point of fact, modern improvements belong chiefly to the latter.

§ 354. Let us look at this matter in detail. Suppose that it were thus possible to divide goods into two classes; one used by the rich, the other by the poor. An improvement in the production of goods consumed by the rich would cheapen the price of such goods and enable the rich to get more for their money. This would be the only effect. It would not increase the amount of real capital available for the support of labor, except in a very slight degree, by an indirect process of redistribution of producers in different employments. The surplus available for laborers would probably remain unchanged. The activity of capital in giving employment to labor would find itself restricted within narrow limits.

Suppose, on the other hand, that the increase is confined to things which laborers use. Under such a condition the rich would find themselves practically compelled to reinvest the whole surplus. They would have no use for the increased production. They would be forced to convert it into capital. The benefit of the surplus would accrue to the laborers in the form of a direct and immediate increase of real wages. Barring losses from waste, and from the consumption of this increased product by idlers instead of laborers, the wage-fund theory in a case like this would be substantially the true one.

What we actually see is something intermediate between these two cases, but nearer the second than the first. Improved methods have not cheapened the products which are used by the rich exclusively. Champagne and yachts and race horses are as costly as ever. They cheapen products which are used by poor as well as rich. Nearly all the large improvements in modern industry have depended for their success upon the creation of a wide market (§ 179), appealing not only to those who have accumulated large fortunes, but to those who live more or less prosperously on the results of their labor. Under these circumstances we find an active competition, both for the services of the laborer as a producer and for the money of the laborer as a consumer ; *especially the latter.* The laborer is the residual claimant in modern industry, not solely nor chiefly on account of his profit in the increase of production, but on account of his profit in the increase of consumption.

§ 355. If the effect of increased efficiency in production is to enlarge the amount of products available to the laborer as a consumer, the question at once arises, what he will do with the surplus. Four possibilities are open to any group of laborers :

1. They may increase their numbers, making the average size of their families larger.

2. They may shorten their hours of labor.

3. They may enlarge their consumption of the products of other laborers.

4. They may save money ; that is, they may waive the enjoyment of a part of their income and put it at the disposal of other members of the community, for the

sake of a future return which they anticipate from such present abstinence.

The choice between these alternatives depends largely upon the character of the laborer himself.

If he is influenced by the force of custom, and is not in the habit of reasoning at all, he will unconsciously choose the first alternative, supporting an increased family in the old standard of comfort and bringing up a number of children who in the next generation will increase the intensity of competition of laborers with one another.

If he pursues short-sighted lines of reasoning, he will take advantage of the improvement to lessen his hours of labor, being able to obtain the old amount of comfort with less expenditure of effort. Whether this change is a gain or a loss to the community will depend largely on the way in which he uses his leisure. If the time is spent in loafing, with its habitual concomitants, it will be a loss; if it is spent in rational enjoyment, it will pave the way for the third alternative of diversified consumption, and will be a means of real gain to the individual and progress to the community as a whole.

If he is in the habit of far-sighted reasoning, he will choose either the third or the fourth alternative. Reducing his labor very little, and making up by increased speed for any slight reduction in hours, the far-sighted man will take the fullest advantage of his gain as a consumer and will utilize the change to secure more enjoyment, either present or future, rather than to do less work. He will not increase his family or diminish his output, but will increase his comfort for the present and his provision for the future.

§ 356. These differences may be illustrated mathematically as follows:

On the line $OX$ (Fig. 10) lay off equal parts representing units of time of labor—say hours of work per day. At each of these points draw a line parallel to $OY$, representing the intensity of enjoyment derived from the results of the labor of that hour; or, what is substan-

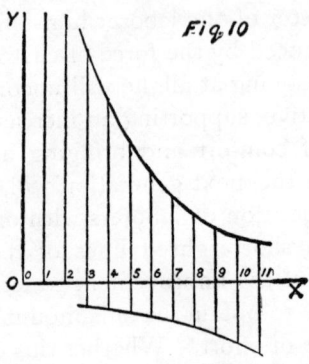

Fig. 10

tially the same thing, the sacrifice which would be involved in going without them. As the number of hours increases, the intensity of enjoyment tends to diminish. The first hours represent the difference between death and life, and their product may be said to have infinite [1] utility. Longer hours mean an increase in the total comfort available; but this increment becomes less marked as the working day grows longer. If we connect the extremes of these lines measuring satisfaction, we obtain a curve whose height at any point represents the degree of enjoyment secured by the last unit of labor time, while the total area between the curve and the two axes represents the total enjoyment which the individual obtains by his work.

If we represent the pain of successive hours of labor in like manner, by lines drawn downward from $OX$, we can construct a similar curve, below the axis, representing the

---

[1] Patten uses the term "absolute" instead of "infinite," which is perfectly proper; but he measures it by zero instead of infinity, which hardly seems right. For the thing which is barely distinguishable from a necessity involves a very great sacrifice, when people are forced to give it up, not a very small one, and thus approximates to infinity instead of to zero.

sacrifices, direct and indirect [1] which the laborer undergoes. These sacrifices during the early hours will be comparatively slight; there may even be, as Jevons suggests, a balance of pleasure in working rather than in not working, in which case the curve of labor will rise above the axis. But, as the hours increase, the pain and sacrifice also increase. The laborer who exercises free judgment will go on working until the (diminishing) increment of satisfaction from the product just balances the increasing pain and sacrifice from the labor. At that point he will stop. In the illustration given, this condition of things comes into play at the end of the ninth hour. Everything before that gives a balance of satisfaction over pain and sacrifice. Everything after that gives a balance in the other direction.

§ 357. What will be the effect on this balance, if the laborer, either through his own increase of efficiency or through the cheapening of the products of others, is able to get more products and services for a given duration of labor? Will the enlarged quantity of possible return for the tenth hour's work serve as a stimulus to make him increase his time? Or will the larger product which he has obtained from earlier hours so appease the intensity of his desires that he will stop at the eighth or seventh hour? Which will prove the stronger force, the increase of the amount to be obtained, which makes additional labor seem more remunerative, or the increased amount of comfort already in his possession, which makes it seem less so?

The answer to this question will depend largely upon the kind of use which he makes of his wages. Assume that a laborer spends part of his earnings for food, part for comforts, part for luxuries, and part for social advance-

---

[1] Direct sacrifice means pain; indirect means loss of pleasure. Patten has developed some of the bearings of the difference between the two in an interesting manner; but in our elementary treatment of the subject it seems hardly worth while to distinguish them.

ment. While Weber's law, that increased consumption is attended with diminished satisfaction (§ 92), perhaps applies in some measure to all of these things, the rapidity of the diminution is very different in the four cases. It is most marked in connection with food. Hunger is the most exacting of wants; but when hunger is satisfied, the enjoyment connected with additional expenditures for eating rapidly diminishes, and the point of satiety may soon be reached. In the case of comforts like clothing, fuel, or shelter, the first want is not so imperative as that of hunger; but the utility of added supplies of these things does not diminish so rapidly as in the case of food. While two suits of clothes do not represent twice as much utility to the wearer as one suit of clothes, the gain in enjoyment from their possession is relatively greater than that which results from eating double the accustomed number of meals. In the case of luxuries the first necessity is much less than that for food or clothing; but when people have once begun to spend money on luxuries they can go on for a long time before they find themselves even approximately satiated. Expenditures for social advancement are not a necessity at all, but they are accompanied with almost undiminished enjoyment as their amount increases.

§ 358. Suppose that a laborer under old conditions, working nine hours a day, spends the product of five hours' labor on food, that of three hours' labor on comforts, and that of one hour's labor on luxuries; and that by some industrial change his purchasing power in all these lines is doubled. What will happen? He will quite certainly reduce the time devoted to the production of means of purchasing food. He can get more food by three hours' labor than he previously got by five; and this so far satisfies his hunger that the promise of increased supplies from the fourth and fifth hour does not constitute a motive to work for that purpose. The time devoted to the acquisition of comforts is not so certain to diminish. Not improbably it will remain nearly stationary. If he continues to work three hours for fuel, clothing, and house-rent, it will show that as the amount of these things has doubled, the intensity of enjoyment from additional supplies has halved—a probable enough result. The labor-time devoted to securing luxuries is likely to increase, because the increased amount of commodities which he can buy gives a large enjoyment with which the possession of other luxuries hardly interferes. What is true of luxuries is even more conspicuously true of means of social advancement. The more of these a man can get for any given time of labor, the more will he try to secure them independently of the amount he already possesses. We are thus likely to see a redistribution of hours somewhat as follows :

|  | Old Conditions. | New Conditions. |
| --- | --- | --- |
| Food | 5 | 3 |
| Comforts | 3 | 3 |
| Luxuries | 1 | 2 |
| Ambitions | 0 | 1 |

§ 359. This is not mere theory. It is verified by two independent lines of observation :

1. The Prussian statistician, Dr. Engel, has developed the fact that the greater the wages a group of laborers receives, the smaller will be the percentage of those wages which is spent for food. This generalization, known as Engel's Law, has been confirmed by investigations in a great many different countries, and has been supplemented by observation as to other groups of expenditure corresponding to the view just stated.

2. It has also been noted that an increase in the volume of food products, while population remains unchanged, produces a fall in price more than corresponding to the increase of supply, so that the aggregate payment for such products by the consumers tends to diminish. This in-

dicates that consumers, when they can get a larger amount of food for the same amount of labor, tend to reduce the hours devoted to the work of securing food supplies. On the other hand, in most manufactured articles, which are matters of comfort or luxury, an increase in quantity produced is accompanied by a fall in price less than corresponding to the increase in supply, so that the aggregate payment for such products by the consumer tends to increase. This shows that consumers, when they are enabled to get a larger amount of manufactured products for the same amount of labor, so increase their consumption as to devote more labor instead of less to procuring things of this kind.

This result is even more conspicuously seen when we come to luxuries like travel. A moderate reduction in price has been sufficient to cause a great increase in the use of transportation agencies, and to make the total amount paid for their services much larger than it was a few years ago. When the invention of the railroad enabled one man to do work which formerly required a hundred or a thousand hands, it was supposed that the demand for labor in moving goods and passengers would be greatly diminished. But the railroad system employs far more laborers in proportion to the population than were employed on roads in the old days ; and this proves that the people as a whole spends a larger part of its income for transportation at low rates than it ever did at high rates.[1]

---

[1] These conditions are illustrated in the differing forms of the demand curve (§ 91) for different articles. In the case of necessities, or things which are regarded as necessities, a change in price is accompanied by less than the proportionate change in quantity consumed. The demand curve in these cases approaches more nearly to a horizontal line. Especially is this true of an article like tobacco, so distinct from others in its character that nothing else can be substituted for it. On the other hand, with things which are not popularly regarded as necessities, a change in price is accompanied by a more than proportionate change in quantity demanded, and

§ 360. We have thus far assumed the hours of labor to remain unchanged while the use made of the earnings of those hours was redistributed. But it will generally happen that any increase of real wages, like that which has been described, is attended with some reduction in the hours of labor.

There are two different causes, operating on different classes of laborers, which combine to produce this effect. The low-grade laborer who cares much for food and drink and comparatively little for other things, when he finds himself able to get his accustomed living in fewer hours is strongly tempted to reduce his working time; or if he continues to work as many hours as before, he reduces speed in such a way as to have virtually the same effect on the industrial community. Until his consumption has become diversified and his ambition developed, the motives for reducing his labor are stronger than those for increasing his earnings. On the other hand, the high-grade laborer, though anxious to increase his consumption, finds that time is necessary for the enjoyment of the new opportunities of diversified consumption which progress has placed within his reach. The long hours of labor interfere with the enjoyment of the results of that labor. He sets a limit to his working day, not so much on account of the direct pain of labor as on account of the indirect sacrifices connected with its long continuance. He may try to combine both the means and the opportunity for enjoyment by reducing hours and increasing his speed—in which case the reduction of the working day is more apparent than real.

§ 361. But will not the progress of those who wish to shorten their hours or increase their enjoyments be de-

the demand curve approaches more nearly to the vertical line. At high prices the demand will be trifling; at low prices it will be many times greater. Commodities of this kind are said to be *sensitive*; those of the former class are said to be *insensitive*.

feated by the less intelligent laborers, who go on irration-
ally increasing their numbers? Will not the whole vantage
ground be lost in the next generation, when a larger population is competing for a limited supply of food products
and disregarding opportunities for diversified enjoyment?
Is not the gain to the laboring classes in its nature a temporary one, which will be destroyed by increase of numbers on the part of the less intelligent members of the
class? In some lines of production it will. In these lines
the competitive system results in having our work done by
a large number of low-grade laborers, instead of by a relatively small number of high-grade laborers. The ready-
made clothing trade in our cities furnishes perhaps the
most conspicuous instance. It is served by people who
are underpaid, underfed, and undersupplied with everything which contributes to civilized life. The effort to
realize economy of production has in such cases led to the
employment of cheap labor in the bad sense—of labor
which is cheap because it does little, and which receives
correspondingly little.

§ 362. But while low grade labor is the cheapest labor
in some employments, it is not cheap in others. To enable a man to do hard work he must be reasonably well
fed. The economy of increased power overbalances any
apparent loss from increased consumption. Even where
work requires physical strength only, the man who receives low wages per day is so much less efficient that
his labor may be very costly per unit of product. In employments which require mental ability as well as physical
strength, the inadequacy of the so-called cheap labor, and
its real dearness when measured on the basis of work
done, becomes even more conspicuously apparent. The
brain worker, to do his work properly, must have not
merely the necessary amount of food and shelter and
fuel, but the necessary amount of comfort and travel and

education to keep the brain in working order.[1]  A surgeon or a lawyer who earns only one dollar a day is a very bad man to employ.  The cheap laborer cannot compete with the dear laborer in lines requiring special strength or special skill.

§ 363. Different men require different feeding; different trades require different men.  If we go into a machine shop where many steam-engines are built, we find some large ones and some small ones.  The small ones burn little fuel, but they also furnish very little power.  The large ones burn ten or one hundred times the amount of fuel, and require correspondingly greater care and expenditure in every direction; but the difference in work done by large engines is such that, in those lines where they can be used, the apparent waste represents a true economy.  So it is in the diversified industries of modern life.  There are some men whose maximum efficiency per unit of food is obtained with small consumption and small output.  These go into the lines requiring neither exceptional strength nor exceptional skill, and remain poor because the best commercial economy in such lines is obtained by a combination of low output and low consumption.  There are others who require for their maximum efficiency a greater amount of food and a considerable diversity of enjoyment.  These go into lines where the maximum efficiency is obtained by moderate but not immoderate consumption.  Finally, we have a smaller number of men in yet higher walks of industry, whose economy is like that of the engines of the *Lucania;* whose power can be obtained only by an enormous consumption of the products of others, past and present, but

---

[1] A large manufacturing concern, within the author's knowledge, offered to defray half the expenses of a visit to the Chicago Exposition for any of its foremen who would make the trip, believing that the increased value of their services to the concern would make the investment a paying one.

is, if properly directed, capable of rendering services more than proportionate to this consumption.

§ 364. It is in this differentiation of employment that we are to seek the cause of poverty. People will have small earnings per day if they are so constituted that their maximum service in the community is obtained under conditions analogous to those of the small steam-engine. The multiplication of numbers which is characteristic of laborers of this grade drives the price of their services so low that it becomes impossible for men with a higher standard of living to compete with them in doing work which requires no special qualifications, either physical or mental. The high-grade man who competes with an increasing number of low-grade men finds himself forced to the alternative of rising or dying. The competition of those who multiply their numbers instead of shortening their hours or diversifying their consumption, drives the higher class of laborers out of some things and up into others. The men thus driven out cannôt always maintain themselves in any higher grade of employment, and from this fact there results a great deal of hardship to those upon whom the changed conditions come when they are advanced in years; but, on the whole, a surprisingly large number of the workmen who appear to suffer most from the competition of cheap labor are forced upward in spite of themselves,—forced to do a higher grade of work and to become richer and stronger than they could have hoped to be under the old conditions. The day-laborers in the United States have always feared and tried to obstruct the immigration of men whose habits of living were lower than their own, and whose influx would apparently take the bread out of the mouths of those who had previously done the cheapest grades of work. But there can be no doubt that the successive waves of immigration have improved rather than debased the condition of those with whom they came into competition. The Irishman in 1830 forced the American up; the Italian and the Canadian have forced the Irishman up. The cheapening of the lowest grade of product, while it has operated as a disadvantage to those who compete in producing it, has served as an advantage to every consumer, and has made all those in the higher industrial groups better off from being relieved from the necessity of doing the work which could more economically be done by cheap labor and poor men.

Each group of laborers contributes to the supply of one particular kind of goods or services, and to the demand for goods and services of many other kinds. Every laborer who adds himself to one of these groups increases the supply and lowers the price in the line which he chooses. The greater the number of men in a group, the smaller will be the price of their services, and the larger the amounts which they have to pay for services rendered by men in other groups. An addition to the numbers of any given group makes life harder for those within its pale and easier for those without it.

§ 365. Many men find themselves bound to a certain group by a custom or habit which they cannot override, or by special tastes which are the result of such habit. Others are free to choose their line of work as they please. With some reservations, they will choose the line where they think they can make the most money per year. A man of given physical and mental traits will try to adopt the business where those traits are most efficient—where the value due to their possession outweighs the cost of their maintenance. But if too many men go into the same group, some must go to the wall. If a profession is overcrowded, this fact reduces the amount which its members can earn, until there comes a time when some are forced into other trades where there is no such overcrowding. The differences of wages in different employments are not due to differences in the pleasure or pain

in the work, except so far as this pleasure or pain increases or diminishes the number of those who enter the
field. They are due to the reciprocal demand of different
groups for one another's products or services.[1] The relative prices paid for the products of different groups must
be such as to secure a grade of workers within each group
which can give the required product at the minimum of
waste to society.

§ 366. While the characteristics of each individual are
the chief factor in determining to which of these groups
he shall belong, there are always some producers who
stand on the verge between a lower and a higher group,
and who are drafted to the one or the other by slight
changes in the public demand. If the majority of men
and women throughout the community are intelligent in
their consumption, spending a relatively small proportion
of their money for the bare necessaries of life and a large
proportion for comforts and enjoyments, of higher as
well as lower grades, we can have a large number of producers engaged in furnishing these enjoyments without
driving their remuneration below the necessary minimum.
In this way the education of the community in diversified
consumption becomes of the highest importance to all
classes in society. The qualities of an individual man
will determine to a great extent whether he is to be rich
or poor; but the general standard of consumption of the

---

[1] Down to the time of Mill it was generally said that the price of articles
tended to conform to their labor cost. Mill showed that in international
trade this process was reversed; that the remuneration of the producers of
goods for the export trade of different nations was determined by their
"reciprocal demand" for one another's products. Cairnes extended this
theory of reciprocal demand to explain the relative remuneration of men of
different social antecedents—"non-competing groups." About 1870 Walras, Jevons, and Menger, working almost simultaneously and quite independently, showed that what Mill had treated as an exception was really a
rule. "I hold labor to be essentially variable," says Jevons, 'so that its
value must be determined by the value of the produce, not the value of the
produce by that of the labor."

community will be the dominant factor in determining how large a proportion of the community shall be rich or poor. If the bulk of the people live on the minimum of cheap food, multiply or at any rate maintain their numbers as long as such cheap food is forthcoming, and spend comparatively little for comforts and luxuries, we shall find that most of the labor of such a community is employed in obtaining subsistence for the masses. Under such circumstances the proportion of low grade labor will probably be very great. If, however, a large part of the community has been educated to demand something besides cheap food and to exercise self-restraint in the multiplication of numbers until it is possible to provide a high standard of comfort, we shall have a relatively smaller demand for food and a relatively larger demand for those comforts and luxuries which are the product of higher intelligence and require a higher rate of pay in order to enable the producer to furnish them to advantage. In this way, any increase in intelligence of consumption on the part of the masses increases the average rate of real wages, by making it possible for a larger proportion of the producers to live in employments where the conditions of economical production are favorable to comfort, education, and wealth, rather than to poverty and numerical increase.

§ 367. This must not be understood as involving indiscriminate commendation of luxury. If luxury lays many men and many things under contribution for the enjoyment of one man only, it is bad for the community. If it leads one man to monopolize the product of a larger amount of land than is necessary for his own support, it prevents others from getting food. If it causes an unnecessary amount of labor to be spent for one man's enjoyment, it prevents the labor from furnishing means of enjoyment to many others. If, as frequently happens, the product of this labor harms the efficiency of the man who enjoys it, it involves an additional source of weak-

ness to the community.  We have seen the fallacy of
the attempt to excuse such luxury on the pretext that it
gives employment to labor.  But in their well-grounded
protest against selfish excesses of luxury, and against the
excuses made to palliate them, some economists have
gone too far in discountenancing all unnecessary expenditure for personal comfort.  " The Puritans objected to
bear-baiting, not because it gave pain to the bear, but because it gave pleasure to the spectators."  This judgment
is as unwarranted as the other.  The intellectual progress
connected with using things that are not necessary is quite
as important to the community as the industrial progress
connected with producing things that are.  The distinction between productive and unproductive consumption is
often drawn in such a way as to emphasize purely material advances and ignore other things which are quite
as essential.  The lack of intelligent enjoyment, in the
Anglo-Saxon race at any rate, involves more pressing
danger than the lack of readiness to save capital.  If a
man spends his money for luxuries which do no harm,
and whose production does not involve a waste of land or
labor disproportionate to the enjoyment which they furnish to him and to others, he is presumably helping rather
than hindering the progress of the community at large.

§ 368.  There are many schemes of social reform, whose
promoters expect to lessen poverty by increasing the
laborers' intelligence in production, but whose actual
promise of good to society is far more dependent upon
their influence on intelligence in consumption.  Popular
education may serve as a type.  This has some effect in
making a laborer more skilful and in enabling him to contribute a larger share to the public income.  But it does
not directly promote the man's earning power to a degree
commensurate with the time spent by the schoolboy or
the money spent by the taxpayer.  The more advanced
the education, the greater is the force of this complaint.

A high school course is most useful to those who reach the higher walks of life; but all men cannot reach these walks without overcrowding them: and in the lower spheres of industry it often seems to do the recipient little good. The greatest gain from public education lies in the fact that a people which grows up with wide views of life, develops wider demands for consumption. Instead of a large population chiefly engaged in supplying itself with a bare living, we have a somewhat smaller total population, demanding and receiving more complex services which their education has led them to regard as indispensable, and in whose purveyance the high grade laborer has an advantage over his low grade competitor. Somewhat the same thing can be said of the grounds for regulating the liquor traffic. The waste of productive power due to indulgence in drink is only a part, and perhaps not the largest part, of the evils chargeable to drunkenness. Where the passion for excess in drink stands in the way of intelligent enjoyment, it promotes poverty, not only by making the drinking men poor producers, but by making the public a poor consumer.

# CHAPTER XI.

## MACHINERY AND LABOR.

Alleged Displacement and Degradation of Labor—Factory Acts—Labor
Organizations—Old and New Methods—Compulsory Arbitration—
The Living Wage.

W. S. Jevons. "The State in Relation to Labor." London, 1882.
J. A. Hobson : "The Evolution of Modern Capitalism." London, 1894.
G. v. Schulze-Gaevernitz: "Der Grossbetrieb." Leipzig, 1892.
The older motives and ideas of English Trades-Unions are well presented
by G. Howell, "Conflicts of Capital and Labor," 2d ed. London, 1890.
The views of the new unionism are given by Sidney and Beatrice Webb,
"History of Trade Unionism," London, 1894. There is no correspond-
ingly complete history of American labor movements ; perhaps the most
available is R. T. Ely, "The Labor Movement in America," New York,
1886.

§ 369. WE have thus far assumed that improvements
in the efficiency of labor were not accompanied by any
radical alteration in the industrial system ; that the conditions of employment remained substantially the same,
while the power of the individual workman was increased.
But in point of fact, the greater part of the increase in
the efficiency of modern labor has been connected with
the use of modern machinery and improved productive
methods which are under the control of the employer and
not of the laborer. Some people who admit that the
laborer gains by the increase of his own powers are disposed to doubt whether a similar gain is possible for the
laborer when the means of increased production are held
in the hands of the capitalist. Especially doubtful does

the case seem in those large industries where combination has made the greatest progress, and where the protection which the workman receives from the competition of different capitalists is apparently reduced to a minimum.

§ 370. There are three evils which the opponents of private capital charge against machinery, as now managed and operated :

1. That it displaces a large amount of human labor, thus taking income away from employees and giving it to employers.

2. That when it does not actually drive human labor out of use, it employs it in circumstances unfavorable to efficiency, health, and morals.

3. That under the best conditions it deprives the workman of independence, making him a specialized machine instead of a broad-minded man.

§ 371. The first charge, in its wider shape, is obviously belied by the facts. Machinery has not displaced labor. On the contrary, there has been a most conspicuous increase of employment in those lines where improvements in machinery have been greatest. The number of persons engaged in manufacturing and transportation to-day bears a far larger proportion to those engaged in agriculture than was the case two or three generations ago. The urban population makes more use of machinery than the rural population ; and it is a conspicuous fact that our cities have grown faster than the country as a whole. Whatever else machinery may have done, it certainly has not kept labor out of mechanical industries.

Nowhere have modern methods been more strikingly exemplified than in transportation industries. By the use of the railroad a single man is enabled to do work which formerly would have been hardly within the capacity of a thousand men. On this very account the introduction of railroads was regarded with distrust by large classes of the community. It was thought that teamsters, hostlers, and innkeepers would be thrown out of employment, and that there would be no work left for them to do. But it has turned out that the development of the railroad has given additional work to the very classes which it was expected to antagonize. While the efficiency of human labor in transportation has increased a thousand-fold, the volume of goods and passengers transported has increased much more than this. The services of collection and delivery of freight at stations now employ as many men and horses as were engaged in the whole movement of freight a century ago. The entertainment of modern travellers affords occupation to a larger number of inn-keepers than were supported by the few passengers who ventured to take long journeys in ancient times. The cheapening of transportation attendant upon the use of improved appliances has called forth a development of travel and of freight shipment more than proportionate to the increased efficiency of service. The aggregate demand for labor in these lines has become greater instead of less.

Nor is this experience with railroad travel an isolated or accidental one. It is characteristic of the effects of modern mechanical processes, wherever they have been applied on a large scale. The work of machinery is generally of such a kind that it can be made profitable only by extensive public use. If a community can buy but ten pairs of shoes in a year, it will be more economical to have shoes made by hand, no matter what machinery may be invented. In order to obtain the advantage of the best modern processes of manufacture, we must make a hundred thousand pairs a year. The economy of the introduction of a machine consists, not in making the old product at less expense and with less labor, but in making a much larger product with the same labor. What is called labor-saving machinery is in fact not labor-saving, but product-making. It can only become profitable by meeting the wants of the community as a whole, and not those of a few rich men.

§ 372. Some detailed results of improvement in machinery from 1840 to 1883 are well illustrated by figures which Atkinson has collected from cotton mills. For purposes of comparison he chose two mills which had been in operation throughout this period, which employed substantially the same number of operatives in 1883 that they did in 1840, and which had not changed the valuation of their capital. During the period in question, the output of these mills had almost exactly trebled. This increase had made it necessary to reduce the price charged for the services in manufacturing (*i. e.*, the margin between selling price and cost of material) from about three cents per yard in 1840 to about one cent and a half in 1883. The wages paid had fallen from 1.82 cents per yard in 1840 to 1.08 cents in 1883 ; but the profits had fallen from 1.18 cents in 1840 to 0.43 cents in 1883. The share of the laborers in the total product had risen from less than 61 per cent in the former case to more than 68 per cent in the latter, in the face of a decided reduction in the hours of labor, and an even more decided increase in the number of looms and spindles per operative. The actual profits on the total capital had remained about the same, but the wages per operative per year had increased 64 per cent. Other instances like this, which have been collected from different lines of business, seem to indicate that under the modern industrial system there is a tendency toward increase of wages and relative diminution of profits.

To this optimistic view, that machinery benefits the laborer rather than the employer, there are certain objections which must be carefully examined.

§ 373. The increase of large fortunes on the part of the owners of capital while so many of their operatives have accumulated little or nothing is held by many to prove that the capitalists have been the chief gainers in modern industrial progress. The growing contrast between wealth and poverty seems to indicate that the rich are growing richer and the poor poorer. In a new community, few are very rich, but few are in danger of starvation. As the community becomes older, the disparity between the richest and the poorest becomes greater with each succeeding year. This fact of itself is thought sufficient to prove that progress increases the advantages of capital as compared with those of labor.

This reasoning is inconclusive. Differences of accumulated wealth of different members of the community prove nothing as to ratios of income of different classes.

The disparity in the accumulations of different men is likely to become more marked as the amount of wealth in any community grows larger. There is always a number of people who stand at the zero point in the matter of accumulation. Some men gamble and get rid of their property at once ; some men drink and get rid of it almost as speedily. Some without either gambling or drinking are so shiftless that they refuse to work as long as they have a dollar in their pockets. Some, again, are unfortunate, through no fault of their own, and fall into the fate of the shiftless unless relieved by charity. If property were evenly divided to-day, there would soon be some men who had none and others who had a great deal. The successful gambler and the saloon keeper will benefit by the losses of their victims; the industrious or fortunate man will find himself gradually drawing ahead of the shiftless or unfortunate. The more capital there is in the community the greater these differences are sure to become. With the increasing wealth of modern nations there has inevitably been an increasing disparity between the accumulations of those who have most and of those who have least.

But this does not always represent a difference in income. The income of the man who has saved nothing may be larger than that of the man who has saved a hundred or a thousand dollars a year. Nor does it represent a difference in enjoyment. The enjoyment of different classes and different individuals in the community is measured by their expenditure, not by their accumulations. The most careful calculations show, that side by side with the increase of accumulations, and partly as its direct consequence, the proportion of enjoyment which goes to labor is becoming larger, and the proportion which accrues to capital relatively smaller. Just as increased numbers of laborers mean increased competition for employment, forcing the position of the laboring classes downward, so increased accumulations of capital mean increased competition for the services of the laborers, forcing the relative income of the capitalists downward and that of the laborers upward. It is in large measure because of the enormous investments of capital and the resulting keenness of competition among employers, that the proportion of the public income going to the laborers has steadily increased.[1]

[1] Several attempts have been made to measure the relative shares of the annual product received by capitalists and laborers at different times. Rae has made an estimate for England on the basis of figures furnished by Gregory King for 1688 and by Dudley Baxter for 1867. Using the term "working class" somewhat narrowly, so as to exclude those receiving salaries or fees, he calculates that in 1688 74 per cent of the population belonged to the working class, and earned collectively 26 per cent of the entire income of the country ; while in 1867 somewhat less than 80 per cent belonged to the working class and earned collectively 40 per cent of the income of the community. Atkinson has made a similar estimate for the United States in 1880 in which he has included with the working class the salary-receivers as well as the wage-receivers. Taking his figures from the United States census of 1880, he estimates the value of the commercial product of the country at $10,000,000,000, while the amount paid in wages and salaries of every kind was $9,000,000,000. As 1880 was very nearly a normal year, not conspicuously marked by either inflation or depression, and as the census of 1880 was better managed than any other in the history of the United States, he believes that this represented very nearly the ratio of wages to profits. The

§ 374. It is urged as proof of the diminishing share of labor in the industrial product, that modern methods cause more time to elapse between the rendering of labor and the receipt of the product; that while the *rate* of profit has doubtless fallen, this fall is not proportionate to the increase in the average duration of the process; and that the ratio of total profits to total wages must therefore have increased.

To this view it may be answered, first, that the rate of profit (as distinct from the rate of interest) has fallen most conspicuously in large industries with much fixed capital. Goods are produced and sold on far narrower margins. A few large employers can make more accurate calculations of cost than a number of small ones; and the very scale on which the work is done, while it often seems to preclude competition, really gives publicity to the facts with regard to production and sale in a way to ensure more fully both to laborers and consumers the benefit of the one-price system. It may be added in the second place, that instances of mistaken investment in machinery which gives no profit at all, tend to reduce the gains of the capitalist classes to a far greater degree than any one would assume who did not make the calculation in detail.

§ 375. Another objection to the view that the benefit of machinery has gone chiefly to the laboring classes is based on the fact that the hours of labor have not been reduced in proportion to the increased efficiency which

small proportion of profits under this estimate has excited general surprise, and Hawley, in his criticism of Atkinson's methods, points out that the total current product of the year 1880 should include the value of services rendered, as well as goods consumed. Adding $2,000,000,000 on this ground, Hawley makes the total sum to be divided between labor and capital $12,000,000,000, and the proportion of wages to profits 3 to 1 instead of 9 to 1,— a much more plausible result. But all estimates of this kind, however carefully made, are beset with difficulties, both theoretical and practical. For the product which is distributed between laborers and capitalists is to be measured as income, not as capital; it is a flow, and not a fund; and this fact enormously enhances the difficulties of observing and measuring it.

the new mechanical methods have given. Marx and his followers make a great deal of this argument. They say that the inventions and appliances of the nineteenth century have increased the power of labor in every line, and that its average productiveness to-day can hardly be less than three times what it was in 1800. Therefore, if the laborer at the beginning of the present century worked twelve hours a day to obtain a bare living, he ought now to be able to secure the same result in four hours. If, in spite of improvements, he continues to work ten or eleven hours for starvation wages, it shows that the result of six or seven hours' time has been quietly appropriated by the capitalist.

The answer to this argument has been indicated in a previous chapter. When a larger amount of products is placed at the disposal of the community, different classes of laborers utilize that increase in three or four distinct ways. Some employ it in shortening their hours of labor, some in extending their consumption of comforts and luxuries or their control of industrial enterprises. Progress has been made in all these directions. Some laborers have become capitalists. Many more have increased their consumption of comforts and luxuries. The hours of labor have been considerably shortened. But a large class of laborers has been content to increase its numbers, and has fallen into those lines of industry where the maximum economy is obtained by employing a large number of people for a small daily wage. The effect of machinery on the laboring classes as a whole is not to be judged by its effect on those sections of the laboring class which, either by fault or misfortune, have placed themselves in the position to obtain a minimum benefit, either as producers or as consumers.

§ 376. Another argument of those who believe that machinery has hurt the laborer is based on the facts observed in every commercial crisis. The most conspicuous, if not the most serious, distress connected with hard times is found in those lines where there has been great duplication of machinery; lines where the machines and the laborers together are far more than able to supply the popular demand for products and services at rates which will keep the workman and his family alive. This criticism is not to be set aside like the two already noticed. The suffering from this source is terribly severe. The best that can be said is, that the evil is due, not so much to the introduction of machinery as to variations in the rate of its introduction, and that it is one which, after a comparatively short period, works its own cure.

§ 377. Let us examine the nature of the process by which machinery leads to over-production and throws men out of employment.

While a new machine is in process of construction, there is a large temporary demand for labor in making it. The capitalist is spending money which he hopes gradually to recoup by the sale of the products or services of this machine. Until it is finished it causes an increased demand for labor in the coal and iron trades, which are chiefly concerned with the production of machinery; after it is finished, it creates a permanently increased supply of consumable products or services in its own particular line of work. The capitalist expects that a moderate reduction in the price of those products will cause an increase in their consumption sufficient to enable him to sell them.

If as a result of a commercial panic there is a sudden cessation of investment in new machinery, we have a stoppage of demand for labor in the coal and iron trades, while the supply of consumable products of machinery remains unimpaired. The loss of employment in the trades concerned with the production of machinery operates to check consumption, since these laborers—no small percentage of the whole people—find themselves without money to spend. The manufacturers are left with a large surplus of unsalable products on their hands. In order to avoid an accumulation of unsold stock they are obliged to limit the output of their mills, and thus the reduction of employment extends far beyond the sphere of the trades that were first affected and causes great suffering to laborers in almost every line of industry.

§ 378. This suffering constitutes perhaps the most serious ground for the indictments of the socialists against the capitalistic system of production. It is not, however, chargeable to machinery; nor even to the private ownership of machinery, for we find similar irregularities of employment in industrial enterprises managed by government. It is due to variations in the rate at which machinery is introduced; variations stimulated sometimes by inflation in the currency, sometimes by unwise tariff legislation, sometimes by the abuse of commercial credit and the reaction which inevitably follows it. Nor is the position of the laborers permanently depressed by these misfortunes. The chief ultimate loss falls on the capitalists. Fixed capital is almost always permanently reduced in value by the readjustments of a commercial crisis, while wages return to their old figure in the next recurring period of prosperity.

§ 379. The second great charge made (§ 370) against the factory system is that it displaces a higher grade of labor by a lower grade; sometimes substituting the work of women and children for that of men; sometimes substituting work under conditions physically or morally unhealthful, for work under healthful conditions; sometimes substituting specialized and mechanical work for diversified occupation which contributes to general intelligence.

§ 380. In point of fact, the introduction of machinery has not been attended with an increase in the proportion of labor done by women and children, but with a diminution. If we wish to find the place where the largest amount of work is done by the weaker members of society, we must look to the peoples whose civilization is least advanced. A much larger proportion of industrial work is done by women in the unprogressive parts of Europe, where modern machinery is little known, than in those which have felt the fullest effects of economic progress. As we examine the changes in the United States from one decade to another, we find that successive censuses show an increasing proportion of men engaged in manufactures, a nearly stationary proportion of women, and an actually decreasing proportion of children. While there is probably much more employment of women and children in factories than is desirable for the best interests of the community, the facts which we have at command indicate that we are better off in this respect to-day than we have been in previous generations.

§ 381. Those who hold the opposite view and think that the use of machinery increases the proportion of women's and children's labor, rely on two arguments to prove their position. In the first place, they say that the introduction of machinery dispenses with the necessity of physical strength, and enables the weaker members of the community to do many things which formerly required the direct attention of the stronger. This is true as far as it goes, but it is inconclusive. Machinery in its complicated forms may lessen the demand for physical strength, but it greatly increases the demand for responsibility in handling it. The races which are successful in dealing with machinery are those which have the mental and moral qualities that enable them to operate it without destruction. A lessened demand for strength which might increase the use of child labor is counterbalanced by an increasing demand for continuity of attention and intelligent care which makes such labor inapplicable.

§ 382. Another argument of those who believe that the factory system has increased the employment of women is founded on the high rate of infant mortality which prevails in large cities. It is said that this points clearly to the employment of married women in factories when they should be attending to their children at home. This inference is not fairly warranted. The conditions of city life are so far adverse to the health of little children that we may expect to see a high infant death-rate in cities, whether the mother stays at home or goes out to work. In England, where the vital statistics are far more accurately kept than in this country, the largest percentage of infant mortality is seen in Liverpool, which among all the leading English cities is probably least devoted to manufacturing. So far as the factory system has caused people to crowd in cities it may be held responsible for the increase of infant mortality; but it is through the lack of air and sunlight that this effect seems to be produced, rather than through the employment of married women in factories.

§ 383. The charge that factory labor is physically unhealthful is so vague as to be difficult to discuss. Some factory employments are of course injurious to health; so are some home employments. If we wish to see labor in its most abject circumstances we must look, not to the large factory, but to those survivals of the earlier domestic system of industry which are exemplified in the tenement-house districts of New York or the East End of London. The crowding in factories with insufficient air space or bad ventilation is sometimes a great evil; but the air space and ventilation of factories are as a rule indefinitely better than the air space and ventilation to which the operatives are elsewhere accustomed. "The trouble," says Colonel Wright in his monograph on the factory system of the United States, " is not in the air space of the factories but in that of the homes. The air of a cotton factory is better than that of a lecture room." The statistics of mortality in the various occupations are not

at all decisive as to the healthfulness or unhealthfulness
of factory life. According to Colonel Wright's observation, they "prove the one or the other conclusion, as the
motive of the person using the statistics may indicate."

§ 384. Nor are the moral results of the factory system
as bad as those of the domestic system which it super-
seded. The intemperance of manufacturing towns seems
to be a result of town life rather than of manufacturing.
It has been proved in France that drunkenness among
factory operatives is less than among laborers of other
kinds; and it is believed by Colonel Wright that the same
thing can be said of the United States. It is still clearer
that the factory system does not promote prostitution.
The small number of prostitutes coming from the ranks
of factory operatives is most conspicuous in every investigation of the subject.

§ 385. "The great evils which became apparent during
the early days of the factory system were simply the results
of bringing together the labor which had become pauperized under the domestic system and in agricultural districts. The factory brought these evils to light; and the
employment of women and children became an offence in
the eyes of the public, not because it was severer than
under the old system, but because under the new the
evils of such employment could be seen." When these
things were brought to the notice of the public, measures
were at once taken to remedy them, not as a rule by the
workmen themselves but by sections of the public which
now became cognizant for the first time of wrongs which
had existed for centuries. The larger the factory, the
more visible are the evils and the more effectively does it
become possible to control them, either by law or by public
opinion. The factory system has not created the abuses
which are charged against it; it has created the opportunity of holding employers responsible for their prevention. This opportunity has been most effectively utilized

in England, the birthplace of modern manufacturing; while of all the United States, Massachusetts, which was the first to establish factories, has done the most to regulate their methods and to improve the condition of their operatives.

§ 386. Much has already been accomplished in these lines. The labor of very young children has been prohibited, and that of older ones restricted in such a way as to enable them to attend school. Female labor has been subjected to regulations which are at once effective and salutary. Even for adult men, the hours of employment have been decidedly reduced, to some degree by law and much more by public sentiment. Half a century ago, thirteen hours was not an uncommon working day for a factory operative. Now, eleven represents a maximum in progressive communities, while the average working time in such places is under rather than over ten hours.[1]

An equally important branch of factory legislation deals with unhealthful methods of conducting business. It would be tedious to enumerate provisions made in the statutes of different states and countries, with regard to ventilation, protection from fire, and provision against various forms of accident to which those who use machinery are liable. Apart from any system of statutory enactments, much has been done by the enlightened self-interest of the factory owners. Manufacturers' mutual insurance companies (§ 431) have sought to reduce losses by avoiding all preventable causes of fire, and have succeeded to an astonishing degree. Associations for boiler inspection are able to use a vigilance which in most districts far surpasses that which can be expected from the public officials, and have prevented much loss of life to the workmen, as well as loss of property to the employer.

[1] A fuller discussion of laws regulating the hours of labor, not as means to public health, but as efforts to reduce the labor supply and create employment for those now out of work, will be found in ch. xiii.

§ 387. Meantime there has been a great change in the views which prevail with regard to employers' liability in the matter of accidents. The common-law doctrine on this subject was exceedingly unfavorable to the workman. It generally made him responsible for injuries which he suffered in the exercise of his trade. It was held that in accepting the employment he took the risks incident to it. A special hardship in this matter arose from the provision that a workman could get no compensation for harm sustained through the negligence of a fellow workman. The old doctrine appears to have assumed that the employee, and not the employer, was in a position to tell what was going on; that the way to prevent carelessness was to hold the workman responsible for the results of such carelessness on the part of himself or his fellows. In the modern factory a policy of this kind does not put the responsibility where it belongs. In a very large class of accidents arising from defects of ways, works, or machinery, the employer is usually in a better position than the workman to know what is wrong and to take effective measures to prevent accidents. Even in those cases where injuries are caused by the negligence of a fellow workman, the organization of modern industry gives the employer power to prevent such casualties more effectively than the employee. There is a strong tendency to place increased responsibility on the owner of the works both for defects of his buildings or machinery and for negligence of his subordinates; a tendency which has found most marked expression in the Employer's Liability Law of Great Britain.

§ 388. The charge that the factory system tends to deprive the laborer of independence, and reduce him to the position of a machine, is not so easily set aside. The substitution of mechanical for intelligent labor is often a very serious evil in modern manufacturing. Not only are individual forms of acquired skill, like that of the hand-loom

weavers at the beginning of this century, made useless by
the introduction of new machinery, but large classes of
men who were most useful citizens in the past are being
driven out of existence by the stress of modern competition. The increasing efficiency connected with the division
and organization of labor has crowded out those men who
exercised a diversified industry. It is not merely the
jack-of-all-trades, but the master of one trade, that finds
it difficult to compete with the employees who subdivide
his trade into a hundred different parts. The village blacksmith finds his occupation gone when so large a part of
his product can be made by machinery at one-tenth of
the old cost. We have secured diversification of consumption through the cheapening of products, but it has
been obtained at the sacrifice of diversified industrial
activity on the part of the men who make those products.
It is undeniable that labor is becoming more and more
specialized, and that many of the occupations of the
modern laborer have a narrowing effect upon those who
practise them.

§ 389. Nevertheless we may safely deny that this change
is causing an intellectual decline among the masses. The
gain in opportunities for travel and for varied enjoyment
has outweighed the loss in opportunity for changes of
occupation. We may regret the disappearance of certain
attractive qualities, as the frontiersman gives place to the
farmer, the farmer to the craftsman, the craftsman to the
modern workman. There is a progressive loss of independence and self-sufficiency, and sometimes of self-
reliance. Yet, on the whole, we find that advancing
civilization brings gains which more than make up for the
losses. The agricultural people has more to make life
worth living than the tribe of hunters. The craftsmen
dwelling in cities have more variety than the purely
agricultural peoples. The change from handicraft to
manufacture, in spite of its attendant dangers, yields the

public a gain, not only in material wealth, but in breadth
and variety of civilization.

§ 390. This improvement in the material and intellectual
condition of the laborers has not made the movements
toward combination of labor any less active. In fact, it
has probably tended to stimulate them. Just because the
laborer has so many advantages as a consumer, he is
often led to feel more keenly his lack of independence as
a producer. Increased comfort is attended with increased
ambition. Even if combinations of capital give relatively
good wages, combinations of labor may seem necessary to
insure the laborers against the loss of all industrial and
social power.

§ 391. There was probably a slender historical connection between the remnants of the old trade gilds and the
first trades-unions of modern times.[1] But the tie was an
accidental and unimportant one. The modern organizations differ in principle from their mediæval predecessors.
The gilds were really organizations of capital quite as
much as of labor. They controlled what little machinery
was used in the manufacturing processes of early days.
They broke down not so much because other laborers
competed with them, as because other capitalists had
better methods by which they were prepared to serve the
community cheaper. The modern union is distinctively
a combination of labor and not of capital. It is an out-
growth of the factory system; an effort to meet concentration of power on the part of employers by similar
concentration on the part of the employed.

§ 392. At the beginning of the present century the law
and the public sentiment among the property-owning
classes were both unfavorable to the organization of
labor. This was conspicuously the case in England. To
say that laborers were not allowed to combine in defence
of their rights is to put the matter altogether too mildly.

---

[1] Brentano's evidence on this point seems conclusive.

The slightest attempt at concurrent action to increase the price of their services was visited by the severest penalties. As late as 1834, six Dorchester laborers were sent as convicts to Botany Bay for the mere act of forming a labor organization which had not even asked for an advance of wages. But with the growth of democratic spirit and democratic power, a more liberal policy began to prevail.[1] Not the least important among the series of English factory acts were those which gave increasing recognition of the right of laborers to combine.

§ 393. The change in public sentiment toward trades-unions has not quite kept pace with the changes in the law. In the minds of a large section of the public, labor unions are chiefly associated with strikes. It is believed by many who ought to know better, that such organizations exist for the purpose of striking, and that if the organizations were suppressed, industrial peace would be secured.

The first of these ideas is a distorted one; the second is wholly unfounded. Even in their severest days, combination laws did not prevent strikes. Where a number of operatives are bound together by a common feeling they will take united action for what they deem to be their rights, even if they have had no chance for previous agreement or discussion. The attempt to prevent such previous discussion tends to make the strike more violent by putting it wholly under the control of feeling and giving no place for reason among those who take part in it. Under such circumstances we shall have recklessness and terrorism, if not actual bloodshed or arson. Where all organization of labor is placed under the ban of the law, such unions as continue to exist in defiance of the law are forced to develop their worst sides. The recog-

---

[1] A similar change which took place in the United States was much less conspicuous, because combination laws in America had never been administered in as severe a spirit as that which prevailed on the other side of the Atlantic.

23

nition of the right of labor to combine has made a decided change for the better in trades-union policy. It has substituted open methods of warfare for secret ones. It has allowed the more cool-headed workman to take a prominent part in guiding his fellow-laborers in their conflicts with capital. It has tended to make strikes more rational, and therefore more dangerous to those who resist them.

§ 394. A union whose primary object is conflict rarely has funds enough to carry its conflicts to a successful issue.[1] The stronger and better unions are organized for purposes of insurance and other forms of mutual benefit no less than for conflict. They are responsible bodies, prepared to make contracts with capital as well as to fight against it. It is the possession of this permanent organization and the control of the funds connected with it which make these unions such dangerous enemies in time of war. But this same permanence of organization renders them less ready to engage in conflicts without carefully computing the chance of bringing those conflicts to a successful issue. They have acquired a store of past experience both in victory and in defeat. They have in many instances become holders of considerable property of their own. They show the conservative spirit, not to say the exclusiveness, to which the possession of experience and the ownership of property so often give rise. It is a constant complaint of the more radical agitators in England that the older trades-unionists have no sympathy with labor as a whole, but are interested only in the prosperity of a small body of laborers. The same charge is made in the United States against the conduct of some of the organizations which represent skilled labor only. Many of the workmen who are most in need of help find as little sympathy from a high grade union as from a

---

[1] The apparent exceptions in recent English experience have hardly lasted long enough to be quoted in disproof of this statement.

landowner or a capitalist. Under such circumstances, a " new unionism " has grown up, which seeks to advance the cause of all laborers, instead of that of the favored few. In England this movement numbers among its adherents nearly all of the most distinguished among the younger members of the labor party. In the United States, the ideas underlying this movement were set forth by the Knights of Labor, an organization which in the years 1885 and 1886 grew to almost unprecedented magnitude. The Knights of Labor were not organized according to trade,—though it might readily happen that all the members of one local assembly might be working in the same trade,—but according to locality. They were not occupied with advancing the interests of a particular class of laborers, except so far as the interest of that class was thought to be a part of the common interest of labor against capital. On the continent of Europe, where labor unions have been from the first largely under the dominion of socialistic ideas, the revolt against the exclusiveness of the older unions finds even more unquestioning sympathy than in England or America.[1]

[1] The labor movements on the continent of Europe are political rather than economic in their character. Their leaders are far more occupied with the overthrow of oligarchic institutions than with the improvement of industrial conditions. The " social democrat " is a democrat first and a socialist afterward. Much of the odium and misunderstanding attaching to the name " socialist " is due to the fact that it has in practice been appropriated by revolutionists of every shade of economic belief. Working side by side and under a common banner, we find (1) true socialists, whose programme contemplates an increase of the powers of the general government ; (2) communists, who wish the local governments to do nearly everything, reducing to a minimum the powers both of the general government and the individual ; (3) anarchists, who distrust all governments, local as well as national, and wish their powers reduced to a minimum ; (4) nihilists, whose objections to the existing governments are so great that they do not think it worth while to delay over the discussion of a constructive programme in times when destructive work is all-important.

So loosely has the word socialism been used, that non-revolutionary socialists deem it necessary to distinguish themselves by such terms as " collectivists," " nationalists," or " socialists of the [professorial] chair."

§ 395. With the leaders of the new unionism, insurance and benefit systems count for little or nothing. They are quite ready to support strikes ; they are even more ready to engage in political agitation. They believe with a great deal of reason that they are stronger politically than they are industrially. They rely less on the power of the individual strikers to enforce their demands, and more on the collective power to influence public sentiment and legislation which is possessed by laborers as a class. They think that the growth of the democratic spirit in politics and industry has left the older trades-union leaders far behind the times. They would transfer the field of conflict from the place where capital is strongest to the place where numbers are strongest ; from the factory to the polling place, from the counting room to the council chamber.

§ 396. One of the most important objects which the new unionism proposes to attain is the enforcement of compulsory arbitration in lieu of protracted strikes.

In spite of the frequency with which they are inaugurated, strikes are not a particularly successful means of giving force to the demands of organized labor. The capitalist is usually so situated that he can await the issue of a conflict with less suffering, if not less actual loss, than the labor union which seeks to fight him. He can maintain his family in comfort from the savings of past years, while the funds of the laborers that oppose him are gradually exhausted by a protracted struggle. He can keep large masses of machinery idle through the exercise of his own individual will, while workmen are drifting in from other districts to take the place of the strikers. The attempt to prevent such laborers from accepting employment is beset with difficulty. The penalty of social ostracism, which is the most powerful one that strikers have at their command, may suffice to control the supply of home labor, but it does not stop the importation of laborers from other places. The attempt to intimidate the new men puts those who practise it outside of the pale of the law and alienates public sympathy from the side of the strikers. In exceptional cases, where the wages previously paid have been flagrantly inadequate, the competition of other capitalists may compel an employer to yield to the demands of the strikers in order to prevent large profits from going into other hands; but, except in these instances, the labor leaders are in the position of men who are attempting to corner the labor market with inadequate capital. Such a policy is doomed to failure in the long run.

If, however, the employer can be prevented from protracting the dispute, the position of the strikers is different. They have only to hold together for a short time in order to be assured of success. They are placed on the kind of vantage ground enjoyed by the man who makes a corner in wheat when a large number of people have contracts which they must fulfil within a limited period (§ 175). This is the most potent motive with those who demand compulsory arbitration.

§ 397. They support this demand with strong arguments. They urge that the capitalist who builds a railroad must undertake to serve the public continuously. The more complete the monopoly, the greater is the public necessity for uninterrupted service. This public need is paramount to all other considerations. The capitalist should not be allowed to withhold the necessary service from the public, merely because he cannot agree with his workmen as to the terms of payment. If a railroad company professes itself unable on this account to deliver goods or to run trains, it should be compelled to do so by public authority. If it pleads inability to secure labor at fair rates, courts of arbitration should be established to decide what rates are fair

§ 398. To this argument there is an equally strong

reply.  If capital is to be compelled to maintain continuous service on terms like these, it will be difficult to find
investors who are ready to put their money into business
enterprises which are subject to this liability.  Such an
arrangement as the one proposed, while apparently fair
to both laborers and capitalists, is really quite one-sided.
It could be enforced against the employer but not
against the employee.  Laborers cannot be compelled to
work on the basis of an arbitrator's award.  They have
not, as a rule, property enough to be held to such an
agreement by the threat of pecuniary damages.  No one
would put them in prison if they refused to accept the
rates offered.  Even if they could be thus compelled to
work against their own will, the service rendered under
such terms would resemble slave labor, and might become
dangerous alike to the property of the employer and to
the safety of the public.

If capitalists are afraid to invest their money in new
enterprises, both laborers and consumers suffer ; the consumer for lack of new sources of supply, the laborer for
lack of new fields of employment.  The loss to the
laborer from this cause more than neutralizes any good
which he may have obtained from the temporary enforcement of his demands by a board of arbitrators.  This is
illustrated by the history of the years 1885 and 1886,
when the industries of the United States were virtually
under a regime of compulsory arbitration.  The Knights
of Labor were able so effectually to boycott the goods of
obnoxious manufacturers that employers were forced to
submit to their demands in this matter or suffer financial
ruin.  A boycott was a far more formidable weapon than
a strike.  It precipitated a contest at a point where the
laborers enjoyed the advantage which is possessed by the
holder of ready money as compared with the man who
offers specific goods or services for sale.  The holder of
money can find new places to buy what he wants far more

quickly than the man who has either labor or goods to sell can find new purchasers to take them. In a strike the employer had the money and the laborers the commodity. In a boycott the positions were reversed. By refusing to buy his goods, the laborers attacked the employer at his weakest point. If he remained unmoved by their refusal to purchase, the Knights of Labor could go to the dealers who handled those goods and threaten them with a boycott unless they supplied themselves from other makers. These dealers were often indisposed to defy such a threat for the sake of another man's quarrel. Cut off from his markets, the employer was compelled to submit the disputed matters to arbitration. Yet the result was by no means advantageous to laborers as a class. The hands of the capitalists were so tied that productive industry suffered severely. Compulsory arbitration created more troubles than it settled. After a comparatively short experience, not only courts and capitalists, but laborers of the better class, united in condemning the boycott and the system of arbitration enforced by its use.

It may be objected that the system of arbitration as administered by the Knights of Labor was a one-sided one, and that no conclusion can properly be drawn from such an instance as to the effect of equitable arbitration under public authority. But reasons have been already given to show that arbitration under public authority is likely to be one-sided. It is sought by the laborers and not by the capitalists. It deals with conditions which are as yet unknown and cannot be predicted with assurance by any board of arbitrators. If the decision of such a board is unfavorable to the workmen, they have it in their power to nullify it. If it is unfavorable to the capitalist, he must nevertheless accept it. While public arbitration may be so organized as to avoid intentional unfairness, it can hardly fail to be one-sided in its effects, because we can enforce it against one party and not against the other.

§ 399. We are placed in an awkward dilemma. If we do not admit the principle of compulsory arbitration we are liable to interruptions of public service at points where its continuous maintenance is essential to the comfort and prosperity of the community. If, on the other hand, we adopt compulsory arbitration as a principle, we are liable to an interruption of the investment of capital where it is essential to social and industrial progress. The public is the sufferer in any event. We cannot assume, as was done two or three generations ago, that a conflict between labor and capital is one which the parties immediately interested may be left to settle for themselves. When there were a dozen independent capitalists and a hundred or a thousand independent laborers, a dispute between an employer and those who worked for him was a matter of very little public account. But where the combination of capitalists and laborers has become so complete that a single strike may interrupt the transportation service of a whole district and threaten large communities with famine and suffering, the case is wholly altered. We are, as Jevons says, working on the assumption that individuals will act as individuals, when in point of fact the exigencies of modern industry compel them to act in masses.

§ 400. There are some who advocate government ownership of all monopolies as the only way out of this dilemma. But this remedy (aside from the other dangers connected with its adoption, which will be discussed in the next chapter) is by no means certain to meet the exigencies of the case. If a government avoids labor troubles by yielding to the demands of the organization in every instance, the want of discipline resulting from this practice will be serious if not destructive. We shall live under the rule, not of the people, but of a small section of organized labor. If, on the other hand, government resists the demands of the organization, it will have no means for maintaining its ground which will prove much more effective than those which capitalists now possess. The superior respect of the workman for a government agency might count for something; but our experience with railroads which are operated by the United States Courts under receiverships, shows that government authority is not enough to prevent strikes in cases of serious wage disputes.

§ 401. Fortunately, the practical chance of escape from our dilemma is rather better than the theoretical one. Every strike teaches either workmen or capitalists some useful lessons for the future. There is a process of natural selection, under which leadership, both in organizations of labor and organizations of capital, must come more and more into the hands of men who are competent to exercise it. The time is past when the noisiest orator can control the labor organization or when the closest-fisted miser can succeed in the management of capital. So far as the managers on either side become in the true sense leaders of men, there is a chance for reducing labor disputes to a minimum. This may be a slow and unsatisfactory remedy for present troubles; but it is the only one which appears to promise much hope of permanent success.

§ 402. Government agencies for arbitration can be arranged either to help or hinder this consummation. If they are so organized as to seem to give the laborer rights which cannot be put in force without public disaster, they will simply retard progress in these matters by inviting the repetition of experiments which are foredoomed to failure. If, on the other hand, they attempt to avoid trouble by giving opportunities for mutual understanding between employer and employed, and aim at preventing disputes rather than settling them, they strengthen the hands of those who are really competent to lead the forces on either side. The history of boards of arbitration, both in Europe and America, shows how little can be accomplished by the exercise of political authority after a fight has once begun. The work of courts of conciliation, on the other hand, shows how much can be done to prevent misunderstandings which lead to disputes, if they are taken in hand before matters have reached the stage of open hostility. The French *Conseils de Prud' hommes* have perhaps furnished the best though by no means the only examples of what can be done by courts of industrial conciliation.

A very considerable proportion of the disputes between labor and capital may be characterized as wholly unnecessary. They are the outcome, not of direct quarrels, but of misunderstandings. The employer wants to do one thing, the laborers think he wants something else ; they object to the latter, and he believes that they are taking exception to the former. Or it may happen that the men protest against a reduction in wages without knowing what the conditions of trade really warrant ; the employer insists on the reduction without giving facts to sustain his position ; the workmen strike in the belief that he is wilfully refusing to give the wages they demand, when the truth is that he is prevented by sheer inability. After the strike is once inaugurated, it is often too late for further explanations. But a board of conciliation, whether organized by the government or by the voluntary action of employers and employed, can render the greatest service, in enabling each side to get a clear understanding of the other's position before matters have gone so far as to render cool action on the basis of such an understanding impossible.

§ 403. If, before any dispute arises, both parties can settle upon a satisfactory scheme for the determination of wages, and make a long-time contract on this basis, it precludes much of the danger of labor troubles. The system which has seemed best adapted to this end is known as the *sliding scale*. By this method the workman's earnings, instead of being made proportionate to the product, as in ordinary piece-work, are made to depend somewhat upon its selling price; the rate of pay increasing as the price of the product increases, and *vice versa*. It has been extensively applied in mining, and to a less degree in some other lines of industry. Where the conditions will admit of its use, it has a decided influence in preventing labor troubles, by settling in advance the share in which the laborer and capitalist shall divide the advantages of a rising market or the burdens of a falling one; nor is it, under favorable conditions, so complicated as to give rise to misunderstanding and suspicion.[1]

§ 404. From the employer's standpoint no exception can be taken to the principle of the sliding scale. It undertakes to do for non-competitive labor what economic forces do for competitive labor—to give the workman the total value of what he makes, less a deduction for the necessary profits of capital. But from the workman's standpoint there is always a possible objection which may prove very serious. What if the price of the product, less the necessary deductions, fails to give him the income he needs in order to keep himself and his family alive? Looking at the matter from this side he proposes another standard as a basis of just remuneration—the standard of the *living wage*. According to this view, labor should be paid enough to maintain it at a good grade of efficiency; the amount necessary for this purpose being determined by the habits of life of the workers themselves.[2]

[1] If we go one step farther, and give the workman, in addition to his wages, an interest in the net profits of the business, we have a case of profit sharing. The operation of this system is described in the next chapter.

[2] The principle of the living wage was applied in England in past centuries by action of the magistrates, who from year to year fixed wages as low as they dared. Even this minimum is thought by Webb to have been in some degree a protection to the laborer.

The present bearings of the agitation for a living wage are well treated by W. Smart, "Studies in Economics," London, 1895.

§ 405. The question, which is often asked and seldom answered, whether labor should be treated as a mere commodity, is simply a rhetorical method of bringing forward the issue between the principles involved in the " sliding scale" and the "living wage" as bases of determination of just payment.

If the price of labor is determined by competition, labor is treated as a commodity; if it is determined by the needs of the man himself, labor is not treated as a commodity. If arbitrators act on the principle of the sliding scale, they commit themselves to the former view ; if they apply the principle of the living wage, they adopt the latter. In the one case, they allow every laborer to get what he can ; in the other, they forbid the laborer to take less than a specified sum, even though the refusal should force him to starve or at any rate to become dependent on public support. Either alternative involves widespread hardship, which every serious student of the problem finds it hard to contemplate. Any one who has looked at the matter in all its difficulty is warranted in protesting against the uncritical use of phrases concerning the treatment of labor as a commodity, which have the effect of prejudging the whole case by placing a rhetorical emphasis on the evils of one alternative in such a way as to preclude dispassionate consideration of the relative merits of both.

§ 406. There is no doubt about the possibility of applying the principle of the living wage if the public is prepared to take the consequences. If those who do not earn a living wage are left to starve,[1] those who are

---

[1] This danger is strikingly exemplified if we examine the effect of professional etiquette upon the employment of men who are just making their start in life. Every profession has its customary scale of charges based in large measure upon the supposed cost of education and maintenance of men who can keep a high standard of professional attainment. The man who is beginning life is not allowed to underbid his established competitor. Without discussing the *pros* and *cons* of rigid adherence to such an established scale

more efficient can get what they demand. But this is hardly what is proposed by the advocates of the system. They do not believe that the consistent adoption of their principle would result in any considerable amount of starvation. Some of them think that the gain to society in the avoidance of disease and vagrancy, of prostitution and crime, which would result from paying better minimum wages, would more than compensate any deficiency in the value of the product of those whose wages were raised. This would be hard to prove; and it is difficult to see what practical measures could be devised for testing its truth, short of absolute socialism. Others, probably more numerous, think that if the producers only stand together they can dictate prices for the whole amount now consumed and get higher pay by simply demanding it. But in point of fact, if the producer dictates the price, the consumer responds by varying the amount which he purchases. If every laborer makes his product worth a living wage by rendering society what *it* regards as an equivalent for the food, clothing, fuel, shelter, and other things represented by that wage, he can get it. If he attempts to insist on the wage while not rendering the equivalent— or, what amounts to the same thing, rendering that which he deems an equivalent but which the consumer does not —no amount of combination will enable him to enforce his demands. He may refuse to work for less; he cannot insist on being employed at a price which he deems fair, if the consumer views the matter otherwise.

If the men who demand a "living wage" are prepared to increase their working efficiency as a means of making

of charges, it is enough for the present purpose to point to the hardships which it inflicts upon many who are striving to maintain a foothold in medicine, in law, or in art. Not being free to sell his work for what the public will pay, the young professional man in the majority of cases finds his first years marked by a record of working-time unemployed except so far as he may use it for his own study, and of wants unsatisfied except so far as he can meet them from the previous accumulations of himself or of his friends.

good their claim, their demand is effective in securing its object and salutary in its influence upon industrial life. But to believe that the wages can be paid without the work, or even that the increased efficiency of work necessarily results from improvement in wages, seems a dangerous fallacy.

§ 407. The majority of trades-union leaders appear to underrate the closeness of the competition of capital and the narrowness of the margin of profit. They do not realize how closely actual piece wages have been forced up to the limit which prices will allow. They believe that more is to be expected from combination of labor than from competition of capital. They sometimes support their position by the claim that machinery has destroyed competition between capitalists and allows them to pay unfairly low wages. We have seen in a former chapter (§§ 176–180) how often similar statements made concerning the effect of machinery upon consumers have proved to be exaggerated. Even where the individual consumer is not well protected, the general rate which the capitalist can charge is limited by causes less obvious than immediate competition, but hardly less effective. The same thing holds true in regard to labor. A time might conceivably come when capitalists would be closely enough united to offer labor less than the value of its products, employ a few laborers at that rate, leave the rest to starve, and appropriate the large margin of profit to themselves; but this state of things is very far from being realized at present.[1]

§ 408. Under these circumstances the substitution of a bargain between united labor and capital, for the inde-

---

[1] The common assertion that competition is more intense as the number of competitors becomes greater, seems to be a loose inference from the fact that prices are apt to be higher as the demand for an article becomes greater. It is easy to see that these two things really have nothing to do with one another. As a rule, the closest competition is that which prevails between two well matched rivals.

pendent competition of laborers and capitalists with one another, could hardly prove a gain to the laborer. In a bargain, the capitalist's superior strength and intelligence must tell against the laborer. In competition, the laborer has the advantage of the strength and intelligence of different capitalists to secure him a market rate of wages. In trying to substitute the former system for the latter, the workman foregoes the advantage which he receives from the strength of the capitalists in a competition, and submits to the disadvantage which this strength imposes upon him in a contest of wits or endurance.

§ 409. He finds himself at an equally serious disadvantage in attempting to set a monopoly price on labor, and to reduce the supply as a means of maintaining the price thus fixed. We have seen how universal is the failure of combinations of capitalists when they attempt to carry out this policy. Where the capitalists fail, with every advantage in their favor, it is hardly to be expected that the labor organizations should succeed. The gilds were unable to maintain a labor monopoly ; and the gilds had many circumstances on their side which modern labor organizations have not. To begin with, they did not pretend to care for the interests of labor in general ; they were occupied with securing special advantages for their own labor. Moreover they had the full support of the ruling powers. Their interests were in many respects identical with those of the landowners, who possessed dominant political authority. The landowners wanted agricultural wages low; the gilds wanted municipal wages high. Both objects could be accomplished by a policy which kept large numbers of laborers in the country and prevented them from flocking to the towns. Accordingly we find that gilds and landowners worked in harmony in most measures of industrial legislation. Almost all chance of bettering his condition was cut off from the agricultural laborer by acts of settlement, which prevented his moving from one parish to another unless he could give the authorities in his new home satisfactory assurance that he would not become a burden on the rate payers. The consequence was that an over-supplied labor market in one district could not find relief by migration to another and possibly more favorable farming region. Change of occupation was yet more effectively cut off from the farmer's son by restrictions on the right to exercise a trade. Under the pretext of compelling a workman to learn a trade thoroughly, the statutes of apprenticeship were often used to prevent most applicants from entering it at all and to force those who did enter to become rigidly bound down to antiquated methods. All these measures helped the leaders of the gild to limit the labor supply in their several trades. But no monopoly, however fortified by traditional rights and political alliances, could prosper by refusing to do public service; and as soon as Europe became peaceful enough to admit of investments of capital, the industrial power passed from gilds who were trying to restrict production, to capitalists who were ready to increase it.

§ 410. The political position of the modern labor organization is so much less strong than that of the gild, that its mistakes are not likely to be so wide-reaching in their consequences. But the same tendencies which made the gilds a burden on society show themselves in the management of trades-unions; and this is the chief reason why thoughtful men look on these organizations with so much distrust. It is not because they promote strikes, but because they discourage industrial efficiency. This is not true of all unions, but it is unfortunately true of a very large number. They seek their interest, not in doing as much as possible, but in doing as little as possible. Instead of trying to make their members useful to capitalists and consumers alike, they undertake to drive a bargain with the capitalist, and they thereby antagonize the interests of the consumer. While they honestly attempt to promote good work, they are yet more occupied with promoting slow work. Such a policy not only gives society short service, but handicaps the strong men who would otherwise take the lead in industrial progress. Until the representatives of organized labor recognize the evils involved in this course, the dangers involved in labor organizations are likely to outweigh their possibilities of good.

# CHAPTER XII.

## COÖPERATION.

Profit-Sharing—Producers' Coöperation—Forms of Consumers' Coöperation —Government Management of Industrial Enterprises.

D. F. Schloss: "Methods of Industrial Remuneration." London and New York, 1892.

N. P. Gilman: "Profit-Sharing between Employer and Employee." Boston, 1889.

G. J. Holyoake: "The History of Coöperation in England." London, 1875, 1879.

[Johns Hopkins University] "History of Coöperation in the United States." Baltimore, 1888.

§ 411. The relation between labor and capital is most satisfactory when there is no sharp separation into classes; where many of the capitalists have risen from the ranks of labor, and many of the laborers themselves hope to become capitalists. Under such circumstances we have every stimulus for efficient production, and little or no opportunity for misunderstandings and conflicts. It is this state of things, quite as much as the abundance of free land, which gives the inhabitants of a new country their economic advantages.

§ 412. Unfortunately, this condition is far from being realized in Europe in the nineteenth century; and America, though better off than Europe, is making progress in the wrong direction. The business men in the present generation have in large part risen from the ranks of labor to their existing position of leadership; but whether the same thing can be predicted for the next generation is very doubtful. Certain it is that the prospect of becoming capitalists does not act as so powerful a motive on the laborers of to-day as it did on those of a generation ago. The opportunities to save are as great or greater; but the amount which has to be saved before a man can hope to become his own employer, has increased enormously. When a man who had accumulated a thousand dollars could set up in business for himself, the prospect of independence appealed to him most powerfully; when he can do nothing but lend it to some richer man, the incentives and ambitions connected with saving are far weaker—too weak, in many cases, to lead the man to save at all, except through the medium of a friendly society or trades-union. We thus have a separation of the community into more and more rigidly defined groups, different in industrial condition, distinct in ideals, and oftentimes antagonistic in their ambitions and sympathies. This separation of laborers and capitalists into distinct classes involves serious dangers to society as a whole.

1. It increases the liability of industrial conflicts, producing strikes and lockouts, which throw laborers out of employment and machinery out of productive use. The harm done by these conflicts is by no means confined to the individual contestants, but may occasion misfortune to the whole body of consumers.

2. It neutralizes a large part of the advantages of the institution of private property. If a laborer does not expect to accumulate money and become a property owner, he loses an incentive to hard and efficient work which makes his service most valuable to society.

3. It involves a contradiction between our political theories and the facts of industrial life. A republican government is organized on the assumption that all men are free and equal. If the political power is thus equally distributed while the industrial power is in the hands of a

few, it creates danger of class struggles and class legisla-.
tion which menace both our political and our industrial
order.

§ 413. Some look for the solution of these difficulties
in a paternal policy on the part of employers toward those
whom they employ. It is said, with a fair measure of
truth, that much of the existing industrial friction arises
from the fact that men are treated as machines. The
employer tries to make as good a bargain with his workmen as he can, and does nothing more than this. It is
urged that manufacturers should make provision for the
well-being of their operatives by public improvements, by
the erection of sanitary dwellings, by the establishment of
insurance funds, and by a number of other agencies which
shall bind the interests of labor and capital together.
Much good can undoubtedly be done in this way. We
see this exemplified in an institution like the *familistère*
at Guise or in some of the factory towns of the United
States where the capitalists have taken a living interest in
the welfare of their employees. But the remedy is by no
means a sure one. The modern workman is apt to chafe
under the feeling that his insurance funds are in the hands
of his employer. Nor does he always like to live in houses
owned by the corporation for which he works, even when
such houses are well built and rented at a fair price.
There is a feeling of dependence which often proves irk-
some, and may give rise to serious misunderstanding.
Events like the Pullman strike of 1894 show the dangers
to which a system of this kind is liable. And even when
these experiments are thoroughly successful, they only
touch the surface of the difficulty. They meet the first
of the evils enumerated, but not the second and the third.
They diminish the possibility of open warfare between
laborer and employer; but they do not, to any conspicuous degree, arouse the ambition of the laborer or avoid
the conflict between industrial facts and political theories.

Indeed, the system of paternal care and provision, unless administered with the utmost wisdom, leads to flagrant violations of the modern doctrine of social equality.

§ 414. Another way of meeting these dangers is by encouraging workmen to become owners of stock in the companies for which they work. Many employers give their hands every facility for thus becoming stockholders, on terms more favorable than those which are open to the general public. Such employers believe, and with a great deal of reason, that the gain to the company in assuring itself of the devotion of its men, is one which will more than balance an apparent loss of money on the sale of the stock. But a measure of this kind, though good as far as it goes, is somewhat limited in its application. It is a difficult one to put in practice where the concern is so large that the employer does not come into direct contact with his hands; for in the absence of such contact, the privilege of buying stock at less than market rates is almost certain to be abused. It is thus inapplicable in just those cases where a remedy for labor troubles is most needed. Nor does it, in any real sense, make the workman his own employer. It gives him a fractional share in electing the people who say how he is to be employed—a very different thing, both in theory and in fact, and one which is far from putting the laborer in a position of independence.

§ 415. A third remedy, which has a little wider application, is found in profit-sharing. Under this system the workman, in addition to his regular wages, receives a dividend from the net profits of the business in which he is employed. This stimulates him to make the interests of the employer his own, and gives him, in some measure at any rate, the ambitions and motives of a property owner. This plan was brought prominently into notice by the success of Leclaire, a Parisian house decorator, who adopted it in 1842 and placed it on a permanently efficient basis, making his own fortune, as well as that of many of his workmen, by its results. Profit-sharing has been carried on with a fair measure of success by many other houses in France, particularly since 1870, as well as in Switzerland and in Germany. In England and in the United States the results have not been so good. Though we find some isolated instances of successful profit-sharing, the system has not proved its power to stand a severe strain or to prevent the occurrence of destructive strikes.

§ 416. The most noted experiment in profit-sharing in England was that of the Briggs collieries, near Leeds. Its apparent success was so great that Jevons at one time pronounced it a decisive proof of the ability of the system of profit-sharing to accomplish what its advocates claimed. But in 1875, under the stress of hard times, the whole scheme was wrecked. As long as trade was prosperous and wages were advancing, all went well. But when trade conditions changed, the men struck against reductions in wages. The wage dispute was referred to arbitration, and the arbitrator decided in favor of the employers. But the experiment in profit-sharing was at an end. The bulk of the shareholders objected to the continuance of a system under which they shared profits with their workmen, but which did not make those workmen any more ready to share losses or prevent them from resorting to the old method of warfare between capital and labor, which it was confidently hoped that industrial partnership had forever banished. Various explanations have been given of the failure of this experiment. It is said that while the Briggs family were heartily and loyally in favor of the system of profit-sharing, the outside stockholders, who owned a majority of the capital of the concern, were not. It is also stated that serious mistakes of policy were made during the years of great industrial prosperity, by which the success of the enterprise was unnecessarily endangered. Even granting the truth of all this, it is clear that the system did not do what was expected of it. It did not prevent a strike on the first occasion when its usefulness was put to any serious test. The claim that the experiment would have been continued if the bulk of the shareholders had been sympathetically interested in its success, is a virtual admission that it did not succeed when judged on business principles alone. The fact is that the workmen did not heartily care for it. They were glad to see it in operation when it increased their wages ; but the past experience and future anticipation of its benefits did not enlist them in its support strongly enough to prevent a strike when there appeared to be a prospect of present gain by the employment of that means. A similar comment may be made on the failure of an almost equally noted American experiment —that of Brewster & Co., in carriage manufacturing. For two or three years the employees enjoyed the increase of wages which the system afforded them, but they could not resist the pressure which their fellow workmen brought to bear upon them to enter upon an ill-advised and unjustified conflict with their employers.

§ 417. There has been a sufficient number of successful experiments in profit-sharing to turn the hopes of many economic reformers in this direction. But it must be confessed that it has accomplished far less than its advocates have prophesied, and perhaps less than the majority of unprejudiced critics were disposed to anticipate. There are reasons which do not appear on the surface, which too often make the expected benefits prove illusory.

If it were true, as many people suppose, that ordinary business offered a large surplus of profit, which would give room for the distribution of a handsome addition to the workman's wages without involving the employer in bankruptcy, there would be a better chance to apply the system of profit-sharing as a panacea for labor troubles.

But we have seen that this is far from being the case. The competition of capitalists with one another has in the majority of cases cut down profits to so low a figure as to leave little if any room to increase wages *at the expense of the employer*. If the laborer is to receive a bonus in addition to his wages, one of two things must happen. Either his efficiency, care, and steadiness must be so increased as to create the additional profit from which this bonus is paid; or he must be prepared to accept a lower minimum wage to compensate for his chance of a higher maximum, and leave the average where it now is.

§ 418. The advocates of profit-sharing generally accept the former alternative. They believe that the laborer, in a profit-sharing industry, will do more work, exercise more care, and abstain more surely from labor disputes than he would under the traditional wage system ; and that in this way he will create the profit to be divided. The facts hardly warrant this belief, especially in the case of the American workman. In the list of profit-sharing industries, one of the most conspicuous features is the large proportion of them which report no profit to divide.[1] Nor is this to be wondered at. In the complicated industry of modern times, the connection between the individual effort of a single workman and the general profit of the business as a whole is too remote to act as a very powerful stimulus. If all the operatives simultaneously can be nerved to a higher degree of effort or of care, the results will unques-

---

[1] It should also be remembered that these lists, from the very nature of the case, make the percentage of successes appear too large. The records of failure are never as well preserved as those of success. The successful experiments of the last ten years can be tabulated with tolerable completeness. They are known, and their promoters are anxious to have them known. The failures are far harder to discover and tabulate. They are forgotten, and their promoters are anxious to have them forgotten. It is very difficult to hear about experiments which were quietly abandoned five or ten years ago, unless there were some unusual conditions in their history which placed their failure on record at the time.

tionably be gratifying. But if many of them are already working up to the limit of their powers either in the matter of output or of economy, there is no chance for such general improvement. The gain from the increased efficiency of any individual will be distributed among those who have done comparatively little to deserve it. The smallness of the quotient and the inequity of distribution both interfere with the attainment of good results from the system. They may do even worse than this. If a man has worked much harder than before and received little or no increase of pay, he is sometimes in danger of suspecting the good faith of his employer. Even if he has access to the employer's books, he has not the knowledge of bookkeeping which would enable him to test the conclusiveness of what they show. Where there are no profits to divide, the system of profit-sharing may breed those very misunderstandings between capital and labor which it is designed to prevent.

§ 419. Where the laborers under the old wage system are not working up to a high standard of efficiency, there is more chance for the success of profit-sharing. This seems to be the reason why it works better on the Continent than in England, and better in England than in America. There is a greater chance for increase in the general output in those countries where the men have habitually been working far below their physical capacity; and profit-sharing, like anything else which contributes to such an increase, is a first-rate thing for the workmen.

§ 420. Profit-sharing without such probable increase of output must be unqualifiedly condemned. It makes the workman a sharer in gains and losses which are essentially speculative in their character. For it must be remembered that only a part, and not the larger part, of the variations in profit is due to variations in cost of production. Most of these variations are due to changes in the selling price of the product—a thing over which the workman has no control whatever. To make his wages depend on net profits, under these circumstances, is to force him to participate in the speculations of his employer—a result neither equitable as between individuals nor desirable for society as a whole.[1]

§ 421. To avoid this difficulty, the attempt is sometimes made to determine how much of the gain in a business is due to the work of the operatives, and how much to the speculative power of the capitalists and their representatives ; crediting the operatives with the profit under the former head, and not making them liable to the contingencies which affect the latter. Sometimes this is accomplished by premiums on coal economy, such as are offered by certain railroad companies ; sometimes by a carefully arranged computation of expenses, under which a bonus can be added to the regular wages of the operatives in case the normal standard of cost is diminished. The chief difficulty of these computations is found in their complexity. It is hard to ascertain which items of expense should be charged to the labor cost of a product ; it is perhaps equally hard to persuade the laborers that the employer is accurately following out the apportionment on which he has agreed.

---

[1] " It is quite possible that the workman who, in the hope of earning bonus to labor,' has done work 10 per cent in excess of the normal standard, may, even under a liberal scheme of profit-sharing, find that, instead of receiving an addition to his normal wages of, say 5 per cent, the bad management of his employer has reduced his bonus to so low a level that he has to be content with a supplement equivalent to only 2 per cent on his wages, or that no bonus whatever is available. If I am to do 10 per cent more and better work than I did last year, why not offer me a 10 per cent increase in my wages, subject only to its being shown that my work exhibits a 10 per cent improvement? Why tempt a working-man to gamble by staking part of the reward of his labor upon the financial results of a business over the conduct of whose financial operations he is not allowed to possess any control, and would, perhaps, seldom be competent, even if he were allowed, to exercise any useful control ? " (Schloss, " Methods of Industrial Remuneration," pp. 189, 190.)

§ 422. A more radical reform in the condition of the employees is contemplated by the advocates of coöperation.

Coöperation is often confounded with profit-sharing; but the two things are radically distinct in their nature. Profit-sharing is a change in the method of payment, which is intended to induce the workman to identify his own interests with those of his employer, but which leaves the direction and management of the industry unaltered. Coöperation, on the other hand, involves a change of management. A coöperative enterprise is controlled, not by the representatives of the investor, but by the representatives either of the laborers or of the consumers. In the former case it is known as productive coöperation; in the latter, as distributive or consumptive coöperation.

§ 423. The history of productive coöperation goes back to a very early period. The mediæval gilds were coöperative enterprises. They were managed, not by capitalist employers, but by associations of workmen who contributed from their own funds whatever capital was required for the conduct of the industry. But their conservatism of method led to their displacement by capitalistic industry; and it is not until about the middle of the present century that we find widespread attempts to reestablish the system of coöperative association. Many coöperative societies were established in France in connection with the revolution of 1848. Unfortunately, these enterprises were directed by popular enthusiasm rather than by careful business calculation. A few, notably among masons and piano makers, were successful. The majority were total failures. Those which survived have as a rule abandoned the coöperative form and have become joint stock companies owned by workmen. More recent French coöperative movements, though often discussed in economic literature, do not appear to possess great industrial importance. A number of English experiments in coöperative production were made in cotton manufacturing between 1850 and 1860. But the difficulties consequent upon the American civil war ruined most of these enterprises, nor have they subsequently been revived on any large scale. Of American attempts in productive coöperation the most conspicuous instance has been furnished by the coopers of Minneapolis. A number of journeymen organized a shop of their own in 1868, which has extended its work from year to year and has found many imitators. Its methods have been admirable, its credit high, and it has had the effect of developing business capacity in men who were not aware that they possessed it. There have been also instances of successful organizations of this sort among wood-workers in St. Louis and among boot and shoe companies in Massachusetts. But the whole number is small in proportion to the amount that has been said about them.

§ 424. It is always doubtful whether the operatives will choose as good a manager as the stockholders of a corporation, or whether the manager whom they choose can enforce good discipline among those on whom he depends for his place. It is often hard for workmen to realize the value of the services of a responsible and efficient manager. They are not willing to pay him a high salary; and this false economy too often wastes more money than it saves. The lines of business in which productive coöperation is most successful are those of comparatively simple character, where industry counts for most and management for least; where the connection between the efficiency of the labor and its result is most obvious, and where the necessity for organizing power and speculative foresight are reduced to a minimum. In such industries the superior ambition of a workman who feels that he is his own employer may stimulate him to an increased amount of work and increased care in the use of materials, which will outweigh any lack of speculative skill. This is conspicuously the case in the countries of Continental Europe, where the ordinary standard of work is so low as to leave great room for gain in those directions. The more completely the workman is in the habit of utilizing his powers under the old system, the less chance is there for gain under the new. For this reason the United States furnishes, in some respects, the least promising field for enterprise of this kind.

§ 425. It is believed by many socialists that the chief present hindrance to productive coöperation is the difficulty which workmen meet in their efforts to obtain capital. An association of laborers cannot work to the best advantage unless it controls modern machinery ; and modern machinery costs a great deal of money. Ferdinand Lassalle proposed that the government should meet this difficulty by advancing capital to associations of workmen, who would guarantee to make good its value at the close of the period of production. In this way he thought that the present monopoly of capitalists in the control of industry would be abolished. A man who had no capital, but was willing to work, would be put on an equality with one who had inherited capital from his father or saved it from his business. But the history of productive coöperation gives us little encouragement to expect much good from a project of this kind.

In speculative investments of capital it is quite impossible for any association, of laborers or of any other men, to guarantee that the value of their product to society will equal the value of the goods consumed by the laborers in the course of its production. As business is carried on to-day the losses from unsuccessful investments are very frequent indeed. They would inevitably be even more frequent if these investments, instead of being made by capitalists at their own risk, were made by laborers at the public risk. There is every reason to believe that the waste of public capital under Lassalle's system would many times outweigh any public gain from increased freedom and energy on the part of the laborers.

Where the return on an investment is reasonably sure, it is quite easy to find the money to set an enterprise in motion without government aid. It is not scarcity of capital, so much as scarcity of business ability, which makes productive coöperation so difficult at the present day. So disinterested an observer as Schloss regards the ideal of a self-governing workshop as " a curious mixture of unsound economics and ill-directed philanthropy," and he asserts that the measure of the success which the coöperative movement has attained and of the improvement which it has effected in the position of the working classes has been in proportion to their abandonment of the ideals and methods of producers' coöperation for those of consumers' coöperation.

§ 426. The latter system has certain theoretical advantages which the former does not enjoy. When consumers are managing a business they have it in their power to avoid many difficulties to which the capitalist employer is subject. Consumers can impose upon themselves a set of rules which they would not tolerate if imposed from outside. By obedience to these rules they can secure great gain in economy of production, without diminishing the utility of the goods and services received. By their experience in adopting and enforcing these rules they can educate themselves to a far higher degree of economic forethought than they would otherwise be likely to possess, and can obtain a decided increase of comfort, both for themselves and for the community as a whole.

The three most important forms of consumers' coöpera tion are coöperative purchase, coöperative insurance, and coöperative banking.

§ 427. Coöperative purchasing agencies, through which the buyer gives orders for what he wants instead of waiting for the seller to come and show him a variety of goods, have proved of the highest value.  This has been conspicuously the case in country districts, where buyers are scattered, stocks of goods inaccessible, and travelling agents more or less irresponsible in their acts because of the absence of competition.  The Patrons of Husbandry have secured much advantage for their members and for the public by a system of coöperative purchase, and the same thing may be said with even more emphasis of the agricultural syndicates in France, Germany, and other parts of Europe.

§ 428.  Where the coöperators have stores as well as purchasing agencies—in other words, where they aim to keep a stock of goods on hand to supply current demands —any success which they may achieve is more conspicuous, but the danger of failure is at the same time indefinitely multiplied.  One of the earliest and most successful of the coöperative stores was started at Rochdale, in England, in 1844, by the modest attempt of a number of workmen to buy a few ordinary supplies for their own use. The economy which resulted from this undertaking was so great that their example was rapidly followed in other English towns.  At the present day the coöperative societies of this kind in the United Kingdom have a membership of about a million, a capital amounting to about ten million pounds sterling, and annual sales of three times that amount.

The great gain in economy realized by the English coöperative stores was due to their adoption of a system of cash payments.  The retail business of the United Kingdom had been burdened with the practice of giving long credits, many of which offered no prospect of collection. The cost of this method of doing business ultimately fell on the solvent consumers, who had to pay for the insolvent as well as for themselves.  This credit system also interfered with competition, because many customers became bound to a particular store at which they kept their account, and were not readily able to go elsewhere. A coöperative society avoided all loss from bad debts by insisting on cash payments, and was thus able to give its members a reduction from the current retail prices which covered both the loss from bad debts and the gain which the storekeepers had been accustomed to exact on the basis of their partial immunity from competition. In the United States, where retail credits were less abused than in England, and where competition had probably been more universal, there was less chance of economy from this source, and the success of coöperative stores was therefore much less conspicuous. Though the Patrons of Husbandry have established large numbers of successful purchasing agencies, their losses from coöperative stores have been very serious. Even more noticeable was the failure of an organization known as the Sovereigns of Industry, established in New England in 1874 with the avowed purpose of maintaining coöperative stores. Their purchases were not judiciously made, and in a short time the societies were loaded with unsold goods. They tried to economize in the wrong direction, by lowering the salaries of their managers; and only too late did they find that cheap management wasted much more than it saved.

§ 429. A coöperative establishment has the advantage of avoiding many expenses of advertising and of being sure of a regular flow of business. Where the conditions of sale and purchase are comparatively simple, as in co-öperative creameries and other enterprises which render a restricted range of services, these advantages are great enough to make the chance of success very considerable. But for ordinary commercial purposes the indications are that capitalistic enterprise does better than coöperation, unless there is some specific reform in methods of purchase or supply, like the abolition of the credit system, which the coöperators are prepared to inaugurate.

§ 430. Some of these reforms are promised by the advocates of coöperative insurance. In the competition of different insurance companies with one another, large commissions are paid to agents for their services in securing business. These commissions represent a factitious element in cost, due to the strife of rival companies, and are wholly unprofitable to the public, except so far as the activity of agents leads people to make a fuller use of the advantages which insurance offers. Even this modicum of good is probably neutralized by the evils of over-insurance for which agents are often accountable. People are induced to insure their lives at a higher rate than they can properly afford, or to insure their houses for a larger sum than the company can ever be compelled to pay. When the amount of insurance can be thus artificially inflated there is a temptation to the agents of the company to accept improper risks for the sake of the commission involved, and to the parties insured to be careless with regard to fires and other sources of loss. It is claimed that a coöperative company can avoid these dangers, and by a system of mutual watchfulness can lessen risks instead of increasing them.

§ 431. The history of fire insurance in the United States affords a conspicuous example of what can be done in this way, though not one which has any direct bearing on the relations between labor and capital. About 1870 certain factories, which previously had to pay very high rates of insurance, undertook to insure one another through a coöperative organization which should have in view, not only the adjustment of losses, but the reduction of such losses to a minimum. Its members volunteered to submit to certain rules of construction and operation which should render the liability of fire as slight as possible. Under the efficient guidance of its secretary, Mr. Edward Atkinson, the first of these companies speedily reduced the rate of insurance for its members to a

small fraction of what it had been under the old system.
This saving represented a gain in public as well as in
private wealth.  Anything which can reduce the number
of fires avoids at once the loss of property which the manufacturer feels, and the loss of comfort which the workman suffers from interruption of business and the resulting irregularity of employment.  Never was there a more
signal instance of the good possibilities of coöperation.
The old companies had been content to adjust risks.
The manufacturers' mutual companies succeeded, not
only in adjusting them at far less cost, but in reducing
them to a figure which a few years ago would have been
thought impossible.[1]

§ 432.  In life insurance, the friendly societies of England and fraternal societies of the United States have
had a considerable measure of success in reducing expenses of management, and have been able to give their
members a variety of forms of benefit which the joint-
stock companies could not have undertaken without
serious danger of abuse.  Whether combined with trade
societies or not, they have afforded many indirect advantages more or less separate from the main purpose of the
organization.  As an offset to these benefits we must note
the disadvantage due to the inferior financial responsibility of many coöperative companies.  In the early years
of any such organization the assessments are apt to be
made too low, and a corresponding burden is placed on
the survivors during its later history—a burden which
has in many instances proved too hard for the society
to carry.

§ 433.  Coöperative banking is perhaps even more im-

---

[1] The obvious advantage of combining fire insurance with fire prevention
has led to a demand that municipalities, which take charge of the latter,
should also assume the risks and profits of the former.  But this does not
distribute the risks over a sufficiently large area.  A fire like that of Chicago
a quarter of a century ago would bankrupt a municipality that undertook to
insure its citizens.

portant than coöperative insurance. The essential feature
of a coöperative bank is that a body of men, many of
whom expect to become borrowers, should furnish the
capital and regulate the conditions of its lending and repayment. The largest experiment of this kind was made
in Germany, under the leadership of Schulze-Delitzsch.
His first coöperative bank was established in 1849. The
progress of the system was slow until 1860, but much
more rapid after that date. In 1889 the German coöperative banking associations had 490,000 members, a capital of over $30,000,000, and deposits of twelve times that
amount. The underlying idea of the system of Schulze-
Delitzsch is that a body of laborers shall enable itself to
obtain credit by collecting a small capital in the hands of
the association, shall attract outside investors by the offer
of a fair rate of interest, and shall then loan funds to its
members after direct personal examination of the circumstances of the borrower. In the earlier associations, the
liability of the members was unlimited; of late years this
feature has been changed. The educational effect of
these companies, both in stimulating workmen to save,
and in teaching them the conditions governing the conduct of business, has been incalculably good. Perhaps
the strongest tribute to their efficiency is furnished by
the opposition of the socialists, who see in the success
of plans like this the most insuperable barrier to the
acceptance of their doctrines among an intelligent and
powerful section of German workingmen.

§ 434. In England and the United States coöperative
banking has been chiefly confined to a more restricted
field. It has dealt almost exclusively with loans intended
for building purposes. The first building society was organized in England in 1781 ; the first legal recognition of
such societies dates from 1836. There are now some
2,500 such companies, with aggregate assets of nearly
sixty million pounds sterling. The first building society

in America was organized near Philadelphia, in 1831. In 1890 there were over 5,000 such companies in the United States, with members numbering more than a million, not quite one third of whom are borrowers, and with assets of perhaps $400,000,000. As these societies are commonly organized, the paid-up value of the shares is fixed at $200 each, payable in instalments of $1 a month. If no interest accrued, it would take 200 months for these payments to amount to the face value of the share. But as the subscribers are credited with the amount of interest earned by their funds, they pay for their shares in about two thirds of that time. The money thus obtained from month to month is loaned to shareholders, who agree to use it in building houses under the supervision of the officers of the society. The amount which any man can borrow is limited by the maturity value of the shares for which he has subscribed. Thus, the man who has subscribed to five two-hundred dollar shares may borrow as much as $1,000, if the funds are on hand for the purpose. When, as generally happens, the amount in the treasury is inadequate to meet the wants of all those who wish to borrow, the loan is usually awarded to the man who will, directly or indirectly, offer the highest interest. The board of managers is charged with the duty of seeing that the money is invested in a safe and secure manner. The workman pays, besides interest, his monthly subscription to his shares. If he keeps up these payments regularly, he will in a few years find himself in the possession of paid-up shares which will cancel the principal of the debt when it becomes due and leave him owner of his house without incumbrance.

§ 435. Great as are the advantages of these societies, they are of quite a different character from those with which they are popularly credited. They do not, as a rule, enable a workman to get a home cheaper than he could obtain it without them. The borrowers in these societies, in competing for loans, are tempted to offer unduly high premiums. The chief commercial profit of such societies goes to the outside investors, who do not intend to borrow. It will generally happen that the workman who puts money in a savings bank until he has a sufficient amount to pay part of the cost of a home, and then borrows the remainder from the savings bank, with the view of gradually paying the debt from year to year, gets his house at less expense than he could through membership in a building society. The coöperative society undoubtedly stimulates many workmen to save who otherwise would not; but this advantage is offset by the danger that in case of sickness such compulsory saving, instead of helping a man, will weigh him down by a burden too heavy to bear. What these societies do for the public is, first, to lead workmen to become holders of real estate much sooner than they otherwise would do, and second, to teach them the difficulties and the possibilities attendant on the conduct of banking business. Both of these things are of great public value. The man who owns real estate becomes thereby a gainer in happiness and self-respect. Even if it involves effort and self-denial, the "magic of property" lightens the burdens and sacrifices involved. And besides the moral gain to the real-estate owners themselves, there is an equally important gain to the community as a whole in having the ownership of lands and houses widely distributed among its members. It puts a larger number of citizens on the side of law and order, in opposition to the destructive tendencies of modern industrial life. It makes them acquainted with business methods and with the responsibility of business control, and thus lessens the danger of reckless financial legislation and the possibility of any political warfare of classes. It is in this educational influence that building societies have their chief value. When this is absent, the form of coöperative organization has no virtue. The so-called national associations, which simply provide a means of investment and borrowing without direct personal control, are always a source of danger and often of serious evil. The recent history of building societies in England, as well as in the United States, has furnished conspicuous examples of the abuse of coöperative forms of enterprise, and emphasizes the necessity of direct control by the coöperators themselves, as an essential condition for securing the benefits of the system.

§ 436. By far the most important form of consumers' coöperation is exemplified in government management of industrial enterprises. This differs in two important particulars from the coöperative agencies already described. In the first place the choice of managers of a government business enterprise is connected with the general political machinery of the country, and regulated by constitutional law instead of by statutes of incorporation. In the second place, these managers are likely to fall back on the taxing powers of the government to make up any deficit which may arise in the operations of a public business enterprise; or in the converse case to devote any surplus above expenses to the relief of tax burdens elsewhere. A government enterprise is managed by people who represent, or are supposed to represent, the consumers ; but the good or bad economy of its management does not necessarily redound to the profit or loss of those who most use it.[1]

It is impossible within the limits of a book like this to

---

[1] It is sometime said that public business management is neither more nor less than *compulsory* coöperation. But it must be noted that the compulsion is exercised against the taxpayers in general, rather than against the consumers of goods or services provided. Where is the compulsion applied in the management of a government railroad? Not in compelling people to use the road, but in compelling taxpayers to make up any deficit which arises in its operations. Of course the government may exercise an indirect compulsion upon the users of railroads, if it prohibits the building of private lines, and thus forces people to use its services or none at all ; but this is an accidental rather than a universal feature of state railroad management.

examine in detail the successes or failures of government management of industry in the various lines where it has been tried. But it seems both possible and desirable to group together the general causes which have given force to the demand for such management in some directions and have limited its practical usefulness in others.

§ 437. In the beginning of history, the government is the power that controls the army. When tribes were in a state of warfare with one another, defense against foreign enemies was the matter of primary importance. No man could let his private convenience stand in the way of effective military operations. The discipline and subordination necessary to wage successful war were all-important ; and all the powers necessary to maintain such discipline were entrusted to the leaders of the army.

Somewhat later the military authorities undertook the work of maintaining discipline in time of peace as well as of war, and of defining and enforcing the rights of members of the tribe against one another, no less than against foreign enemies. This function was not accorded to them without a struggle. The priests, under whose tutelage the religious sanction for tribal customs had grown up, tried to keep in their own hands the responsibility of upholding these customs and the physical power connected with it. In some races they succeeded ; but among European peoples the military authorities took the work of enforcing and defining laws out of the hands of the priests, and made it a function of the state as distinct from the church. As security from foreign enemies increased, this law-making power became more and more important. The government was less exclusively identified with the army, and more occupied with the courts, the legislatures, and the internal police. Its judicial and legislative functions assumed a prominence at least as great as its military function.

The growth of private property was almost coincident

with the development of these domestic functions of government. In fact the two things reinforced one another. The production and accumulation of capital, to which private property gave so vigorous an impulse, placed the strong men of the community in a position where they had less to gain by war and more by peace. It put them on the side of internal tranquility. It thus made the government more powerful; and this in turn still further increased the accumulations of capital. But along with this mutual help, which strong domestic government and strong property right rendered one another, there was an element of mutual antagonism. The very fulfilment of those functions which made the accumulation of capital possible, rendered it impossible for the government to do its work except at the expense of the capitalists. It was no longer possible to support armies by booty, or courts by fines and forfeitures. The expense of maintaining order had to be paid by its friends instead of its enemies. The growth of private property was followed by the development of a system of taxation, which, in theory at any rate, involved the power to destroy such property.

The existence of such a system of taxation, with the machinery for collecting money in this way, allows the government more freedom of industrial action than any private individual can command. It can make up a deficit by compulsory payments; and this gives it a wider range of power in deciding what services it will undertake and what prices it will charge—a power which affords almost unlimited opportunity for good or bad use, according to the degree of skill and integrity with which it is exercised.

§ 438. Every extension of government activity into new fields restricts private enterprise in two ways; first by limiting the field for investment of private capital, and second, by possibly, if not probably, appropriating through taxation a part of the returns from private enterprise in all other fields. The question whether a government should manage an industry reduces itself to this: Are the deficiencies or evils connected with private management such that it is wise to give government officials the taxing power which constitutes the distinctive feature of public industrial management?

§ 439. In one class of cases there is no doubt whatever. The expenses for the army, the courts, and the legislature, with the administrative work which they involve, must be defrayed in this way. There may be a question how large an army and navy we should have, or how much legislation; whether we should extend legislative activity to cover a great many points of health and morals, or confine it as far as possible to a few essential matters of public security. But once having established an army or made a law, we have to pay for it by taxation. We have to meet the cost not only of soldiers and sailors, but of forts and ships; not only of congressmen and judges, but of policemen, prisons, and other physical means necessary to make their decisions operative. Every extension of legislative power extends the scope of these expenditures. Regulation of money almost necessarily involves public mints; health ordinances involve public sanitation; compulsory education involves public schools. All of these agencies may be partly supported by fees for the services rendered; but their compulsory character involves the necessity of applying them in cases where the collection of an adequate fee is impossible.

§ 440. This last point leads us to the fundamental characteristic of a second class of circumstances which justify goverment enterprise. It will often happen that an expenditure of money promises a public good out of all proportion to the amount which its promoter can collect from the beneficiaries in case it proves successful. Under such circumstances the government may take hold of an industry, just because it cannot be made to pay by ordinary commercial means. Roads, bridges, canals, wharves, and lighthouses furnish conspicuous instances of this sort. It is an absolute necessity for the public to have lighthouses; but it is, in ordinary cases, impossible for the owner of a lighthouse to collect toll for its maintenance, either from the ships which are not wrecked or from those which are. It is of the utmost importance for the community to have good roads ; but the vexation connected with the imposition of tolls for the use of the highway, and the impossibility of maintaining a highway system by such tolls, force the government to take this matter into its own hands.

Irrigation works in desert lands are likely to furnish another important example of this kind; especially if it be true that the storage and distribution of water produces a rainfall in districts previously arid, so that those who pay nothing for the works can nevertheless get a share in these benefits. An instance of a little different character, but which comes under the same general head, is furnished by forestry. The public need of forests for the sake of securing a regular rainfall is one in which the whole community has an interest, but which is not a matter of personal profit to any one. Each man will, therefore, often destroy his own forests for the sake of the lumber, and trust to others to leave theirs for the sake of the rainfall. In a case like this, government interference has been abundantly justified.

§ 441. In supplying these needs, the government serves a public necessity. But there are two opposite causes which often prevent it from doing its work judiciously. Either the taxpayers know that they are paying for these improvements, or they do not. If they know it, as in the case of country roads, they will grudge every penny of necessary expense, and will waste in horseflesh and wagon-wheels many times the amount of capital which would have sufficed to put the road system in proper shape. Seeing no pecuniary return for the money which they spend, they will cause themselves great pecuniary loss by their shortsighted economy. If, on the other hand, the taxpayers do not see whose money is being spent, as in the case of ship canals and other works of national importance, they will look only at the question of convenience, and will fail to see that somebody must pay for this convenience by taxation. They will commit the fallacy of confounding government property with public wealth, and will ignore the fact that unwise expenditures on government property lessen the public wealth instead of increasing it.

The danger of this mistake is intensified by the fact that so many people believe the expenditure of money to be in itself a positive benefit, without considering the source whence it is drawn ; and are ready to make appropriations for objects of slight value, because they can see the money which is spent and cannot see the losses involved in collecting it.[1] The history of river and harbor improvements has often been a public scandal. Some of them are recklessly made, without the remotest prospect of permanent benefit to any one. Others, which promise a benefit, are begun without anything like a careful estimate of the probable cost. Many an advocate of canal projects claims that a canal is a cheaper means of transportation than a railroad ; basing his argument on figures which include interest and maintenance in the expense of railroad transportation and exclude interest and maintenance from the cost of canal transportation. The comparison is made in this fashion because the government habitually pays interest and maintenance on the canal,

[1] This danger is by no means confined to expenditures for industrial enterprises. It is exemplified in the demand for pensions of various forms (compare § 75). In the United States there is a strong pressure toward regarding military and naval pensions not as a means of support to those disabled in the service of the government, but as a means of distributing public money as widely as possible among private individuals.

so that this is supposed to be no part of the expense of the shipment. But it represents a cost to the public just as much as if it were paid by private individuals, and any legislation which ignores this element of cost is blindly increasing public burdens.

§ 442. A third class of cases brings us into much more doubtful ground. There are many enterprises whose control by private individuals or corporations seems to give those individuals or corporations an arbitrary power over the industrial interests of the country ; which forms a menace to public wealth, and destroys whatever presumption may exist in favor of private control of industry.

Let us see what constitutes the real basis of this presumption.

Each consumer probably knows better than any one else whether he wants an article enough to pay a specified price for it. Each producer presumably knows better than any one else whether he can do a thing cheaply enough to meet the consumer's wants. Competition allows any man to get an article if he is willing to pay the the market price for it, and offers inducements to any man to make an article if he can do it for less than the market price. In so doing, it at once puts goods where they are wanted, makes every producer do his best work, and stimulates progress by giving every incentive for new methods. Even if many mistakes are made in trying these new methods, the gain to the community from the permanent application of those that succeed outweighs the loss from the immediate cost of those that fail. Finally, the rivalry of different producers causes them to sell their products at low rates, and gives the benefit of new methods to the consumers as a body instead of allowing it to be appropriated by a few capitalists.

But it is obvious that these advantages are largely, if not wholly, dependent upon the existence of free competition.[1] In the case of a monopolized industry, the chance for experiments is less wide, the stimulus to producers' energies less effective. Instead of putting prices so low as to bring the product within reach of every consumer who can pay the cost, a monopoly may use its power to fix unfairly high rates, thus increasing its own profits but lessening the sphere of its public service. This danger is present to a noticeable degree in the case of waterworks, of lighting, whether by gas or electricity, and in many of the industries occupied with the conveyance either of intelligence, of passengers, or of general traffic. It is hard to avoid these dangers by legislative control of rates, owing to the inherent difficulty of allowing anybody to fix the charges for a service except those who risk their own capital in so doing. If the government allows corporations to make unduly high charges, it subjects the public to the danger of extortion. If it insists on their making charges which turn out to be unfairly low, it deprives the investors of the control and enjoyment of their property. Why should it not meet the difficulty directly, by owning and managing these enterprises, and making changes in rates with a free hand, at its own risk?

The answer to this question will depend partly on the industry involved, and partly on the financial ability of the government which seeks to take control.

§ 443. The criteria laid down by Jevons[2] to determine when an industry can advantageously be managed by the government, are as follows:

1. Where numberless widespread operations can only be evenly connected, united, and coördinated in a single all-extensive government system.

---

[1] H. C. Adams says that the presumption in favor of private control is lessened if not destroyed where the " law of increasing return " holds good. But we have seen (§ 168, note) the danger involved in making too much of this distinction.

[2] " Methods of Social Reform," p. 279.

2. Where the operations possess an invariable routine-like character.

3. Where they are performed under the public eye, or for the service of individuals who will immediately detect and expose any failure or laxity.

4. Where there is but little capital expenditure, so that each year's revenue and expense account shall represent, with sufficient accuracy, the real commercial conditions of the development.

All this is good as far as it goes; but it leaves the heart of the difficulty untouched. Passing over the first of these points, which really begs the whole question, we have before us, not an indication of the conditions under which a government can manage an industry with the best advantage, but of those under which its management is attended with the least danger. Jevons's principles are restrictive and not positive. They show how far you can trust the government without serious danger of financial mismanagement. Assuming the existence of a political or fiscal motive for extending the sphere of official action, these criteria show in which direction such an extension can be made with the least probability of loss and corruption.[1] Judged on this basis, waterworks form an excellent field for municipal activity, gas works a more doubtful one, and electricity in its various applications quite an unsuitable one. For the national government, these conditions indicate that the post-office is suitable as a field of employment, the telegraph a little more doubtful, and the railroad much more conspicuously so. Unfortunately, these criteria as a rule apply best where the initial necessity for government ownership is least. They indicate that the government may properly own industries where

[1] Even on this restricted basis, a fifth criterion should be added to those of Jevons : namely, that the public management has special advantages where the government is itself a large consumer, as in the case of municipal water supply, so that questions of price will be looked at by the financial authorities from two points of view.

it could easily enough regulate a private company, and may not so properly control industries where it is difficult to regulate a private company. With regard to the *relative* merits of the two systems, administrative ownership or legislative control, in a really perplexing case like railroads, Jevons's principles furnish us no help. Just where the difficulties attendant upon private ownership are greatest, these tests shut the door most hopelessly against state purchase, and leave us no alternative whatsoever.

§ 444. In an industry like the railroad, both private ownership and state ownership, even under the best of circumstances, are likely to be attended with a great deal of dissatisfaction. Neither system is free from serious abuses. The choice between the two is in some measure a choice of evils. Under private ownership we have rapid development of effective methods and processes, and a high degree of industrial efficiency; but side by side with this we have great discriminations and fluctuations in rates, which no system of legislation seems able to keep within bounds. If the government owns all the railroads of a country it will meet many of these difficulties about rates. It will make them steady, and as a rule low. To offset these advantages, it will give a service which, to a country accustomed to the freer system of private management, will seem seriously defective. Germany furnishes a most conspicuous example of a well managed state railroad system. The rates of the German railroads are on the whole quite satisfactory. But the amount of train service in proportion to the population, and the quickness of the trains themselves, whether for passengers or freight, are, according to English and American standards, miserably inadequate.

§ 445. On the whole, private ownership of monopolies tends to rapid development and utilization of improvements. With all the talent that has been put into the public administration of industry it is a salient fact that

the important inventions have been made in countries
enjoying private enterprise. The telegraph, the telephone, the electric light, the railroad track, the locomotive, the air brake, the block-signal system, were all
introduced by private companies. In most cases it took
government experts from ten to twenty-five years to discover them after they had been in successful use on private lines. We also find that the efficiency and quantity
of service is generally higher than we see it under government management. In spite of the ability of the Prussian
civil service the fact remains conspicuous that England
and America have more trains in proportion to the population than Prussia, and that they run them faster.[1]

§ 446. With regard to the relative effect of state and
private ownership in making prices high or low, no general
propositions can be maintained. The United States and
England are the two most conspicuous examples of
countries that have private railroads. The United States
has the lowest freight rates of any important commercial
country in the world. England has the highest. In
either case, if we go below the surface, we find reasons
for the conditions that prevail. The long hauls of cheap
freight give the American railroads an opportunity to
reduce rates, of which they have been quick to avail themselves. In England just the opposite conditions prevail,
and the opposite results naturally follow. On the other
hand, the high American passenger rates are fully explained by the small density of population and the high
average earning power, which make it worth while for
passengers to pay high rates in order to have trains run
when they want them. The same kind of explanation
accounts for most of the glaring differences in charge for

[1] If the government protects private companies from competition these
advantages of private enterprise do not make themselves felt. The French
railroads, which enjoy a guaranteed monopoly, stand in about the same condition as the state-owned roads of Germany, with regard both to train service
and train speeds, besides charging rather higher rates.

telegraph service, lighting, and other objects of industrial monopoly, which are adduced by extremé partisans either of state or of private ownership as arguments for their respective views.

§ 447. Both the advantages and the dangers of government management of industry depend largely upon the form of the government itself; while the possibility of securing the one and avoiding the other is largely dependent upon the character of public men and methods.

In a country like Prussia, where the military element of the government remains the dominant one, we may expect to find public enterprises managed with strict discipline, good economy—at any rate in the narrower sense of the word,—and freedom from glaring abuses. The chief errors of such a government come from not responding quickly to the needs of industrial progress. It is apt to be slow in utilizing improvements or making changes of method : while there is always a danger, which only the best governments are able to avoid, that the monopoly will be used to tax the public instead of to help it.

In a government where the legislative element is more prominent, and especially in a democratic one, the case is reversed. Such a government prides itself on responding to popular needs. Its legislators are chosen to give expression to the public will, and too often pride themselves on their subserviency to the people. Under such conditions we are likely to have reductions in rates to the lowest limit which a regard for the budget will allow, and activity in making obvious improvements and popular changes of method. On the other hand we are in the gravest danger of sacrificing discipline and economy, and of making subserviency to the popular will a cloak to cover abuses of trust and violations of commercial honesty.

§ 448. The chance of securing the advantages and avoiding the evils of either form of government is better

26

in a municipality than in a nation. For the municipality is neither a military body nor in its main functions a legislative body, but an administrative one ; and while the character of the administration chosen is likely to reflect in some measure the traditions of the central government, there is no necessary connection between the two. Moreover, the responsibility for the success or failure of municipal administration is less hopelessly obscure than is apt to be the case with national administration. This being the case, the chance for successful and economical control of enterprises by municipalities is better than the chance under national authorities.

§ 449. If any government agency, local or national, is to be entrusted with the management of an industrial enterprise, a non-partisan civil service is absolutely essential for success. Even in so simple a case as the post office, the abuses of patronage have been great, and only the enforced monopoly of the government which shuts out private competition in letter carriage prevents us from seeing how great is the waste which arises from this source. Much more must this danger make itself felt in industries with large capital accounts. Only where the traditions of the civil service are such that the best men of the country seek and gain admission to it, independent of party, can we hope that the advantages from government management of these industries might outweigh the evils. With the conditions as they exist in the United States, political reasons compel us to reduce government ownership of fixed capital to a minimum. Any extension of party patronage to a new, lucrative, and complex field must involve serious dangers to the already inadequate powers of our Civil Service Commission. The Italian authorities fifteen years ago, after the fullest investigation, came to a decision adverse to government management of railroads ; and this decision was based largely on the ground that politics would corrupt the railroad management and the railroad management would corrupt politics. So long as an administration is to any considerable degree swayed by partisan considerations instead of industrial ones, every extension of government activity to new fields must be regarded with grave apprehension.

# CHAPTER XIII.

## PROTECTIVE LEGISLATION.

The Eight-Hour Movement—The Contract System—Prison Labor—Foreign Immigration—Protective Tariffs—The Popular Argument—The Development of Infant Industries—Political and Military Questions Involved.

John Rae : "Eight Hours for Work." London, 1894.

R. Mayo-Smith : "Emigration and Immigration : a Study in Social Science." New York, 1890.

Leone Levi : "The History of Commerce and of the Economic Progress of the British Nation, 1763–1878." London, 1880.

F. W. Taussig: "The Tariff History of the United States." 2d ed. New York, 1892.

No student of the theory of protection should fail to read the fourth book of Smith's *Wealth of Nations*. The more recent controversial literature on the subject is almost as disappointing as that on bimetallism

§ 450. IT is a natural consequence of the popular doctrine of wages (§ 344) that its adherents try to make use of legislative authority to diminish the apparent oversupply of labor ; sometimes by forced reductions of hours, sometimes by prohibiting the employment of certain classes of laborers, sometimes by restricting the importation of foreign products with a view to the creation of new fields for home industry. They see that the different workmen in an industrial community compete with one another; they fail to see that they consume one another's products. In consequence of this one-sided view, they favor almost any policy that reduces the intensity of competition among workmen as producers, even though it may ultimately reduce the amount of wealth that can be divided among the workmen as consumers.

As a result of this fallacy, even the most wholesome measures are defended on false grounds. There is a disposition to find the reason for prohibiting child labor, not in its real effect on the health and morals of the community, but in its supposed effect in diminishing the employment of adults; to seek grounds for the restriction of foreign immigration, not in the political dangers attendant upon it, but in its industrial consequences in taking away the bread from home labor; to argue for shorter hours of labor, not as a means of improving the quality of the operatives, but as a means of giving work to a larger number of hands.

§ 451. The advocates of the eight-hour movement generally hold that a restriction on the quantity produced by each individual laborer places the laborers as a class in a better position to bargain with those who desire to employ them. They believe, or at least imply, that a diminution in the supply of labor by legislative enactment tends to increase the competition of capitalists for the laborers' services. They claim that enforced reduction of hours of work would create (1) a demand for the labor of men who are now unemployed, and (2) an increase in the price of work per hour, which would enable those who were previously working ten hours to get the old rate of wages for eight hours' work instead of ten.

§ 452. This course of events is most improbable. The proportion of the unemployed is not likely to be diminished by a forced reduction in the hours of labor. Among the many causes of "unemployment," the two most important are the shiftlessness of individual laborers and the fluctuations of commercial credit. The first of these causes would not be affected by legislative reduction of the hours of labor; the second would, for the moment at any rate, be adversely affected. The experience of France after the revolution of 1848, indicates that a sudden change in conditions of employment, devised in the interest of the laboring classes, may so far paralyze credit as to increase the proportion of the idle rather than to diminish it.

If the number of the unemployed remains approximately the same and the product of the employed diminishes as a result of the reduction of time, a loss in real wages is apparently inevitable  The margin of profit in modern industry is so narrow that any considerable gain made by the laborers at the expense of the capitalists so far diminishes the investment of capital in the immediate future as to hurt the laboring classes in the long run more than it helps them for the moment.  This would be the obvious effect if one nation adopted the system and its competitors did not.  For this reason, many advocates of the eight-hour movement are disposed to insist that it should be made an international measure, and that if any nation should refuse to take part in applying it, other nations should defend themselves against the recalcitrant by imposing discriminating duties upon its products.

This removal of international competition puts the difficulties of the eight-hour movement a little way out of sight ; it does not by any means meet them.  No international arrangements or protective tariffs will make one loaf of bread serve the purpose of two.  An eight-hour law either applies to agriculture, or it does not.  If it applies to agriculture, it will make food products scarce. Any one who is inclined to doubt this will soon be convinced of its truth if he watches the actual operations of farm life.[1]  If food products are scarce, some people will surely starve.  If, on the other hand, the eight-hour law does not apply to agriculture, the city laborers who have

---

[1] If an eight-hour day for farm work was once the rule in England, as Rogers thinks, it must have been accompanied by a great deal of overtime.

hoped to maintain a high price for manufactured products, or to give work to the unemployed by a restriction in the output *per capita*, will find themselves wofully deceived. For if the attractions which now draw men from the country to the city are supplemented by a shortening of hours of labor which applies to the latter and not to the former, we shall have more laborers competing for the city work, and more supplies of manufactures to exchange for food. We shall see a larger number of laborers working at starvation rates which the strong man is not allowed to better by working overtime. He must see his children die because the law prohibits him from earning the food they need. If this is to be the result of the eight-hour movement it may well be termed suicidal.

§ 453. The really strong arguments for reduction of the hours of labor are advanced by those who do not believe that the product of labor will be greatly diminished by such a policy. There is much that they can urge in support of this view. They can show that in times past the gradual reduction of the working day, from twelve and thirteen hours to ten or nine, has not caused the expected diminution of output. A shortening of the duration of labor has been accompanied by increased speed, which very soon brings the *per capita* production up to the old level.

Shortened hours combined with increased speed make the conditions of employment more favorable for high grade labor and less favorable for low grade labor. The better laborer does not dislike the speed and enjoys the time saved. Where one country or state has reduced the hours of labor, while another has retained the longer working day, there has been a noticeable differentiation of the character of the employment in the two localities. There was a time when, as a result of legislative enactment, Massachusetts mills were running ten hours a day, while Connecticut mills were running eleven hours. This did not mean that mill hands in Connecticut earned higher wages than those in Massachusetts, or made more products ; nor did it mean that Connecticut mill owners earned larger dividends. The Massachusetts mills ran at greater speed, employed a higher character of operatives, produced on the whole a higher grade of goods, and earned a fair rate of profit in so doing. The Connecticut mills ran at lower rates of speed, and employed operatives of somewhat lower grade than those of Massachusetts, at no higher rates of wages to the laborer or profits to the employer.

It may fairly be asked why the reduction of hours, if it involves no loss of profit, may not be left to the voluntary action of the employer. The answer is this: Industrial history has proved that employers are not, as a rule, ready to take the initiative in these reductions. The unenlightened members of the employing class are often able to dictate the policy of the whole body in this matter. If the employees were united in a universal strike in the whole trade, for the sake of reduction of hours, they could force a compliance with their demands ; but such a result could only be accomplished at great sacrifice to the community as a whole, and in many trades a minority of unintelligent employees could defeat the change altogether. Under these circumstances, recourse must sometimes be had to legislative enactments.

§ 454. For success in legislation of this kind it is necessary that the prescribed reductions be moderate in amount, keeping well within the limits of what the public sentiment of the community will sustain. Otherwise, any statute becomes a dead letter. The eight-hour law of the United States is a monumental instance of failure. To be successfully applied, a law reducing hours of labor must be strictly mandatory and not permissive or optional. The conditions under which overtime is to be allowed must be accurately defined; and the provisions of the law on this subject must be enforced, even in cases where its enforcement involves hardship. It is fatal to the success of an act if public sentiment justifies individuals in taking the matter of exceptions into their own hands. The Fabian Society of England, in its advocacy of the eight-hour day, seems inclined to be satisfied with a law based on the principle of *trade option*. Such a law would provide that where it is proved to the satisfaction of a Secretary of State that the majority of persons employed in any one trade favors a statutory reduction in the hours of labor, this may be made the basis of an order for such reduction. There seems no great reason to apprehend much evil from the adoption of a policy of this kind, in a country where workmen are at once so well organized and so well educated as in England. The danger that a good workman will voluntarily cause a reduction in his earnings for the sake of shortening his working hours is not very serious. But it must constantly be borne in mind that reductions of hours, even more conspicuously perhaps than other forms of labor legislation, bear heaviest, not on the employer, not on the man who has money to spend, but on the labor of those who cannot stand the increased speed and are therefore forced to a choice between a lower standard of comfort or an intensity of strain which they cannot bear.

§ 455. The argument for restricting the employment of certain classes of labor is obviously far stronger than that for general restrictions on the labor supply as a whole. Prohibition of child labor is unquestionably justified on public grounds, because, if the children go to work in the factory at too early an age they are deprived of the chance of health and education which would enable them to make the most of themselves. The community is not always better off for the moment, from keeping them out of the mills; but it is far better off in the long run from having strong citizens instead of weak ones. The gain to the laborers from such a policy is to be sought not in the momentary reduction of the labor supply, but in the ultimate increase of that supply as the children grow to a more efficient manhood.

§ 456. It is very hard to tell at what age the prohibition of child labor should cease. If a boy of thirteen or fourteen is strong enough to earn his living, his gain from the food and other comforts which he earns, is probably greater than his loss from confinement at his labor. In cases like this, the harm from keeping him out of work is likely to outweigh the good. The same difficulty in even more perplexing shape is involved in the regulation of women's labor. There are many women who work for lower wages than those which men in corresponding employments are willing to accept. Some of them live in homes where they are supported by their parents, and where any income which they may earn represents an addition to the family income. Others have families dependent upon them and are ready to kill themselves rather than see their children starve. Each of these classes contributes to the increase of the labor supply in certain lines, and allows wages in those lines to fall below the figure necessary to keep the laborer alive. Men will not, as a rule, take these low wages. They are not allowed to remain in dependence on their parents; they will not go as far as women in killing themselves for the sake of their children. They have a standard of wages which they insist on receiving; in default of such wages they will take to the road. Hence the decided difference between the recognized minimum of wages for the two sexes.[1]

As long as reckless marriage remains the rule, it is hard

[1] Smart ( " Studies in Economics " ) explains this difference on the theory that men have been strong enough to secure industrial gains which modern competition offers them, while women's wages reflect the industrial conditions of a hundred years ago.

to see an escape from this state of things. To forbid a mother to work while her little children starve is out of question. To have the taxpayers assume the support of all such cases would result in placing new burdens upon a number of workers who find it hard enough to maintain themselves at present (compare § 59). The attempt to raise women's wages, either by combination or by law, to a figure equal to those of men, would apparently so diminish the demand for their labor as to leave many with nothing to do. Nor could any reduction in the hours of female labor make work enough to supply all the competitors at remunerative rates. A certain amount of restriction on the labor of women, especially married women, seems necessary on grounds of public health ; but the growing pressure to equalize the legal position of both sexes is likely to reduce such special legislation to a minimum rather than to allow it to expand into an important limitation of the labor supply.

§ 457. A more distinct case for public interference is found in the low wages which prevail under the "sweating system."

An employer who desires to get his work done as cheaply as possible, and at the same time to free himself from the trouble of supervising it, will often make contracts with his subordinates by which he furnishes them whatever materials they may need, and pays them a stipulated price for their product, after deducting the cost of the materials used. Where this contract is made with the workmen as a body, the system is a good one. It gives them a stimulus to use the materials effectively and economically. Where it is made with an individual workman, or *subcontractor*, who hires his help at whatever rates he can persuade them to accept, its benefit is more doubtful. It is good for the employer and the subcontractor; but the men themselves claim that the work is harder and the pay more niggardly than when they are hired by the capitalist directly. They complain that when every penny saved in the workrooms goes to the foreman—which is what the subcontract system accomplishes—his supervision is so intense and his bargaining so close as to make the lot of those under him a hard one. But as long as the labor is performed in the factory itself, the system does not develop its worst features. These are shown when the work is done outside, in isolated shops or in tenements which some people are so unfortunate as to call homes. This method of employment is known as the sweating system. It is perhaps seen at its worst in the ready-made clothing trade, where the length of the hours, the shortness of the wages, and the unsanitary conditions of the employment combine to form an appalling picture.

§ 458. The evils of the sweating system, by which the contractor makes money from the misery of those below him, are made the ground of a severe indictment against free competition. Yet the sweating system is really an illustration of the evils which arise from the absence of competition, not from its presence. Put people in a factory where there is a market rate of wages and they obtain the benefit of the modern competitive process. Leave them isolated and they become the victims of the employer's shrewdness in bargaining. We hear much said about the advantage of the capitalist in his competition with the laborer. The capitalist does *not* compete with the laborer. Laborer competes with laborer and capitalist with capitalist. Where competition exists, the laborer gets the benefit of a market rate made by different capitalists. Their strength is a source of benefit to him. It is where competition does not exist, and bargaining takes its place, that the relative weakness of the laborer makes itself felt. The absence of competition in wages gives rise to oppression as unjustifiable as that which arises from the absence of competition in loans: and laws for the protection of the laborer in these cases may have the same justification as those for protecting the ignorant borrower (§ 155).

The sweating system is in fact a remnant of the domestic system of industry which prevailed until the development of the steam engine concentrated so much of our labor in factories. It represents a survival into modern times of the evils incident to earlier conditions of employment; evils which are doubtless increased by every narrowing of the margin of general profits that gives the contractor an excuse for correspondingly depressing wages, and which are accentuated by the contrast in prosperity between those who have gained the benefits of competition and those who remain under the severer bondage of the older methods.

§ 459. The evils thus far described can probably best be dealt with by the sanitary and educational authorities, rather than by special labor legislation. The dangers to public health in child labor, in unregulated female labor, and in the worst form of contract labor, are so conspicuous that proposals for legislative restriction can most effectively be based on this ground. But there are other forms of cheap labor where the evils, real or alleged, are more distinctively economic. One of these is convict labor.

In order to relieve the taxpayers of a part of the burden of supporting prisoners, it is in many places customary to set those prisoners at work for private contractors. There are three ways in which this is done. Either the convicts are placed directly under the charge of a contractor at a fixed rate per day, the contractor taking the responsibility for the care of the prisoners and getting all the work he can out of them (*lease system*); or labor within the prison walls is placed at the disposal of the contractor, at a fixed rate per day, the contractor having agents in the prison to see that the work is properly carried on (*contract system*); or the results of the labor are offered to the contractor at a fixed price per unit of product, the supervision being in the hands of the prison authorities (*piece price system*). The first of these methods is undoubtedly the worst for the criminals, as it gives all sorts of opportunities for abuse. The third is probably the best; but the difficulty of securing prison supervisors who have at once the qualities of good manufacturers and good wardens is so great that it prevails less frequently than the contract system. The effect of the three systems on outside labor is substantially the same.

§ 460. Convict labor is not a very important matter in actual bulk. The number of convicts set at work in the United States in 1886 was only 45,000, and their output per day was on an average less than half that of free laborers. But the effect of this convict labor in depressing wages may be much greater than that of a corresponding amount of free labor. There are two reasons for this. In the first place, convict labor is pauperized. The community pays for its maintenance whether it is efficient or not. If one free laborer competes with another and his wages fall below the price necessary for his support, he ceases to be a competitor. He must die, migrate, or find some other occupation; and his removal enables the more efficient laborer to command a higher price. But the supply of convict labor is subject to no such restrictions. If the convict, as is habitually the case, earns too little for his own support, the deficiency is made up at the taxpayer's expense and the competition continues with unremitting vigor. It is a subsidized contest of worse elements against better ones. And, in the second place, this pauperized labor can be arbitrarily thrown from one trade to another, while free labor cannot. An increase in the supply of free labor in any particular line is usually a gradual one. If free laborers come into a trade in larger numbers than usual, we may be almost certain that this trade affords exceptional opportunities for earning money and that the laborers already engaged in that trade enjoy more than an average share of prosperity. But in the case of convict labor we have no such certainty. The manufacturers may employ a large number of convict laborers in a trade where the rate of wages offered no special inducements to free labor and where those who are already in the trade suffer severely from the additional supply.

§ 461. Several remedies have been proposed for this evil. There are some who advocate the total abolition of prison labor. This would be extremely undesirable. It would have a bad effect on the convicts themselves, because it would lead to an increase of idleness inside the prison walls, and would not leave the prisoner with a means of earning a living when he has completed his sentence. It would thus make him a permanent burden on society, and would increase the probability of his relapsing into criminal habits from lack of any honest chance of supporting himself. It would also have a bad effect on the taxpayers. The additional expense of maintaining the prison, due to the abolition of the contract system, would cause a reduction in the amount of funds that would otherwise be added to the capital of the community and that would become available for the support of free labor in the year following. While the abolition of the contract system might thus raise wages in the particular trade that had felt its influence adversely, it would be almost certain to lower general wages by increasing the expenses and lessening the receipts of the community as a whole.

Others advocate the restriction of prison labor to work which can be carried on by hand. The prisoner would thus be unable to compete with machine labor, because he would have less useful appliances at command. The objections to this plan differ only in degree from those which have been urged against abolition of prison labor.

It would not provide the prisoner with a means of livelihood when he leaves the prison, because he would have
learned only antiquated methods of work which cannot
compete with those in use to-day.  Nor would it give the
taxpayers as great a relief from burden as is obtained
under the existing system.  It would therefore involve a
loss of capital to the community as a whole, which, though
not so great as that which we should suffer through entire
abolition of industrial labor in prisons, would nevertheless
be very considerable.

Others advocate the retention of prison labor, but propose doing away with the contractor altogether.  They
would have the laborers supervised by the prison authorities,
as under the piece price system ; but instead of selling the
product to a contractor at a fixed rate they would put it
on the market at whatever price it could command.  This
method, which is known as the public account system,
would intensify any evils which result from contract labor.
It would have an opposite effect from the one intended.
It would virtually pauperize the capital as well as the
labor employed.  The state would sell the goods for
what it could get, whether the price covered the expense
of production or not,—a thing which the contractor cannot continue to do for any considerable length of time.
Where the private contractor for prison labor loses
money through the low efficiency of prison labor, he ultimately has to stop business ; but the state, working on
the public account system, would be subject to no such
restriction and might continue indefinitely to produce and
sell goods at a loss.

It is urged in favor of the public account system that
the profits now obtained by private contractors would
accrue to the state.  But these profits are for the most
part illusory.  Experience shows that employers of prison
labor are not conspicuously successful.  Its apparent
cheapness when measured by the day, does not prove

that its results are cheap when measured by the piece. The prison laborer at fifty cents a day usually makes less than one third as many products as the free laborer at a dollar and a half. Only where prison labor is employed in work to be used by the government itself, has the public account system proved even moderately satisfactory.

The best means of guarding against the evils of convict labor is to distribute it among different industries in such a way that no one trade shall suffer unduly from a sudden influx of prison competition. If this matter is attended to, the loss to laborers in any particular trade from the application of the contract or piece price system is relatively slight. It is outweighed by the gain to the public in utilizing men who would otherwise be idle, and in teaching the means of earning an honest living to those who would otherwise be forced to relapse into a criminal career.

§ 462. The case of immigration under contract bears some analogy to that of prison labor. An employer may readily import a large number of foreign laborers into a trade where wages are not particularly high, but where he sees an opportunity of utilizing more labor to advantage. The fact that the employers and not the laborers take the initiative in such contracts, makes this case different from that of the ordinary migrations of labor from place to place or trade to trade. It may be argued that if the employer can profitably contract for foreign labor of this kind, it proves that the country wants such labor. But there are a considerable number of instances which go to show that the country does not always want such labor; that the private gain to the employer is not attended by corresponding gain to the community as a whole; and that, to the laborers already working in the trade, the sudden loss, against which they have not had time to make provision, may prove a very serious one. Advocates of unrestricted immigration say that this loss

27

is one of the incidents of industrial progress, and that the laborers are subjected to precisely the same evils by the sudden introduction of new machinery. But as a matter of equity between different classes of the community the cases of immigration and of machinery are not parallel. In using new machinery, the employer takes far greater risks of failure upon himself. If the experiment proves unprofitable, he bears the whole loss. But in importing foreign laborers under contract, his loss in case of ill-success is not necessarily much greater than the price he has paid for their passage. The community must bear the burden of their subsequent support. On grounds of economic expediency there is at least a fair case in favor of legislation which shall restrict the right of the capitalist to import contract labor.

§ 463. In the case of immigration without contract, the dangers are political and social rather than economic in their character. The worst form of immigration is that which has been "assisted." The authorities in certain parts of Europe, either from a wish to get rid of their superfluous population, or in the hope of relieving themselves of the support of criminals, paupers, or insane persons, have in times past sent their undesirable members to foreign parts, finding it cheaper to spend a few dollars outright in paying their steamship fare than to continue supporting them at home. Every community has a right to defend itself against immigration of this kind. Down to the close of the last century this right was exercised with the utmost vigilance. By the English Acts of Settlement each parish was given protection against the danger of assisted migration from neighboring parishes, and similar restrictions were applied with much greater severity in Continental Europe. The nineteenth century has witnessed a reaction against this policy of repressing free movements of population; but the necessity for vigilance in these matters has not wholly passed. While the growth of international comity may have lessened the danger of an influx of foreign criminals, the development of cheap transportation has increased the danger of an even greater influx of foreign paupers. We have to deal with a large number of immigrants who, though not assisted by foreign governments, have been induced by false representations of agents of the steamship companies to take tickets to the United States, although they had no good prospect of supporting themselves on this side of the water. The laws of the United States against convict and pauper labor seem amply justified by the facts,—far more clearly so than the contract labor law.

§ 464. To a popular government large foreign immigration, even when otherwise unobjectionable, is attended with special evils which arise from the admission of immigrants to political power. When the Irish began to emigrate in large numbers in the fifth decade of our national existence, a great many good people thought that the whole country would go over to Catholicism, and that before the end of the nineteenth century the Roman Pontificate and the Spanish Inquisition would both have their headquarters in New York City. But the Irish immigration has been gradually assimilated without any revolution or any serious change of institutions. It has doubtless increased the difficulties of municipal government in some of our large cities, but it has not rendered it impossible for the country as a whole to remain self-governing and free. Nor does it seem likely that the existing immigration of races of lower grades than the Irish is so large as to prevent our country from dealing with them successfully. The ability of the United States to assimilate foreign elements has proved far greater than was anticipated by many observers. But this ability is by no means unlimited. Every nation needs to have a certain homogeneity of law and morals. It can assimilate a certain number of immigrants who have not been brought up in its own traditions ; but if the rate of such immigration becomes too rapid there is danger that the old national habits will be destroyed. The more alien the thoughts and habits of the immigrant races, the more serious is this danger. The agitation against Chinese immigration, so far as it was justified at all, was justified on this ground.

§ 465. On purely economic grounds, the case in favor of unrestricted immigration is much stronger than people commonly suppose. Voluntary and unassisted immigration is generally of a pretty high grade. It may be fallacious to compute the value of an immigrant to the United States by what it has cost to produce him at home or by what it would have cost to produce and train him here ; but there can be no doubt that the man who has saved money enough and has shown enterprise enough to take a journey of three or four thousand miles, has certain first-rate qualities that are likely to make him a useful citizen to the United States. Though the exhaustion of our public land supply is diminishing the immediate and visible need for such laborers, we still have enough un-used land and unused opportunities to make every able-bodied workman constitute an addition to our industrial strength.

Even the immigrants of a lower class, when they are not so weak or dependent as to constitute a political and social menace to our national life, can render services which are of great value to the community. By doing the low-grade work they may diminish the chance for Americans of low grade to maintain themselves ; but they correspondingly increase the opportunities for Americans of higher grade. If we get our poorest work done cheaply, by men who are able to do it economically, all the rest of the country has the benefit of the products of their labor at less sacrifice than would otherwise be involved. It is hardly fair to say that "the competition that comes through immigration has the tendency to lower the standard of living in this country," or that " the outcome of such competition will be to reduce our whole laboring class to the standard of life of these newcomers." This has certainly not been its outcome in the past. The result of the introduction of a number of low-grade laborers has been not inaptly compared to the effect produced on a pyramid by introducing a new layer at the bottom. The pressure at this bottom layer becomes more intense than ever before, but the general mass is raised instead of being lowered.

With immigration and with the stimulus which it has given to progress by compelling native workers to rise or to die, the country as a whole has been rising. It is doubtful whether it would have risen nearly as fast without such a stimulus. The removal of a cause which has done so much for our industrial progress in the past might well lead to stagnation rather than to higher civilization. Much of the opposition to immigration comes from the men who stand in the way of such progress; men who are incapable of rising into the higher grades; men who, if they work at all, are fitted only for such work as foreign immigrants do, and who fail to do that work well. There may have been good reasons for putting a stop to Chinese immigration; but the average Chinese immigrant, industrious and sober, was far more useful to the community at the time and had far more possibilities of serving the community in the future, than the average persecutor who threw stones at him.

§ 466. The movement to shut out foreign products by a high tariff has generally proved stronger than the movement to shut out foreign labor by laws regulating immigration. In restricting immigration the superficial and immediate interests of the capitalists have been opposed to those of the laborers ; in restricting the importation of the products of industry the interests of the two classes have seemed to go hand in hand. If the legislature threatens to prevent the importation of foreign laborers it antagonizes the man who wishes to employ them. But if it offers to prevent the importation of foreign products it gives the employer who has money to invest in the production of similar goods an interest in behalf of the proposed measure fully as great as that of the laborers. Therefore many capitalists who have been inclined to oppose laws which restrict the movements of laborers, as being violations of the principles of free government, have been equally inclined to welcome laws which restrict the importation of products, as part of a system of *protection* to home industry (compare § 150).

§ 467. It is beyond the scope of this book to give anything like a history of the world's tariff policy. Down to the end of the last century protective taxes were accepted as a matter of course. The country was fortunate that had custom houses on its national borders only, and did not find district separated from district by barriers against trade. The work of the physiocrats and of Adam Smith paved the way for reform in this matter; the French Revolution and the Napoleonic wars, by uniting people into larger political groups, helped to bring more liberal ideas into play; while the great English Free Trade movement, effectively pressed by Cobden and his friends, which culminated in the Sir Robert Peel's Corn Law of 1846, gave the world an example of radical departure from a time-honored method of protective taxation. Napoleon III. and his minister Chevalier made a still further progress in the same direction, by a system of reciprocity treaties devised with the intention of guiding the commercial world in the direction of freer trade. The United States, which had oscillated between high and low duties, seemed committed to the latter policy by the undoubted success of the tariff of 1847 and of the Canadian reciprocity treaty of 1854. But a general reaction set in when it was least anticipated. Wars on both sides of the Atlantic brought out feelings of national antagonism with unexpected force, and led to the adoption of a tariff policy which reflected these feelings. It was first and most conspicuously exemplified in the United States: where the war duties of 1861, 1862, and 1864, originally levied for purposes of revenue, were allowed to stand after the restoration of peace and the abolition of the corresponding internal revenue taxes; where the efforts at reduction in 1872 proved transient, and the acts of 1882 and 1891 only emphasized the protective features of the tariff system. It has been manifested both in France and Germany with increasing force in the years since the war of 1870; nor has any large power in Continental Europe been exempt from its influence. The English colonies have felt the effect of the same movement; and even in England itself under the guise of an agitation for "fair trade," there have been a few appeals for the renewal of protective duties.

§ 468. There are three distinct lines of argument for a protective tariff. The first, which claims that protection makes high wages by keeping money at home and by directly creating an increased demand for labor, is popular and superficial. The second, which urges the indirect economic advantages of diversification of industry, is less popular but more substantial; and the same may be said of the third, which looks at protection as a military necessity forced upon a nation by the rivalry or hostility of its neighbors.

§ 469. The popular argument for protection is a survival of the mercantile theory of political economy. This theory holds that a nation grows rich by making money, —by having a large income and small expenses. The exports of a nation correspond to the income of an individual; the imports of the nation correspond to the expenses of an individual. The national wealth is therefore promoted by an increase of exports and a diminution of imports. Every excess of exports over imports represents an addition to the accumulated capital of the country. A tariff laid for the purpose of preventing the import of things which can be made at home is a means of increasing this capital. Such a tariff, it is urged, is not only beneficial to the community as a whole, but especially so to the laborers. For money, which was formerly employed in buying goods from abroad, will, under the operation of a protective tariff, be used to give employment to laborers at home. All such avoidance of foreign expenditure means, therefore, an increase in the wealth of the country and in the income of the laborers.

Carrying the same principle still further it is urged that bounties should be given in those industries where an effective tariff would make the price to the consumer too high,—for instance, in the case of sugar,—or where it is desired to stimulate our production for foreign trade as well as for domestic trade. But there is more reluctance to give bounties than to impose tariffs, because the tax arising from a high tariff is, directly at any rate, a source of revenue to the government ; while the payment of a large bounty involves an expenditure which can be met only by levying taxes whose burden is more obvious than that of a tariff and therefore more unpopular.[1]

§ 470. This view of the effects of protection is a very superficial one. In the great majority of cases it is impracticable for a nation to " make money " in this way. It will pay for its imports by its exports and *vice versa.*

---

[1] The subject of bounties (and indeed the whole theory of protection) is well treated by C. Gide, " Principles of Political Economy," book ii., ch. vii. For bounties to shipping see § 490.

A bounty brings the burden of supporting the favored industry upon the shoulders of the whole body of taxpayers. It is therefore theoretically more equitable than a protective tariff which taxes the consumers of certain articles only. But all our methods of taxation are so bad in many of their workings that this theoretical equity is not very well realized in practice.

An attempt to diminish the imports and maintain or increase the exports for any considerable period of years is generally futile. The accumulation of money in one country and its withdrawal from another will cause high prices to prevail in the former country and low prices in the latter. The former country thus becomes a good market to sell in and a bad market to buy in. People will ship more goods to such a country than they would if the high prices did not prevail, and will take fewer goods from it. They will withdraw gold from the place where prices are high, for use in the place where prices are low. The experience of four centuries has demonstrated the futility of trying to interfere with this movement of specie. Although the exportation of gold has often been prohibited under the severest penalties, it has nevertheless continued. Although statesmen have made every effort to modify or prevent the operation of this automatic movement, by which prices in different communities seek their natural level, the results of their efforts have been strikingly small.

§ 471. In the few cases where these efforts to accumulate money are in any degree successful, most of the expected good proves illusory. Higher nominal wages combined with higher prices leave the different classes of the community in the same relative position that they held before. The real demand for labor is not measured by the accumulated supply of money, but by the commodities which the laborer can buy with the money he receives. If every dollar in the United States were cut in halves and each half were called a dollar, there would be a larger nominal supply of money but no real increase in wages. When an increase of money is the result of better business methods, it is a good thing; but when we seek to reverse this process and obtain better business by putting more money into circulation, we are simply playing with figures.

So far as the increase of money is obtained at a sacrifice of useful things which the money would buy, it may prove a positive disadvantage to the laborer. If we succeed for a few years in arbitrarily checking our imports, we may find ourselves with more money and less of certain other things which would help our productive laborers more than money does. In this respect, the mercantile system of political economy may not inaptly be characterized as a miserly system. It would make the policy of the nation similar to that of a miser rather than that of a wise merchant. The successful business man is not the one who sells the most and spends the least, but the one who spends his income on things which will permanently increase his earning capacity in the future. The successful nation is not the one which strives to get the most money, but the one which invests most of its income in increased productive resources, by purchasing things which other nations are able to place at its disposal, that will either increase the real wages of the laborer to-day or give better chances for efficient exercise of labor in the immediate future.

§ 472. But it may be urged that countries like the United States, which have borrowed large amounts of capital, may profitably employ an excess of exports over imports in paying their debts. A debtor should undertake to sell more than he buys, and spend the difference, not in extending his personal consumption, not in making additional investments, but in cancelling past obligations and placing himself in a position of independence. This is in a measure true. But the adoption of such a policy by an individual indicates that his business has pretty nearly reached the limit of its growth. Until this point is attained, he will find it more profitable to use his surplus income in widening the scope of his operations than in paying his debts. The conspicuously successful leader in commercial enterprise is not occupied with restricting his liabilities, but with increasing his assets. As long as he can borrow capital at a low rate and use it with large profit, he will care less to diminish his obligations than to enlarge his means of meeting them. The United States is in a position of this kind. While it is a satisfaction to pay our debts, it is a greater satisfaction to increase our resources. The years which show the greatest excess of exports over imports have not always been the years of conspicuous industrial prosperity.

§ 473. The evils resulting from an adverse balance of trade,—*i. e.*, an excess of imports over exports—are much exaggerated. As was clearly pointed out by Daniel Webster, a slight adverse balance represents a normal and healthful condition of commerce. If we ship goods worth $1,000,000 at New York and sell them for $1,100,000 in London, we are in a position to bring back goods worth $100,000 more than those we shipped. The possibility of selling our goods at a profit is the best indication of demand for the products of our labor. Of course it is conceivable that we should bring back the $100,000 in specie. But a very slight movement of this kind would cause a redundance of money in New York and a scarcity in London. The difference of price levels thus created would make further exports difficult, and would diminish instead of increasing the demand for the products of our labor. There may be times when, owing to the precarious condition of its currency, a nation needs specie more than goods, and when imports of coin are of more consequence to it than any other form of capital. But these cases are exceptional. The history of the mercantile system (§ 9), enforced as it was by the efforts of the ablest European statesmen for two centuries, goes to show the fatuity of trying to increase a country's supply of gold by statutory restrictions either on the movement of the metal or on that of the commodities for which it is exchanged.

A country which mines more gold than it needs for its immediate use, purchases other forms of capital with the surplus. This creates an apparent adverse balance of trade—an import of goods and an export of gold;—yet gold mines are a source of industrial prosperity and strength. Even when the United States has an adverse balance greater than the product of its mines, it does not necessarily mean that we are losing gold; it may mean that foreign countries are using their capital to develop our natural advantages and are taking their pay in securities. We are increasing our indebtedness ; but we are yet more rapidly increasing our productive assets and our effective employment of labor.

All payments to foreigners—freights, interest, investment, foreign travel—tend to make our balance of trade look more favorable, because we are usually compelled to export goods to meet them. All receipts from foreigners from the same sources tend to make our balance look less favorable, because foreigners generally cannot pay them in gold without causing redundance and therefore ship goods instead. Yet the payments on the whole represent sources of weakness, and the receipts are all but universally sources of strength. England habitually imports more than she exports because other nations owe her so much for interest and freight charges ; in other words, because she has large invested capital and a large merchant marine.

§ 474. Unless a country is in some very exceptional financial position stoppage of imports means stoppage of exports, because other nations cannot continue to buy its goods unless they sell it their own goods in return. The apparent widening of the home market and increase of the demand for labor caused by a protective tariff is accompanied by a narrowing of the foreign market and a diminution in the production of goods for export which was profitable under the old system. What is called the creation of a new industry is generally nothing but the diversion of capital and labor from one industry to another. The exceptions to this rule are more apparent than real. We see the opportunity for profitable employment of foreign capital and immigration of foreign labor in a new line; we fail to see with equal clearness the loss of some of the opportunities which made foreign investment and foreign immigration in old lines most profitable. If the imposition of a high tariff is followed by prosperity in manufactures and adversity in agriculture, everybody credits it with the former results, while few look far enough below the surface to hold it accountable for the latter.

§ 475. This diversion of labor and capital is, presumably at any rate, from a line where it is more efficient to one where it is less so. If there is one line of industry where an American can compete with the whole world without the aid of a protective tariff, and can sell his goods in foreign markets though he pays double the wages given by his competitors, it shows that his natural advantages are such that his labor is more than twice as efficient as theirs. If there is another line where he cannot compete with the foreigner because of the difference in American wages, it shows that his natural advantages are less than this difference. The man who exports goods must produce so much more than his foreign competitors that the superior efficiency of each individual laborer covers not merely the difference in wages, but the cost of transportation also; while the man who is shut out from the home market by his foreign competitor is employing labor whose efficiency is so much less than the difference in wages that the foreign producer can pay the cost of transportation [1] and continue to undersell him.

[1] The current argument, that protection produces economy by having goods consumed near the point of production, is in large measure fallacious, for if people import an article from a distance it shows that the difference in economy between the producers of an article in two countries more than covers its cost of transportation.

§ 476. The popular argument, that by admitting goods free of duty we subject ourselves to the competition of pauper labor, ignores the fact that the chief reason for the difference between American and European wages lies in the difference of efficiency of American and European workmen. The American gets higher wages than the European competitor, because he does more work in a day (§ 362). The cost per unit of product in the United States, which is the thing that determines power of competition, is low in some lines and high in others. In general, it is lower than that of Europe in the unprotected industries, and higher in those which are protected either by a tariff or, as in the case of personal services, by the impossibility of transportation.

If American locomotive works are competing with English locomotive works in neutral markets, it shows that the labor cost per locomotive in the two countries is substantially the same; for if the English labor cost were higher, the American locomotive builders would drive the Englishmen out of the market; and conversely, if the American labor cost were higher, the English builders would drive out their American competitors. Therefore, if the wages per day of the American workmen in these lines are higher than those of the Englishmen, it follows that their efficiency, as measured by amount of work done, is also correspondingly higher. If American clockmakers compete not only in neutral markets, but in England itself, it shows that we have an advantage in efficiency which more than makes up for any difference in wages. Industries of this kind have nothing to fear from pauper labor. What is apparently the dearest labor is really the cheapest. This superior efficiency of the American workman in these lines is the cause of the high wages which he receives.

There are some forms of labor, like that which is employed in the building trades or like personal and professional services, whose results must be utilized on the spot. Laborers in these lines will share in the high wages enjoyed by workmen in those industries where we have natural advantages, because if the wages in services or building trades were low while those in exporting trades were high, the workmen would nearly all desert the former line of employment and gravitate toward the latter. The demand for services at home on the part of the men who make goods for export, forces them to offer sufficiently high wages to induce men to render those services.[1] This result must ensue whether we have a tariff or not. We cannot have our meat cooked in Paris, our boots blacked in London, or our houses built in Berlin, no matter how cheap these services may be in foreign countries. The cook, the boot-black, and the house-builder therefore share in the high wages due to the efficiency of labor in lines for which we have a natural advantage. But there are other forms of industry, like the manufacture of woollen cloth, where we have the option of having the work done at home or abroad. In the production of woollen cloth we have little or no advantage over our foreign competitors; much less than our advantage in some other lines of productive industry. If we leave trade free, we shall export wheat and cotton, metals and certain lines of manufactures for which we are particularly skilled, and shall import woollen goods from abroad. If we place a tariff on woollen manufactures which prevents their importation, we shall divert a part of our labor from wheat and cotton and mining and specially profitable manufactures to a line of industry where we have no especial advantage, and shall thereby reduce the average efficiency of our labor. When we are threatened with severe evils as a result of admitting the

---

[1] In a mining camp the cook will receive wages at least as high as the average of miner's earnings, because if offered less than this, he will prefer to seek for gold on his own account, instead of staying at home to cook.

pauper labor of Europe to compete in our own markets, we
must remember that the chief effect of such competition
will be to force our labor into lines where it is more productive.  We shall make it impossible for men to live in
some lines; we shall make it more profitable to divert
their work to other lines.

§ 477.  It is sometimes said by protectionists that they
do not want us to diminish our imports as a whole; they
want us to make all the things we can and use our money
in importing things we cannot get otherwise.  But the
question of ability or inability to make a thing is one of
degree.  If we try to make things for which we have
only moderate advantages, and in so doing divert labor
and capital from those where we have extraordinary ones,
we do not, in general, make money; we lose more than
we gain.  The attempt to do everything ourselves for the
sake of shutting out the competition of pauper labor from
abroad is in its results not unlike the attempt of a surgeon
to make money by shovelling his own snow.  The surgeon
has a physical and mental education which enables him
to shovel snow with less expenditure of time and force
than the laborer who offers to do it for him.   Why, then,
does he hire the laborer instead of doing the work himself?  Why does he say that he cannot *afford* to shovel
his own snow?  Because there is a line of industry open
to him in which he can make ten dollars an hour, and he
cannot afford to waste his strength in competing with
men who earn one dollar an hour.  The diversion of force
to the unprofitable employment is a loss instead of a gain.
If an ordinance were passed compelling every surgeon to
shovel his own snow, he would gain one dollar and lose
ten.  He would avoid the competition of pauper labor,
but at the expense of a large reduction in his aggregate
income.  His high rate of pay is the result, not of legislative restrictions, but of a difference in industrial efficiency;
an advantage which he may forego if he chooses, for the

sake of diversifying his employment, but at an economic loss rather than an economic gain.

§ 478. In the second group of arguments for a protective tariff, it is frankly admitted that the so-called creation of new industries is really a diversion of labor and capital from one employment to another; but it is maintained that the indirect advantages which may accrue from such a policy are great enough to warrant any temporary sacrifice which it involves. Its advocates urge, in the first place, that the apparent profit in the exercise of unprotected industries is often not a real or permanent one. An industry may apparently be very profitable, when private individuals are being allowed to appropriate the natural resources of the country and to weaken it by sending those resources abroad for their own pecuniary advantage. This is true conspicuously of mining and timber cutting; it is in somewhat less degree true of food production. Systems of agriculture under which the owners seek to get all that they can out of virgin soil, exporting a large product for a few years without making proper returns to the land in the form of manure, may result in impoverishing the home country for the benefit of foreign consumers. If by a well devised tariff a part of the labor and capital thus used in agriculture is diverted to manufacturing, the advocates of protection say that it will result in supporting more people at home with less exhaustion of the soil, and on a basis which, though perhaps temporarily less remunerative, will be far more profitable in the long run.

They urge that under these circumstances the tariff may conceivably give increased employment to labor from the outset. If a country is engaged in agriculture, and in that alone, the differences in the character of the land used will show themselves in the form of economic rent. This is a surplus which goes to the landowners and is not necessarily distributed among the laborers at all;

28

especially if the landowner uses his income to import foreign articles of luxury. If a change in tariff policy causes less agricultural land to be used and makes industry more diversified, there will be smaller differences which can be appropriated as rent. Even where the momentary efficiency of labor in earning a return for its employer is slightly diminished, it is quite conceivable that the amount actually distributed to labor may increase, and the social condition of the community be benefited rather than injured.

§ 479. If this is conceivable as a momentary result, it is still more possible in the long run. The introduction of a new industry is attended with great difficulties, which make its returns during the first years quite uncertain. A tariff arranged to protect an *infant industry* may be sufficient to overcome this initial uncertainty which makes it impossible for individuals to start such an enterprise; and may after a brief time provide the country not only with profitable investments of capital in diversified lines, but with useful employment for laborers whose skill would otherwise have remained undeveloped.

Such investments, it is said, give a chance for the employment of high-grade labor, which would otherwise be compelled to accept what it could earn in lower grades of work where its special powers would be less perfectly utilized. If a country like England has special industrial advantages in the way of established connections and large capital, it may force other nations to engage in less complicated forms of labor which do not properly utilize their more intelligent members. This argument, which is strongly urged by writers like List or Gunton, is the opposite of the pauper labor argument. In this view, a country needs protection, not from the weakest laborers of other countries, who would crowd its own citizens up into higher lines, but from the strongest laborers of other countries, who would crowd them down into lower ones.

§ 480. On the theoretical merits of this argument for protection, it is difficult and unnecessary to pronounce a definite judgment. If we could assume that the legislature would be wise and incorruptible, we might hope that it could frame a tariff which would be of positive benefit to the community ; and it is altogether probable that it could devise one which would produce more good and less evil than any system of national taxation which is now in use. But in actual practice we do not have to deal with an all-wise and incorruptible legislature. The chance for mistakes in the adjustment of industrial burdens, whether made in good faith or otherwise, is extremely great. The legislature sees the new industries which are developed ; it fails to see the old ones which are handicapped. It may produce unforeseen losses which outweigh the expected gains. Our increase of manufacturing in the years succeeding the Civil War is heralded as a result of a high tariff, by many who overlook the effects of that tariff as manifested in the accompanying diminution in the ocean marine and ocean shipbuilding industries.

§ 481. The apparent prosperity which often attends the first operation of a protective tariff increases the probability of these mistakes. The policy of shutting out foreign goods means that the protected country duplicates the plant by which they were made. The persons who were saving money have, for the time being, a profitable method of utilizing their surplus—and, incidentally, of damaging the foreigner by so doing. But after a short time this special chance for investment ceases. The laborers employed in making machinery are thrown out of work. The whole industrial world suffers from the effects of a policy which has duplicated means of production and restricted facilities of exchange.

§ 482. Far from preventing exhaustion of the soil, actual tariff legislation is apt to stimulate it. We have for many years had a tariff on copper not justified by any difference in its cost of production—for no mines in the world can produce so cheaply as those of the Lake Superior region —but acting as a bonus on the unnatural extension of mining operations. American copper has habitually been sold in London in competition with foreign copper, at a price less than was paid by American consumers at home. We have put a positive premium on the exhaustion of American mines for the benefit of the foreign consumer. Equally conspicuous is the case of lumber. Without any good pretext in connection with the necessity of paying high wages to American labor—for the labor that is employed in the lumber business is very largely composed of Canadians who come to this country temporarily and return to their homes at the end of a season—we have exhausted our northern forests at a rate which has proved dangerous, not merely to the resources of the country as timber land, but to the rainfall and other conditions connected with public health.

§ 483. Under these circumstances, the argument about increasing the share of the national income that goes to the laborer and diminishing the proportion that goes to the landowner has no practical application. A duty like that which was imposed on copper shows its results, not in the increased proportion of wages paid in the copper industry, but in the very high value of the shares of well situated copper mines. A tariff which is accurately adjusted to counterbalance any difference in labor cost in two countries may have the theoretical effect of increasing the laborer's share at the expense of the landowner's; a tariff rate higher than this is likely to have the opposite effect. The manufacturers in protected lines of industry always protest against public attempts to ascertain their labor cost per unit of product. This protest creates a presumption that the tariff is higher than can be justified on grounds of protection to labor alone.

§ 484. Protection to infant industries has unquestionably proved successful in certain cases. But it is open to doubt whether the number of instances of success has been sufficient to justify the expense involved. The period of industrial infancy, and the taxation connected with it, almost always continues longer than was at first anticipated. Very few industries have been in a position to submit to a removal of a protective tariff within the time originally contemplated. In many the rate of protection has tended to increase rather than to diminish. If a duty is "specific" (§ 507), *i. e.* based on the *quantity* of a product imported rather than on its *value*, the cheapening of the protected article through new processes of manufacture makes the rate of protection constantly increase. Even where successive tariff bills reduce the specific duty per yard or per pound, we do not generally find any continuous reduction in the ratio between the duty levied and the value of the article at the time of passage of the different acts. The steel rail industry of the United States is often cited as an instance of successful protection and falling tariff rates; but the actual percentage of duty levied has on the whole increased. The tariff rate per ton has fallen; but the price of rails has fallen still faster. Nor has this diminution in price been the result, as some persons would have us believe, of the development of industry in the United States under the tariff itself. The prices have been habitually much lower in England than in the United States; and in countries which manufacture no rails of their own they have been quite as low as in England. What is claimed as an effect of the protective tariff in cheapening prices is usually only the natural result of modern improvements in the arts, which we should have enjoyed quite as fully without the tariff as with it.[1]

[1] The only convincing proof that protection has ceased to be a burden upon the consumer of any particular article (in other words, that an industry

§ 485. Advocates of protection to infant industries often make the mistake of assuming that the foreigner is a single person who can shift prices up and down at will; that he will charge high prices for articles which the home producers do not make, but accept much lower ones when the development of a protected industry has made a nation independent of his power. But the competition of one foreigner with another prevents extortionate rates and arbitrary shifting of prices, whether there be any home production or not. Foreign trade is the hardest field in which to exact monopoly prices, because it is open to competition from the whole industrial world. The home producer is on the whole far more likely to make arbitrary prices than the foreigner, because the difficulty of forming a pool which includes all the capital engaged in a given line of business in any one country is far less than the difficulty of doing the same thing for the whole world. This point was illustrated by the history of the steel rail traffic, where a strong combination was formed that for ten years succeeded in keeping up the price of steel rails in those countries which produced them. During a large part of this period Italy, which produced no rails, obtained its supplies from Germany, at rates thirty per cent lower than those which were exacted from German purchasers.

§ 486. Any good effect of a tariff in promoting the development of higher grades of productive industry is offset by its bad effect in retarding the development of varied consumption. It is a matter of prime importance for the community in general, and the laborers in particular, to have cheap goods placed within their reach. The educational effect of cheapness in increasing consumption and diversifying the enjoyments of a community is very great. A tariff which temporarily enhances prices for the sake of

has outgrown the stage of infancy) is furnished by a readiness to have the tariff removed.

indirect effects on producers is liable to have an adverse effect on consumers which outweighs the possible good that it might otherwise afford.[1]

§ 487. A tariff to protect infant industry, being avowedly temporary in its nature, is liable to be removed; and the doubt as to the time of this removal constitutes a serious economic burden. The great majority of business men agree that the worst evil in a tariff is uncertainty; that industry will adjust itself to almost any schedule of duties, high or low, if it is continued long enough, but that the possibility of a change in the future has a paralyzing effect on trade of every kind. Any tariff which is temporary in its nature and variable in its amount is apt to produce the spasmodic demand for labor and irregular investment of capital in machinery, whose evils have been clearly described in a previous chapter. It cannot be expected that people will agree as to the time when an industry should be left to stand alone. If there has been an over-investment of capital in any industry it will suffer severely when finally exposed to foreign competition. The more completely the height of a tariff has been left to the discretion of the manufacturers, the greater is the danger of such over-investment, and of organized political opposition to the removal of the duty when the pretext for it has been outgrown. A system of taxation which is arranged with a view to the needs of particular industries, rather than those of the treasury department, is liable to be upset by a change of party, if the leaders of the new legislature are not in touch with the business men in industries or localities which have enjoyed protection. Here we have what is perhaps the most serious evil connected with the protective system. It makes the success or failure of business enterprise depend upon the

---

[1] It is strange that Patten, who has so emphasized the importance of diversified consumption, should have overlooked this point in his very ingenious arguments on the "Economic Basis of Protection."

retention of a particular set of men in office. Whether it actually produces corruption or not, it furnishes a powerful motive for subscription to campaign funds, and a temptation to corrupt practices. The less the average congressman understands the needs of business, the greater is the danger that his vote may be shaped by the results of improper influences, even when his own personal character is above suspicion. With legislatures as they are actually constituted and elections as they are actually managed, the danger to popular government as a whole, arising from this source, outweighs the good which can be expected to result from the application of protection for the sake of diversifying industry. If the business men of the country were unenterprising and short-sighted, while its statesmen were able to take a wider and clearer view of the future, many of these theoretical arguments for protection would deserve careful consideration. With matters as they stand, it seems much the safer economic policy to adjust the tariff for purposes of revenue.

§ 488. The third group of arguments for protection is based on military necessity. If there were no such thing as war, and all countries could settle their disputes amicably, many protectionists say they would at once become free traders; but as long as there is a possibility of armed conflict which may exclude a nation from its outside sources of supply, they believe it necessary to be prepared for such an emergency. They adduce in confirmation of their view instances like the American Civil War. The North had already established manufactures; the South had to improvise them. This difference had a great effect on the issue of the conflict. Of still more importance in the same connection was the disparity between the naval forces of the North and South. The North had a reserve of seamen trained in her merchant marine, and was able to establish an effective blockade, which Southern steamers were sometimes able to elude but never really to break. As long as the control of sea power exercises such decisive influence on the results of warfare, it is claimed that every nation which would preserve its independence must maintain not only diversified industries which will make it independent of foreign supplies, but an effective navy, a merchant marine, and a shipbuilding industry by which the navy can be rapidly increased in an emergency.

So far as this argument is based on political grounds rather than industrial ones, it hardly falls within the purview of an economist to criticise it ; except perhaps by the suggestion that a very small part of the proceeds of a revenue tariff, placed directly at the disposal of the military authorities, would do more to prepare a nation for war than is accomplished by a protective tariff. But the policy of protection to the foreign *carrying trade* is advocated for its results in the commercial rivalry of nations no less than in their trials of military strength ; and no economic discussion of the subject is at all complete unless it deals with these claims.

§ 489. Under the influence of the mercantile system of political economy, the leading commercial nations tried to protect their shipping by *navigation acts*, which confined the carrying trade between any two powers to the ships belonging to those powers. Thus the trade between England and France was open to English and French ships, but not to Dutch ships. The application of these laws caused great inconvenience, involving the shipowners in roundabout voyages, and often preventing merchants from forwarding their cargoes as quickly and cheaply as they might otherwise have done. Before the middle of the present century, these laws were gradually done away with ; though the United States still confines its coasting trade to its own vessels.

All direct protection being thus abandoned, the carrying trade of the world tended to fall into the hands of the nations that could build and run ships most cheaply. For a time, England and the United States were closely matched in the race. As long as ships were built of wood the United States had a slight advantage. But with the substitution of iron or steel for wood and steam for sail, the conditions were reversed; and a protective policy which enhanced the cost of shipbuilding materials tended to increase the disadvantage under which American ship-owners labored, compelled as they were by law to buy their ships at home. They were thus handicapped on either side, receiving no protection against foreign competitors, and being compelled to buy vessels in a dearer market in case they wished to run them under the American flag. As a result the ocean tonnage of America fell rapidly behind, in spite of the increased amount of goods to be carried; and England became the unquestioned leader in the world's merchant marine. A considerable amount of American capital is invested in ships sailing under the British flag, because of the economy which is obtained in buying ships where they are cheapest. The requirement that American ships should be built in home yards, which was intended to protect the American ship-builders, only resulted in driving the American flag from the seas.

§ 490. When navigation acts were abandoned, recourse was had to *subsidies* as a means of encouraging the merchant marine. It was inaugurated by Great Britain, whose widely scattered colonial empire made it necessary to maintain communication between the different ports by the quickest possible method, and to utilize steam for this purpose at the earliest possible moment. With this end in view, large postal contracts were made, during the years from 1837 to 1840, with the Peninsular and Oriental Line, the Cunard Line, and the Royal Mail to the West Indies. The system of profitable mail contracts was gradually extended until the time came when the need for them was practically outgrown. The United States adopted a similar policy a few years later (1848), but practically abandoned it just before the Civil War. Since 1880 there has been a tendency on the part of other nations to extend the subsidy system more widely, and to make payments, not for special services in carriage of mails, but for the much less definite service of running steamers under the National flag. France has gone further in this matter than any other nation, having an elaborate system of bounties both for construction and navigation. Italy has adopted somewhat similar methods. Germany, Austria and (since 1891) the United States, pay subsidies in the form of mail compensation, sometimes under general laws and sometimes under special contracts— perhaps the most important of the latter being, that between the United States and the International Navigation Company for a transatlantic service.

These subsidized steamers are useful in providing a reserve in case of war. The commercial success of the policy is more doubtful, whether we look at its effect on the profit of the shipowners or upon the commerce of the nation. French experience seems to indicate that the system of bounties, by calling unnecessary ships into operation, diminishes the regular earnings of the business to a degree for which the government bounty furnishes scant compensation ; while the old proverb that " trade follows the flag " is hardly borne out by recent events. It may have been true in old times that goods went where ships most desired to take them ; but with modern facilities of communication, the owners of the goods make up their minds where they want them to go, and the ships must take them there or nowhere. All things considered, it would be hard to show any commercial gains from subsidies which compensate for the sums spent in this way.

§ 491. A popular form of the military argument for

protection rests in the fact that, by the adoption of restrictions upon trade, we do other nations injury. We
are told that free trade would be all very well if every nation adopted it ; but as long as other people are imposing
tariffs against our goods, we must be prepared to strike
back. Those who hold this view in its milder shape are
content to regard a tariff as a diplomatic means of securing mutual concessions (*reciprocity*)—sometimes treating
these concession as steps toward a general policy of tariff
reduction the world over, which was the plan pursued by
the ministers of Napoleon III. ; sometimes bargaining for
them as special privileges not to be granted to the world
in general, which is the idea underlying the present reciprocity treaties of the United States. But there are not
a few who go farther than this ; who regard injury to
other nations as gain to ourselves, and who say that they
advocate a high tariff for the United States because England desires to have a low tariff.

§ 492. When this view is accepted, a policy of tariff
warfare follows as a matter of course. There are times
when it seems as though a great many nations were carried away with this spirit of commercial hostility. The
years since 1870 have afforded only too clear an illustration of this spirit. But they certainly have not been
a period of prosperity for the nations concerned ; and it
is perhaps safe to regard the policy of these twenty-five
years as a set-back in the general current of economic
events rather than as an indication of the course of that
current. If we look at any long period of time we find
that national intercourse and friendliness are increasing
rather than diminishing. Increased travel and cheapened transportation bring people together more powerfully than armies or custom houses can keep them apart.
The legal disabilities of foreigners are being broken down
by international patent right and international copyright.
The world is on the whole learning that strangers are

not enemies ; and that even in dealings between strangers, each party is helped by the prosperity of the other. It is undoubtedly true that a nation can hurt foreigners by its tariff ; but there is not one whit of evidence to show that it helps itself individually by legislation devised with such a purpose, and every reason to believe that the attitude of mutual hostility thus engendered involves evil, commercially and politically, to all the parties concerned.

§ 493. Colonization as a measure of national protection and a means of finding profitable employment for labor, has had more importance in the past that it has at present. The conspicuous advantages which it affords are, first, an opportunity of employing labor on new land, and thus relieving pressure of population on subsistence ; second, a means of diversifying industry by taking advantage of different climates and of a range of natural resources not likely to be found within the limits of a single compact territory. The older advocates of colonization laid great stress on the second of these points. The English authorities measured the value of a colony by its power of producing things which England must otherwise import. Virginia was highly prized because it could furnish tobacco ; New England was rated lightly, because its products were so nearly the same as those of the mother country. With the downfall of the mercantile system, this argument has been less frequently urged. It is seen that the prosperity of a colony and its utility to the mother country are due to the general efficiency of its labor rather than to the particular form in which that labor is embodied. Colonies are now valued by statesmen as means of relieving the country of its surplus population without weakening it to the degree which is inevitable when emigrants seek refuge under a foreign flag. But even when we look at them in this light, colonies are by no means a source of unmixed strength.

As long as they remain weak, they are apt to involve expense to the home country; when they grow strong they are independent enough to repel the suggestion that they should repay the bounty of earlier days, and to meet any attempt to force such repayment by a declaration of independence. It is on grounds of political rather than of commercial or fiscal advantage that the modern statesman must rest his defense of a policy of colonization.

# CHAPTER XIV.

## GOVERNMENT REVENUE.

Its Different Forms—Principles of Taxation—Certainty the Primary Object
—Incidence of Taxation—Direct and Indirect Taxes—Property and
Income Taxes—Progressive Taxation—The Single Tax—Public Debts.

For American and English readers, the most available general work on
finance is probably C. F. Bastable's "Public Finance." 2d ed. London,
1895. The able writings of Wells and of Seligman are unfortunately somewhat fragmentary.

The French and German literature on the subject is much fuller. It is
enough to refer to the writings of De Parieu and of Leroy-Beaulieu, or to
those of Cohn (translated by Veblen, Chicago, 1895), of Wagner, and of
the contributors to the second volume of Schoenberg's "Handbuch."

§ 494. The ordinary sources of revenue of modern
governments divide themselves into three groups: 1.
Prices. 2. Fees and Assessments. 3. Taxes.

A price is a charge for special services which people are
not compelled to accept unless they choose. A fee or
assessment is a charge for special services which people
are compelled to accept whether they will or no. A tax
is not based on special services, but is a forced contribution to the general expenses of the government.

§ 495. When the government revenue takes the form
of a *price* it is collected by processes like those of private
business. But the range of prices which the government
can charge is far wider than that which is open to a private individual or corporation. It may use its position of
vantage to compel the payment of a higher price than an
individual can charge, as in the case of the tobacco and

salt monopolies of Continental Europe, or the rates of letter postage in the United States. Or, on the other hand, it may make use of its varied fiscal resources to charge a much lower price than an individual would be likely to do or could do without running into bankruptcy. This is illustrated by the sales of public land in the United States, or by the passenger rates of the various European state railroads. Most of the arguments for government ownership of industrial enterprises proceed on the assumption that very low prices will result rather than very high ones—an assumption which is not always borne out by the facts.[1] When the government charges more than individuals could do, the payment exacted is known as a monopoly price, and is treated by most writers on finance as a tax on the consumer. When it charges approximately the same rate that a private individual would do, whether it be under the stress of actual competition or not, the payment is known as a quasi-private price. When it charges less than a private individual would do, the payment is called a public price.

§ 496. The payment of a price to the government is to a certain extent voluntary, since the purchaser has the option of avoiding it by going without the service rendered. When there is no such option, and the payments, though based on special services rendered, are collected by processes different from those which an individual could adopt, it is called an *assessment* or a *fee*. The chief difference between the two things is that an assessment is levied once for all, to meet some extraordinary expense, while fees are charged for services which are constantly recurring in the ordinary course of relations between a government and its subjects. Assessments are levied on property rather than on persons, and there is usually a more careful attempt to make the price conform to benefits rendered than can possibly be carried out in the case of

[1] Compare § 446.

fees. A sewer is built by assessments; lighthouse and hospital service are supported by fees. It is the theory of some writers that fees are based upon cost of service. But license fees (which perhaps should be regarded as taxes) are far in excess of specific cost of service—indeed there is often a conspicuous absence of positive service rendered; while judicial fees are in many cases far below the cost of maintaining the services which they help to support.

§ 497. Whatever part of the current expenses of government cannot be covered by prices, fees or assessments must in general be met by *taxation.*[1]

Taxation is a system of forced contribution to meet the general expenses of the government, whether national or local. Taxes are distinguished from fees and assessments in being a contribution for general services instead of a more or less adequate return for special services. They are distinguished from fines and confiscations in being part of a regular system, publicly arranged as a means of meeting the deficit which the government account or budget would otherwise show.

§ 498. This idea of systematic taxation has been a matter of gradual development. In the earlier stages of political society the government tried to get as much as

---

[1] Seligman, in his extremely interesting treatment of the subject, prefers a classification of the public revenues based, not on the methods of collection, but on the comparative importance of the public and private purpose in the service rendered by the government. A quasi-private price is charged when the public purpose is of subordinate importance, and the special benefit to the individual is the dominant consideration. A fee or a tax is levied when the public purpose becomes the controlling or exclusive consideration of the government in rendering the service while the benefit to the individual assumes correspondingly less importance. But it will be found on examination that Seligman's classification nearly coincides with the one in the text. For if a charge is fixed on a basis of special benefits rendered, it is safe to leave it to individuals to decide whether they care enough for the service to pay for it; while if the public purpose becomes the dominant or exclusive consideration, the basis and method of collection must be correspondingly modified.

it could, without regard to system, while the subjects were trying to pay as little as they could. As late as the seventeenth century the great French financier, Colbert, defined taxation as "the art of so plucking the goose as to secure the largest amount of feathers with the least amount of squealing." It is an unfortunate truth that we have not wholly outgrown the stage of political life which gave this definition its force. But as popular government has made progress,—or, more accurately, as we have gradually come to rely on the consent of the people to give force to legal enactments—we have learned to regard taxes as a self-levied contribution which each man pays according to his ability. Though this ideal is as yet very far from being realized in practice, it has become a fundamental doctrine of political justice among the great mass of civilized men. In fact, the positiveness with which this ideal is asserted, coupled with some uncertainty as to the form in which it would best be realized, and with widespread ignorance as to the means by which it can be best attained, forms at present an obstacle rather than an aid to measures which would really make taxation more equitable.

§ 499. Adam Smith, in a passage frequently quoted,[1] lays down four criteria of a good tax system: equity, certainty, convenience of time of payment, and avoidance of unnecessary cost of collection, direct or indirect. If all these things can be combined, the tax is obviously a good one. But what if they cannot all be combined? What if the first two requirements (which are the most fundamental general principles, the third and fourth being largely matters of administrative detail) be found to conflict with one another? What shall we do if the pursuit of equity demands sacrifice of certainty, and if all the methods of taxation which promise a sure return seem to leave some men untouched who can best afford to pay?

[1] *Wealth of Nations*, Book V., chapter ii., part ii.

By placing equity first, Smith gives countenance to the popular view that we should make this not only our ideal of taxation but our guiding principle in framing tax laws. As an ideal it is undoubtedly right; as a guiding principle, it will be found to defeat the realization of that ideal.

§ 500. It should be said in justification of Smith, that the distinction between ideals and guiding principles in taxation, which has since become so conspicuous, was in his day only just beginning to take shape. In ancient times certainty and equity went hand in hand. The men who held property and enjoyed income had this property and income in forms which rendered it easy of assessment. Their wealth consisted chiefly of real estate. Personal property was small in amount, and consisted largely of visible and tangible objects like plate or jewels, kept for display rather than for income. The persons who could best pay taxes held the property whose value could be ascertained. The attempts to levy taxes on other people, though frequently made, were at once ineffective and unjust. But from the time of Adam Smith downward there has been an increasing divergence from this state of things. The persons who are best able to pay taxes are not now so situated that the assessors can ascertain the exact measure of their ability. Invisible forms of personal property, like stocks or notes, have assumed a dominant importance. The attempt to secure equal contributions by a general income tax, or a general property tax, may result in exempting the dishonest and burdening the honest, in making a tax system whose burdens are wholly out of proportion to the financial results. Under these conditions the tax legislator now has to choose between making equality or certainty his primary end, rather than to keep both in view as coördinate aims.

In the light of experience in modern industrial communities there can scarcely be any doubt as to the proper choice. *Certainty* is the fundamentally important

object, without which all attempts at equality prove illusory.[1] With an uncertain tax no systematic improvement
can be hoped for. With a certain tax any evils which
exist at the outset tend to diminish as time goes on.

§ 501. Uncertainty may result either from failure to
discover the objects which should be taxed; or from
doubt as to their value ; or from the possibility of collusion between the assessor and the person who should
pay the tax by which consent is given to an unduly low
valuation.

§ 502. To avoid the first evil, taxes should be levied,
as far as possible, upon visible and tangible objects. In
general, things should be assessed, rather than persons.
The attempt to rely on personal disclosure as a means of
discovering taxable property results in discrimination of
the worst character. The property or income of widows
and orphans, which is in the hands of trustees whose
reports are matters of public knowledge, is taxed at its
full value; so is that of a few exceptionally conscientious
men. The majority of men make some return of taxable
property, sufficient to satisfy their consciences ; but they
interpret all doubtful points in their own favor, so as to
make as few returns as possible. They take the law into
their own hands ; and, as an English essayist has said, the
law is such a fragile thing that when men take it into

---

[1] If people would carry out to its logical conclusion the modern theory
that taxes are a self-imposed burden, we might make equity our primary object as well as our ultimate goal. Where public sentiment insists that people shall make correct tax returns, and treats laxity in this respect as a
dereliction of public duty, the tax legislator has a comparatively free hand.
There are certain communities where this sentiment is so strong that the
principal of self assessment can be safely adopted, with the knowledge that
crooked tax returns will be as severely condemned by the individual conscience as crooked voting. But with the increasing margin of doubt as to
what constitutes taxable income the difficulty of relying on such sentiment
becomes greater ; and in the absence of such a controlling motive no tax
law can be made effective, unless framed with the immediate purpose of
preventing evasion.

their own hands it is sure to get broken. Finally, there is a considerable class of men who have no conscience at all in the matter, and who, in safe reliance on the certainty that their property will remain undiscovered, escape taxation on everything which the law hopes to discover by their declarations.

We cannot rely on the courts for much help in correcting this injustice. They feel obliged to assume that any law will be obeyed, even when it is notorious that such is not the case. They can only consider theoretical violations of equity ; they leave to the legislator the avoidance of practical ones.

Nor is this an evil that tends to correct itself by time. The success of the bad men in escaping taxation and the impunity with which they defy the law, lowers the public conscience year by year. When we have a tax law which discriminates against honesty, the honesty and the law both suffer in about equal measure.

§ 503. Of the visible and tangible sources of taxation, real estate is probably the most important. It can always be seen ; it can never run away. In order to be sure of taxing its owners, it is only necessary to apply the rule of making no deductions on account of debt. Mortgaged real estate should be assessed at its full value. This may seem to bear hard on the debtor ; but it is really far more equitable than the system of deductions. If such deductions are allowed, a large part of the money loaned on real estate escapes taxation altogether ; while undue burdens are put, first, on the holder of unmortgaged real estate who has to pay a higher tax rate on account of the deductions made from the grand list, and, second, on the honest minority of lenders[1] who pay a high tax rate on their investments, while most other investors make no adequate return of property thus loaned. The holder of mortgaged real estate gets comparatively little benefit from the de-

---

[1] Chiefly those whose property is held in trust.

duction, because the theory that such loans are taxable against the lender drives enough honest investors out of the mortgage loan market to keep the rate of interest higher than it otherwise would be. The only real beneficiary is the unscrupulous investor who profits by the high interest rate and makes no tax return.

The chief obstacle to a change in system—apart from the reluctance of legislators to abandon the old principle of taxing persons instead of things—is found in the apparent loss to communities of lenders, in allowing property which their citizens own to be taxed in the place where it is invested. But the actual amount collected in this way is very small in proportion to the vexation involved.

Another objection urged against this plan is that real estate, which is already overburdened, will suffer still more, while personal property will be correspondingly relieved. But the secondary result of relieving the lender from taxation, owing to increased competition among different lenders, will be a lowering of the rate of interest; and the holders of personal property will thus indirectly pay a larger share of the taxes than they now do. If such loans can be reached by this indirect method, one of the largest items of personal property will be taxed; and a very large part of the remainder can be reached by taxes on corporations.

§ 504. In the assessment of corporate property, as in that of real estate, no deduction should be allowed for indebtedness. If the attempt is made to tax the debt in the hands of the holders, it will fail. The tax should reach the whole property of the corporation without reference to the question of its ownership. In that way, and in that way only, will it be evenly distributed. If the market price of the securities is used as a means of ascertaining the value of such property, bonds as well as stock should be included in the estimate. It affords opportunities for evasion no less than for injustice if two railroads, physically alike, pay different rates of taxes because the capital of the one was largely borrowed while that of the other was subscribed.

§ 505. The attempt to levy taxes on the thing where the value originates, rather than on the person who receives the benefit of such value, is known as the policy of *stoppage at source.* It is the most effective means which has been devised for combining economy in collection with efficiency in reaching those who ought to pay the tax, honest and dishonest alike. Its effects are perhaps even more clearly illustrated in income taxes than in property taxes. It makes comparatively little difference to an honest man whether he receives his full income and deducts the amount necessary to pay the tax, or whether he receives his income less the deductions and then pays nothing. But to the dishonest man it makes a great difference ; for in the former case he has a large chance of avoiding payment, while in the latter case, his burdens are forcibly made equal to those of the honest man—a thing which results in benefit both to the exchequer and to the public. The gain in certainty of collection from stoppage at source is due to three causes. First, the man who makes the payment has no personal interest in giving the government less than its due. Second, the fact that income is earned is usually much more observable at its source, where the transactions that give rise to it are matters of public observation, than at the point of its receipt, where its existence can only be surmised. Third, so many of the payments of income are made by large corporations to a number of shareholders or creditors, that stoppage at source substitutes a single financial transaction, easily and economically controlled, for a whole series of individual transactions involved in collecting the tax from the recipients, whose very number tends to multiply both the uncertainty and the expense of collection.

Of course the adoption of this principle interferes with the possibility of laying progressive income taxes whereby the rich pay a larger percentage than the poor ; but if, as generally happens, the effort to make the rich pay more than their share by a complicated tax system, actually results in letting them pay less than their share, we need not take great account of this objection, in the present stage of industrial society.

§ 506. The second source of uncertainty arises from doubt as to the actual value of the property or transactions assessed.

It is always very difficult to determine the actual net earnings of a business. The gross earnings are comparatively easy to ascertain. The difficulty is to determine what deductions should be made from them before we reach what is available as net income. Take the case of a railroad. It should obviously deduct the expenses of running trains, maintaining stations, equipment, and track, and paying the salaries of its officers. But what constitutes maintenance of track or equipment? Shall the company simply aim to make ordinary repairs ? This will cause the road to deteriorate from year to year as new inventions arise, so that the income will really not be so large as it appears. Or shall it try to pay for all improvements out of earnings? This is going to the other extreme, and will make it appear that a very prosperous road has no net income at all. The conception of net income, simple as it appears, is really very difficult to apply in practice, and involves so much possible litigation that many states prefer to substitute a low tax on the gross earnings of corporations for a somewhat higher tax on their net earnings. The latter would be the more equitable ; for a tax on gross earnings bears hard on a corporation which is doing large business at low rates and a small margin of profit. But the superior certainty of the tax on gross earnings outweighs its theoretical disadvantages.

In like manner there is a tendency among those charged with customs administration to prefer *specific* duties, based on the weight or measure of goods imported, to *ad valorem* duties, calling for a percentage of their value. Although the specific duty is the less equitable in theory, and has the added disadvantage of ·becoming more and more protective as time goes on (§ 484), the multiplication of chances of fraud under the *ad valorem* system is apt to turn the balance in favor of specific duties.

§ 507. The third source of uncertainty arises from danger of collusion between the assessors and those who pay the taxes. This comes about chiefly where minor civil divisions are asked to contribute to the general government on the basis of their assessed valuation. For local purposes it makes no difference to a town whether its citizens pay a tax of one per cent. on a valuation of $2,000,000, or two per cent. on a valuation of $1,000,000. But if they are asked to contribute to the general government, the community with the low valuation will have an advantage ; and the desire to secure such advantages will lead the local authorities to a system of undervaluation which may easily result in great irregularities. No board of equalization can correct such an evil. For certainty of valuation it is indispensable that the objects of national and local taxation should be kept as far as possible separate from one another.

§ 508. It is scarcely necessary to add that double taxation should be avoided, in the interest of certainty no less than of economy and of equity. In the United States the sentiment against double taxation is so strong that each tax is made a pretext for evading the other. In Europe, the objection to double taxation is not so strongly felt and the evasion which results from its application is probably less ; but in any event it can hardly be other than a wasteful method.

§ 509. A tax which meets the requirements of certainty

tends to become more equitable as time goes on. It may impose an unnecessary aggregate burden on the community, which will continue from year to year; but the inequality of the burden will tend to reduce itself. For capital will not be invested in lines or in places where the rate of profit is much lower than the average; and any tax which lowers the rate of profit tends to diminish the supply of products and thus to increase the price, putting the burden largely upon the consumers instead of the producers.

Let us a take a concrete illustration. Assume that railroads were taxed at a higher rate than any other kind of property. At first this would be an injustice to the owners of railroads; but as time went on fewer roads would be built and the managers of those already existing would charge higher prices on account of the demand for transportation which they alone were able to meet. Part of the burden of the tax would thus be placed on the consumers. Meantime the lessened demand for railroad labor would tend to reduce either the number or the wages of railroad employees; and the reduction in the demand for coal and for iron consequent upon the diminished extent of railroad construction would transfer part of the burden to those industries also. As this shifting process extended itself year after year it would include a wider circle of industries within its scope, and it would not cease until the profits of railroad enterprise which were at first reduced by the tax, finally adjusted themselves to the same general level which prevailed in other industries.

If the tax is not thus shifted by a change in the supply of products, it shows that the capitalists were obtaining a monopoly profit before the imposition of the tax; and that the apparent inequality due to the failure to shift such a tax really puts the burdens where they belong—among those who have a distinct surplus under the processes of exchange or distribution.

§ 510. If all taxes were *continuous* in their operation, we might trust to this shifting process to make them equitable. We might fairly assume that in the long run the men who were able to pay the taxes would pay them, while those who were unable to pay would be crowded out of an industry. We could judge of the goodness or badness of a tax by comparing the benefits derived from its proceeds with the evils resulting from this crowding-out process. We could set ourselves to work to devise a tax system which should raise the necessary revenue with a minimum of industrial pressure. But the matter is not thus simple. Taxes are not continuous in their operation. New grounds of expenditure arise which necessitate either an imposition of new taxes or an increase of old ones. Changes in industrial method may intensify this need by rendering the old taxes less productive; or they may operate in the reverse direction and produce a surplus which gives ground for a well-founded claim for reduction in tax rates. But whenever any tax is increased or reduced a change of economic burdens is created, which it takes time to adjust, and which may for months or years impose upon certain individuals an undue share of contributions to the public revenue, before the matter finally adjusts itself in an equitable fashion.

§ 511. It is in this connection that the distinction between direct and indirect taxes becomes one of dominant importance.

A direct tax, as ordinarily defined, is one which is levied upon the person who is expected to pay it; an indirect tax is one whose burden is presumably shifted upon some one else. An income tax is generally of the former class. The man against whom it is charged is expected to pay it at his own loss. A customs duty belongs to the latter class. The importer pays it to the government; but it is expected that he will charge the greater part if not the whole of it to the man who buys the article, so that the tax will ultimately be paid by the consumer instead of the importer.

There is no doubt that there is a real distinction between these two kinds of taxes; but there is a great deal of doubt whether the distinction just drawn (which is that of Smith and of Mill) correctly marks the line between them. Some taxes which are undoubtedly direct are shifted at once by legal authority; for instance when a tax on rents is, as a matter of administrative convenience, collected from the man who pays the rent with the understanding that he will deduct it from what he afterward hands over to the owner under previous contracts. Again, nearly all taxes on income or on property are, as we have seen, gradually shifted, even though the law makes no provision for such a process; and a sharp application of Smith's definition would give the term "direct tax" a meaning very much narrower than that which it has in current usage.

In view of this difficulty, Continental writers have generally preferred to define direct taxes as those which are assessed on persons (or property) and indirect taxes as those which are levied on acts. This is correct enough in its practical applications. But it fails to indicate any real distinction of principle; and therefore, in a considerable number of cases which can be regarded in either light (*e.g.* taxes on occupations) we cannot use the definition as a criterion. We decide on unformulated grounds to which class a tax belongs and interpret our definition accordingly.

§ 512. In order to find the real ground for the distinction, we must consider the different ways in which taxes are shifted.

1. In some cases the transfer is a perfectly simple one. The person who pays the tax to the government deducts the amount of that tax from payments which he would otherwise have been compelled to pay to some one else.

A corporation pays a tax, and correspondingly reduces the amount which would otherwise have gone to the security-holders. A man who occupies a house may be compelled to pay a tax on its rental with the understanding that he is to deduct this tax from the payment which he makes to the owners.

2. Some taxes are transferred by commercial competition. A customs or excise duty is largely paid by the consumers, not voluntarily, but because the dealers find it impossible to furnish the goods at the price which prevailed before the imposition of the duty; and this reduction in current supplies produces competition among buyers, until the price rises high enough to compensate the importers for their expense under the new conditions of trade.

3. Some taxes are transferred only by industrial competition (§ 100), instead of commercial; not by the competition of buyers for a supply of products which the tax suddenly reduces, but by the withdrawal of capital invested in certain lines where the tax has borne heavily, and a slow indirect readjustment of the relations of supply and demand. It is not always possible to distinguish sharply from one another the effects of commercial and industrial competition; but there is a clear general line of distinction between the quick adjustment under the one process and the slow adjustments under the other.

§ 513. With the third of these means of shifting taxes, the distinction between direct and indirect taxation has nothing to do. The terms direct and indirect apply to immediate incidence, not to ultimate incidence. A tax is said to be *direct* when its immediate burden is shifted only by the *first* of these processes, and therefore falls within the prevision of the legislator. It is said to be *indirect* when its immediate burden is shifted by the *second* of these processes, and cannot be at all accurately foreseen by the legislator. To the former class belong property, income, and inheritance taxes, no matter from whom they may be first collected; also poll taxes, and franchise taxes in their various forms. The latter class is exemplified by excise and customs duties.

§ 514. Indirect taxes are not generally available for local purposes. If a locality attempts to tax a certain class of acts while neighboring localities do not, it is apt to result in driving business from the place where it is taxed to that where it is untaxed; disturbing trade while the process of adjustment is going on, and leaving comparatively little revenue after it is completed. There are exceptions to this rule; for instance the *octroi*, or tax on provisions entering the close walled towns of continental Europe. But the general tendency as time goes on is to leave the collection of indirect taxes more and more to the central authorities. The local governments are thus compelled to rely on direct taxation as the chief source of their revenue.

The central government can use either form of taxation it pleases. It will generally collect a large part of its income by indirect taxes, using direct taxation to make up any temporary or fluctuating deficit. It is in some respects desirable to restrict direct national taxation to a minimum; for if the proceeds of a direct tax on the property or income of one locality are used for purposes in which other localities are exclusively interested, there is a feeling of injustice which cannot come up in the same form when each section uses its own taxes for its own purposes. There are, however, certain forms of direct taxation which cannot advantageously be levied by municipal assessment. This is notably the case with taxes on large corporations. The value of a railroad is by no means the sum of the values of the separate pieces of property in the different towns through which it runs. It is much greater than this; and it can only be properly determined by being assessed as a unit. The taxation of corporations in America has mostly been in the hands of the States; but with the rapid growth of industrial consolidation, interstate tax problems are beginning to have increasing importance. Even though the revenues from this source continue to be used for State purposes, it seems inevitable that their assessment and apportionment should be under national control if we are to avoid the double taxation and other evils which prevail in the present system.

§ 515. Most direct taxation is necessarily based upon wealth, because the possession of wealth is the chief criterion of a person's ability to bear an additional tax. But whether such ability is best judged by measuring wealth as capital, and imposing a property tax, or by measuring it as income, and taxing it accordingly, is a question on which there is no unanimity. The bulk of European judgment and practice favors the latter method; in America the former is in more general use.

The theoretical arguments as to the merits of the two methods are rather inconclusive. At first sight, income seems a fairer measure of ability than accumulations; for the receipt of income represents present productive capacity, while the possession of savings does not. But it must be remembered that a man who has a current income of $10,000 and no savings is practically compelled to lay aside a considerable proportion of it for the future; and a system which taxes him at the same rate as the man who has the same income from invested capital creates gross inequality of burden. So conspicuous is this fact that many of those who believe in taxing income rather than property, would levy a lower rate upon personal earnings than upon income from investments.

There is an argument often urged in favor of an income tax which, when carefully examined, appears unsound. It is said to be essential for the community that taxes should be paid out of current income rather than past accumulations; that a tax on property as distinct from income is really a tax on accumulations and a discouragement to saving. This argument depends for its force on the assumption that a tax on income will be paid out of income and a tax on property paid out of capital; an assumption for which there seems to be no warrant. For capital and income are not separate things; they are different ways of measuring the same thing. Capital is constantly being converted into income, and income into capital. A tax is really paid out of capital when its effect is to make the amount of accumulations at the end of the year less than they otherwise would be; it is paid out of income, when the expenditures of the year are reduced to meet the tax, so that the amount of accumulation remains unimpaired.[1] If an income tax bears heavily on the men who would otherwise make savings, it is paid out of the nation's capital; if a property tax causes the property owner to reduce his current expenses, it is paid out of income. There seems to be no direct relation between the form in which taxes are assessed and the choice of means adopted to pay them.

§ 516. Apart from the possibility of progressive or compensatory taxation, (§§ 517, 518) the theoretical advantages and disadvantages of income and property taxes are so closely balanced that the question between them must be decided on the basis of certainty of assessment and ease of collection. In the former respect the property tax has perhaps a slight advantage. The measurement of capital presents fewer theoretical difficulties than the measurement of income; for we have to make a number of uncertain deductions in the latter case which are not involved in the former. But practically our choice depends on the preferences and habits of the people. If they are accustomed to an income tax rather than a property tax

---

[1] The desirableness of this condition is by no means so self-evident as some people suppose. Compare § 161.

we may expect better results to be reached on taxing income. If they are more accustomed to the property tax the case will be reversed. The experience of the United States immediately after the war, contrasted with that of most European states, shows how great may be the difference in productiveness, in equity, and in popularity, of similar taxes in different communities.[1]

§ 517. It is a more important question whether we should strive to have *equality* or *progression* in our direct taxes ; whether we should tax each source of wealth in proportion to its value or whether we should try to tax the strong man at a relatively higher rate than the weak man. The latter policy is urged on two grounds ; first, because in all the early stages of their operation indirect taxes, by raising the price of articles of consumption, affect the poor, who spend their incomes, relatively more than the rich, who have a large surplus which they do not spend ; second and more important, because any increase of direct taxes which may be needed to meet a current emergency hurts the poor man, far more than it hurts the rich man. If a man makes only enough to keep himself and his family alive, the imposition of a tax will cause some of them to starve. The process of adjustment by which wages are raised to meet such a tax will only be brought about after most acute suffering and irreparable loss.

[1] The notorious evils in the working of the general property tax in the United States have created some prejudice against this mode of assessment. But the inequalities of this tax are less than those which the country suffered under the income tax ; and both are more conspicuously the result of want of certainty than of want of equity. The evils were not due to the fact that property was a bad basis of assessment, but to the fact that much property which was nominally subject to assessment was not reached at all. If local expenses were met by taxes on local real estate only, no deduction being made for debts, and if state expenses were largely met by corporation taxes, which the exemption of personal property from local assessment would make possible and equitable, we should be likely to have a tax system which would be efficient, elastic, and reasonably just.

30

These objections do not apply so directly to a tax on property as to a tax on income. Even a small property gives its owner a certain leeway when a new tax is imposed, and prevents him from starving as long as his accumulations hold out. It may be a misfortune and an injustice to deprive him of part of his savings; but it is not, in most instances, a direct deprivation of all immediate means of support. A property tax can therefore be made general without immediate disaster; while an income tax practically involves the exemption of a minimum[1] income necessary for the support of a family.

§ 518. Any such exemption causes the large incomes to be taxed at a higher rate than the smaller ones. Thus if $1000 is exempt from taxation, and the excess above that sum is taxed five per cent,

An income of $1000 pays   $0 or 0   per cent
"      "      "    1500        25   $1\frac{2}{3}$   "     "
"      "      "    2000        50   $2\frac{1}{2}$   "     "
"      "      "    2500        75   3    "     "
"      "      "    3000       100   $3\frac{1}{3}$   "     "

and so on with constantly increasing percentages. But when we come to deal with really large incomes the changes of rate due to this cause are very slight in amount. Thus, an income of $50,000 in the case supposed will pay at the rate of $4\frac{9}{10}$ per cent; while an income of double the amount will pay at the rate of $4\frac{19}{20}$ per cent. The difference between the two rates is hardly noticeable in comparison with the difference in wealth of the two individuals. Under these circumstances, all the more radical champions of progressive taxation insist on an increasing *rate* as well as on the exemption of a fixed minimum. The increasing rate is used in several countries of continental Europe, and is perhaps most conspicuously exemplified in Switzerland.

[1] It depends upon the judgment of the legislature how high this minimum shall be fixed. There is no well-recognized standard in fiscal usage.

There can be no reasonable doubt that a progressive tax, *if collected*, imposes the immediate burdens where they can be borne with least hardship. But it seems equally certain that such a system increases the difficulty of collection. It makes it necessary to assess the tax against the actual recipient of the income in such a way as to make the principal of stoppage at source quite inapplicable. In so far as the uncertainty from this cause makes itself felt, the attempt to secure progression does a permanent harm which outweighs any temporary good. For it must be constantly kept in mind that the need for equalization of burdens which progression aims to meet is a transient one, which will in any event be gradually met by the process of industrial competition ; while the equalization that depends upon certainty is a permanent matter, which will not adjust itself under any law, however well meant, that fails to secure such certainty.

§ 519. An effort is often made to combine certainty of collection with equality of immediate burden by exempting competitive gains and taxing monopolized advantages —especially those of landed property. Some have gone so far as to believe that a single tax, on this basis alone, would afford the government its necessary revenue with a minimum of hardship, and perhaps with a positive incidental gain.

If we make use of the method employed in § 295 (Fig. 9) we shall see that a tax which is made proportionate to the income from a given business usually puts severe burdens on consumers and on laborers.[1] If, to the expense of production $qy + yx$ (wages + interest,) there be added a tax $xt$ (Fig. 11), the quantity sold must gradually fall until a new point of equilibrium between demand

---

[1] The effect here described is most immediate if the tax is placed on the consumer (indirect taxation). It is much slower in the taxation of labor, and probably slower still in the taxation of capital ; but the final adjustment tends to be the same in all cases.

and supply if established.  At this point the price $Op$ will cover wages + interest + taxes $(q'y' + y'x' + x't')$

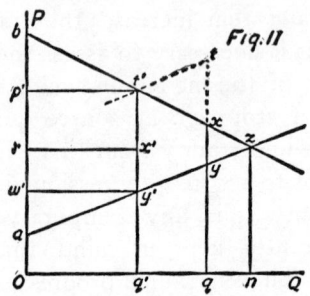

The amount of government revenue will be represented by the rectangle $rx't'p'$.  The losses incident to the collection of this revenue will be as follows :

1. The consumers have to go without a certain amount of goods $q'q$.

2. A rise in price reduces the consumers' surplus from the series of transactions from $pxb$ (Fig. 9) to $p't'b$ (Fig. 11).

3. The labor which produced the goods $q'q$ is thrown out of employment.

4. A fall in wages reduces the producers' surplus from $ayw$ (Fig. 9) to $ay'w'$ (Fig. 11).

5. The field of investment of capital is reduced by the amount of reduction of wages.

§ 520.  According to the advocates of the single tax theory, most of this burden is an unnecessary imposition on society, due to the taxation of competitive gains on the same basis as monopolized gains.

We have seen (§ 319) that in many lines the expense of production of the same article varies widely for different competitors.  Some of those who are engaged in its production obtain a differential gain.  If we can tax this gain and not tax the men who fail to secure it, we shall avoid most of the evils described in the preceding section. The quantity of goods produced will not be altered ; for the tax will only affect those men who produce the goods at a special advantage, and these will prefer to pay the tax rather than abandon an exceptionally profitable business. Therefore all the laborers will be employed at the old wages, and all the consumers served at the old prices; the revenue of the government will be furnished by those who can afford to pay taxes and who will not be led to change their occupation by so doing.

This state of things may be roughly represented as follows (Fig. 12). With a demand curve *bb'* and a price *Op*

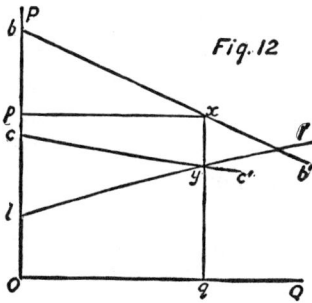

Fig. 12

at which the supply equals the demand we shall find that payments to laborers for producing different parts of the supply vary from a maximum *qy* to a minimum *Ol*. The total profit to the capitalists who advance those wages is *lyxp*. But of this profit there are deductions to be made for interest varying from a maximum *xy*[1] to a minimum *pc*. The total amount chargeable as interest is thus represented by *pxyc*. If we can tax the surplus profit *lyc* without touching wages or interest we shall

---

[1] It will of course often happen that the maximum interest charge does not come on the same unit of product where we have the maximum wages. To take proper account of this fact the figure would have to be made too complicated for our present purposes.

obtain our revenue with the minimum of immediate burdens on producers and consumers and the least disturbance to the channels of trade.[1]

§ 521. We have already seen (ch. ix.) that the differential gain of producers enjoying special advantages is divided into two parts, rent and profits. The advocates of a progressive income tax claim that in a rough way they reach both of these things pretty effectively, since the large fortunes are made up from one or the other of these gains rather than from wages or interest. But the advocates of a single tax object to the attempt to put rent and profits on the same basis. They say that the sums received as profits are really earned. They come to pioneers who have led the way in industrial progress. They are instrumental in putting the control of industry into the hands of men who are competent to take the lead. Rent on the other hand they regard as a dead weight; as an appropriation of the products of present industry by thóse who have laid hands on the results of past service or of natural bounty; sometimes even as a premium to those who stand in the way of progress by keeping land out of use until the growth of population has given it the increased value. They draw a sharp distinction between the profits resulting from the enterprise of the individual, to which that individual may fairly lay claim, and the rent resulting from the movements of population, which equitably belongs to the people. They propose either to make the

---

[1] This will serve to illustrate the important but not very clear proposition often laid down, that rent is not an element in the price of products. Anything that affects wages or interest tends at once to affect the supply at previously existing prices, and to cause a change in the adjustment of supply and demand. A change in economic rent will not produce this result, because it does not affect the marginal producers—those who are just ready to increase or diminish the supply by entering or leaving a business. A remission of English rents would not change the price of wheat materially, because it would not increase either the amount of land cultivated or the amount raised per acre. Rent is a result of variations in demand rather than a cause of changes in supply.

land common property and let this gain accrue to the public (land nationalization [1]) or to leave the title in private hands as at present, but tax economic rent to its full amount in lieu of all other taxes (single tax theory). The latter proposition, in its modern shape,[2] owes its chief importance to the popularity of the writings of Henry George.

§ 522. The first difficulty with the modern single-tax theory arises from the fact that we cannot make any such sharp distinction between rent and profits as it contemplates. They shade into one another by insensible gradations. Though rent is more permanent than profits, we cannot regard it as enduring for all time, since land may lose value as well as gain it. Though rent is chiefly due to the growth of population rather than to the controlling hand of an individual, we find that the man who goes into land speculation without special skill in serving the public (§ 322) is apt to lose rather than gain. The majority of gains in real estate speculation have been made by men who have developed property at considerable risk, instead of waiting for others to do it. Exceptions there are, and numerous ones; but the general rule holds good that large returns on real estate have come to men who used their capital rather than to those who kept it idle. Nor has the proportion of failures been a small one. Superficial observers who see an assured fortune,

---

[1] Land nationalization is more properly treated here than in chapter xii. because its advocates generally propose to leave the actual improvement of the land to private persons (at most, assisted by advances of government credit) and to treat the land as a source of revenue and an instrument of social policy rather than as a field of economic experiment by public authorities.

[2] The "*Impôt Unique,*" advocated by the physiocrats, while superficially resembling George's proposed plan, differed from it radically in principle. The physiocrats proposed to tax the surplus of food above what was necessary for the maintenance of the laborer; while George deals with a surplus of market price above expense of production. The Ricardian idea of a differential gain which is so prominent in the latter proposal had not made itself felt in the former.

are apt to think that it was so assured from the outset, and to overlook the fact that the gains, which we see, are survivals amid the wreck of less successful investments which have been forgotten.

The single tax theory in its more pronounced forms would deprive the man who has made successful investments in real estate of any surplus above the current rate of interest. Would it guarantee him against losses? If it did not do so, it would destroy the motives to invest capital in projects of land improvement. The public could not expect to play with the investor at the well known game of "heads I win, tails you lose." If on the other hand it gave such a guarantee it would find itself compelled to make good an amount of loss so large as to do away with the expected gains from the system. Losses on real estate are large enough at present, when each man acts at his own risk; they would unquestionably be much greater if this risk was shifted to society as a whole. The amount and the certainty of economic rent are both habitually overestimated by the advocates of the single tax theory.

§ 523. The ethical and political difficulties which stand in the way of the application of the single tax theory are even more pronounced than the economic ones. It is not a legal possibility to appropriate the whole unearned increment by any speedy process and to overturn, without compensation, a large number of recognized rights. The existence of law depends on the continuity of its application. The principle that private property must not be taken without compensation is no mere accidental phrase let fall by courts or constitution-makers. It is an axiom of political science. If the progress of society renders the abolition of an institution necessary, compensation follows as a matter of course.[1] A very gradual increase

---

[1] The apparent exception in the matter of slavery in the United States was due to the fact that the slaveholders were in arms against the government.

of taxes on economic rent to which the owners might find time to adjust themselves, represents the utmost stretch of possibility in this matter. Now if the fiscal success of the single tax is questionable when applied to the whole unearned increment, past as well as future, much more must it be so if we leave the past undisturbed and deal with the future only.

This is the critical weakness in land nationalization plans like that with which John Stuart Mill's name was identified. The advocates of this plan proposed that England should buy out the landowners, and appropriate the future gain in value. No fault could be found with the equity of this proposal. But as a fiscal measure it was radically defective. Leaving out of account the inevitable losses due to a scheme of quasi-compulsory purchase, the scheme must have ended in disaster because the lands which it was proposed to buy have fallen in value instead of rising. Nothing could more conspicuously emphasize the fallacy of treating economic rent as an assured source of increasing returns, than the fact that Mill was led astray by it. He recognized that improvements in the arts tended to lower rent; but he assumed that increase in population would more than counteract any such tendency. The effect of modern methods of transportation, which make the whole world compete with the English wheat growers, lay outside the scope of his calculation.

§ 524. These arguments do not militate against reforms in taxation which shall carry us in the general direction indicated by the single-tax theory. Wagner, after an investigation of the subject whose thoroughness is worthy of the highest praise, whether we can accept his conclusions or not, is inclined to look with favor on public appropriation of future increments in the value of *city* real

The measure was recognized as one of confiscation, justified only by a state of war.

estate as distinct from agricultural land.  Without going
so far as Wagner, most economists would be willing to
agree that more taxes should be assessed upon economic
rent and less upon improvements.  The present practice of assessors in this matter is a good illustration of
the misapplication of the principle of taxation according
to ability.  The holder of unimproved real estate gets
no apparent income from it ; he is therefore taxed on only
a small percentage of the market value of the property,
while the owner of improved land must pay a correspondingly heavier tax.  This puts a premium on the worst
sort of land speculation.  The man who serves society is
burdened ; the man who stands in the way and tries to
profit by others' progress is encouraged and helped.

§ 525.  Other forms of direct taxation can be much
more briefly dealt with.

A poll tax is in frequent use ; but it is neither productive
nor equitable, and stands as a relic of past methods rather
than as a subject of present importance.

An inheritance tax has much to recommend it in the
fact that it takes property for the use of the state at the
time when individuals least feel its loss.  It is also easy of
collection because all estates of deceased persons must
come under cognizance of the probate courts, independently of the question of taxation.  It is usually so graded
as to increase with the remoteness of the heir or legatee
from the direct line of kinship with the deceased ; sometimes increasing also, notably in a recent French law, with
the size of the amounts received by each individual.  The
chief objections to such a tax are the possibility of evading
it by donations before death, and the uncertainty of the
amount which it will produce in any given year, which
makes it unavailable as a calculable source of immediate
revenue.  In spite of these objections, an increasing
amount of government income is being collected by this
method.

Taxes on occupations should be counted among direct taxes, though they approach closely to indirect taxes in some of their characteristics.[1] They are less used in England and in the United States than in other countries, because of the double taxation which is involved when a man is taxed both on the value of his business or profession and on the fact of exercising it. Of taxes on occupations in the strict sense of the word, the one of most importance in the United States is the fee charged for licenses to sell liquor. In many communities this is not managed primarily for revenue, but as a means of restricting the number of those engaged in the business by reducing the profits to which it gives rise.

Of greater importance from a fiscal point of view are the various taxes on corporate franchise. The vast amounts of personal property which can be reached in this way and in no other, coupled with the good grounds for special taxation furnished by the rights granted to companies of various kinds, make this a field of great and increasing importance for the tax legislator. A few of the most important practical rules for such assessment have been laid down in connection with the subject of certainty in taxation. The attempt to enter into further details would lead us beyond the scope of this book.

§ 526. Indirect taxes may be divided into three groups: *excise charges, export duties, and import duties.*

Excise or internal revenue charges, when fixed at small amounts, are often hardly distinguishable from fees. When they are large in amount, they constitute a tax on the consumers of the article, so obvious as to be quite unpopular. There is a tendency in the United States to confine the imposition of excise dues to trades connected

---

[1] In some cases they are hardly distinguishable from fees. For instance, the money collected by special taxes on shipping may be regarded as a compensation to the government for the special services which it renders the navigator in connection with harbors, lighthouses, and hydrography.

with the production of alcohol ; in the belief that a high
price of liquor and restriction in its use is likely to be of
advantage to the country.  Nations which have a customs
tariff for revenue, and not for protection, often use excise
duties as a means of preventing the loss of revenue
that results from the establishment of a home industry
which diminishes the importation of articles on which the
tariff is imposed.

Export dues are unpopular because they put the home
producer at a disadvantage in international trade; and
they are falling into disuse on this account.[1]  For the
converse reason, taxes on imports are correspondingly
popular.  The apparent advantage to home industry connected with the imposition of such taxes, coupled with
the convenience of the national frontier as a place of tax
collection, tends to give import duties an over-prominent
place in modern fiscal systems.

§ 527.  For purposes of revenue, indirect taxes have
several disadvantages as compared with direct taxes.  We
have already seen the difficulty of using them for local
purposes.  Even when applied for national objects it is
hard to predict the amount which they will yield.  The
process of shifting the tax is often accompanied by a contraction in the volume of business which makes the return
less than was anticipated.  In years of depression when productive taxes are most needed, this contraction often becomes disastrous.  The loss of revenue from indirect taxes
in bad years is more conspicuous than in the case of direct
taxes and far less easy to remedy.  For if the rate of
indirect taxation is raised to meet the emergency, the
result is sometimes just the opposite of what was intended.  The experience of the United States in taxing
distilled spirits shows that more revenue is often obtained
by a low rate than by a high one.  The high rate at once

---

[1] For a similar reason countries with an extensive excise system usually
refund the tax on articles actually exported.

checks consumption and stimulates evasion; so that any increase in the tax rate beyond a certain moderate figure is more than counterbalanced by a diminution in the amount that pays taxes.

In the case of high import duties a third cause often tends to increase the loss of revenue still further. If the article is one which can be produced in the home country, domestic production tends to take the place of imports. To avoid this loss, England adopts the principle of placing an excise on the home product substantially equal to the import duty. Most countries, however, find the protective feature a popular one. Some content themselves with the " incidental " protection afforded by a tariff framed for revenue purposes. Others, instead of imposing the minimum rates which will secure the required revenue by a low tax on large imports, adopt the maximum rates which will secure this result by a high tax on small imports; thus adopting a system of duties framed for protection with incidental revenue.

§ 528. Closely analogous to the restrictive taxes just described are the *fines*[1] and *forfeitures* exacted from criminals. In former times these constituted a very considerable part of the revenue of powerful governments which stretched their criminal jurisprudence to meet their fiscal necessities. This matter has become much less important to-day. The criminal law is narrower in its scope. The offense of high treason, which has been made the pretext for enforcing most extensive forfeitures, is now for obvious reasons much rarer than under the more anarchic conditions of feudal times. Under the well-grounded feeling that it is unjust to make a man's heirs suffer for his misdoings, penalties are made to attach to his person rather than to his estate. He may be com-

---

[1] Many of the mediæval fines were unconnected with criminal law and were theoretically fees for special services, *e. g.*, those connected with the estates of minors and females.

pelled to make good his damages to another individual ;
but a payment to the government as a punishment for a
crime is often felt to be one which bears too lightly on
the individual and too heavily on his family.

The revenue from confiscation of the property of enemies has also ceased to have the importance which it did
in feudal times.   When war was frequent, and the obligations of international law and justice were unrecognised,
such transactions were a source of much profit to the conqueror.   To-day such appropriation of private property
of enemies as a means of revenue is generally condemned ;
and even the demands for contributions from public
authorities in a hostile nation are at least theoretically
based on the cost incurred by the victor in carrying on
the war.   The very name " indemnity," which is so frequently applied to such contributions, is an illustration of
this theory.

The revenue of governments from failure of property
to find an owner (*escheat*) is of trifling amount where freedom of testamentary bequest is a recognized principle of
law.   That which comes from voluntary contributions is in
modern states almost entirely predestined to special uses,
and need not be treated as a part of the ordinary revenue.

§ 530.  In a well-ordered budget, the taxes will generally
be so arranged that the current revenue of the government is large enough to meet its current expenses.   If
this is not accomplished, a deficit is carried over to subsequent years in some form of *public debt*.

If the government simply leaves its bills unpaid, letting
the creditors get what security they can, the result is an
unfunded or *floating* debt.   If the government pays these
bills by issuing formal obligations to pay interest (and
usually principal also) at dates distinctly specified, and
borrowing money on the basis of these obligations, the
debt is said to be *funded*.   When these obligations set a
date for payment of the principal (*maturity*) they are

known as *bonds*. When the principal is paid 'by the isssue of a new loan, whether at maturity or before it, the operation is known as *refunding*.

§ 531. A nation cannot permanently rely on loans to meet any considerable part of the ordinary expenses of the government. Creditors will not trust the agents of a treasury which is managed in this way. They will either demand payment in advance, as manufacturing firms habitually do in making large sales to semi-civilized governments, or they will insist on exercising so much control over the fiscal machinery of the debtor government as to deprive it of a good deal of its freedom in conducting its own affairs. A government cannot compel foreign customers to give it credit without security. It may exercise a pressure on domestic customers which shall temporarily force them to do this ; but the immediate effect of this is a tax on such customers, thinly veiled under the form of a loan. Such a tax, if persisted in, is almost certain to prove disastrous alike to the customers and to the government. It is a discriminating and destructive tax upon the very people on whom the government most directly depends for its current supplies.

One of the commonest and at the same time most destructive forms of forced loan is an issue of irredeemable currency. Any gain to the government on a few transactions is offset by the greatly increased prices charged by those who deal with it in all subsequent transactions. If such currency is ultimately redeemed, its inflated volume is a long and painful burden on the future taxpayers of the nation ; if it is not redeemed, it carries the government and many of the citizens into virtual bankruptcy.

§ 532. There are apparently but two cases where recourse to loans is necessary or desirable : 1. In an extraordinary emergency like war.[1] 2. In the case of permanent

[1] The only other analogous cases would be those of flood or fire, where present relief must be had at any cost.

productive investments, like state railroads or telegraphs, which are made once for all, and offer the prospect of national and fiscal advantages for a long series of years.

It is thought by some observers that a loan transfers the cost of a war or an improvement from the present to the future. This view is ridiculed by others who say that the cost of a war is borne by the generation which wages it, and that a loan simply shifts this cost from one group of individuals to another. This misunderstanding arises from the two different sources of the word cost. The cost in the public sense is borne by the people who carry on the war, not by their children. The destruction of wealth is a destruction of present means of enjoyment; the pain is present pain. But the individual cost or expense is shifted. The men who loan money to a government enable a certain amount of wealth to be devoted to destruction, just as much as if that money were extorted from them by taxation. But they do not part with their individual wealth or property. On the contrary, they retain, in the form of a government bond or other obligation, the right to ample indemnification from the taxpayers of the future. Wealth is destroyed, but property rights and relations are conserved.

§ 533. The great advantage of loans over taxes as means of waging war is that they enable the government to secure unequal contributions of capital from different citizens. The guarantee of repayment does not lessen to any material degree the aggregate amount of things destroyed; but the government can get those things with far less ill-will, because each citizen does not suspect the treasury of exacting an unfairly large share from him and an unfairly small one from his neighbor. The promised indemnity for the expense makes the cost more easily borne. It becomes possible to secure the aid of foreign capital which could not be obtained by taxation. In fact, the apparent lightness of the burden of loans at the outset

of a war as compared with that of taxes, constitutes one of the chief dangers of the system. The voluntary contributions of the sanguine are exhausted at the beginning, and the government is then compelled to have recourse, under most unfavorable circumstances, to those who are not so well-affected to the national cause. If it calls for additional loans, they are negotiated at very high rates of interest ; if new and burdensome taxes are imposed, they have to be extorted from unwilling hands by a government whose powers are already overstrained by the difficulties of its situation. If a nation goes into a war with its eyes open,[1] its statesmen will strive to impose the maximum of taxation at the outset, and resort to loans only as the power to bear new taxes becomes exhausted. In this way it can command the maximum of capital, both in the form of taxes on the unwilling, and of loans from the willing ; while it can obtain the borrowed capital at relatively low rates of interest, and thus lessen the burden on the future taxpayer.

§ 534. In the case of debts for industrial enterprises which do not promise a commercial return, the same rule should be applied which has been given for war debts. They should be reduced to a minimum ; the only difference being that the extraordinary expenses which these enterprises involve should often be met by increase of assessments rather than by increase of taxes. Sewers, harbor improvements, highways, and other things which cannot pay for themselves commercially, *i. e.*, for whose use the community cannot charge a remunerative price,— should in general be paid for by assessment or not built at all. This may seem a hard rule ; in some cases it really is.

---

[1] The policy of the United States Treasury at the opening of the Civil War was the reverse of this. It was partly justified, though not wholly so, by the fact that the North did not go into the war with its eyes open to the cost, and would have refused to make sacrifices in 1861 which it was ready to make two or three years later.

But the enormous number of mistakes made in borrowing money for things which can not and do not pay for themselves shows how unsafe it is for government authorities to judge whether the public necessity of such enterprises warrants putting heavy burdens on the future taxpayer.

§ 535. Equally bad are the results which arise from borrowing money for enterprises whose commercial profit is speculative. Loans in aid of railroads often promise a return both in public convenience and in fiscal advantage, when in point of fact the road is so tardily completed as to furnish neither. In so conservative a state as Massachusetts, a large part of the municipal subscriptions in aid of railroad building have been given to railroads that either were not built at all, or did not become available for use until many years had elapsed.

§ 536. The case of loans for industrial improvements which promise a sure return is different, at least in theory. Instead of raising as large a part of the expense as possible by taxation it is enough if we keep the loan within such limits that the investment is sure to pay interest and make such slight annual contributions to the payment of the principal as are warranted by the character of the business. If the original form of the capital is liable to become antiquated in twenty years' time, its cost and income should be so adjusted that the current returns will extinguish the principal within twenty years. The agency by which this gradual extinction of debt is accomplished is known as a *sinking fund.*[1]

§ 537. The attempt to apply the sinking fund system

---

[1] The detailed working of various sinking fund systems, and the questions involved in the sale or purchase of bonds above par, belong to a treatise on finance rather than to one on general economics. As a rule, it appears to be a wise provision for a government, as well as for a private corporation, to insert in all its bonds a clause stipulating a right to redeem them before maturity, at a price slightly in advance of their par value ; say at 110. This does not interfere with the readiness of the public to take the original loan, and it often greatly facilitates the operation of repayment or refunding.

to war debts usually involves a good deal of juggling with figures. Nor has it any natural basis in theory. There is no definite time within which a war debt ought to be repaid, because there is no definite date at which a nation can expect another war. If bonds can be placed on the market at a lower rate of interest when they contain a sinking fund provision, such a clause may wisely be inserted.[1] But in general the only safe rule about a war debt is to pay it off as fast as the resources of the country will allow. The slight disturbance to individual investors is more than made up by the reserve strength which freedom from debt gives the government. Had the United States, in 1861, in addition to its other difficulties, labored under an inherited burden of old war debts, it would have been disastrously weakened. Even in the case of debts for industrial improvement it would generally be better if provision were made for paying them off more rapidly. Very few improvements pay for themselves within the time anticipated. For one case like the Erie Canal, which did better than its promoters expected, we have a hundred cases which fail to pay for themselves at all, and which leave a burden of interest with no real increase of the means of repayment. Witness the enormous increase of municipal indebtedness in recent years, and of the burdens connected with it; burdens so great as to lead to the enactment of arbitrary provisions limiting the amount of debts which municipal authorities may legally contract.

§ 538. It must never be forgotten in matters of public finance that the treasurers of our nations and municipalities are dealing with government property and not with

---

[1] The use of *terminable annuities* by which a man gives a certain amount of capital to the government in consideration of receiving a determinate payment during his lifetime, combines the two advantages of attracting the capital of a certain class of investors, who have no families to provide for, and of providing for the gradual extinction of the obligations of the government by the death of the annuitants.

public wealth.  The fact that capital is in the hands of public authorities does not necessarily make the national wealth any greater than it would be if left in the hands of individuals or corporations.  Public authorities may do some good things which private individuals cannot; they may also do some bad things which private individuals can be prevented from doing.  Unless fiscal checks are rigidly applied and fiscal deficits made up by present taxation rather than by promises for the future, the danger of waste far outweighs the probability of good.

# INDEX.

The numbers refer to pages.

485

# THE EVOLUTION
## OF CAPITALISM

Allen, Zachariah. **The Practical Tourist,** Or Sketches of the State of the Useful Arts, and of Society, Scenery, &c. &c. in Great-Britain, France and Holland. Providence, R.I., 1832. Two volumes in one.

Bridge, James Howard. **The Inside History of the Carnegie Steel Company:** A Romance of Millions. New York, 1903.

Brodrick, J[ames]. **The Economic Morals of the Jesuits:** An Answer to Dr. H. M. Robertson. London, 1934.

Burlamaqui, J[ean-] J[acques]. **The Principles of Natural and Politic Law.** Cambridge, Mass., 1807. Two volumes in one.

**Capitalism and Fascism:** Three Right-Wing Tracts, 1937-1941. New York, 1972.

Corey, Lewis. **The Decline of American Capitalism.** New York, 1934.

[Court, Pieter de la]. **The True Interest and Political Maxims, of the Republic of Holland.** Written by that Great Statesman and Patriot, John de Witt. To which is prefixed, (never before printed) Historical Memoirs of the Illustrious Brothers Cornelius and John de Witt, by John Campbell. London, 1746.

Dos Passos, John R. **Commercial Trusts:** The Growth and Rights of Aggregated Capital. An Argument Delivered Before the Industrial Commission at Washington, D.C., December 12, 1899. New York, 1901.

Fanfani, Amintore. **Catholicism, Protestantism and Capitalism.** London, 1935.

Gaskell, P[eter]. **The Manufacturing Population of England:** Its Moral, Social, and Physical Conditions, and the Changes Which Have Arisen From the Use of Steam Machinery; With an Examination of Infant Labour. London, 1833.

Göhre, Paul. **Three Months in a Workshop:** A Practical Study. London, 1895.

Greeley, Horace. **Essays Designed to Elucidate the Science of Political Economy,** While Serving to Explain and Defend the Policy of Protection to Home Industry, As a System of National Cooperation for the Elevation of Labor. Boston, 1870.

Grotius, Hugo. **The Freedom of the Seas, Or, The Right** Which Belongs to the Dutch to Take Part in the East Indian Trade. Translated with Revision of the Latin Text of 1633 by Ralph Van Deman Magoffin. New York, 1916.

Hadley, Arthur Twining. **Economics:** An Account of the Relations Between Private Property and Public Welfare. New York, 1896.

Knight, Charles. **Capital and Labour;** Including *The Results of Machinery*. London, 1845.

de Malynes, Gerrard. **Englands View, in the Unmasking of Two Paradoxes:** With a Replication unto the Answer of Maister John Bodine. London, 1603. New Introduction by Mark Silk.

Marquand, H. A. **The Dynamics of Industrial Combination.** London, 1931.

**Mercantilist Views of Trade and Monopoly:** Four Essays, 1645-1720. New York, 1972.

Morrison, C[harles]. **An Essay on the Relations Between Labour and Capital.** London, 1854.

Nicholson, J. Shield. **The Effects of Machinery on Wages.** London, 1892.

**One Hundred Years' Progress of the United States:** With an Appendix Entitled Marvels That Our Grandchildren Will See; or, One Hundred Years' Progress in the Future. By Eminent Literary Men, Who Have Made the Subjects on Which They Have Written Their Special Study. Hartford, Conn., 1870.

**The Poetry of Industry:** Two Literary Reactions to the Industrial Revolution, 1755/1757. New York, 1972.

**Pre-Capitalist Economic Thought:** Three Modern Interpretations. New York, 1972.

**Promoting Prosperity:** Two Eighteenth Century Tracts. New York, 1972.

Proudhon, P[ierre-] J[oseph]. **System of Economical Contradictions:** Or, The Philosophy of Misery. (Reprinted from *The Works of P. J. Proudhon*, Vol. IV, Part I.) Translated by Benj. R. Tucker. Boston, 1888.

**Religious Attitudes Toward Usury:** Two Early Polemics. New York, 1972.

Roscher, William. **Principles of Political Economy.** New York, 1878. Two volumes in one.

Scoville, Warren C. **Revolution in Glassmaking:** Entrepreneurship and Technological Change in the American Industry, 1880-1920. Cambridge, Mass., 1948.

Selden, John. **Of the Dominion, Or, Ownership of the Sea.** Written at First in Latin, and Entituled *Mare Clausum.* Translated by Marchamont Nedham. London, 1652.

Senior, Nassau W. **Industrial Efficiency and Social Economy.** Original Manuscript Arranged and Edited by S. Leon Levy. New York, 1928. Revised Preface by S. Leon Levy. Two volumes in one.

Spann, Othmar. **The History of Economics.** Translated from the 19th German Edition by Eden and Cedar Paul. New York, 1930.

**The Usury Debate After Adam Smith:** Two Nineteenth Century Essays. New York, 1972. New Introduction by Mark Silk.

**The Usury Debate in the Seventeenth Century:** Three Arguments. New York, 1972.

Varga, E[ugen]. **Twentieth Century Capitalism.** Translated from the Russian by George H. Hanna. Moscow, [1964].

Young, Arthur. **Arthur Young on Industry and Economics:** Being Excerpts from Arthur Young's Observations on the State of Manufactures and His Economic Opinions on Problems Related to Contemporary Industry in England. Arranged by Elizabeth Pinney Hunt. Bryn Mawr, Pa., 1926.